This book
belongs to

# Adventures In Oz

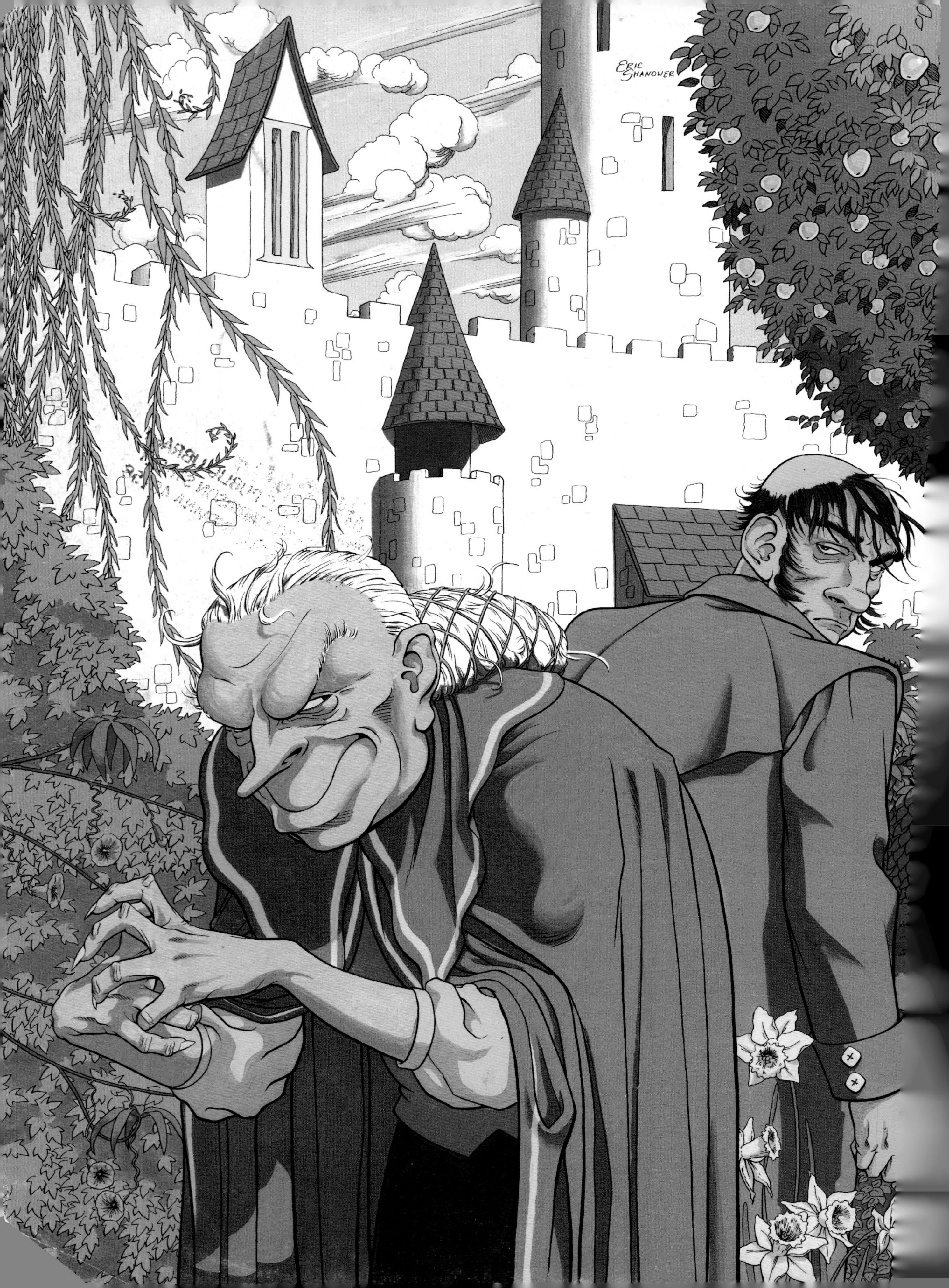
ERIC SHANOWER

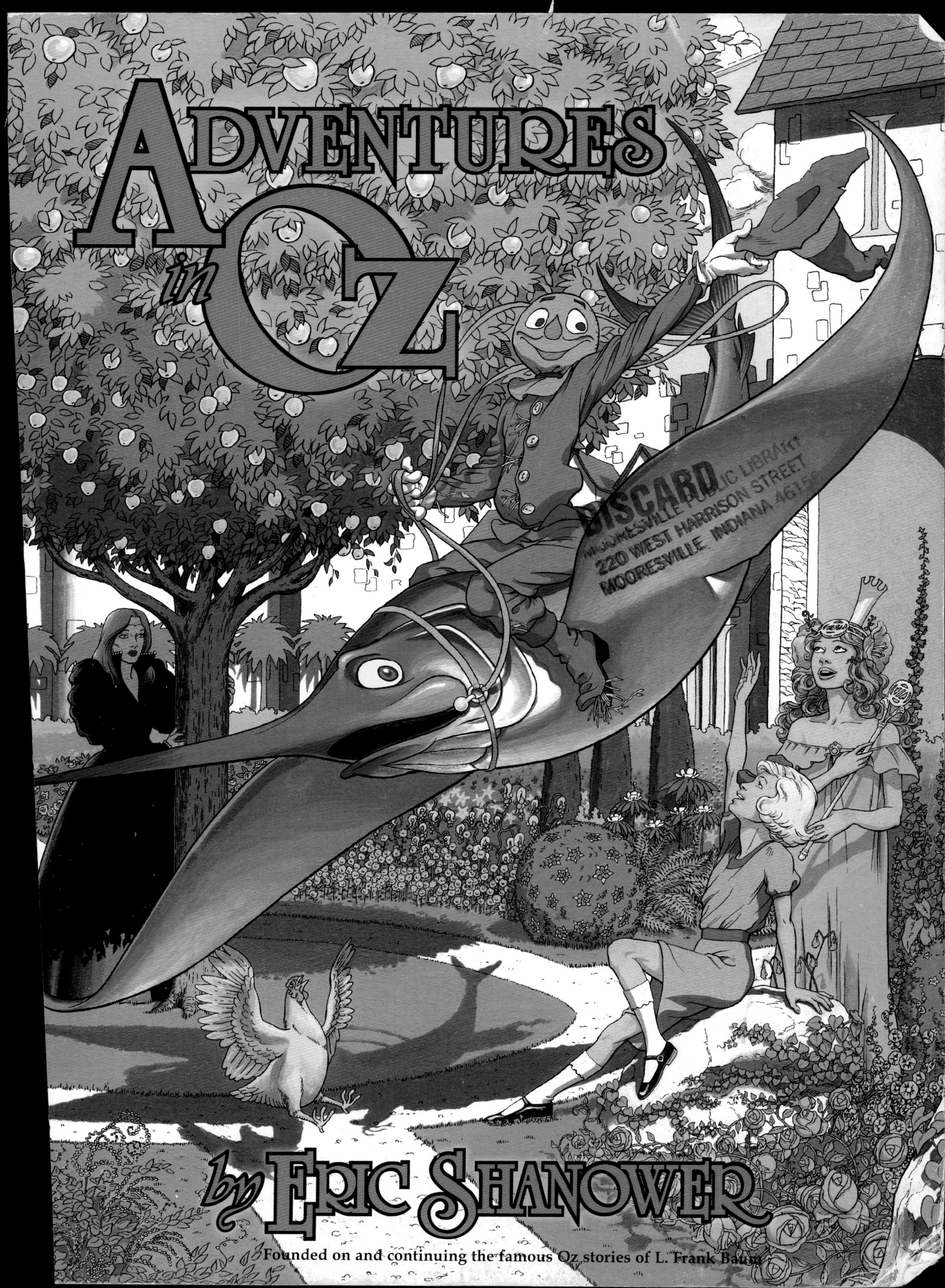
Adventures in Oz
by Eric Shanower
Founded on and continuing the famous Oz stories of L. Frank Baum

**Eric Shanower**
Writer and Illustrator

**John Uhrich**
Production Artist

**Neil Uyetake**
Design Production Director

**Rick Oliver**
Original editor for *The Enchanted Apples of Oz, The Secret Island of Oz, The Ice King of Oz,* and *The Forgotten Forest of Oz*

**Byron Erickson and Anina Bennett**
Original editors for *The Blue Witch of Oz*

**Willie Schubert**
Calligrapher for *The Secret Island of Oz*

**Tom McCraw**
Painting Assistant for *The Secret Island of Oz*

**www.IDWPUBLISHING.com**

Published by:
IDW Publishing
4411 Morena Blvd., Suite 106
San Diego, CA  92117

Softcover: ISBN 1-933239-61-1
Signed & Numbered: 1-60010-003-1

09  08  07  06    5  4  3  2  1

IDW Publishing is:
Robbie Robbins, *President* • Chris Ryall, *Publisher/Editor-in-Chief*
Ted Adams, *Vice President* • Kris Oprisko, *Vice President*
Neil Uyetake, *Art Director* • Dan Taylor, *Editor*
Aaron Myers, *Assistant Editor* • Tom B. Long, *Designer*
Chance Boren, *Editorial Assistant* • Matthew Ruzicka, CPA, *Controller*
Alex Garner, *Creative Director* • Yumiko Miyano, *Business Development*
Rick Privman, *Business Development*

# TABLE OF CONTENTS

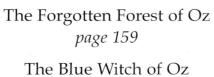

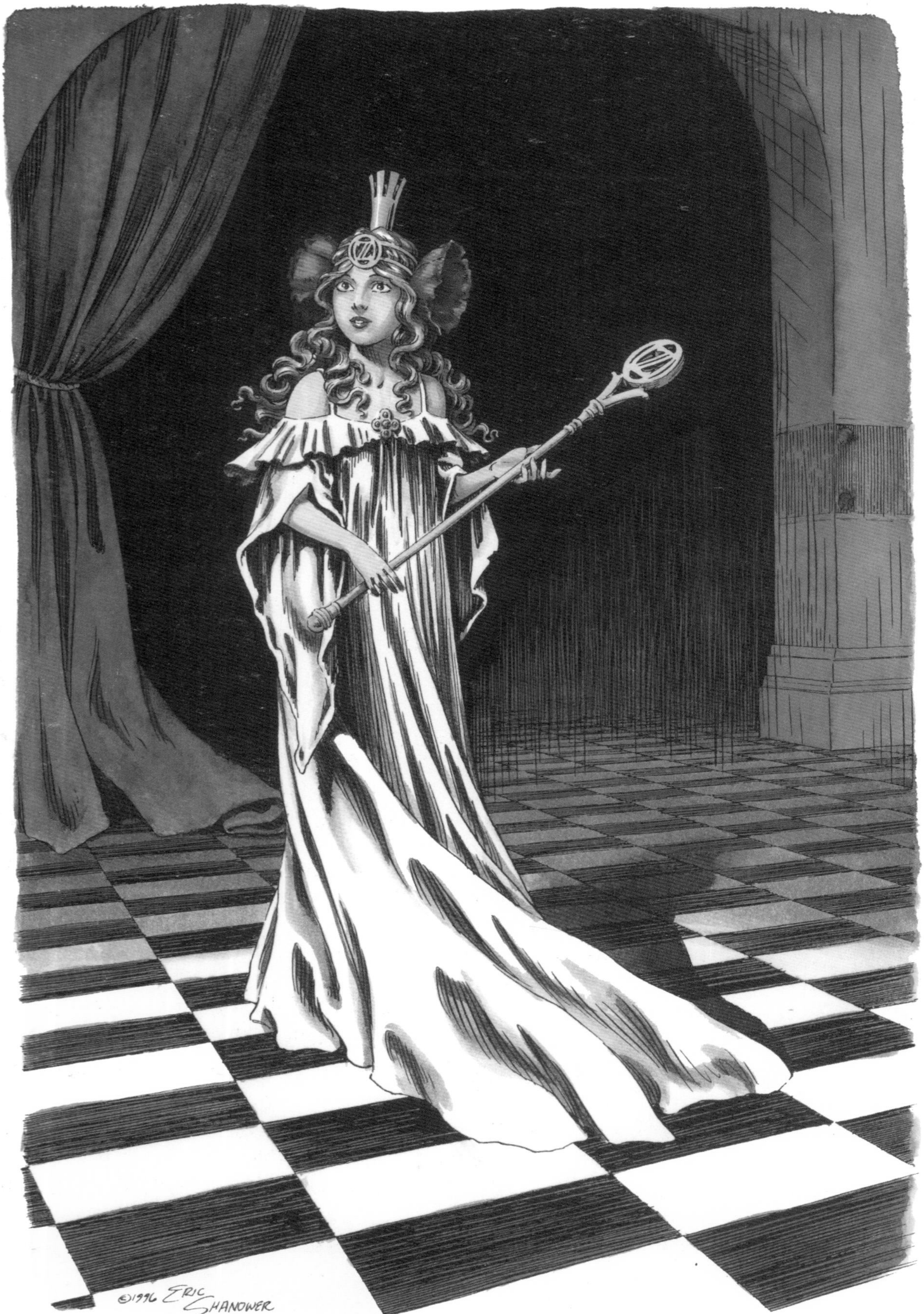
©1996 ERIC SHANOWER

**Ozma of Oz**

# Just a Word Before You Start

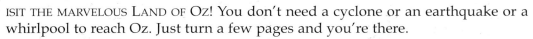ISIT THE MARVELOUS LAND OF OZ! You don't need a cyclone or an earthquake or a whirlpool to reach Oz. Just turn a few pages and you're there.

First, however, you might like to know a few things about the place you'll be visiting. A lot has happened in the Land of Oz since that day years ago when Dorothy Gale first arrived.

Long, long ago, the fairy queen Lurline and her band were flying over Oz. They were so charmed by the lovely country that they decided to enchant it. They turned it into a magical place where no one ever gets sick, people only grow older if they choose to, and no one ever dies. To protect Oz from the rest of the world, Lurline surrounded it with a desert. One touch of the desert's sands turns flesh to dust, so Oz sometimes isn't an easy place to reach.

One day, a man riding in a large balloon sailed down from the clouds above Oz. The people hailed him as a great Wizard and made him their ruler. The Wizard had them build the Emerald City for his capital in the center of the country. From there, he ruled in seclusion until Dorothy Gale exposed him as a simple circus performer from Nebraska.

The rightful ruler of Oz was actually a girl named Ozma. She was descended from a long line of fairy rulers that the fairy queen Lurline appointed to rule Oz. A witch imprisoned Ozma under an enchantment for many years. At last the enchantment was broken, and today, Ozma rules the Land of Oz with sweetness and charm.

Oz is divided into four major countries: the Munchkin Country lies in the east where the favorite color is blue; the Winkie Country lies in the west where the favorite color is yellow; the Quadling Country lies in the south where the favorite color is red; the Gillikin Country lies in the north where the favorite color is purple; and in the center of Oz lies the Emerald City, where the favorite color is green.

Turn the page and you'll see a map of Oz. Notice that the compass directions are different from ours here in the Great Outside World. Oz is a magical place full of mystery and the strange case of Oz's compass directions is merely another of those mysteries.

Each of the four countries of Oz has its own ruler. Nick Chopper is a man made all out of tin who used to be a simple woodman, but now he's the Emperor of the Winkies in the west. In the south, the Quadlings are ruled by one of the most powerful sorceresses ever known, Glinda the Good. The Munchkins and Gillikins have their ruling families as well, but all are subject to the supreme ruler of Oz, Ozma, who lives in a beautiful, emerald-studded marble palace in the Emerald City.

Ozma has gathered many friends and advisors to help her rule her marvelous country. Among them are:

- Dorothy Gale from Kansas, who is Ozma's best friend—Ozma made Dorothy a princess of Oz, but Dorothy is too normal and everyday to let such an exalted title make her conceited
- A living Scarecrow whose brains supplied by the Wizard have made him the most popular man in Oz
- The wonderful Wizard of Oz, who has learned to perform real magic
- The Cowardly Lion and the Hungry Tiger, who are Ozma's bodyguards
- The Soldier with the Green Whiskers, Oz's sole army—he keeps his gun unloaded so that he's in no danger of hurting anyone

You'll meet many other delightful and amusing personalities in this book too. So what are you waiting for? Let's go to Oz!

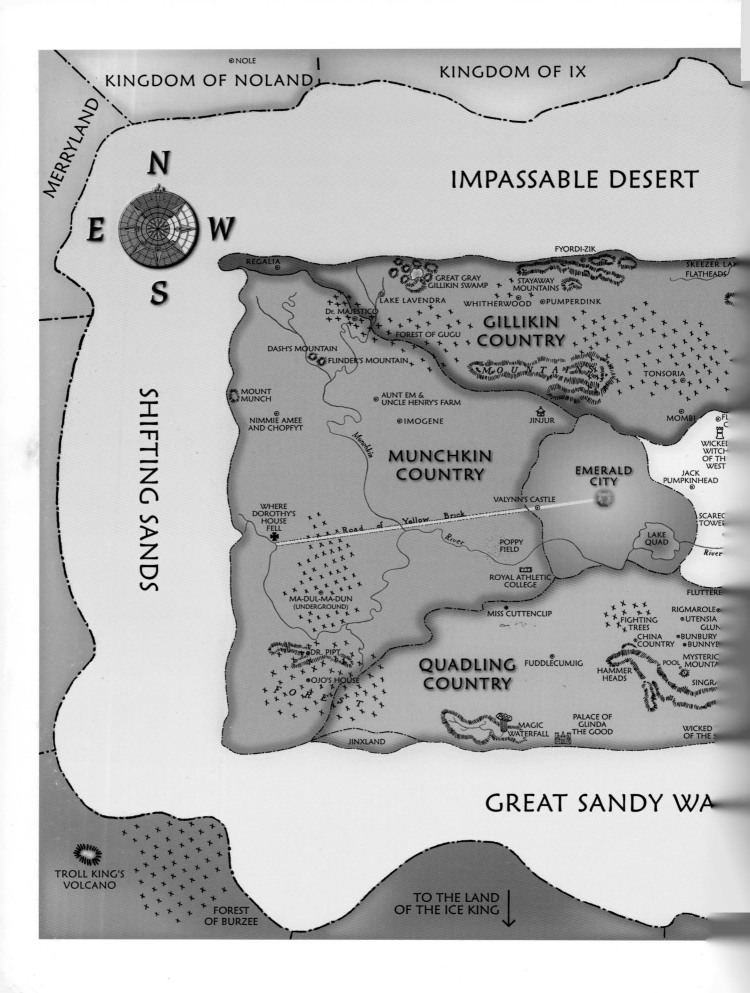

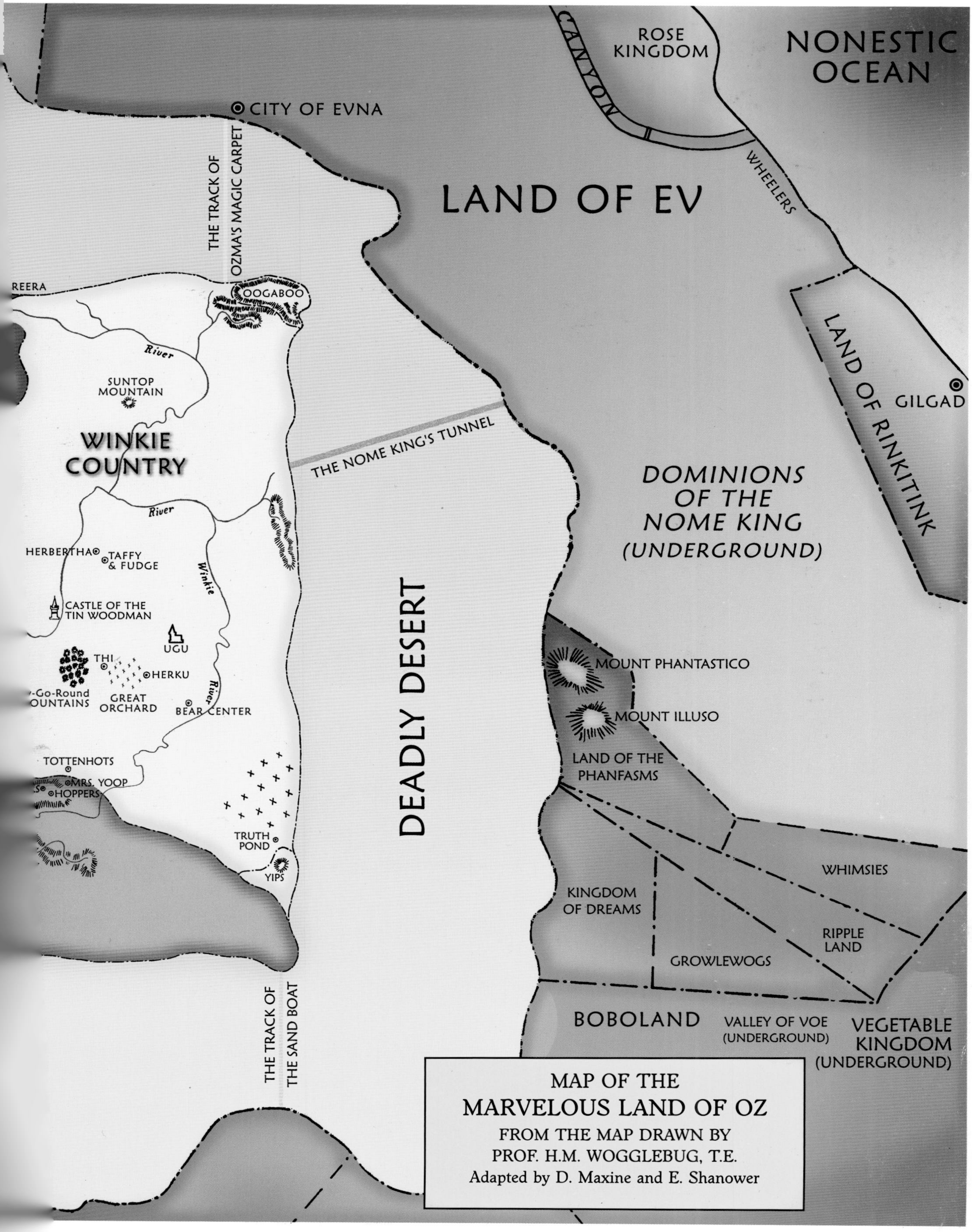
ROSE KINGDOM
CANYON
NONESTIC OCEAN
CITY OF EVNA
WHEELERS
LAND OF EV
THE TRACK OF OZMA'S MAGIC CARPET
REERA
OOGABOO
LAND OF RINKITINK
GILGAD
River
SUNTOP MOUNTAIN
WINKIE COUNTRY
THE NOME KING'S TUNNEL
DOMINIONS OF THE NOME KING (UNDERGROUND)
River
HERBERTHA
TAFFY & FUDGE
Winkie
CASTLE OF THE TIN WOODMAN
UGU
DEADLY DESERT
THI
HERKU
MOUNT PHANTASTICO
-Go-Round OUNTAINS
GREAT ORCHARD
River
BEAR CENTER
MOUNT ILLUSO
TOTTENHOTS
LAND OF THE PHANFASMS
MRS. YOOP
HOPPERS
TRUTH POND
YIPS
WHIMSIES
KINGDOM OF DREAMS
RIPPLE LAND
GROWLEWOGS
BOBOLAND
VALLEY OF VOE (UNDERGROUND)
VEGETABLE KINGDOM (UNDERGROUND)
THE TRACK OF THE SAND BOAT

MAP OF THE
MARVELOUS LAND OF OZ
FROM THE MAP DRAWN BY
PROF. H.M. WOGGLEBUG, T.E.
Adapted by D. Maxine and E. Shanower

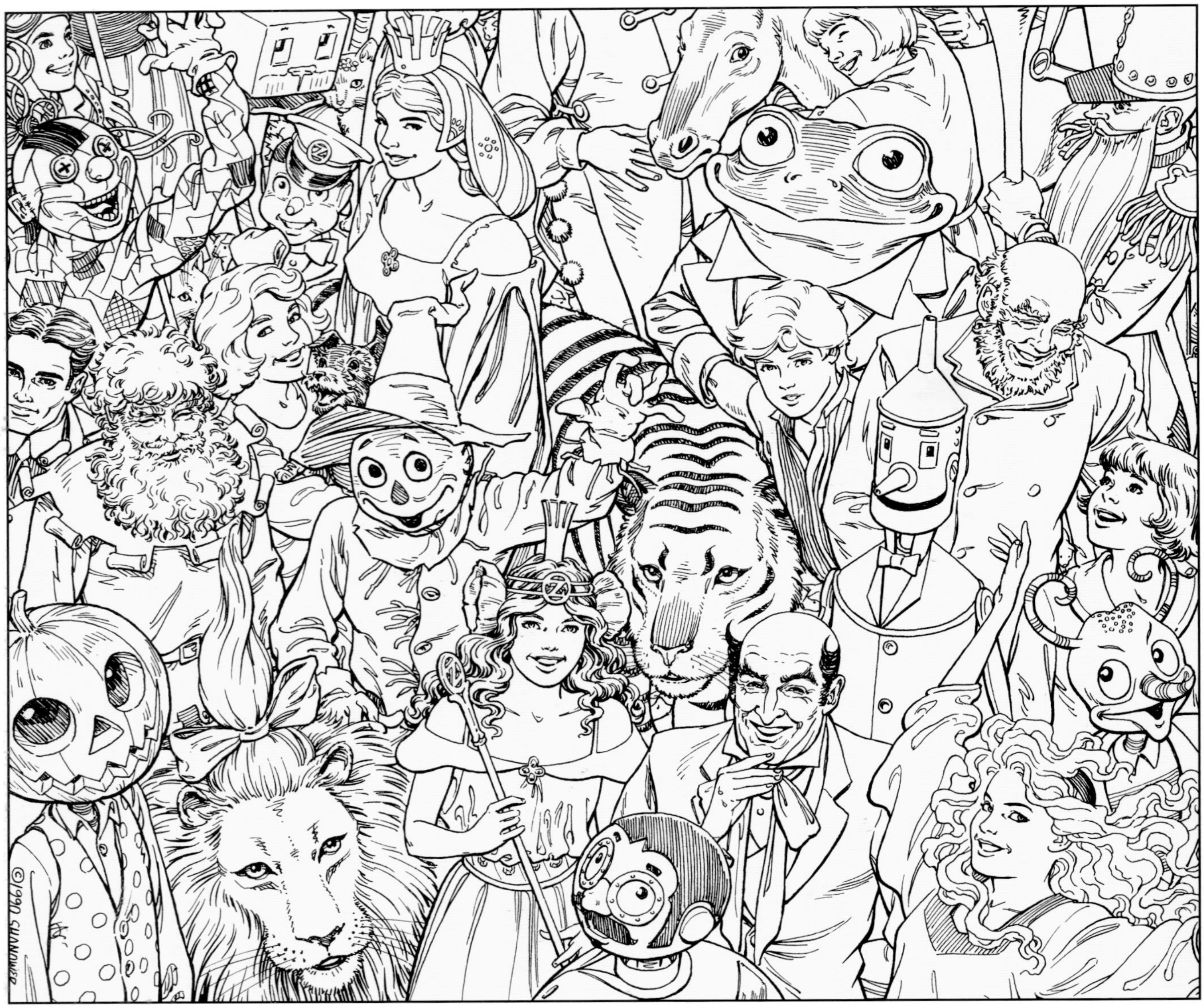
©1990 SHANOWER


## Acknowledgements

I'd like to thank all the people associated with the original printings of the Oz graphic novels: those at First Comics and Dark Horse Comics, particularly my editors Rick Oliver, Byron Erickson, and Anina Bennett; First Comics publisher Rick Obadiah; and my agent at the time, Mike Friedrich.

I'd like to thank Jay Geldhof, Dan Seitler, those of my instructors at the Joe Kubert School of Cartoon and Graphic Art, particularly Joe Kubert, who contributed to my original Oz comic book proposal, Glenn Ingersoll for comments on my plot for *The Enchanted Apples of Oz,* Karen Shanower for her vital last-minute assistance with *Enchanted Apples,* Willie Schubert for lettering *The Secret Island of Oz,* and Ed Brubaker and David Maxine for comments on *The Forgotten Forest of Oz.*

In particular, I thank Tom McCraw for help during *Secret Island,* not only for his assistance with painting, but for it all.

I'd like to thank everyone associated with this new edition as well: Ed Brubaker again for helping IDW and me to get together; everyone at IDW, particularly Ted Adams, Chris Ryall, Robbie Robbins, and Neil Uyetake; and both Tom McCraw and David Maxine again for loaning artwork for reproduction.

I extend my greatest appreciation to John Uhrich for his attention to detail and painstaking effort to make the present volume the definitive printing of my Oz graphic novels.

# The Enchanted Apples of Oz

To Margaret and Chris
for enchantment created.

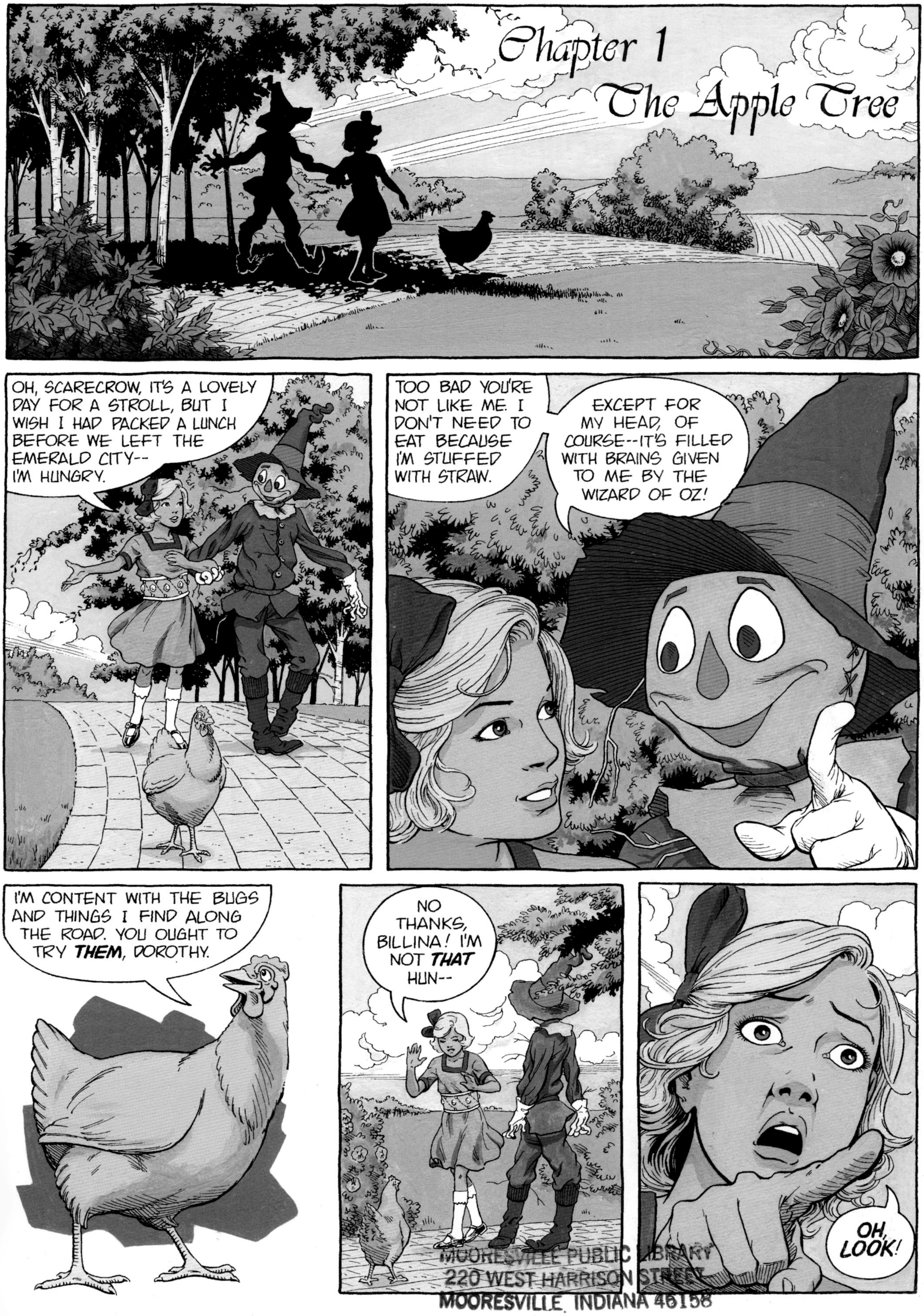
Chapter 1
The Apple Tree
OH, SCARECROW, IT'S A LOVELY DAY FOR A STROLL, BUT I WISH I HAD PACKED A LUNCH BEFORE WE LEFT THE EMERALD CITY-- I'M HUNGRY.
TOO BAD YOU'RE NOT LIKE ME. I DON'T NEED TO EAT BECAUSE I'M STUFFED WITH STRAW.
EXCEPT FOR MY HEAD, OF COURSE--IT'S FILLED WITH BRAINS GIVEN TO ME BY THE WIZARD OF OZ!
I'M CONTENT WITH THE BUGS AND THINGS I FIND ALONG THE ROAD. YOU OUGHT TO TRY *THEM*, DOROTHY.
NO THANKS, BILLINA! I'M NOT *THAT* HUN--
OH, LOOK!

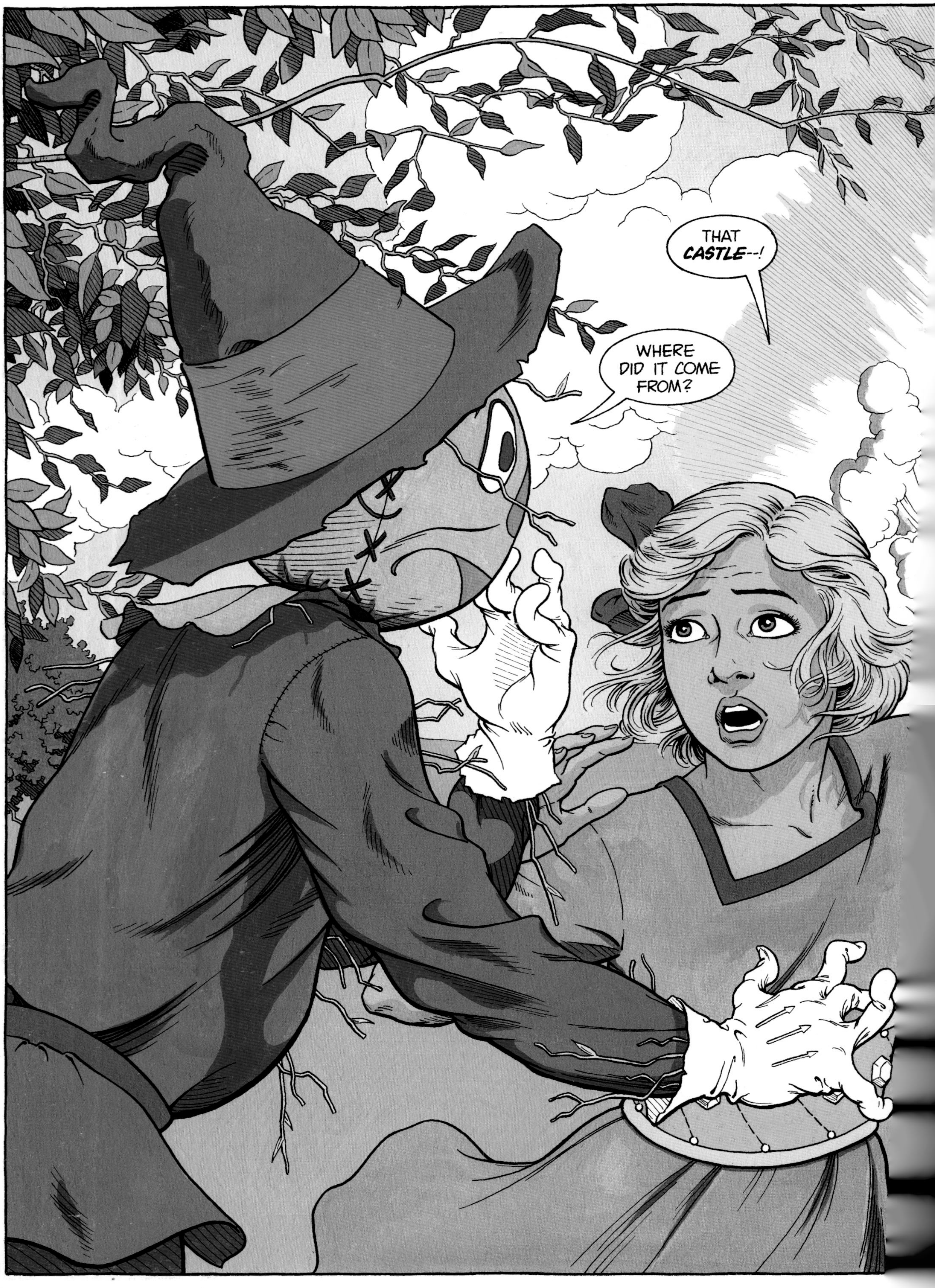
THAT CASTLE--!
WHERE DID IT COME FROM?

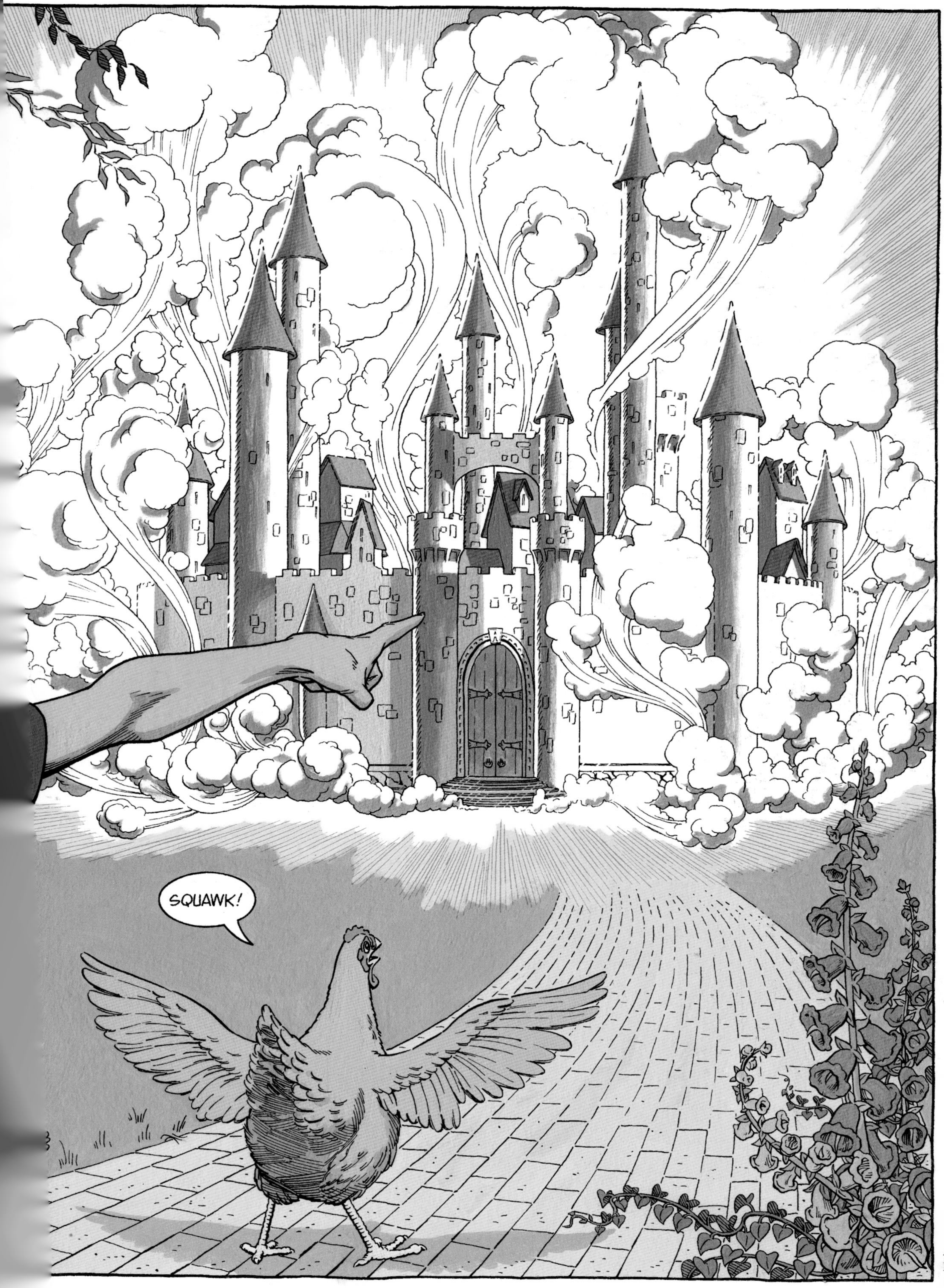
SQUAWK!

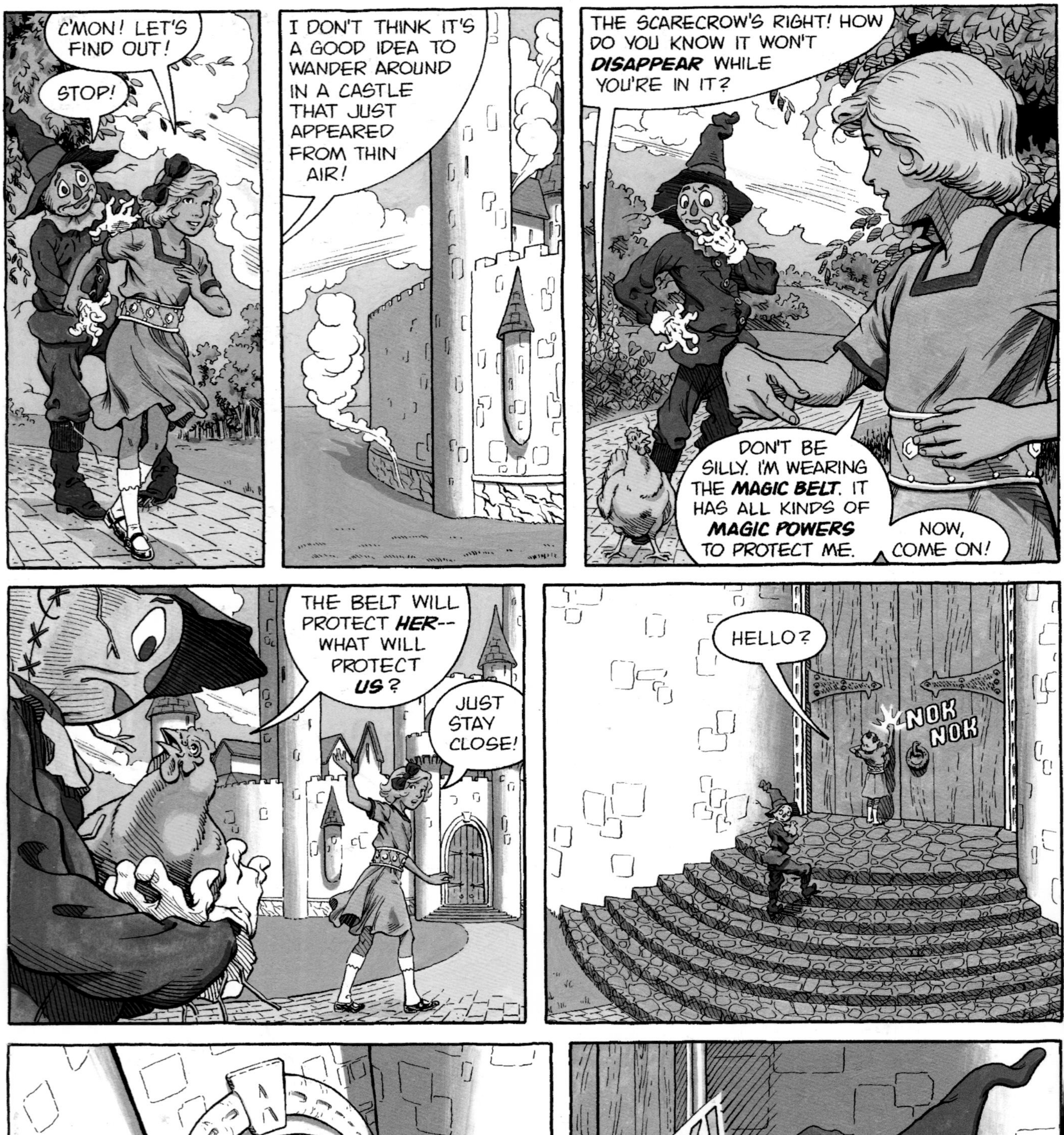
C'MON! LET'S FIND OUT!
STOP!
I DON'T THINK IT'S A GOOD IDEA TO WANDER AROUND IN A CASTLE THAT JUST APPEARED FROM THIN AIR!
THE SCARECROW'S RIGHT! HOW DO YOU KNOW IT WON'T **DISAPPEAR** WHILE YOU'RE IN IT?
DON'T BE SILLY. I'M WEARING THE **MAGIC BELT**. IT HAS ALL KINDS OF **MAGIC POWERS** TO PROTECT ME.
NOW, COME ON!
THE BELT WILL PROTECT **HER**-- WHAT WILL PROTECT **US**?
JUST STAY CLOSE!
HELLO?
NOK NOK
CREAK!

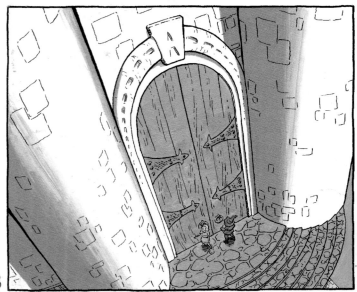

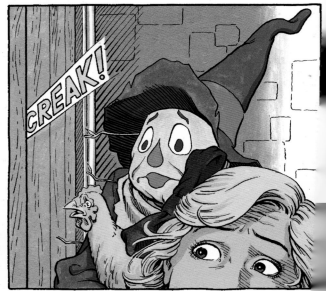

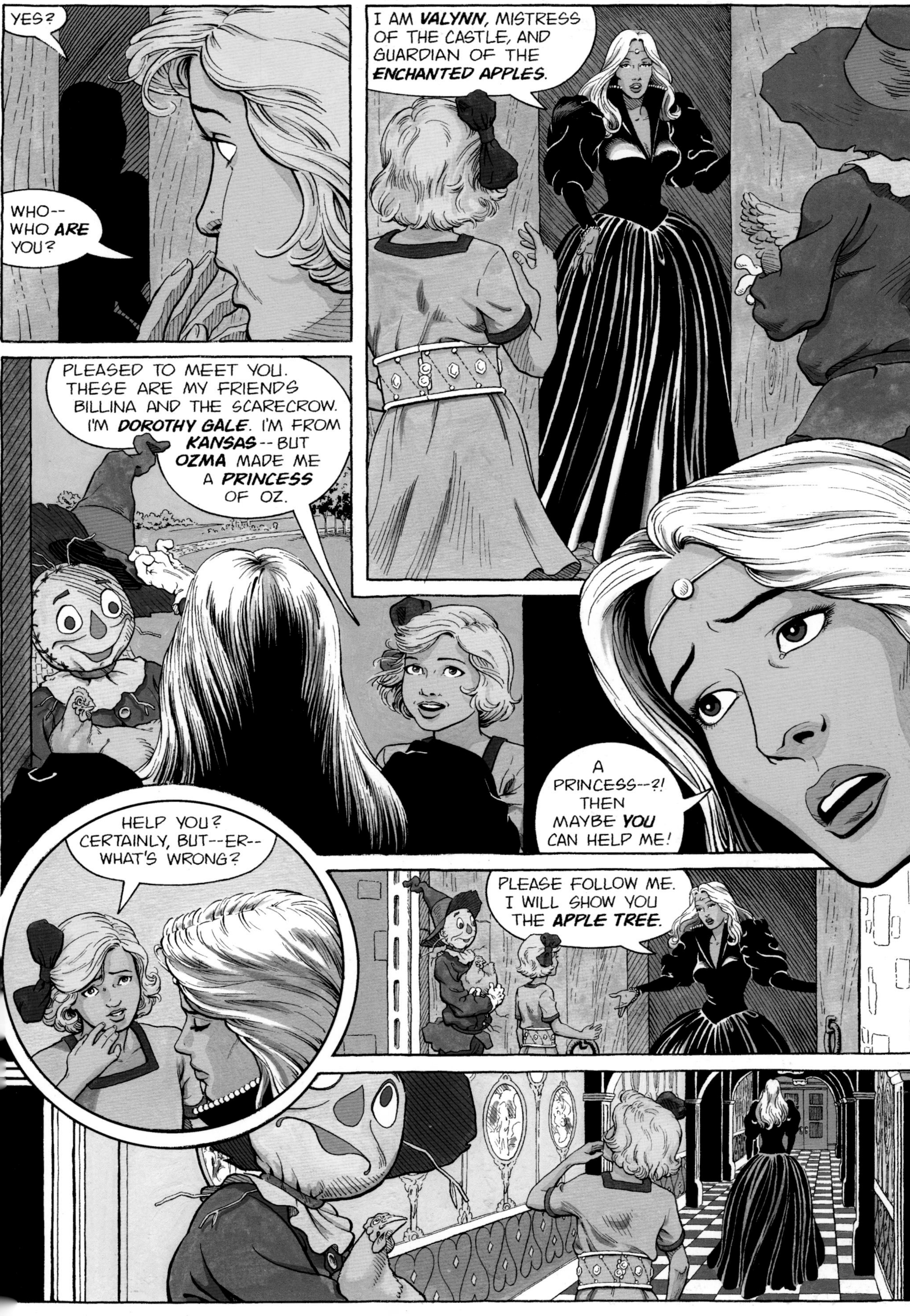
YES?
WHO-- WHO ARE YOU?
I AM VALYNN, MISTRESS OF THE CASTLE, AND GUARDIAN OF THE ENCHANTED APPLES.
PLEASED TO MEET YOU. THESE ARE MY FRIENDS BILLINA AND THE SCARECROW. I'M DOROTHY GALE. I'M FROM KANSAS--BUT OZMA MADE ME A PRINCESS OF OZ.
A PRINCESS--?! THEN MAYBE YOU CAN HELP ME!
HELP YOU? CERTAINLY, BUT--ER-- WHAT'S WRONG?
PLEASE FOLLOW ME. I WILL SHOW YOU THE APPLE TREE.

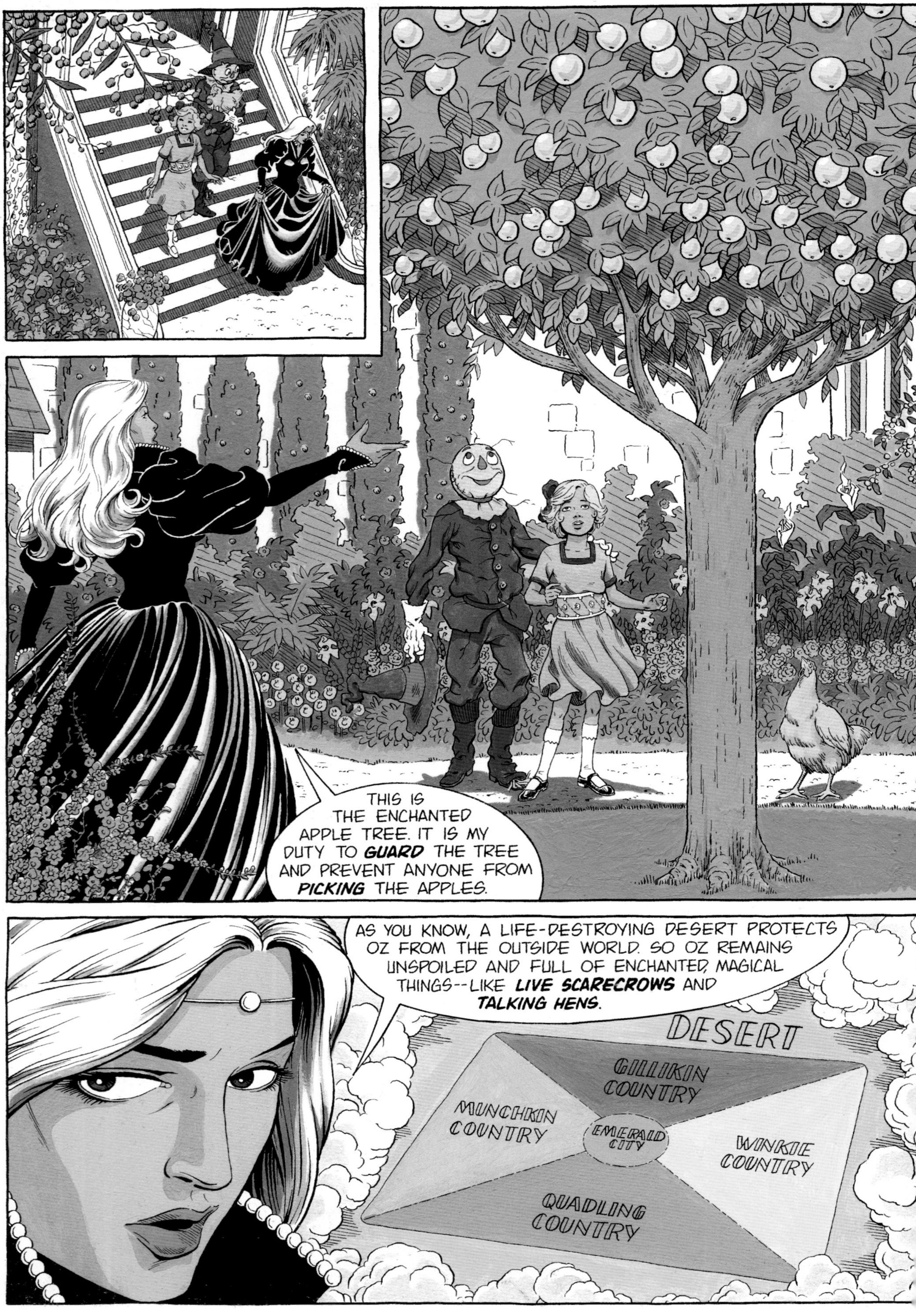
THIS IS THE ENCHANTED APPLE TREE. IT IS MY DUTY TO **GUARD** THE TREE AND PREVENT ANYONE FROM **PICKING** THE APPLES.
AS YOU KNOW, A LIFE-DESTROYING DESERT PROTECTS OZ FROM THE OUTSIDE WORLD. SO OZ REMAINS UNSPOILED AND FULL OF ENCHANTED, MAGICAL THINGS--LIKE **LIVE SCARECROWS** AND **TALKING HENS**.
DESERT
GILLIKIN COUNTRY
MUNCHKIN COUNTRY
EMERALD CITY
WINKIE COUNTRY
QUADLING COUNTRY

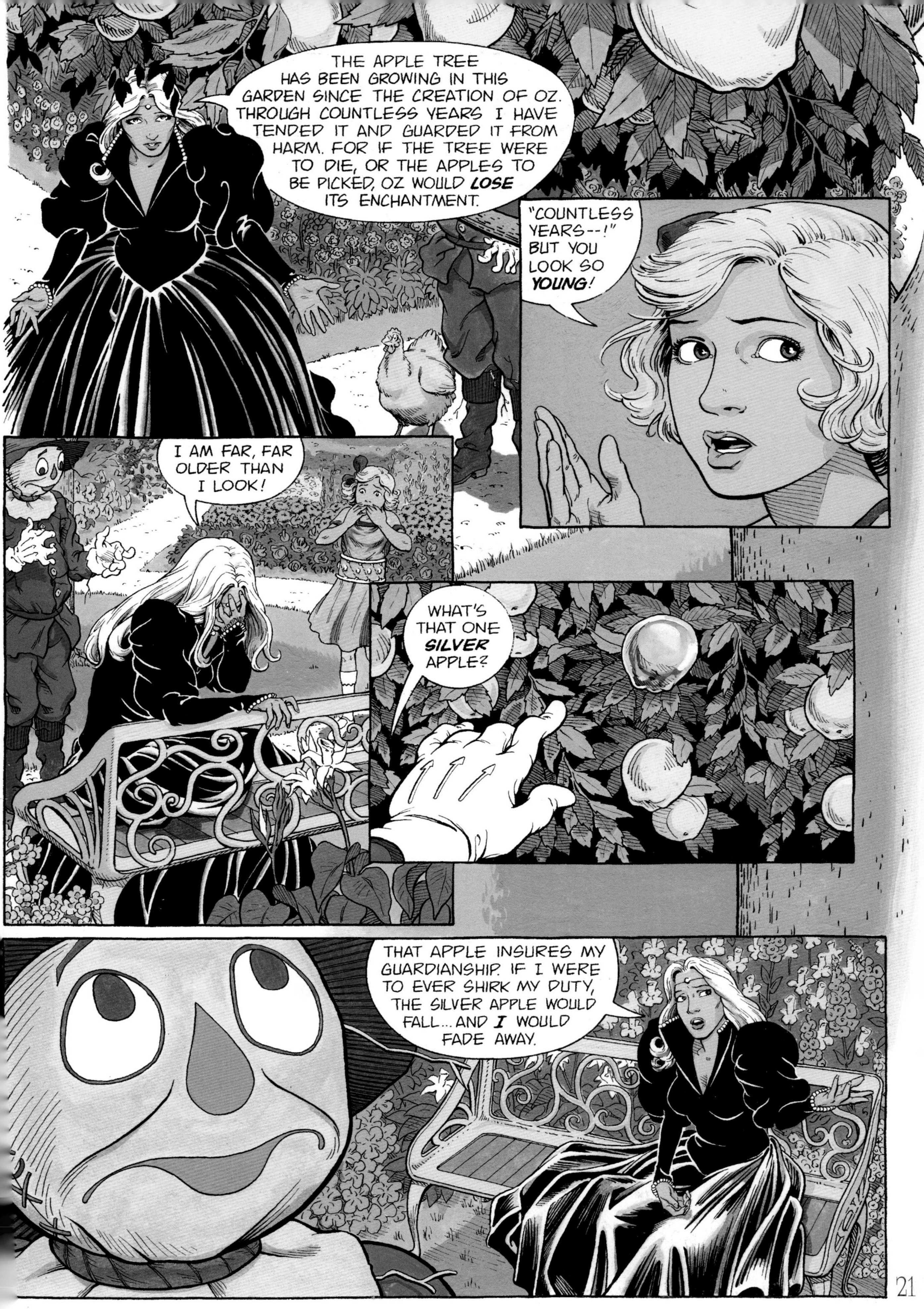
THE APPLE TREE HAS BEEN GROWING IN THIS GARDEN SINCE THE CREATION OF OZ. THROUGH COUNTLESS YEARS I HAVE TENDED IT AND GUARDED IT FROM HARM. FOR IF THE TREE WERE TO DIE, OR THE APPLES TO BE PICKED, OZ WOULD **LOSE** ITS ENCHANTMENT.
"COUNTLESS YEARS--!" BUT YOU LOOK SO **YOUNG**!
I AM FAR, FAR OLDER THAN I LOOK!
WHAT'S THAT ONE **SILVER** APPLE?
THAT APPLE INSURES MY GUARDIANSHIP. IF I WERE TO EVER SHIRK MY DUTY, THE SILVER APPLE WOULD FALL... AND **I** WOULD FADE AWAY.

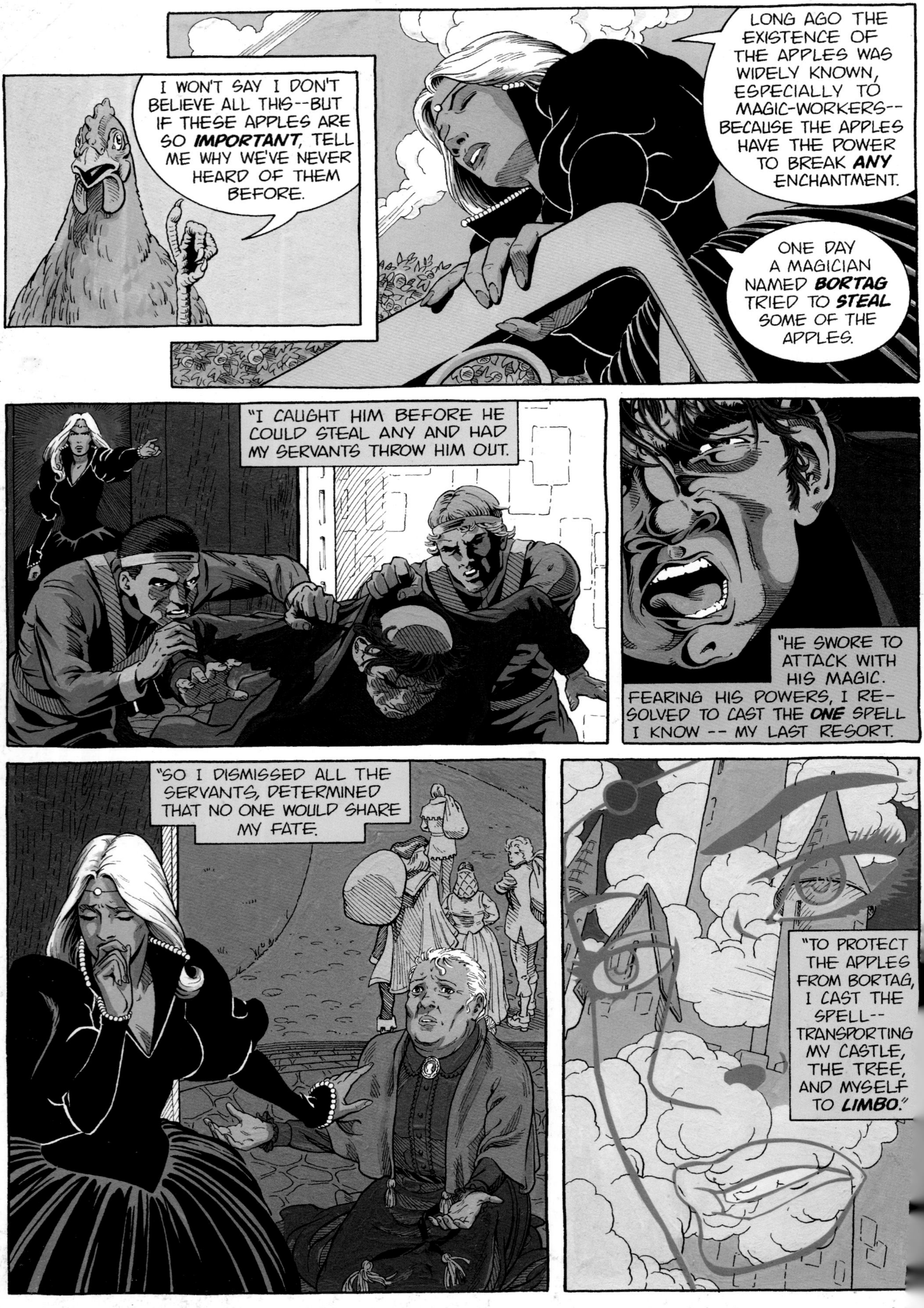
I WON'T SAY I DON'T BELIEVE ALL THIS--BUT IF THESE APPLES ARE SO **IMPORTANT**, TELL ME WHY WE'VE NEVER HEARD OF THEM BEFORE.
LONG AGO THE EXISTENCE OF THE APPLES WAS WIDELY KNOWN, ESPECIALLY TO MAGIC-WORKERS--BECAUSE THE APPLES HAVE THE POWER TO BREAK **ANY** ENCHANTMENT.
ONE DAY A MAGICIAN NAMED **BORTAG** TRIED TO **STEAL** SOME OF THE APPLES.
"I CAUGHT HIM BEFORE HE COULD STEAL ANY AND HAD MY SERVANTS THROW HIM OUT.
"HE SWORE TO ATTACK WITH HIS MAGIC. FEARING HIS POWERS, I RE-SOLVED TO CAST THE **ONE** SPELL I KNOW -- MY LAST RESORT.
"SO I DISMISSED ALL THE SERVANTS, DETERMINED THAT NO ONE WOULD SHARE MY FATE.
"TO PROTECT THE APPLES FROM BORTAG, I CAST THE SPELL--TRANSPORTING MY CASTLE, THE TREE, AND MYSELF TO **LIMBO**."

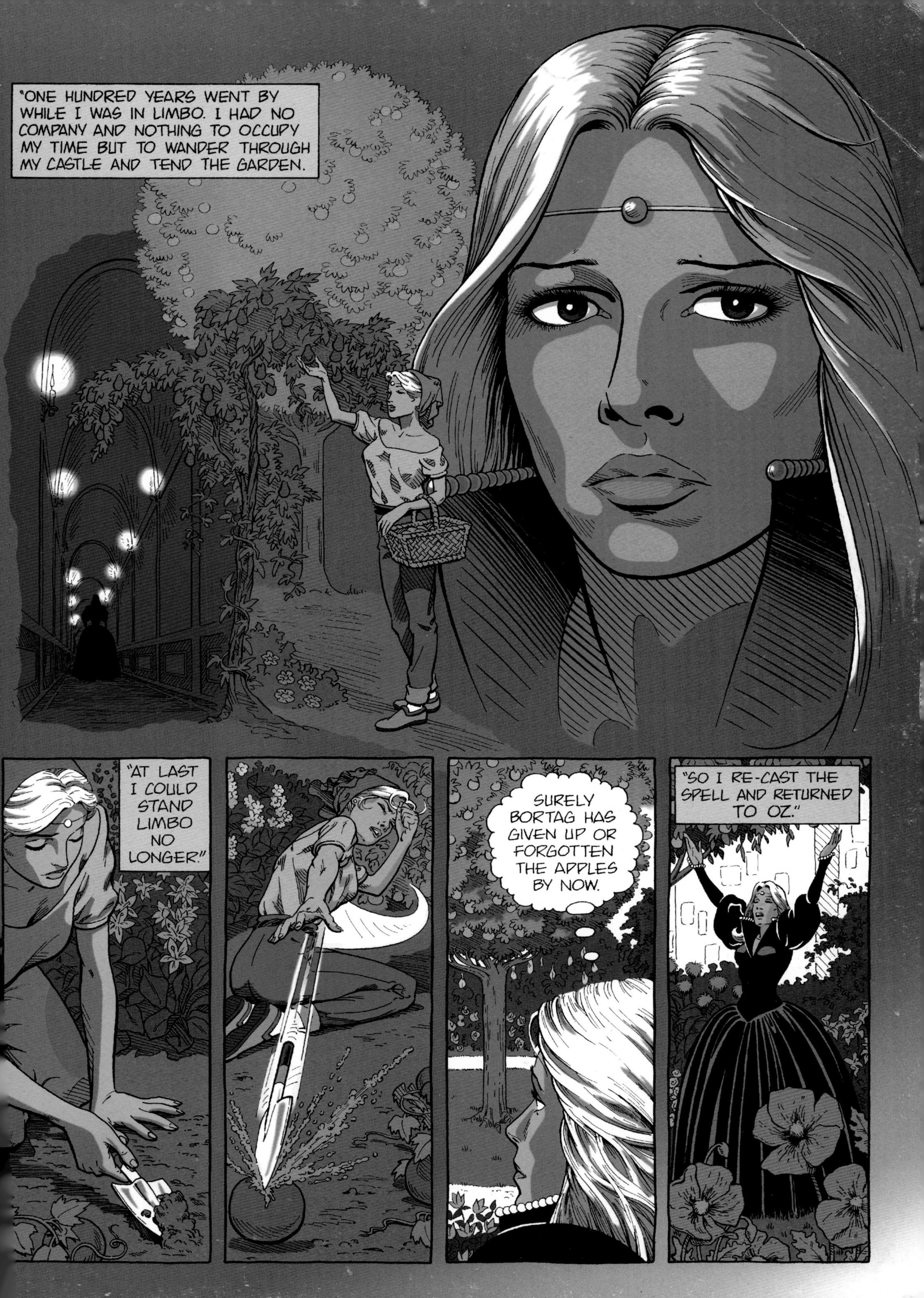
"ONE HUNDRED YEARS WENT BY WHILE I WAS IN LIMBO. I HAD NO COMPANY AND NOTHING TO OCCUPY MY TIME BUT TO WANDER THROUGH MY CASTLE AND TEND THE GARDEN.
"AT LAST I COULD STAND LIMBO NO LONGER."
SURELY BORTAG HAS GIVEN UP OR FORGOTTEN THE APPLES BY NOW.
"SO I RE-CAST THE SPELL AND RETURNED TO OZ."

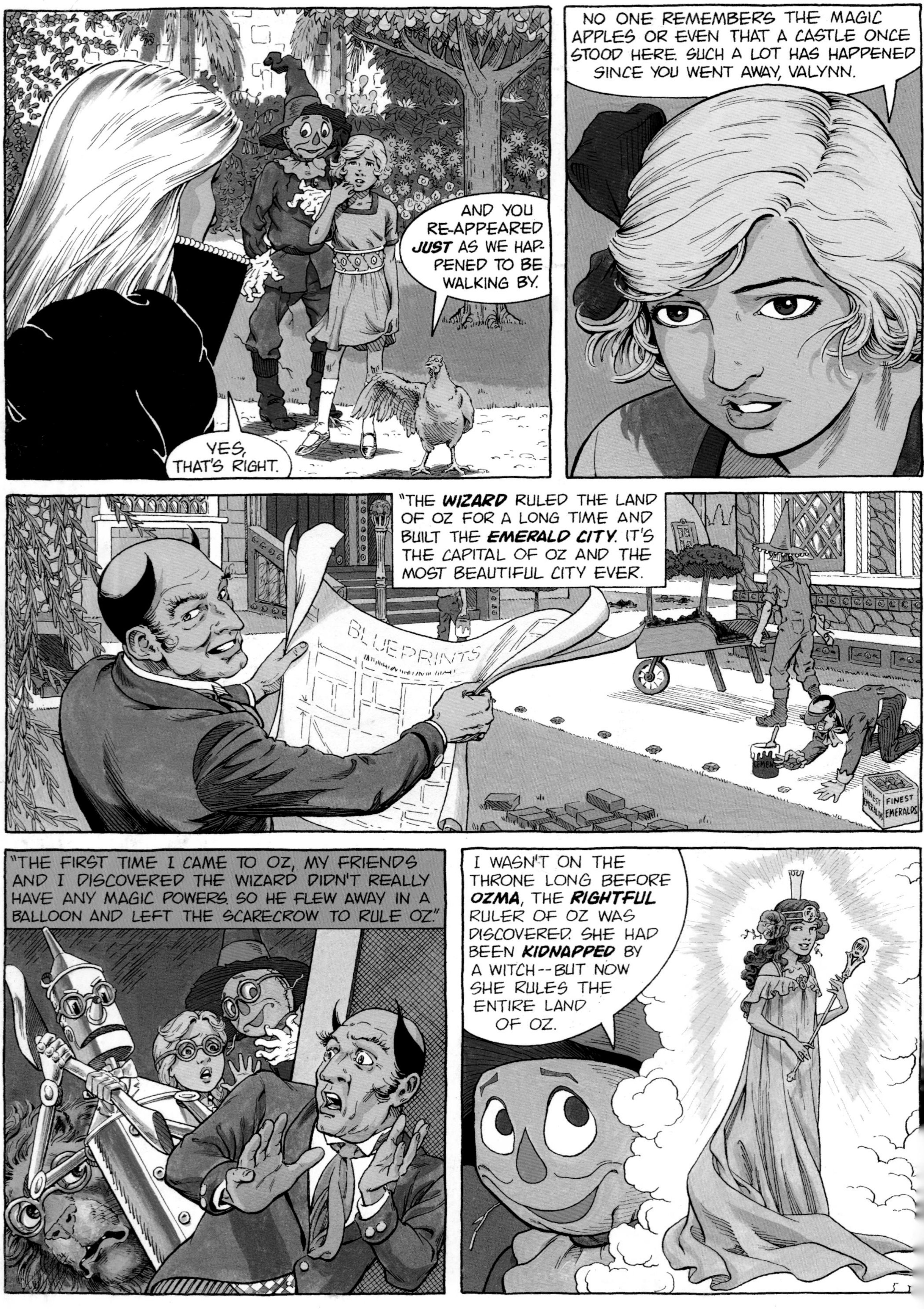
AND YOU RE-APPEARED *JUST* AS WE HAPPENED TO BE WALKING BY.
YES, THAT'S RIGHT.
NO ONE REMEMBERS THE MAGIC APPLES OR EVEN THAT A CASTLE ONCE STOOD HERE. SUCH A LOT HAS HAPPENED SINCE YOU WENT AWAY, VALYNN.
"THE ***WIZARD*** RULED THE LAND OF OZ FOR A LONG TIME AND BUILT THE ***EMERALD CITY***. IT'S THE CAPITAL OF OZ AND THE MOST BEAUTIFUL CITY EVER.
BLUEPRINTS
CEMENT
FINEST EMERALDS
FINEST EMERALDS
"THE FIRST TIME I CAME TO OZ, MY FRIENDS AND I DISCOVERED THE WIZARD DIDN'T REALLY HAVE ANY MAGIC POWERS. SO HE FLEW AWAY IN A BALLOON AND LEFT THE SCARECROW TO RULE OZ."
I WASN'T ON THE THRONE LONG BEFORE ***OZMA***, THE ***RIGHTFUL*** RULER OF OZ WAS DISCOVERED. SHE HAD BEEN ***KIDNAPPED*** BY A WITCH--BUT NOW SHE RULES THE ENTIRE LAND OF OZ.

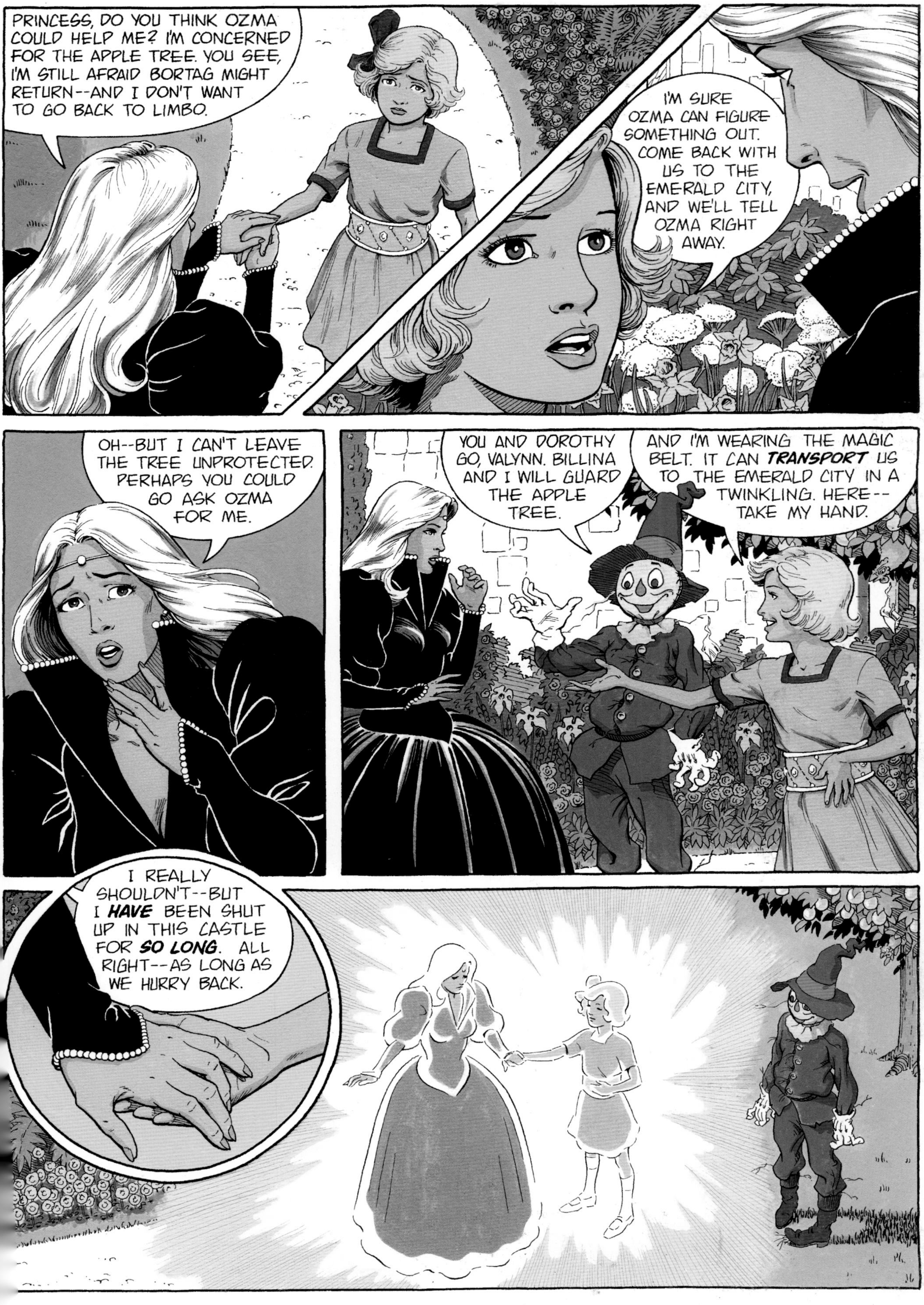
PRINCESS, DO YOU THINK OZMA COULD HELP ME? I'M CONCERNED FOR THE APPLE TREE. YOU SEE, I'M STILL AFRAID BORTAG MIGHT RETURN--AND I DON'T WANT TO GO BACK TO LIMBO.
I'M SURE OZMA CAN FIGURE SOMETHING OUT. COME BACK WITH US TO THE EMERALD CITY, AND WE'LL TELL OZMA RIGHT AWAY.
OH--BUT I CAN'T LEAVE THE TREE UNPROTECTED. PERHAPS YOU COULD GO ASK OZMA FOR ME.
YOU AND DOROTHY GO, VALYNN. BILLINA AND I WILL GUARD THE APPLE TREE.
AND I'M WEARING THE MAGIC BELT. IT CAN **TRANSPORT** US TO THE EMERALD CITY IN A TWINKLING. HERE--TAKE MY HAND.
I REALLY SHOULDN'T--BUT I **HAVE** BEEN SHUT UP IN THIS CASTLE FOR **SO LONG**. ALL RIGHT--AS LONG AS WE HURRY BACK.

# Chapter 2
## The Witch Awakes

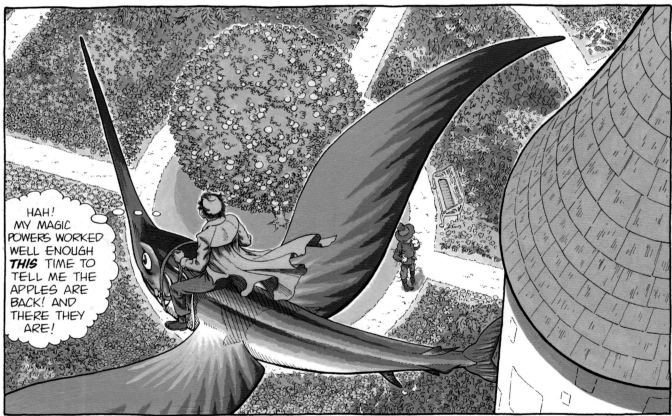

HAH! MY MAGIC POWERS WORKED WELL ENOUGH **THIS** TIME TO TELL ME THE APPLES ARE BACK! AND THERE THEY ARE!

THIS IS PERFECT, DROX--THERE'S NO ONE HERE!

BUT, BORTAG, THERE'S A **MAN** STANDING RIGHT OVER THERE!

THAT'S JUST A SCARECROW-- NOT A **REAL** MAN. AS IF SOMETHING **THAT** SORRY-LOOKING COULD FOOL ME!

NOW, DROX, **DIVE**!

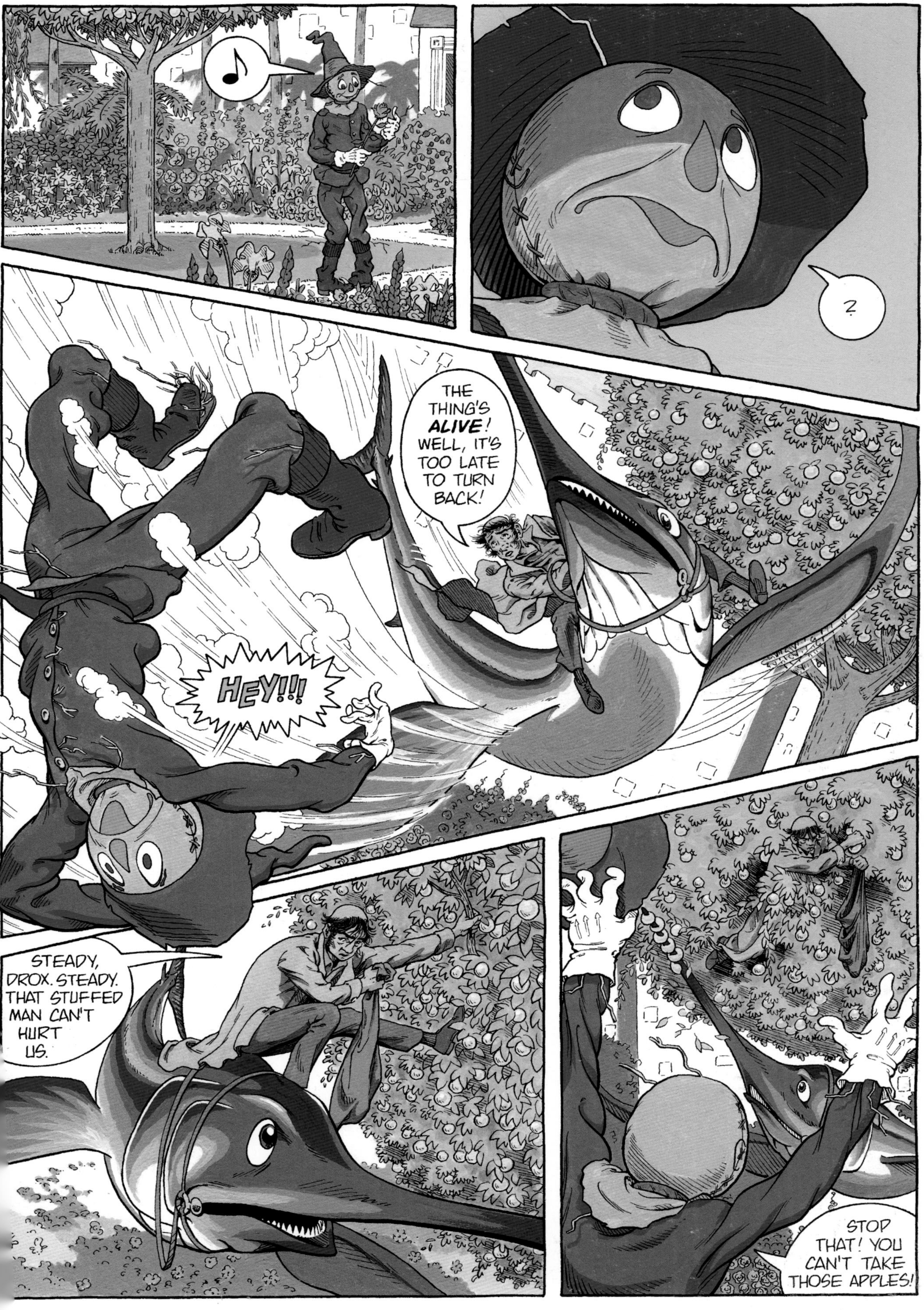

♪
?
THE THING'S **ALIVE**! WELL, IT'S TOO LATE TO TURN BACK!
HEY!!!
STEADY, DROX. STEADY. THAT STUFFED MAN CAN'T HURT US.
STOP THAT! YOU CAN'T TAKE THOSE APPLES!

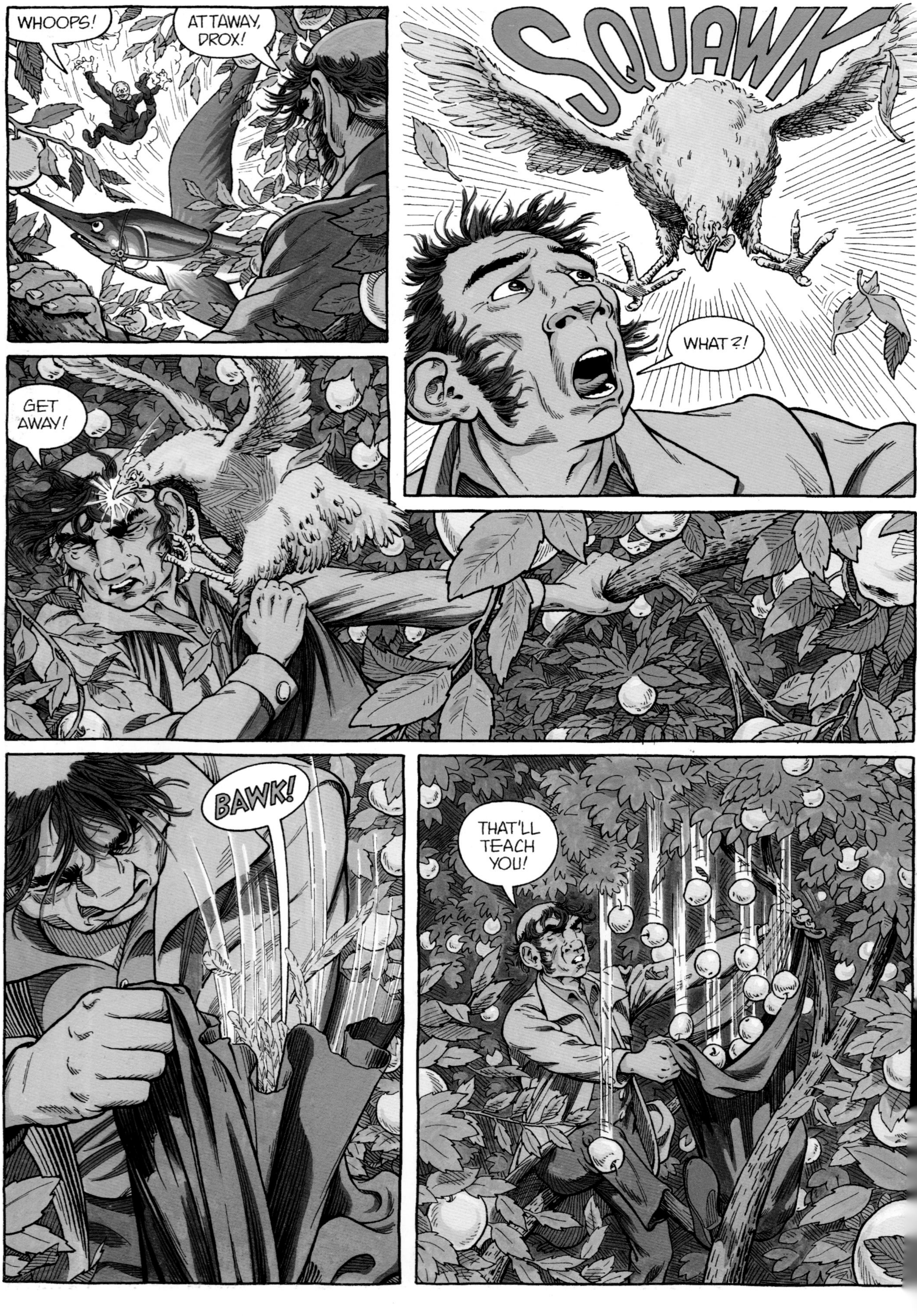
WHOOPS!
ATTAWAY, DROX!
SQUAWK
WHAT?!
GET AWAY!
BAWK!
THAT'LL TEACH YOU!

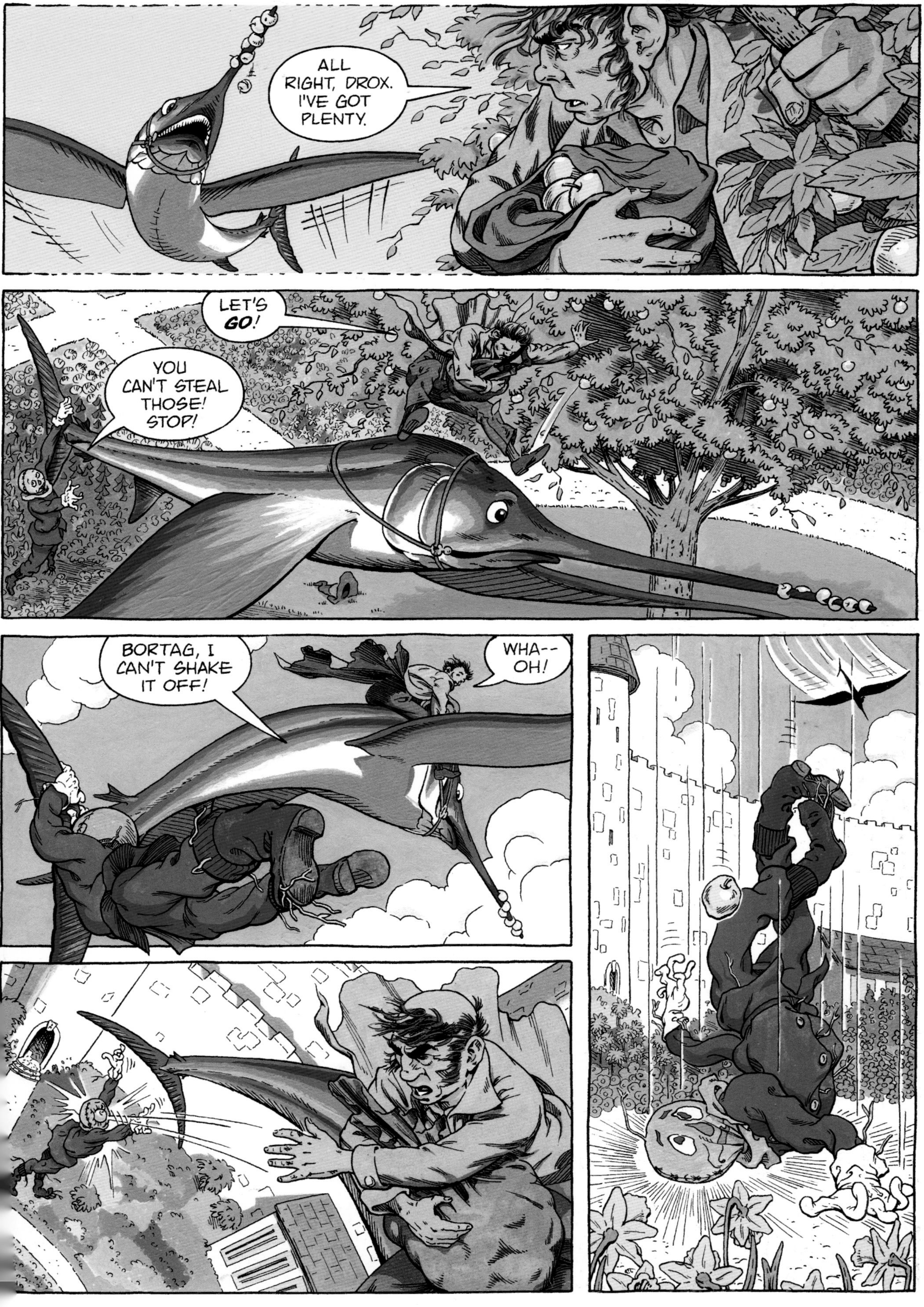
ALL RIGHT, DROX. I'VE GOT PLENTY.
LET'S GO!
YOU CAN'T STEAL THOSE! STOP!
BORTAG, I CAN'T SHAKE IT OFF!
WHA-- OH!

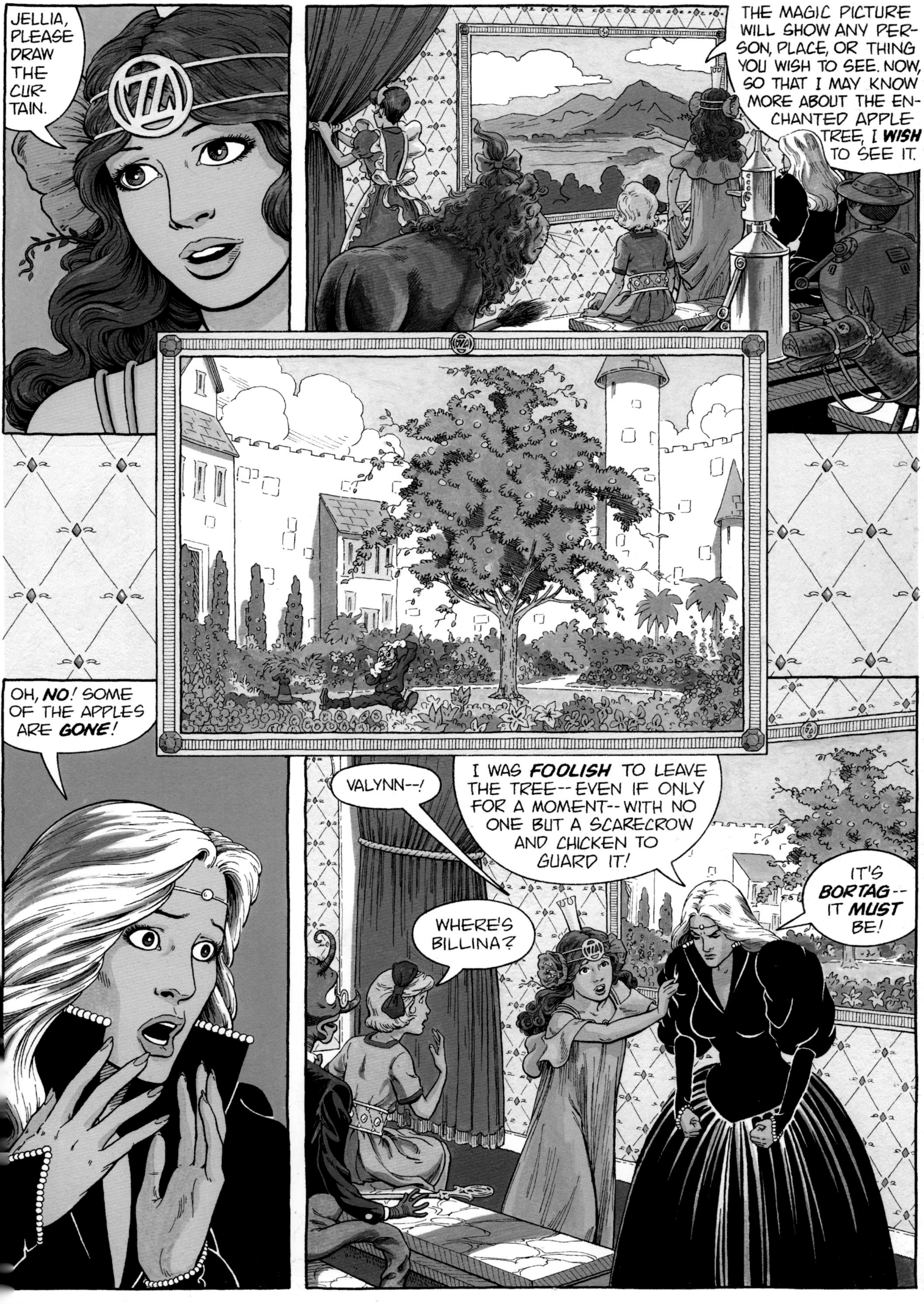
JELLIA, PLEASE DRAW THE CUR-TAIN.
THE MAGIC PICTURE WILL SHOW ANY PER-SON, PLACE, OR THING YOU WISH TO SEE. NOW, SO THAT I MAY KNOW MORE ABOUT THE EN-CHANTED APPLE TREE, I **WISH** TO SEE IT.
OH, **NO**! SOME OF THE APPLES ARE **GONE**!
VALYNN--!
I WAS **FOOLISH** TO LEAVE THE TREE--EVEN IF ONLY FOR A MOMENT--WITH NO ONE BUT A SCARECROW AND CHICKEN TO GUARD IT!
WHERE'S BILLINA?
IT'S **BORTAG**--IT **MUST** BE!

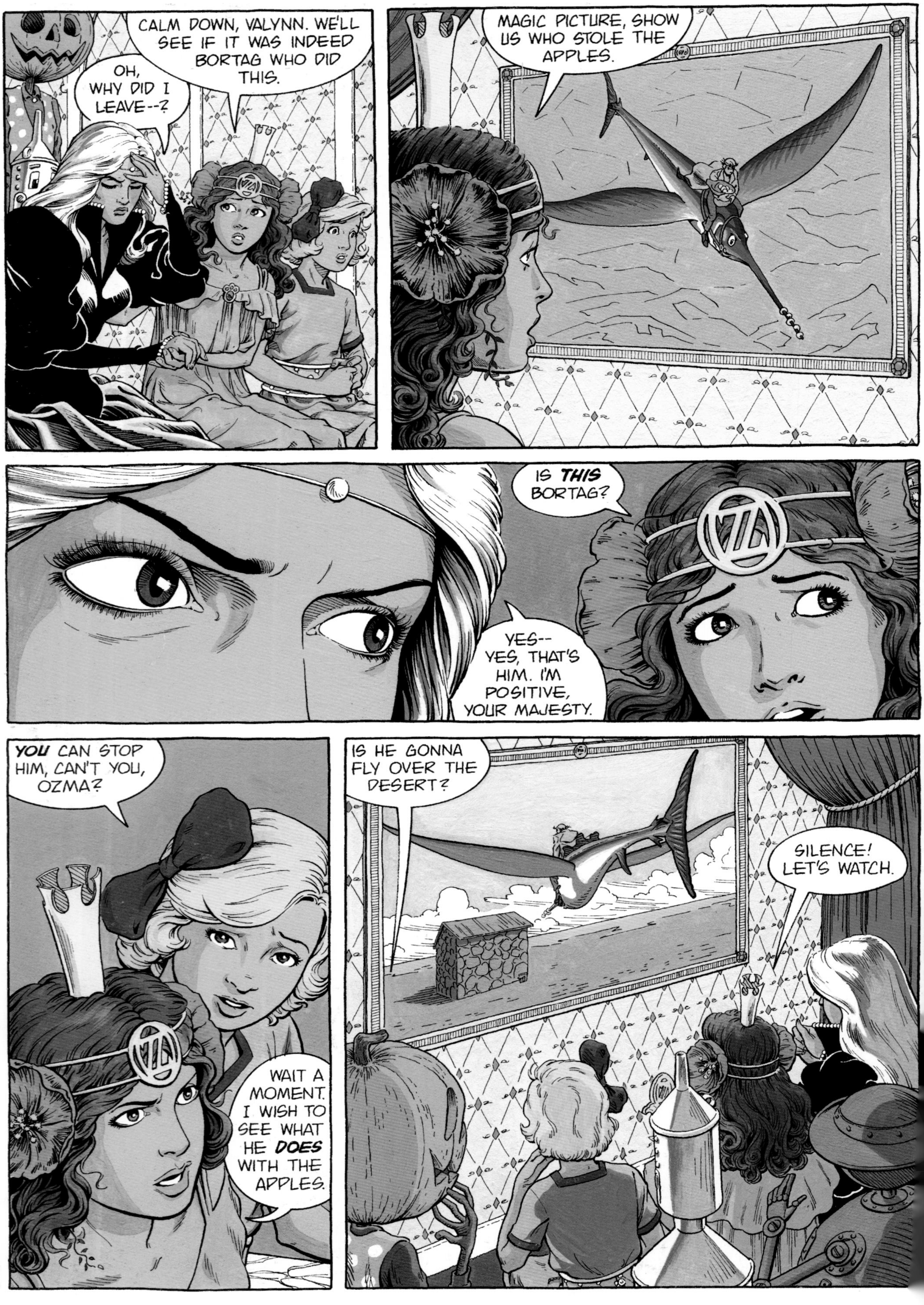
CALM DOWN, VALYNN. WE'LL SEE IF IT WAS INDEED BORTAG WHO DID THIS.
OH, WHY DID I LEAVE--?
MAGIC PICTURE, SHOW US WHO STOLE THE APPLES.
IS **THIS** BORTAG?
YES-- YES, THAT'S HIM. I'M POSITIVE, YOUR MAJESTY.
**YOU** CAN STOP HIM, CAN'T YOU, OZMA?
WAIT A MOMENT. I WISH TO SEE WHAT HE **DOES** WITH THE APPLES.
IS HE GONNA FLY OVER THE DESERT?
SILENCE! LET'S WATCH.

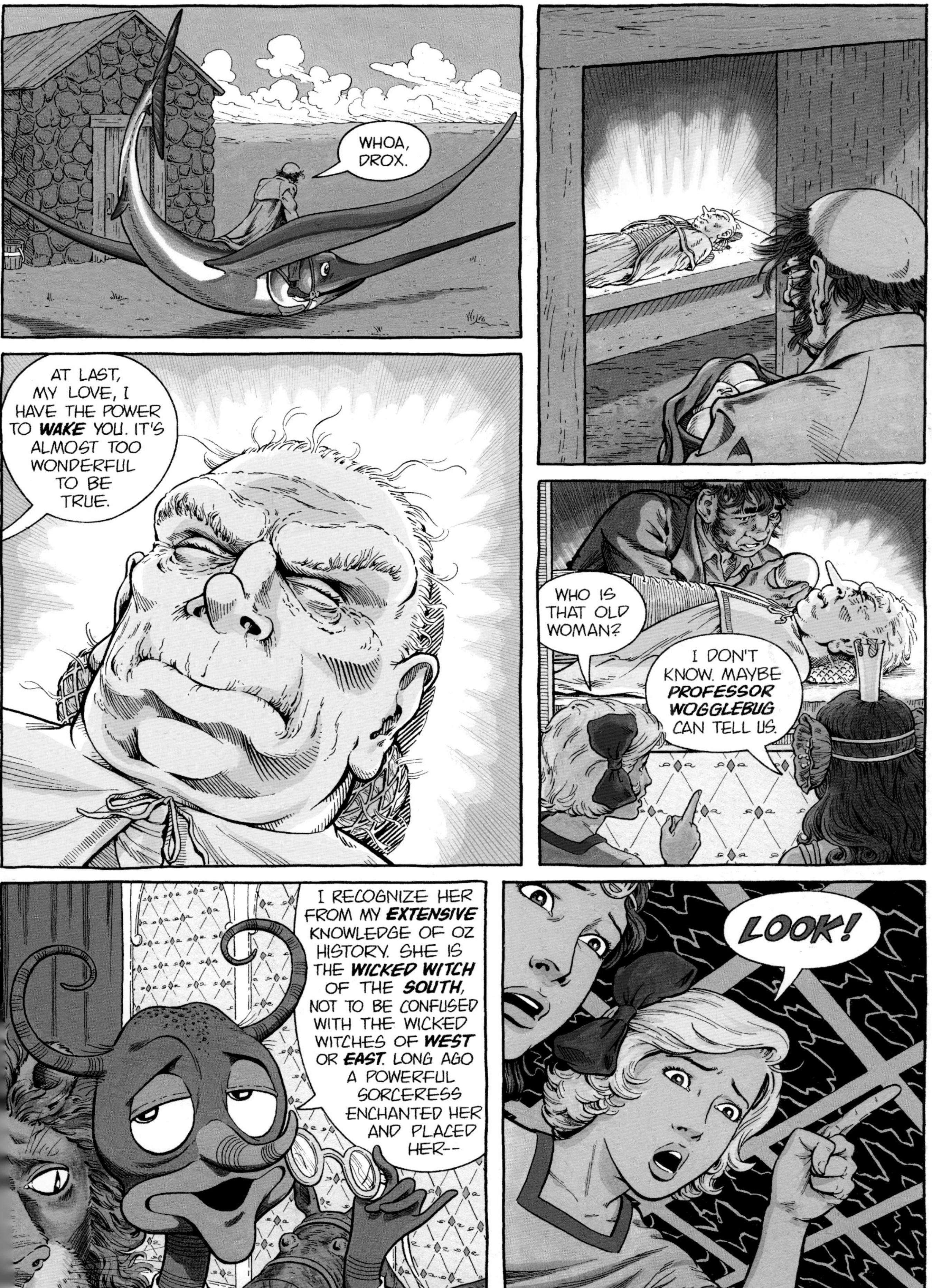
WHOA, DROX.
AT LAST, MY LOVE, I HAVE THE POWER TO **WAKE** YOU. IT'S ALMOST TOO WONDERFUL TO BE TRUE.
WHO IS THAT OLD WOMAN?
I DON'T KNOW. MAYBE **PROFESSOR WOGGLEBUG** CAN TELL US.
I RECOGNIZE HER FROM MY **EXTENSIVE** KNOWLEDGE OF OZ HISTORY. SHE IS THE **WICKED WITCH** OF THE **SOUTH**, NOT TO BE CONFUSED WITH THE WICKED WITCHES OF **WEST** OR **EAST**. LONG AGO A POWERFUL SORCERESS ENCHANTED HER AND PLACED HER--
LOOK!

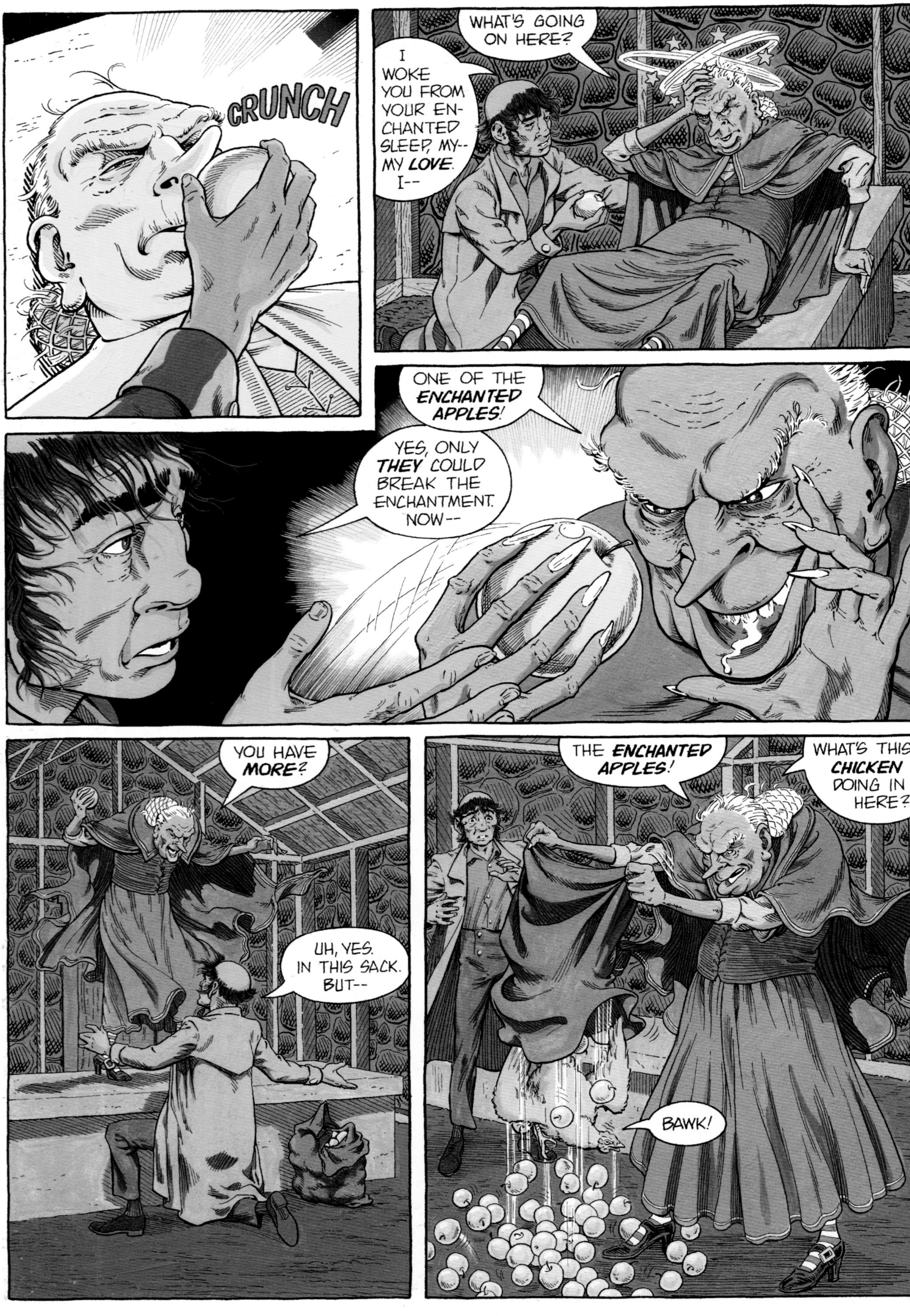
CRUNCH
WHAT'S GOING ON HERE?
I WOKE YOU FROM YOUR EN-CHANTED SLEEP, MY-- MY LOVE. I--
ONE OF THE ENCHANTED APPLES!
YES, ONLY THEY COULD BREAK THE ENCHANTMENT. NOW--
YOU HAVE MORE?
UH, YES. IN THIS SACK. BUT--
THE ENCHANTED APPLES!
WHAT'S THIS CHICKEN DOING IN HERE?
BAWK!

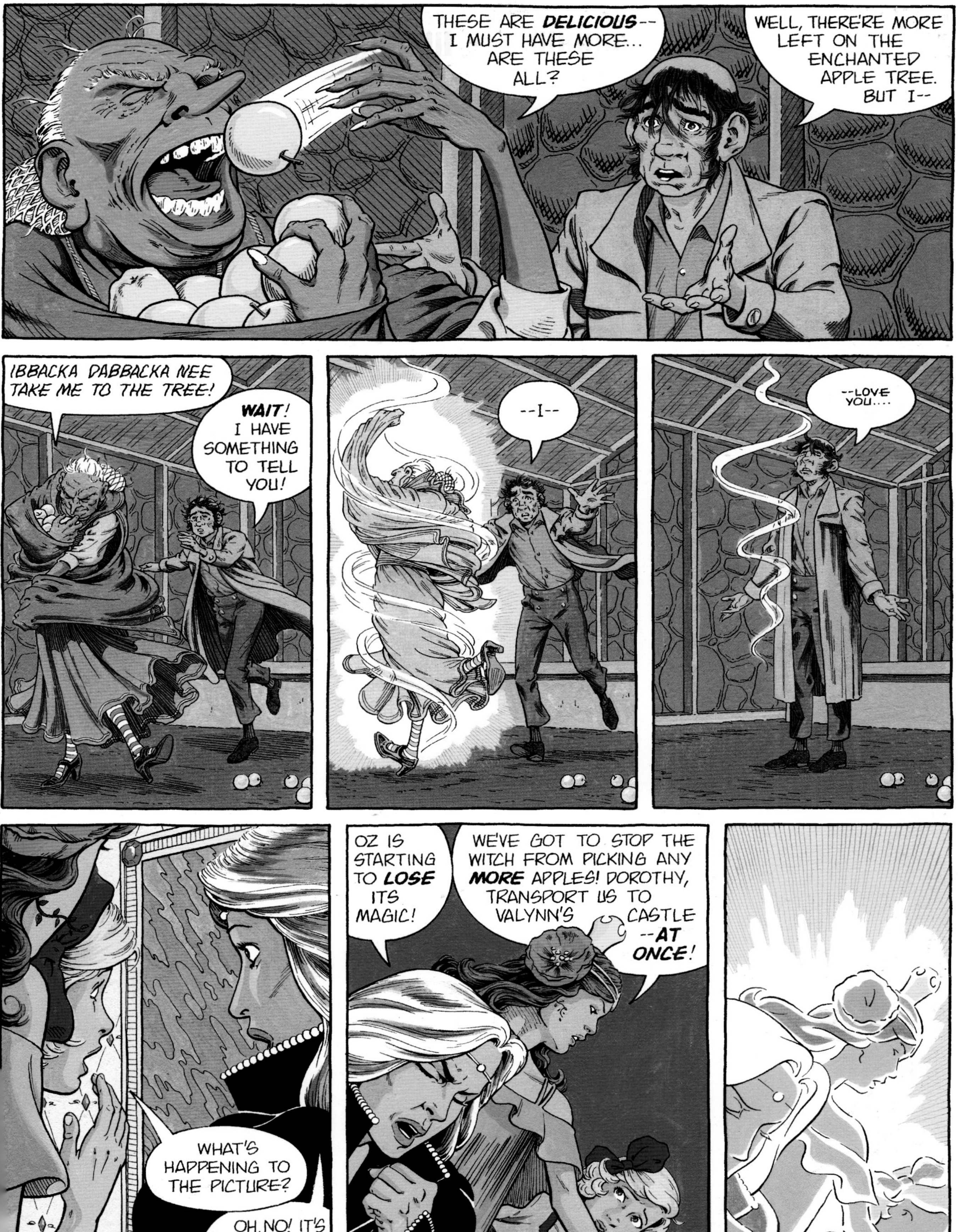
THESE ARE DELICIOUS-- I MUST HAVE MORE... ARE THESE ALL?
WELL, THERE'RE MORE LEFT ON THE ENCHANTED APPLE TREE. BUT I--
IBBACKA DABBACKA NEE TAKE ME TO THE TREE!
WAIT! I HAVE SOMETHING TO TELL YOU!
--I--
--LOVE YOU....
WHAT'S HAPPENING TO THE PICTURE?
OH, NO! IT'S STARTING ALREADY!
WHAT'S STARTING?
OZ IS STARTING TO LOSE ITS MAGIC!
WE'VE GOT TO STOP THE WITCH FROM PICKING ANY MORE APPLES! DOROTHY, TRANSPORT US TO VALYNN'S CASTLE --AT ONCE!

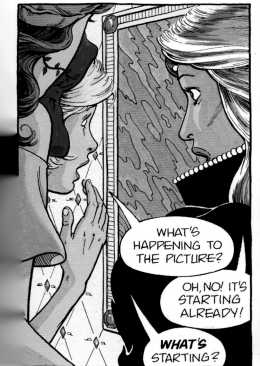

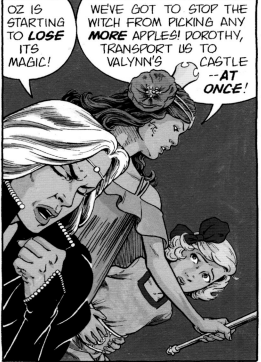

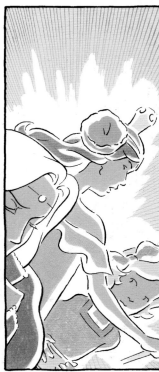

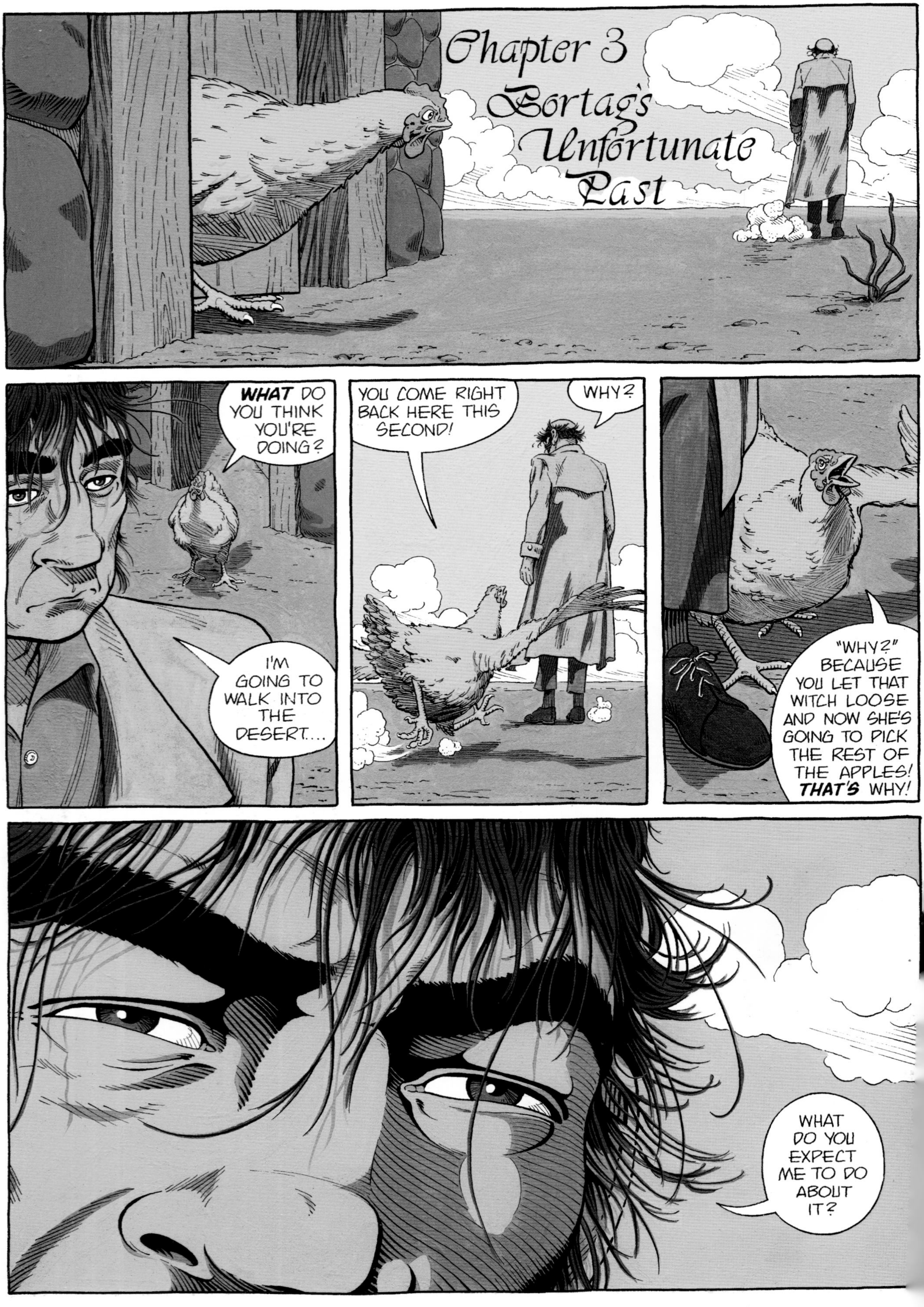

Chapter 3
Bortag's Unfortunate Past
WHAT DO YOU THINK YOU'RE DOING?
I'M GOING TO WALK INTO THE DESERT....
YOU COME RIGHT BACK HERE THIS SECOND!
WHY?
"WHY?" BECAUSE YOU LET THAT WITCH LOOSE AND NOW SHE'S GOING TO PICK THE REST OF THE APPLES! THAT'S WHY!
WHAT DO YOU EXPECT ME TO DO ABOUT IT?

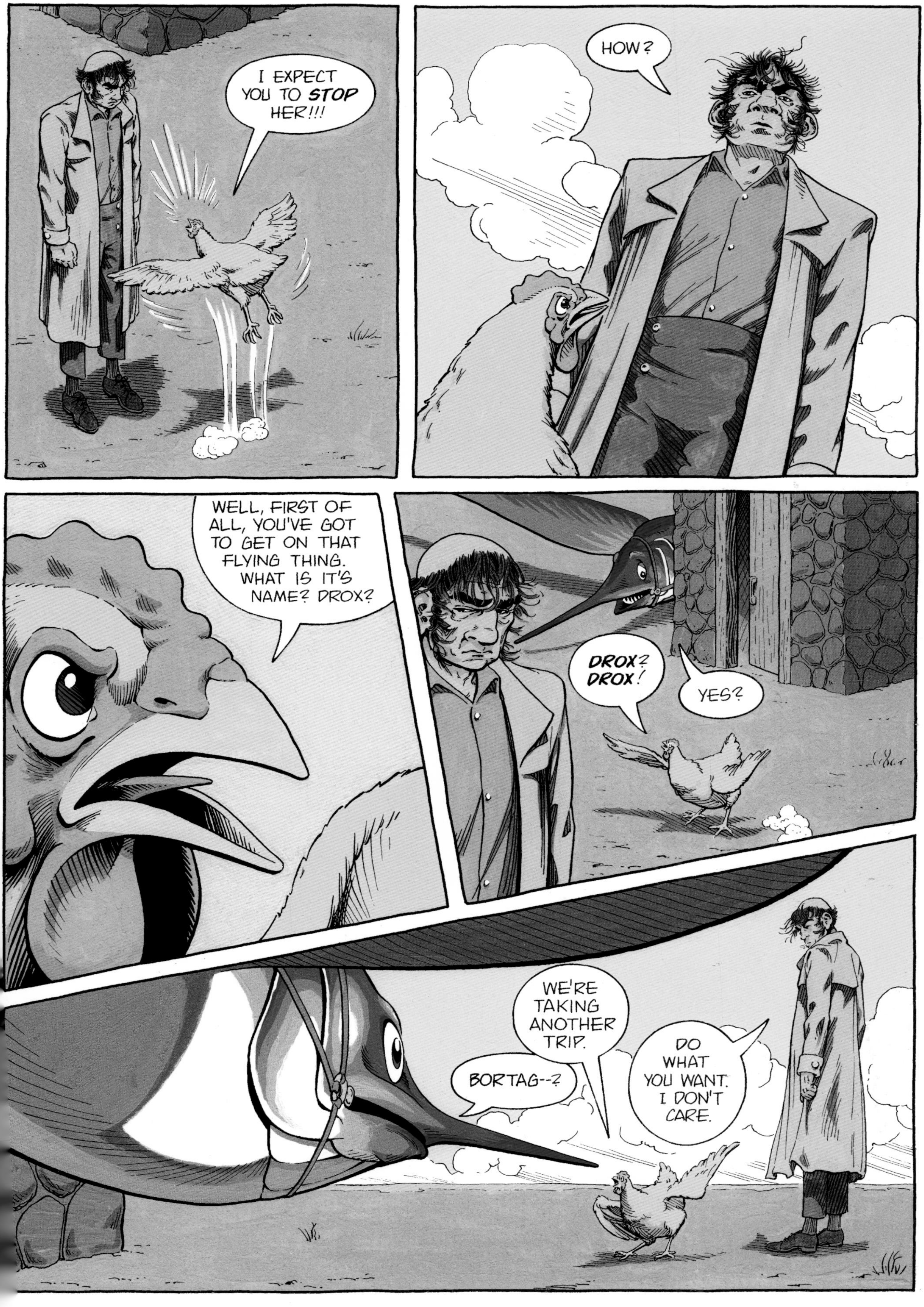
I EXPECT YOU TO **STOP** HER!!!
HOW?
WELL, FIRST OF ALL, YOU'VE GOT TO GET ON THAT FLYING THING. WHAT IS IT'S NAME? DROX?
**DROX? DROX!**
YES?
BORTAG--?
WE'RE TAKING ANOTHER TRIP.
DO WHAT YOU WANT. I DON'T CARE.

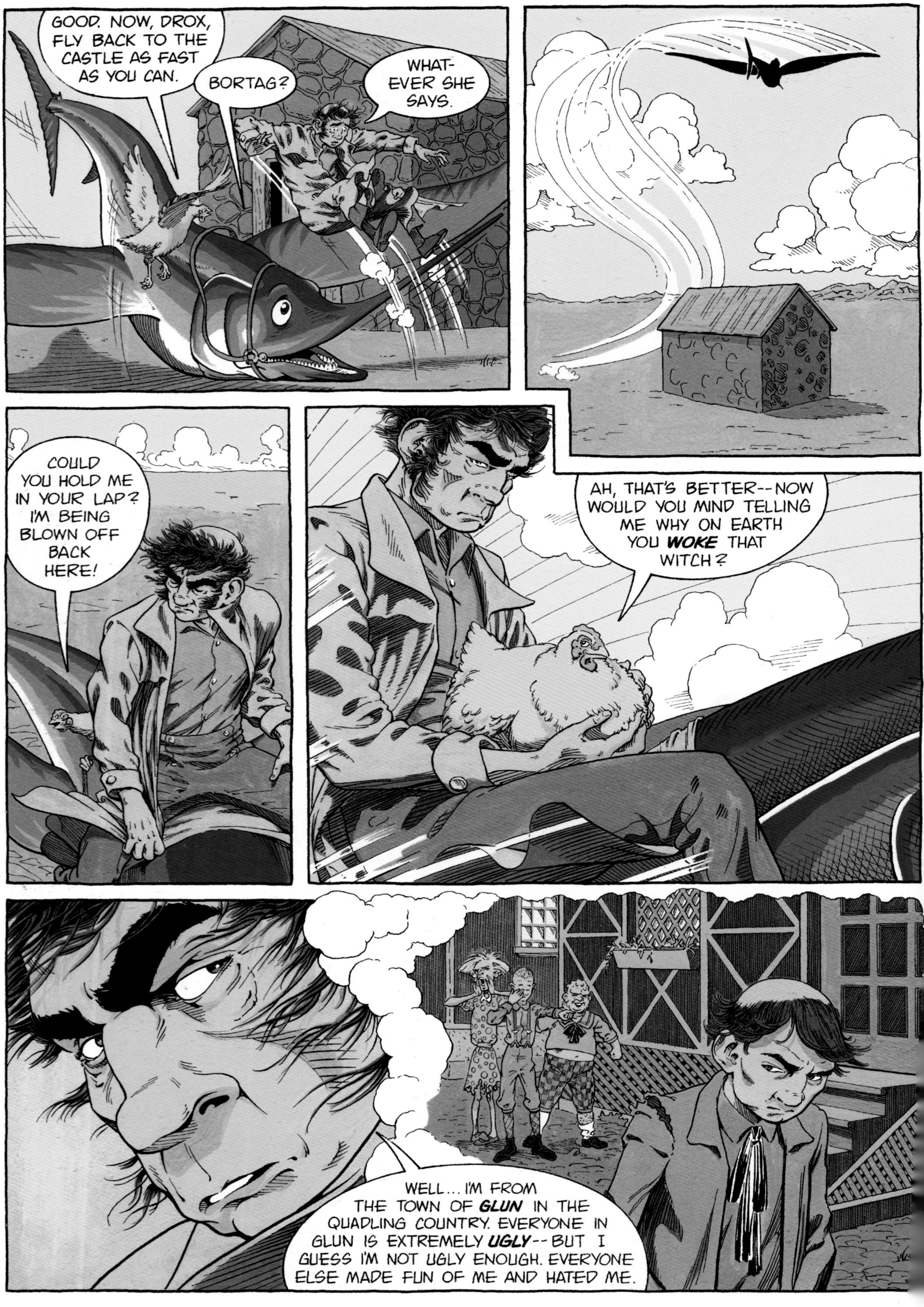
GOOD. NOW, DROX, FLY BACK TO THE CASTLE AS FAST AS YOU CAN.
BORTAG?
WHAT-EVER SHE SAYS.
COULD YOU HOLD ME IN YOUR LAP? I'M BEING BLOWN OFF BACK HERE!
AH, THAT'S BETTER--NOW WOULD YOU MIND TELLING ME WHY ON EARTH YOU **WOKE** THAT WITCH?
WELL... I'M FROM THE TOWN OF **GLUN** IN THE QUADLING COUNTRY. EVERYONE IN GLUN IS EXTREMELY **UGLY**--BUT I GUESS I'M NOT UGLY ENOUGH. EVERYONE ELSE MADE FUN OF ME AND HATED ME.

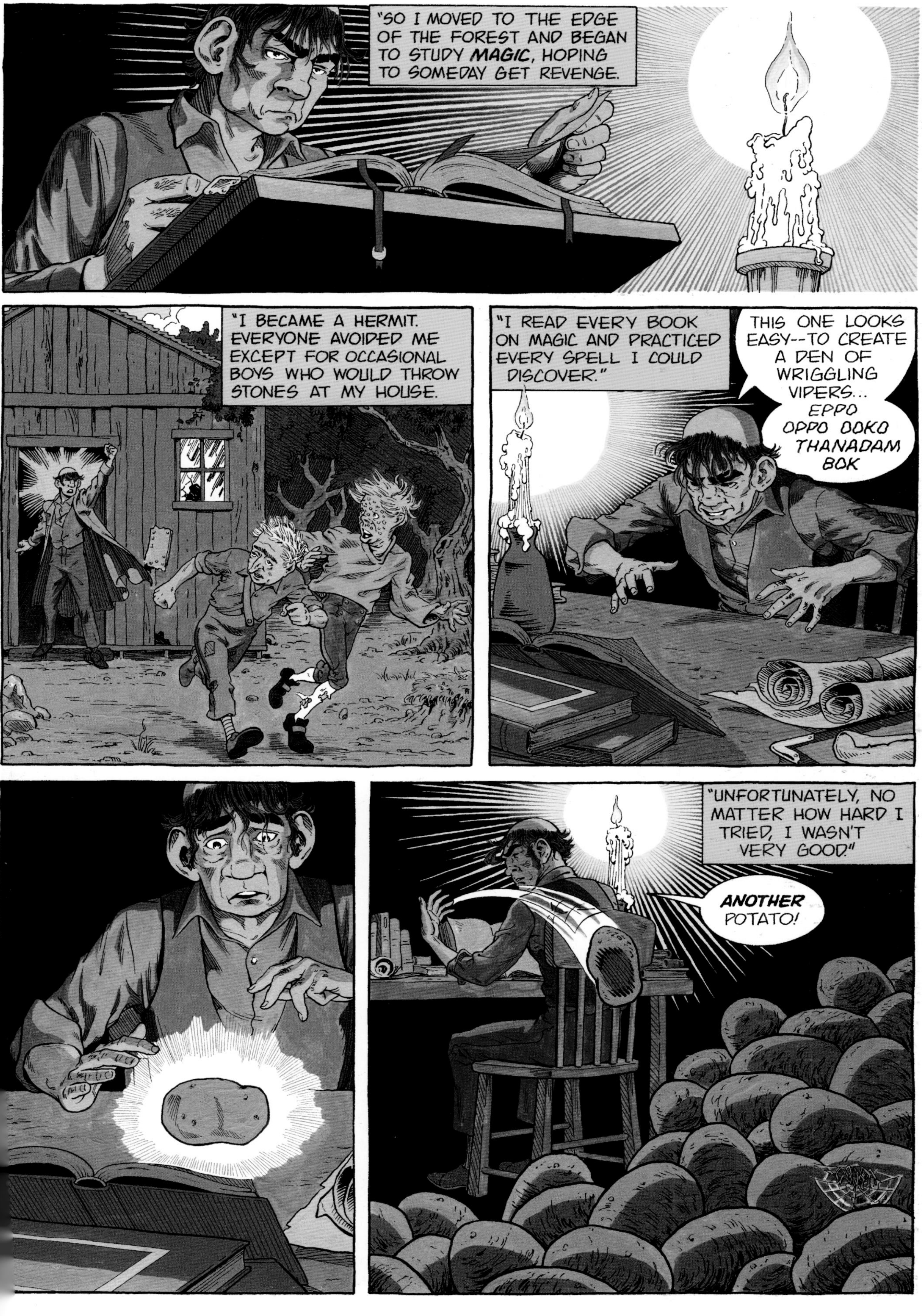
"SO I MOVED TO THE EDGE OF THE FOREST AND BEGAN TO STUDY **MAGIC**, HOPING TO SOMEDAY GET REVENGE.
"I BECAME A HERMIT. EVERYONE AVOIDED ME EXCEPT FOR OCCASIONAL BOYS WHO WOULD THROW STONES AT MY HOUSE.
"I READ EVERY BOOK ON MAGIC AND PRACTICED EVERY SPELL I COULD DISCOVER."
THIS ONE LOOKS EASY--TO CREATE A DEN OF WRIGGLING VIPERS...
*EPPO OPPO OOKO THANADAM BOK*
"UNFORTUNATELY, NO MATTER HOW HARD I TRIED, I WASN'T VERY GOOD."
***ANOTHER*** POTATO!

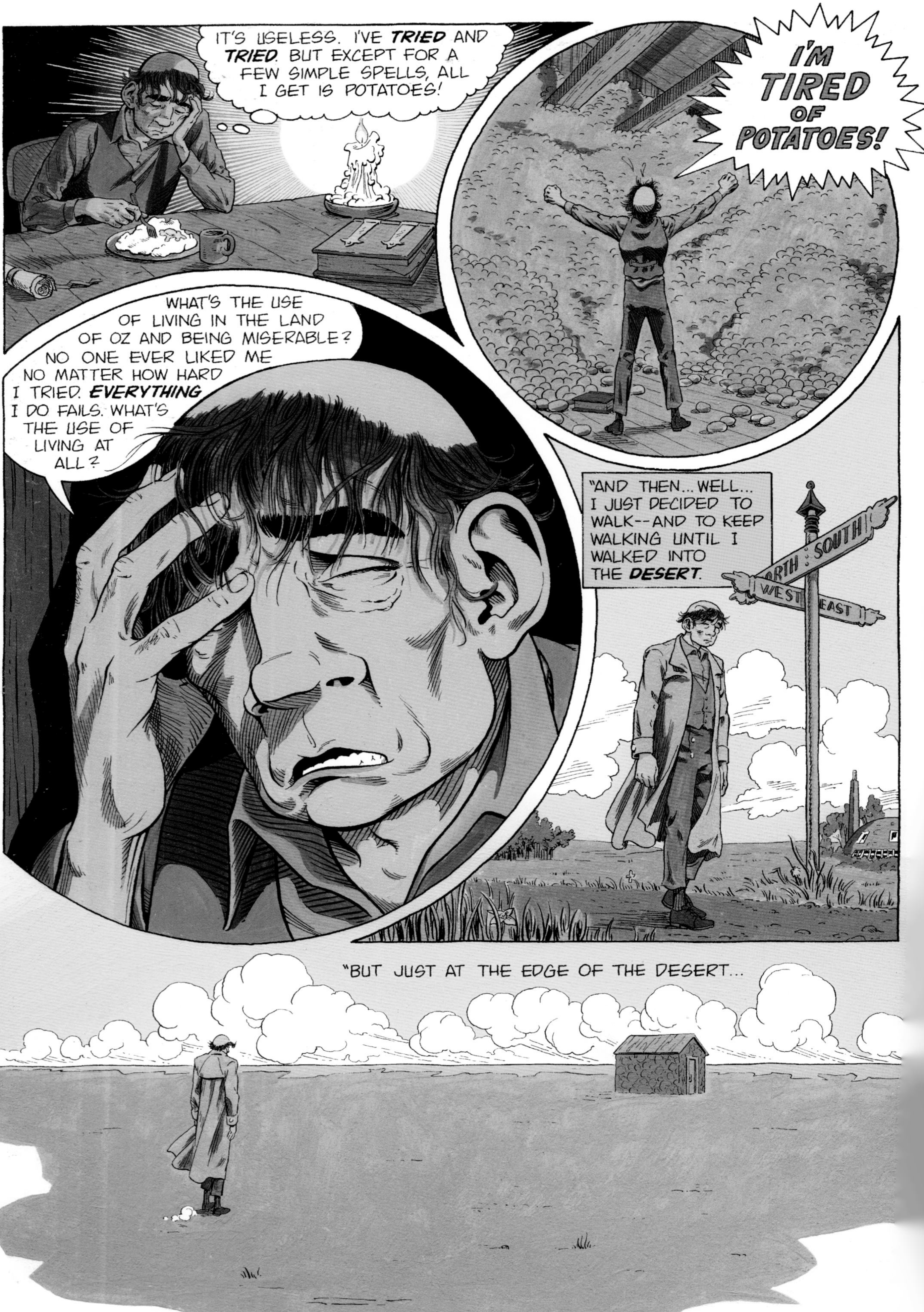
IT'S USELESS. I'VE TRIED AND TRIED. BUT EXCEPT FOR A FEW SIMPLE SPELLS, ALL I GET IS POTATOES!
I'M TIRED OF POTATOES!
WHAT'S THE USE OF LIVING IN THE LAND OF OZ AND BEING MISERABLE? NO ONE EVER LIKED ME NO MATTER HOW HARD I TRIED. EVERYTHING I DO FAILS. WHAT'S THE USE OF LIVING AT ALL?
"AND THEN... WELL... I JUST DECIDED TO WALK--AND TO KEEP WALKING UNTIL I WALKED INTO THE DESERT.
SOUTH
WEST
EAST
"BUT JUST AT THE EDGE OF THE DESERT...

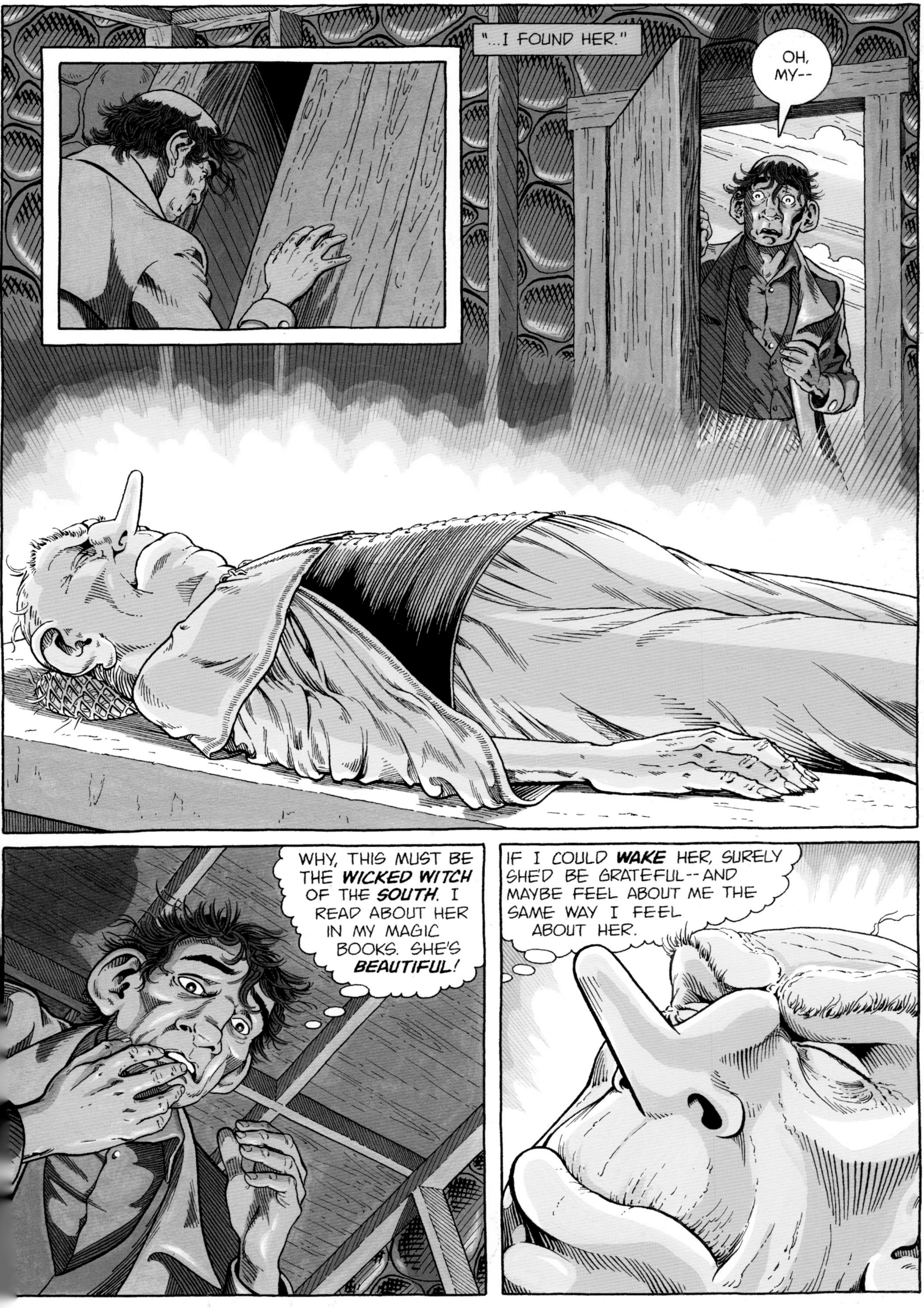
"...I FOUND HER."
OH, MY--
WHY, THIS MUST BE THE ***WICKED WITCH*** OF THE ***SOUTH***. I READ ABOUT HER IN MY MAGIC BOOKS. SHE'S ***BEAUTIFUL***!
IF I COULD ***WAKE*** HER, SURELY SHE'D BE GRATEFUL--AND MAYBE FEEL ABOUT ME THE SAME WAY I FEEL ABOUT HER.

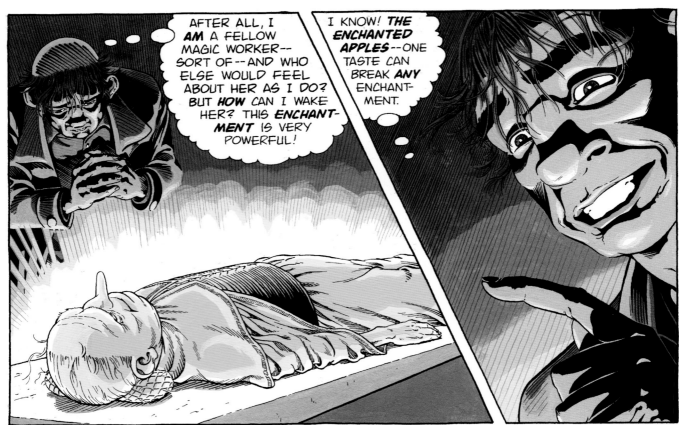

AFTER ALL, I *AM* A FELLOW MAGIC WORKER--SORT OF--AND WHO ELSE WOULD FEEL ABOUT HER AS I DO? BUT *HOW* CAN I WAKE HER? THIS *ENCHANTMENT* IS VERY POWERFUL!

I KNOW! *THE ENCHANTED APPLES*--ONE TASTE CAN BREAK *ANY* ENCHANTMENT.

"SO AGAIN I SET OUT, BUT THIS TIME I WAS *DETERMINED* NOT TO FAIL. I HAD TO GET AN APPLE, THOUGH I KNEW THEY WERE FORBIDDEN.

"I GOT INTO THE CASTLE WITHOUT MUCH TROUBLE...

"...BUT I DIDN'T GET AN APPLE.

"HOPING TO **SCARE** THEM INTO GIVING ME AN APPLE, I THREATENED TO USE MY MAGIC AGAINST THEM. I DIDN'T HAVE MUCH HOPE--A MAGICAL ATTACK WAS BEYOND MY FEW ABILITIES. WHAT COULD I DO, THROW **POTATOES** AT THEM?

"I SCARED THEM, ALL RIGHT, BUT NOT AS I HAD INTENDED.

"SO I WENT BACK TO THE WITCH."

SOMEDAY THE APPLES WILL COME BACK. I DON'T KNOW WHEN, BUT I'LL WAIT--AND WHEN THEY DO, **NOTHING** WILL STOP ME FROM TAKING ONE.

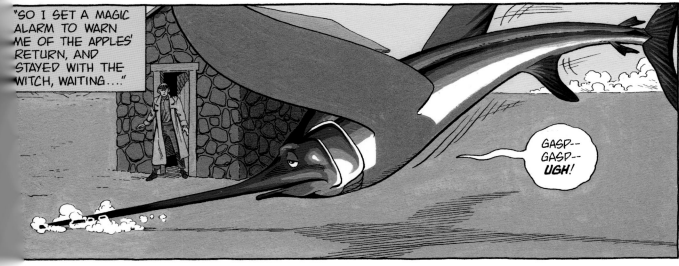

"SO I SET A MAGIC ALARM TO WARN ME OF THE APPLES' RETURN, AND STAYED WITH THE WITCH, WAITING...."

GASP-- GASP-- **UGH!**

43

THIS IS **PERFECT**! I CAN USE THIS FLYING THING--WHATEVER IT IS--TO GET THE ENCHANTED APPLES!

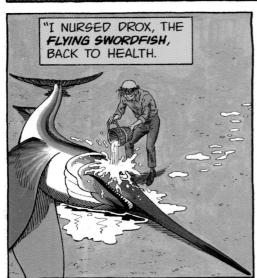

"I NURSED DROX, THE **FLYING SWORDFISH**, BACK TO HEALTH.

"SINCE I HAD SAVED HIS LIFE, DROX WAS CONTENT TO SERVE ME."

FAR BEYOND THE DESERT IS THE OCEAN WHERE I LIVE. I USED TO SWIM AND FLY AROUND WITH MY FRIENDS, THE OTHER FLYING SWORDFISH.

BUT ONE DAY I DECIDED TO SEE **MORE** OF THE WORLD.

"SO I FLEW ACROSS THE LAND. AT FIRST I SAW GREAT CITIES, BUT THEN I GOT LOST OVER THE DESERT. I BARELY CROSSED IT ALIVE AND WOULD BE DEAD NOW-- IF NOT FOR **YOU**, BORTAG."

BUT NOW WITHOUT **OCEAN** WATER, I'LL NEVER BE STRONG ENOUGH TO CROSS THE DESERT AGAIN.

WITH DROX'S HELP I **DID** GET THE APPLES...BUT-- IT DIDN'T TURN OUT THE WAY I FIGURED....

WELL, ALL I HAVE TO SAY IS **CUT-CUT-CUT-KA-DAW!**

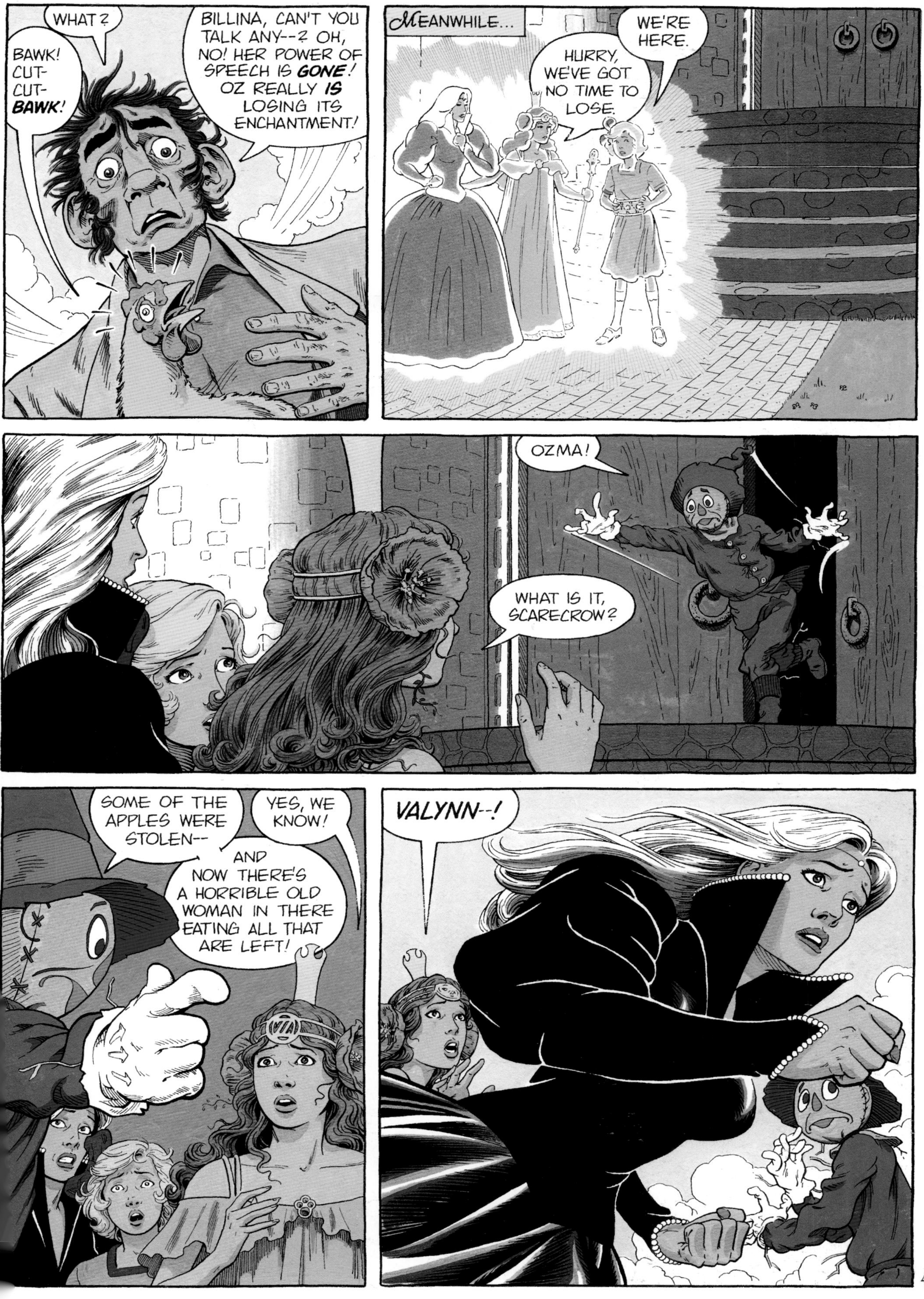
BAWK! CUT-CUT-**BAWK**!
WHAT?
BILLINA, CAN'T YOU TALK ANY--? OH, NO! HER POWER OF SPEECH IS **GONE**! OZ REALLY **IS** LOSING ITS ENCHANTMENT!
MEANWHILE...
HURRY, WE'VE GOT NO TIME TO LOSE.
WE'RE HERE.
OZMA!
WHAT IS IT, SCARECROW?
SOME OF THE APPLES WERE STOLEN--
YES, WE KNOW!
AND NOW THERE'S A HORRIBLE OLD WOMAN IN THERE EATING ALL THAT ARE LEFT!
VALYNN--!

FOLLOW ME! I'M AFRAID VALYNN MAY DO SOMETHING DRASTIC!

WHAT'S THIS? COMPANY?

TOO BAD THERE'S NOT ENOUGH TO GO AROUND!

HEY!

OH, NO!

SCARECROW, WHAT ARE YOU--?

THE SCARECROW'S UNDER HER POWER!

WELL, WELL, THE MAGIC BELT-- *MY* MAGIC BELT. NOW, WHY DON'T YOU THREE RUN ALONG BEFORE I USE IT TO TRANSFORM YOU INTO CORN COBS OR SOMETHING?

I AM OZMA, RULER OF OZ. I *COMMAND* YOU TO SURRENDER AT ONCE.

OH, GO AWAY, LITTLE GIRL. I'M HAVING MUCH TOO DELICIOUS A TIME. HMMM, HERE'S A *SILVER* APPLE...

...THAT LOOKS QUITE TASTY.

*NO!*

MY, SUCH TEMPER! I'LL HAVE TO *CHANGE* THAT!

47

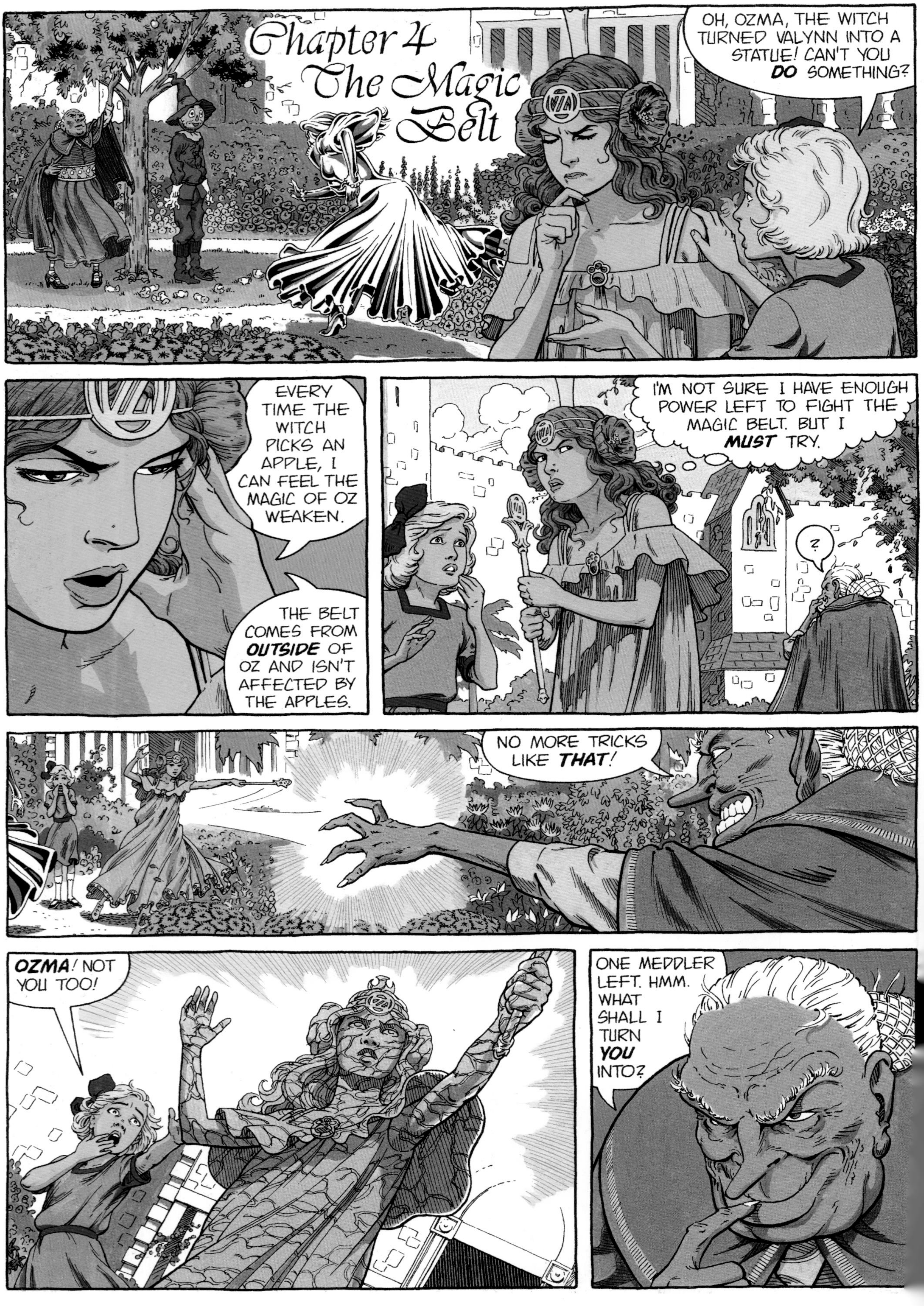
Chapter 4
The Magic Belt
OH, OZMA, THE WITCH TURNED VALYNN INTO A STATUE! CAN'T YOU DO SOMETHING?
EVERY TIME THE WITCH PICKS AN APPLE, I CAN FEEL THE MAGIC OF OZ WEAKEN.
THE BELT COMES FROM OUTSIDE OF OZ AND ISN'T AFFECTED BY THE APPLES.
I'M NOT SURE I HAVE ENOUGH POWER LEFT TO FIGHT THE MAGIC BELT. BUT I MUST TRY.
?
NO MORE TRICKS LIKE THAT!
OZMA! NOT YOU TOO!
ONE MEDDLER LEFT. HMM. WHAT SHALL I TURN YOU INTO?

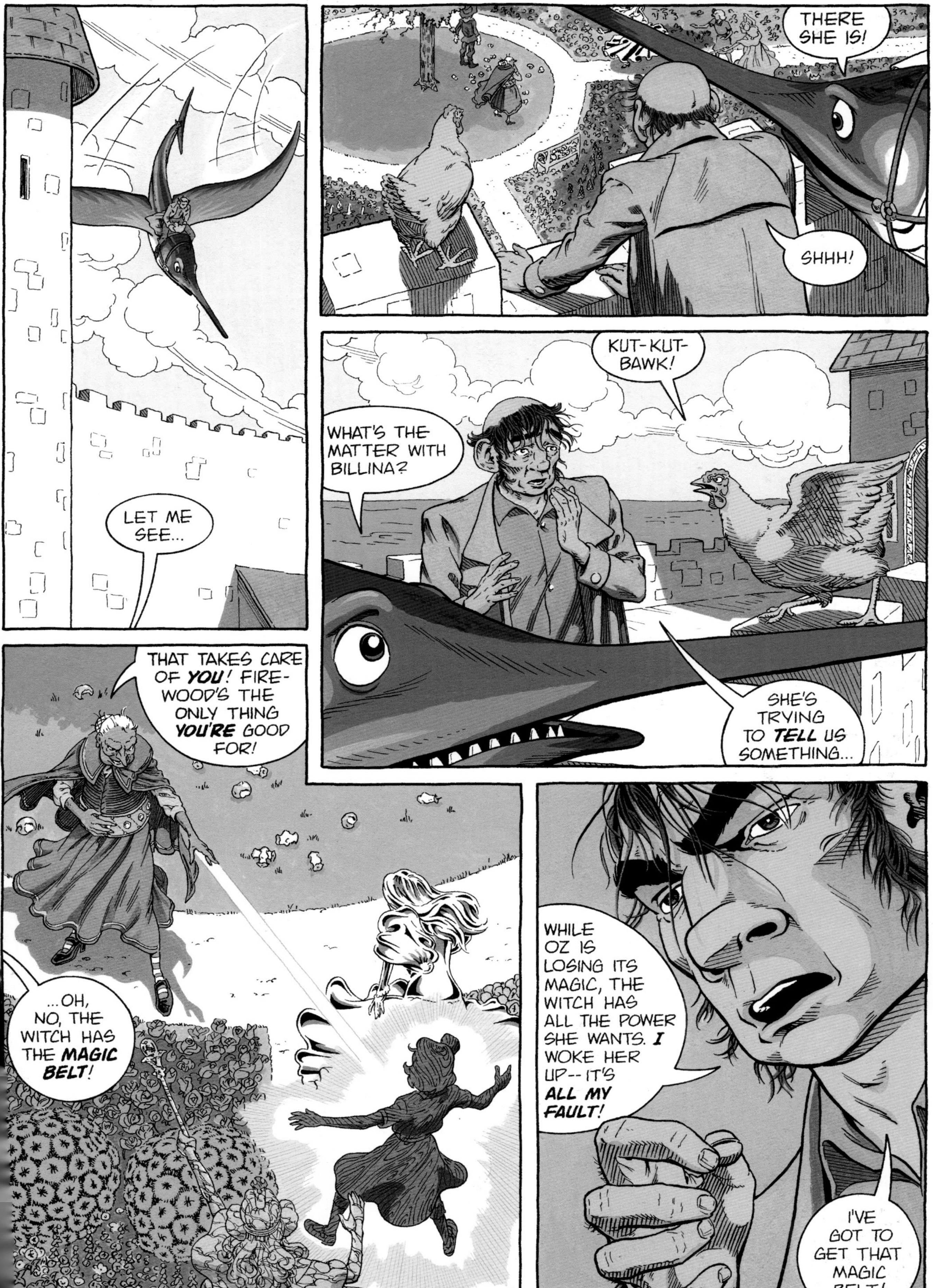
LET ME SEE...
THERE SHE IS!
SHHH!
KUT-KUT-BAWK!
WHAT'S THE MATTER WITH BILLINA?
SHE'S TRYING TO **TELL** US SOMETHING...
THAT TAKES CARE OF ***YOU***! FIRE-WOOD'S THE ONLY THING ***YOU'RE*** GOOD FOR!
...OH, NO, THE WITCH HAS THE ***MAGIC BELT***!
WHILE OZ IS LOSING ITS MAGIC, THE WITCH HAS ALL THE POWER SHE WANTS. ***I*** WOKE HER UP-- IT'S ***ALL MY FAULT***!
I'VE GOT TO GET THAT MAGIC BELT!

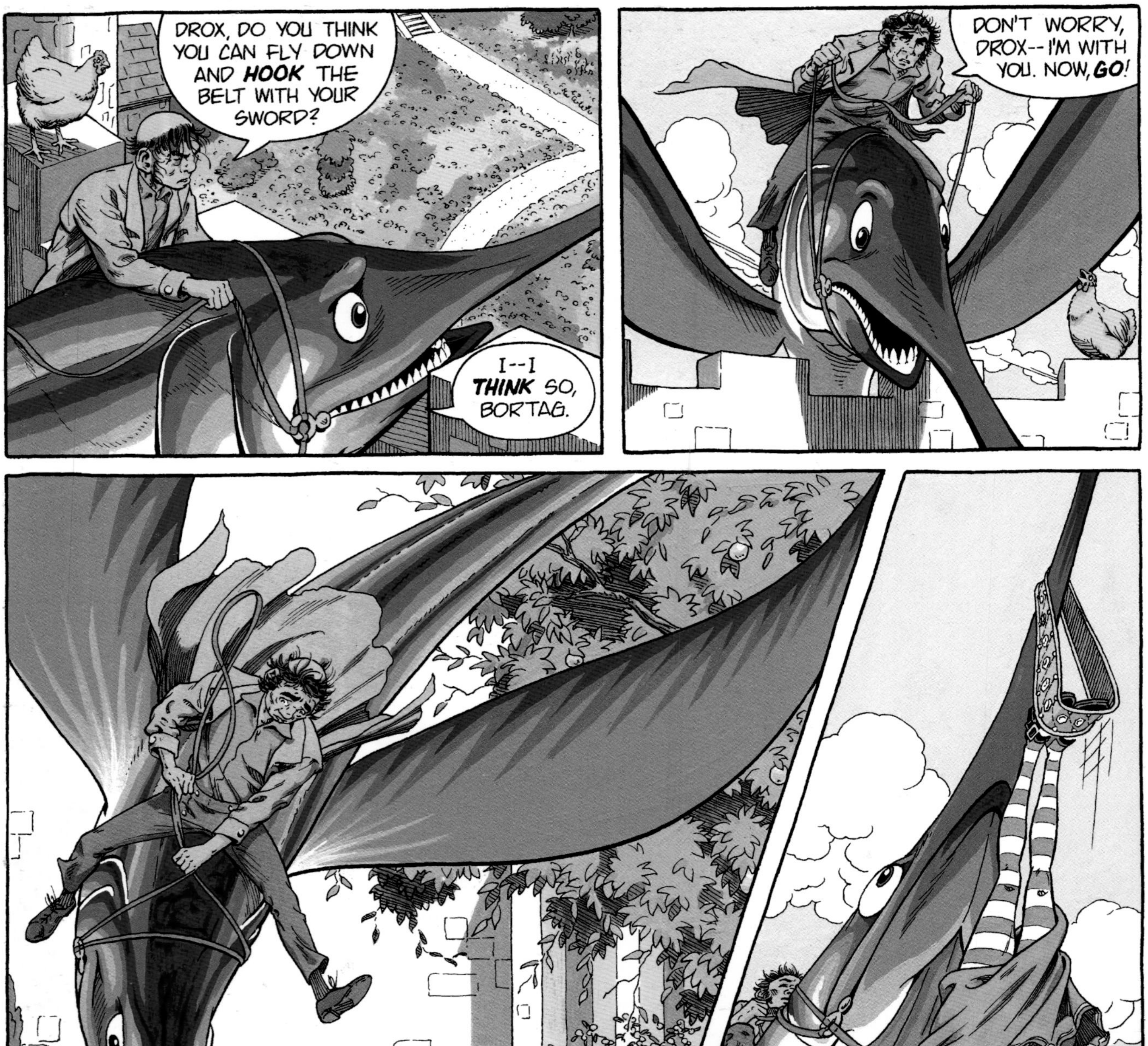

DROX, DO YOU THINK YOU CAN FLY DOWN AND **HOOK** THE BELT WITH YOUR SWORD?
I--I **THINK** SO, BORTAG.
DON'T WORRY, DROX--I'M WITH YOU. NOW, **GO**!
**HEY!**
WHAT'S GOING--
--ONNAAAHHH--

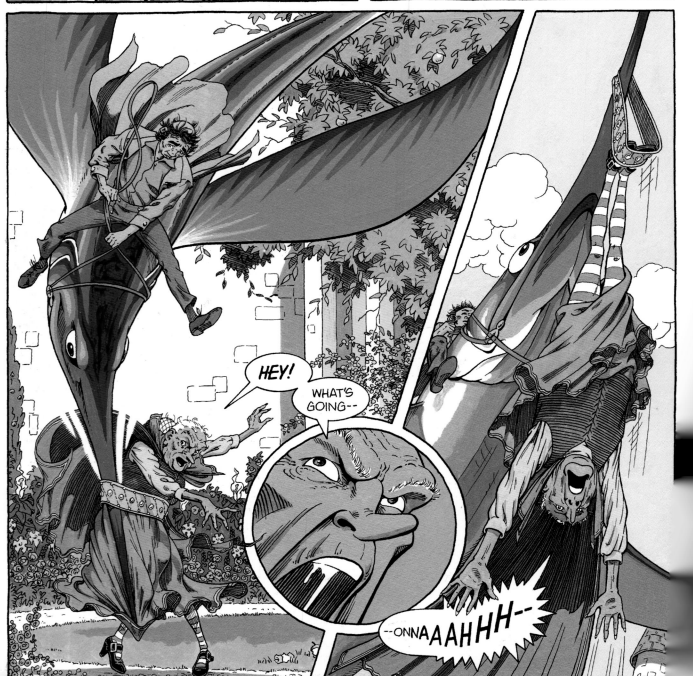

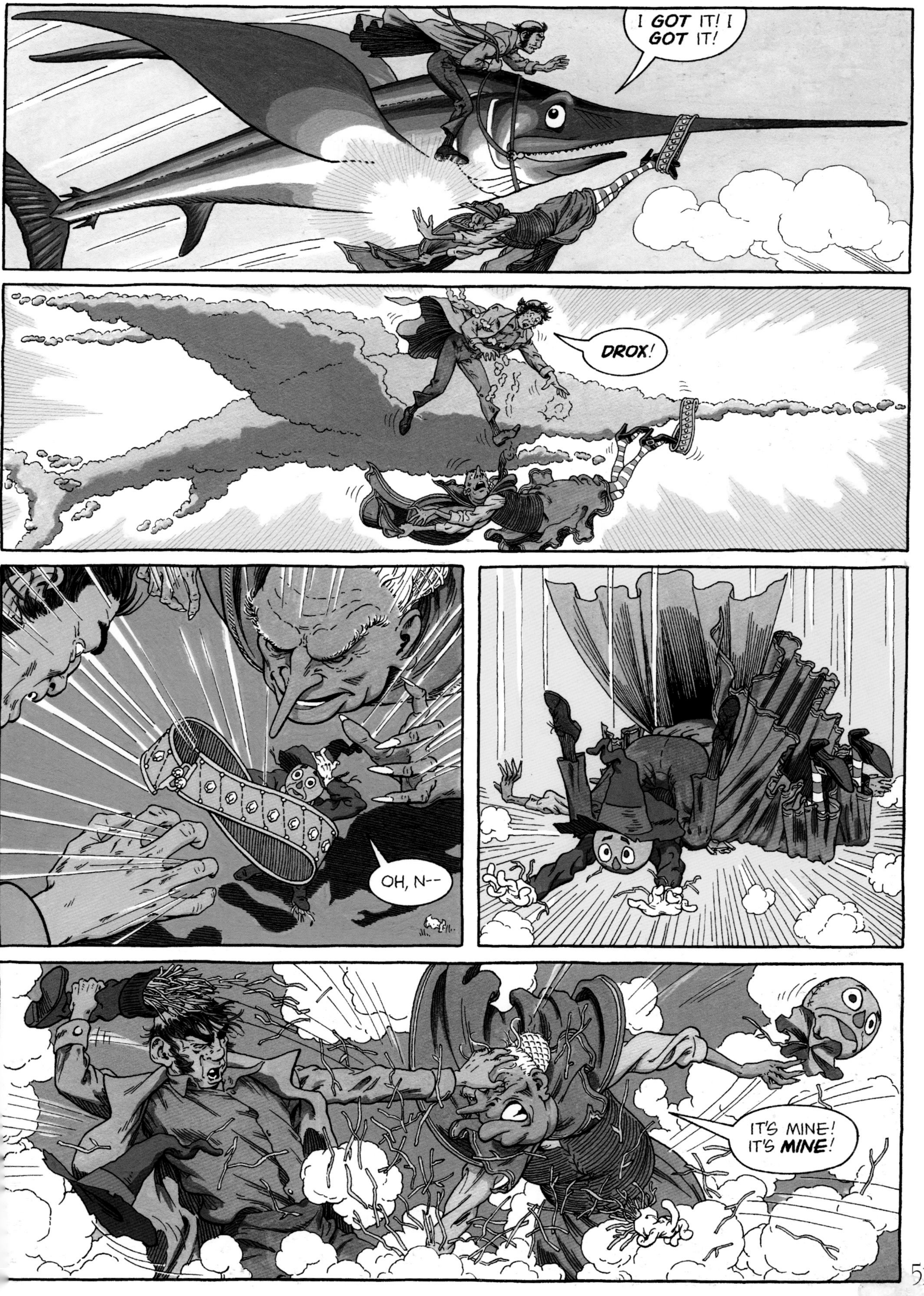
I GOT IT! I GOT IT!
DROX!
OH, N--
IT'S MINE! IT'S MINE!

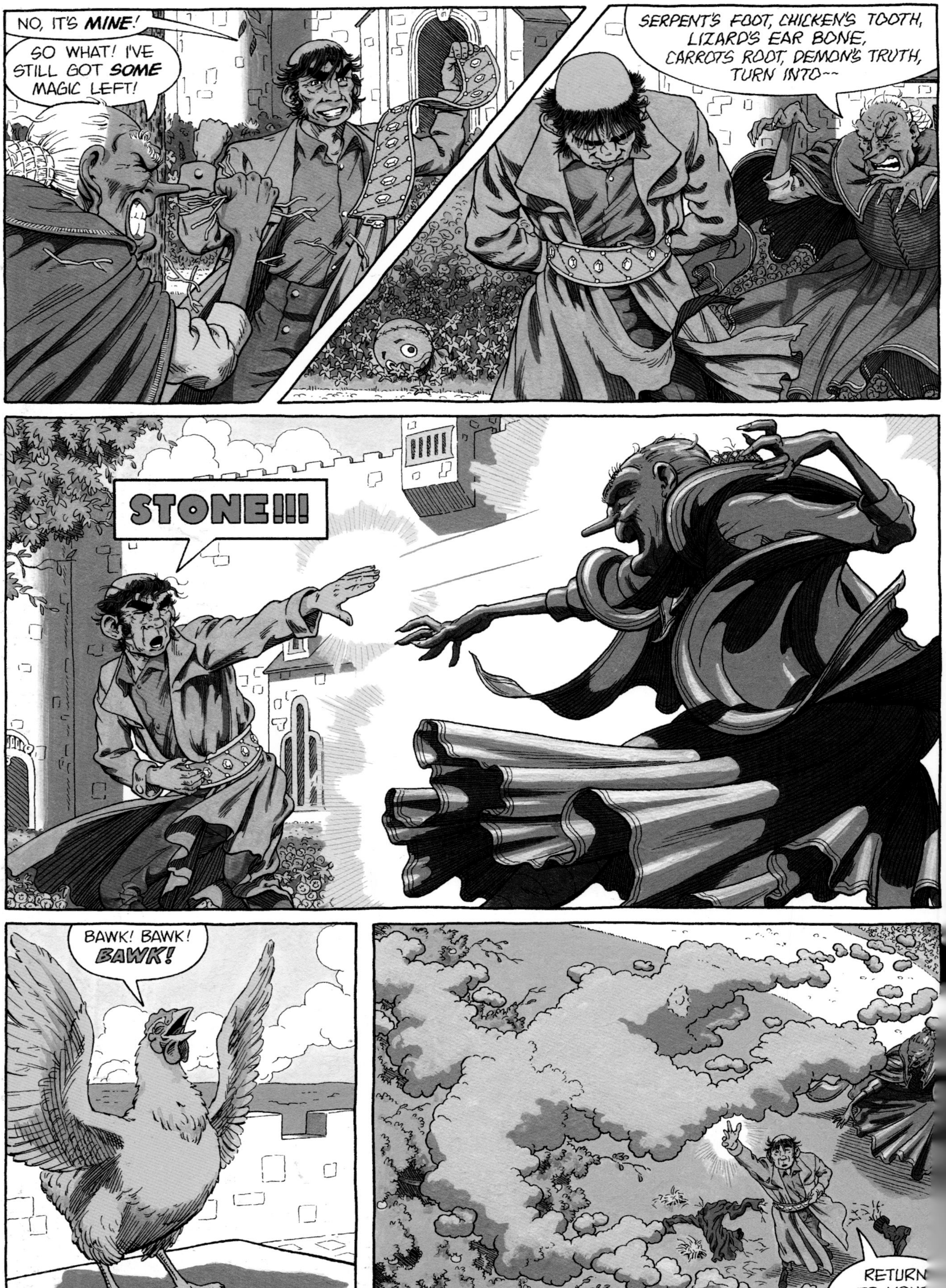
NO, IT'S MINE!
SO WHAT! I'VE STILL GOT SOME MAGIC LEFT!
SERPENT'S FOOT, CHICKEN'S TOOTH, LIZARD'S EAR BONE, CARROTS ROOT, DEMON'S TRUTH, TURN INTO~~
STONE!!!
BAWK! BAWK! BAWK!
RETURN TO YOUR TRUE FORM

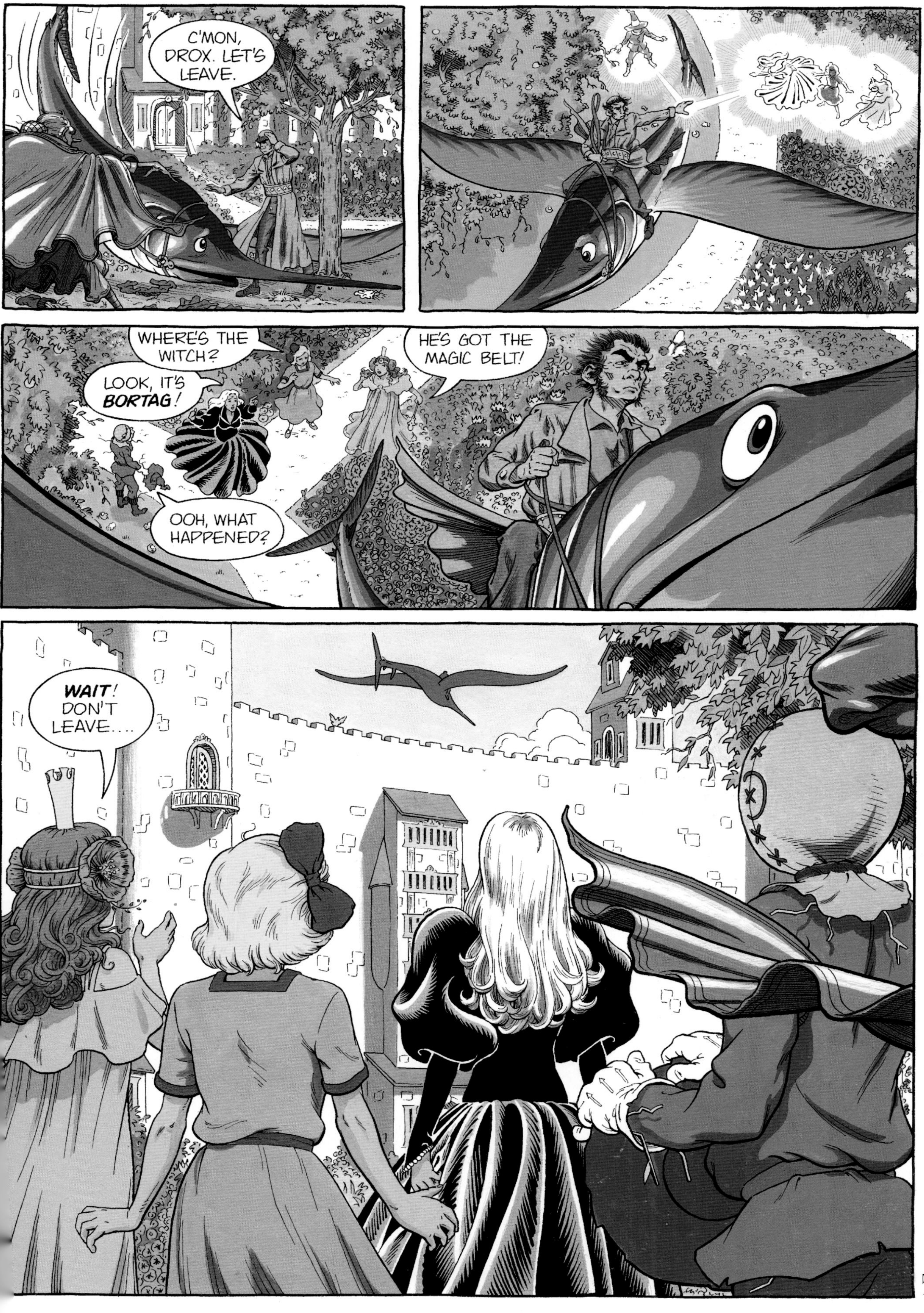
C'MON, DROX. LET'S LEAVE.
WHERE'S THE WITCH?
LOOK, IT'S **BORTAG**!
HE'S GOT THE MAGIC BELT!
OOH, WHAT HAPPENED?
**WAIT**! DON'T LEAVE....

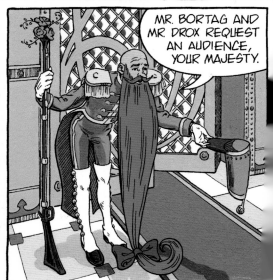

SHOW THEM IN *AT ONCE!*

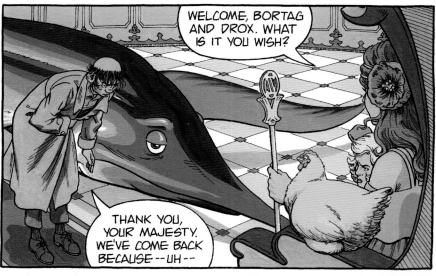

WELCOME, BORTAG AND DROX. WHAT IS IT YOU WISH?

THANK YOU, YOUR MAJESTY. WE'VE COME BACK BECAUSE--UH--

WELL...ER... WE'VE COME TO RETURN *THIS*.

UM, Y'SEE, I THOUGHT THE MAGIC BELT COULD GIVE ME EVERYTHING I EVER WANTED--THAT'S WHY I KEPT IT.

BUT AS SOON AS I HAD IT, I REALIZED THAT ALL I EVER REALLY WANTED WAS FOR SOMEONE TO *LIKE* ME. AND I FOUND THAT I ALREADY HAD WHAT I WANTED--

--A *TRUE FRIEND*--DROX. SO PLEASE, YOUR MAJESTY, I'VE NO RIGHT TO ASK, BUT COULD YOU TRANSPORT HIM BACK TO THE OCEAN AND SEND ME WITH HIM?

55

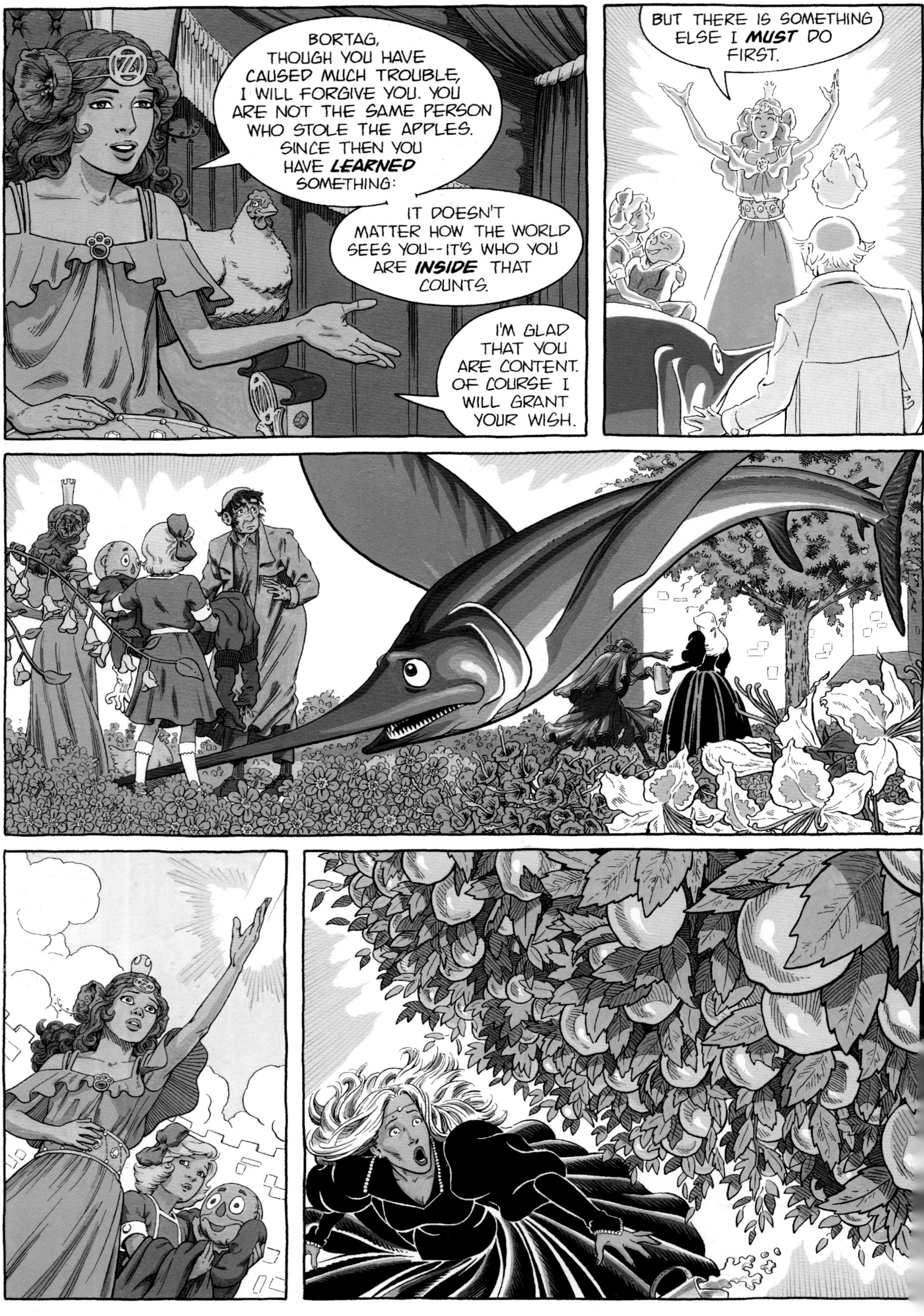
BORTAG, THOUGH YOU HAVE CAUSED MUCH TROUBLE, I WILL FORGIVE YOU. YOU ARE NOT THE SAME PERSON WHO STOLE THE APPLES. SINCE THEN YOU HAVE ***LEARNED*** SOMETHING:
IT DOESN'T MATTER HOW THE WORLD SEES YOU--IT'S WHO YOU ARE ***INSIDE*** THAT COUNTS.
I'M GLAD THAT YOU ARE CONTENT. OF COURSE I WILL GRANT YOUR WISH.
BUT THERE IS SOMETHING ELSE I ***MUST*** DO FIRST.

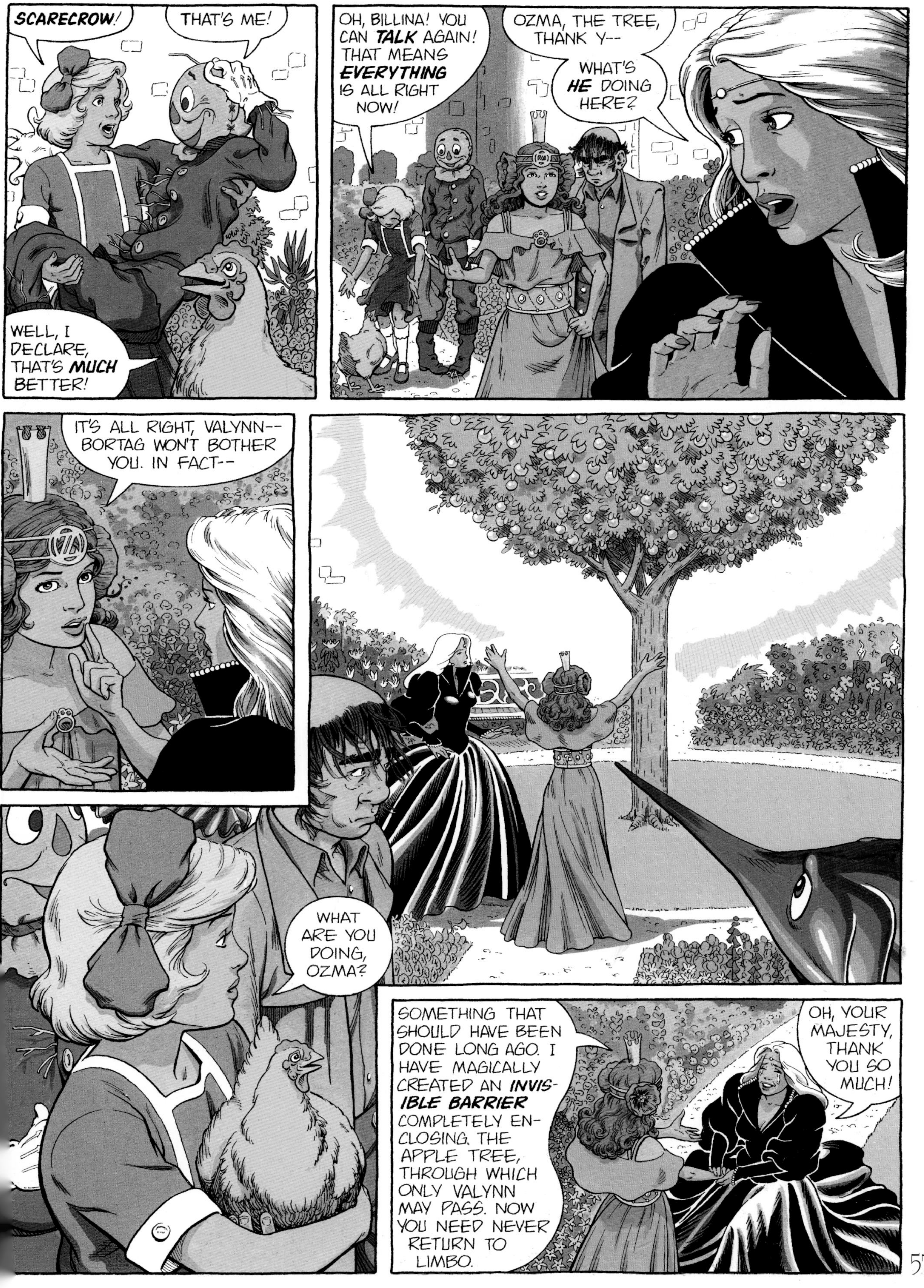
SCARECROW!
THAT'S ME!
WELL, I DECLARE, THAT'S MUCH BETTER!
OH, BILLINA! YOU CAN TALK AGAIN! THAT MEANS EVERYTHING IS ALL RIGHT NOW!
OZMA, THE TREE, THANK Y--
WHAT'S HE DOING HERE?
IT'S ALL RIGHT, VALYNN-- BORTAG WON'T BOTHER YOU. IN FACT--
WHAT ARE YOU DOING, OZMA?
SOMETHING THAT SHOULD HAVE BEEN DONE LONG AGO. I HAVE MAGICALLY CREATED AN INVISIBLE BARRIER COMPLETELY ENCLOSING THE APPLE TREE, THROUGH WHICH ONLY VALYNN MAY PASS. NOW YOU NEED NEVER RETURN TO LIMBO.
OH, YOUR MAJESTY, THANK YOU SO MUCH!

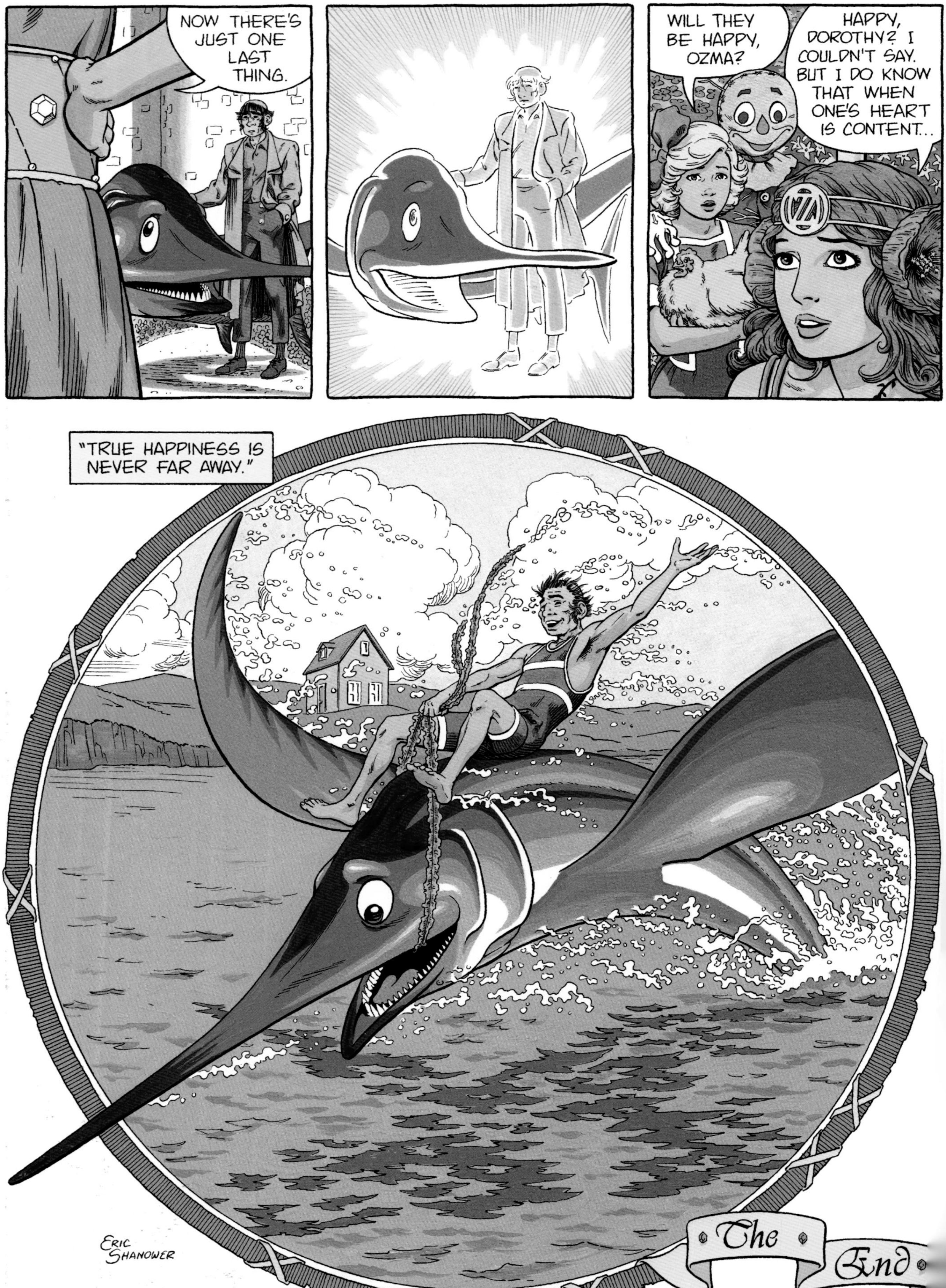
NOW THERE'S JUST ONE LAST THING.
WILL THEY BE HAPPY, OZMA?
HAPPY, DOROTHY? I COULDN'T SAY. BUT I DO KNOW THAT WHEN ONE'S HEART IS CONTENT...
"TRUE HAPPINESS IS NEVER FAR AWAY."
ERIC SHANOWER
The End

# The SECRET ISLAND of Oz

Dedicated
with love
to my parents

# Chapter 1 The Crimson-tailed Quipperug

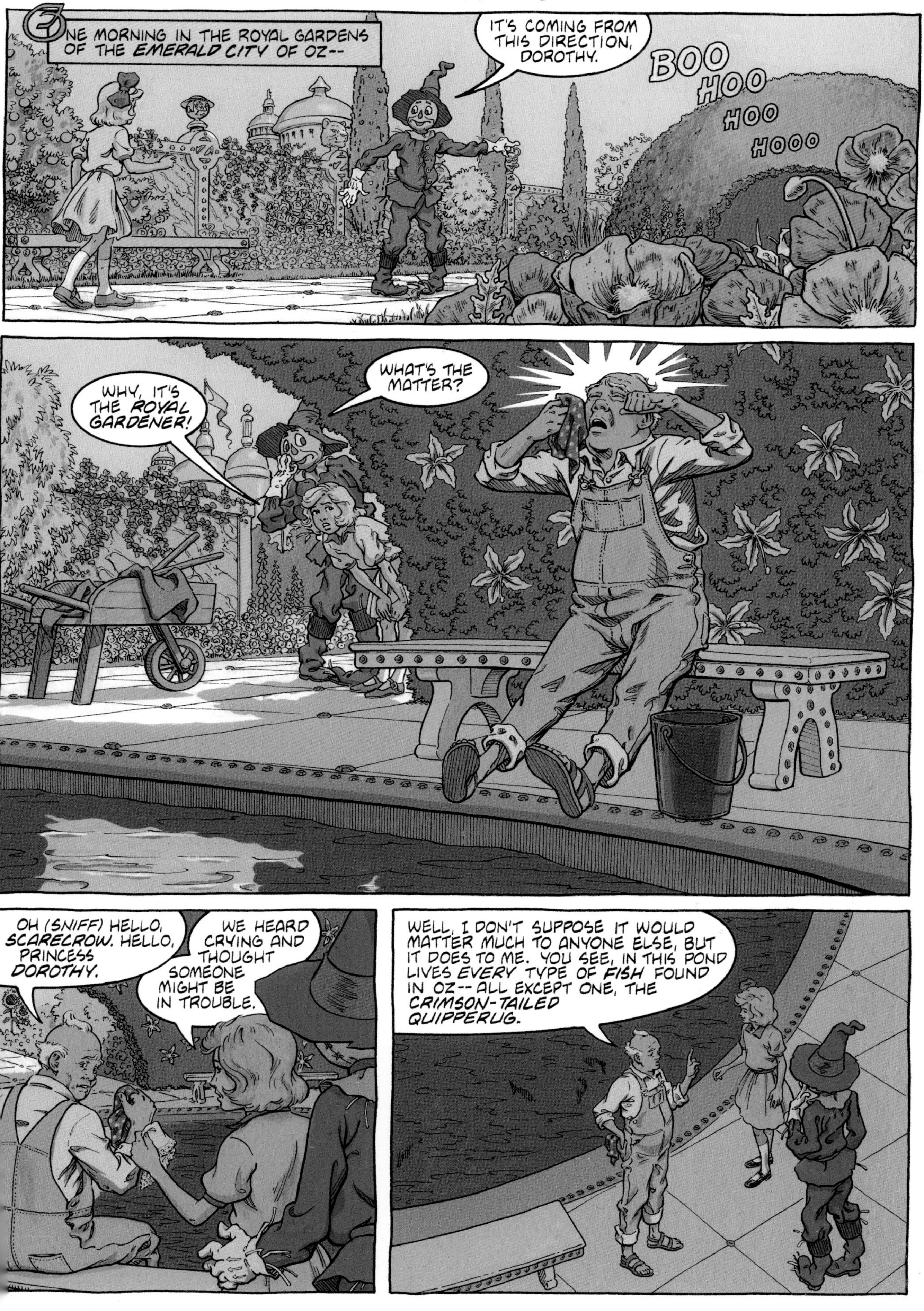
ONE MORNING IN THE ROYAL GARDENS OF THE EMERALD CITY OF OZ--
IT'S COMING FROM THIS DIRECTION, DOROTHY.
BOO HOO HOO HOOO
WHY, IT'S THE ROYAL GARDENER!
WHAT'S THE MATTER?
OH (SNIFF) HELLO, SCARECROW. HELLO, PRINCESS DOROTHY.
WE HEARD CRYING AND THOUGHT SOMEONE MIGHT BE IN TROUBLE.
WELL, I DON'T SUPPOSE IT WOULD MATTER MUCH TO ANYONE ELSE, BUT IT DOES TO ME. YOU SEE, IN THIS POND LIVES EVERY TYPE OF FISH FOUND IN OZ-- ALL EXCEPT ONE, THE CRIMSON-TAILED QUIPPERUG.

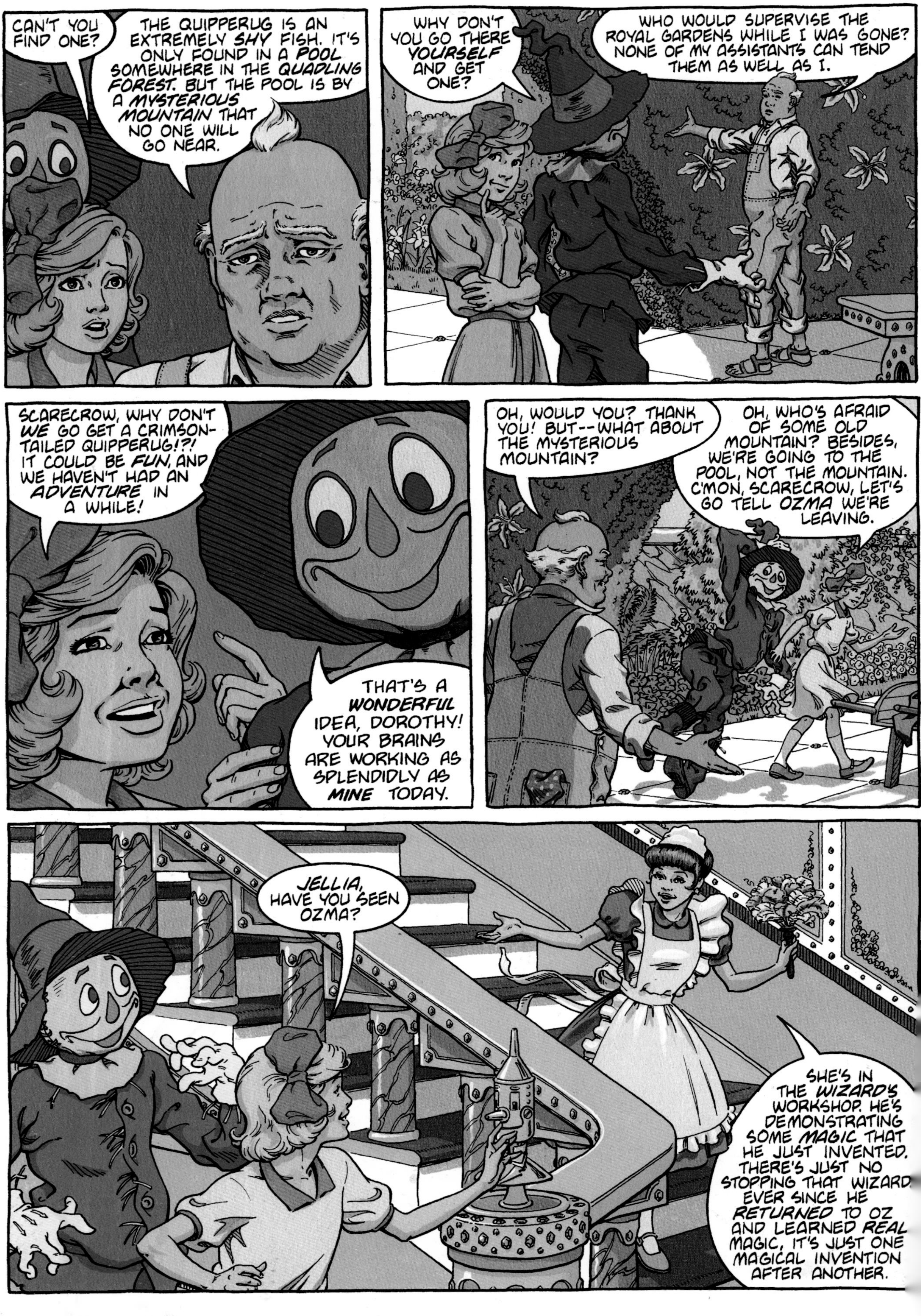
CAN'T YOU FIND ONE?
THE QUIPPERUG IS AN EXTREMELY SHY FISH. IT'S ONLY FOUND IN A POOL SOMEWHERE IN THE QUADLING FOREST. BUT THE POOL IS BY A MYSTERIOUS MOUNTAIN THAT NO ONE WILL GO NEAR.
WHY DON'T YOU GO THERE YOURSELF AND GET ONE?
WHO WOULD SUPERVISE THE ROYAL GARDENS WHILE I WAS GONE? NONE OF MY ASSISTANTS CAN TEND THEM AS WELL AS I.
SCARECROW, WHY DON'T WE GO GET A CRIMSON-TAILED QUIPPERUG!?! IT COULD BE FUN, AND WE HAVEN'T HAD AN ADVENTURE IN A WHILE!
THAT'S A WONDERFUL IDEA, DOROTHY! YOUR BRAINS ARE WORKING AS SPLENDIDLY AS MINE TODAY.
OH, WOULD YOU? THANK YOU! BUT--WHAT ABOUT THE MYSTERIOUS MOUNTAIN?
OH, WHO'S AFRAID OF SOME OLD MOUNTAIN? BESIDES, WE'RE GOING TO THE POOL, NOT THE MOUNTAIN. C'MON, SCARECROW, LET'S GO TELL OZMA WE'RE LEAVING.
JELLIA, HAVE YOU SEEN OZMA?
SHE'S IN THE WIZARD'S WORKSHOP. HE'S DEMONSTRATING SOME MAGIC THAT HE JUST INVENTED. THERE'S JUST NO STOPPING THAT WIZARD. EVER SINCE HE RETURNED TO OZ AND LEARNED REAL MAGIC, IT'S JUST ONE MAGICAL INVENTION AFTER ANOTHER.

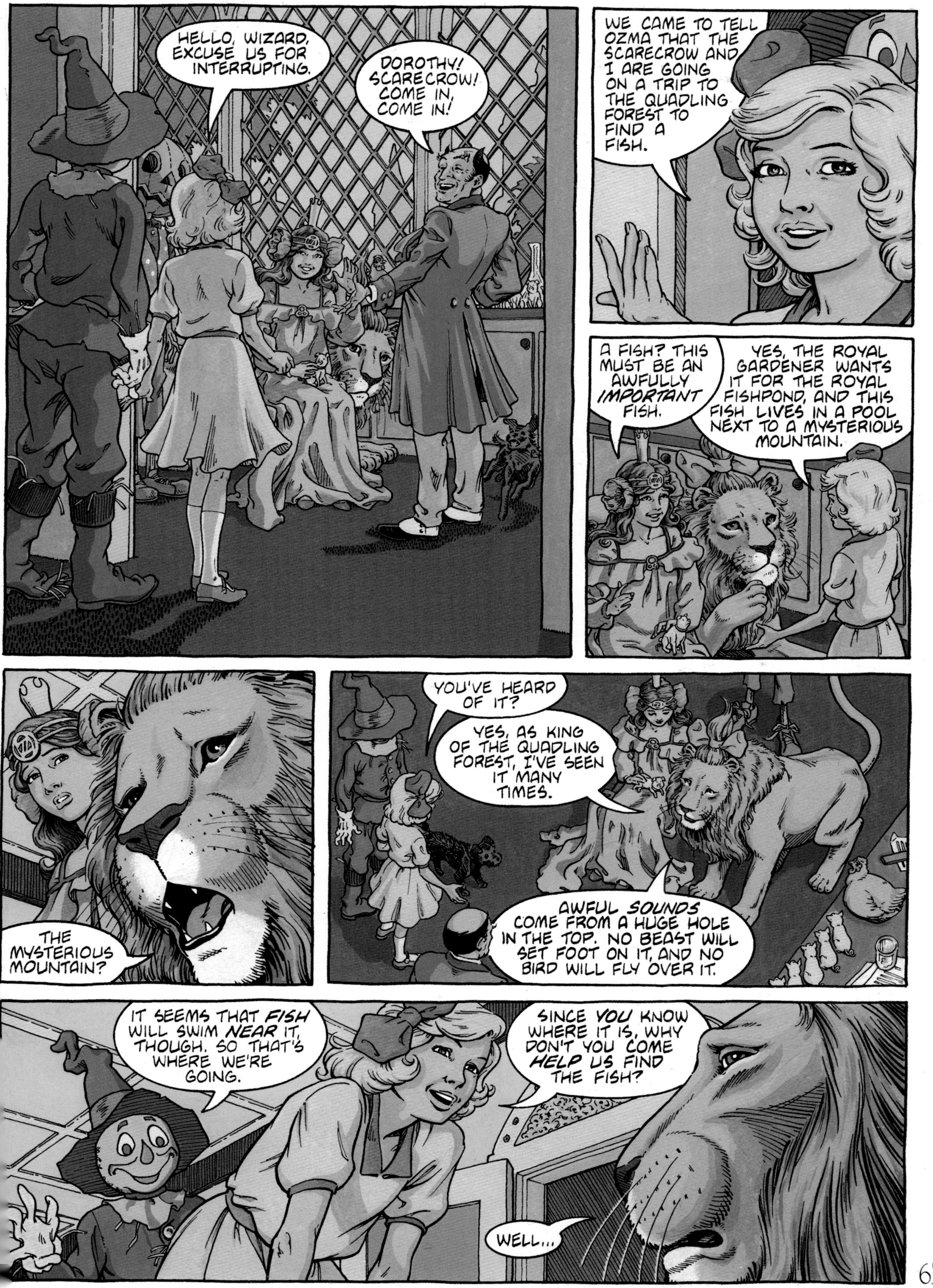
HELLO, WIZARD. EXCUSE US FOR INTERRUPTING.
DOROTHY! SCARECROW! COME IN, COME IN!
WE CAME TO TELL OZMA THAT THE SCARECROW AND I ARE GOING ON A TRIP TO THE QUADLING FOREST TO FIND A FISH.
A FISH? THIS MUST BE AN AWFULLY IMPORTANT FISH.
YES, THE ROYAL GARDENER WANTS IT FOR THE ROYAL FISHPOND, AND THIS FISH LIVES IN A POOL NEXT TO A MYSTERIOUS MOUNTAIN.
THE MYSTERIOUS MOUNTAIN?
YOU'VE HEARD OF IT?
YES, AS KING OF THE QUADLING FOREST, I'VE SEEN IT MANY TIMES.
AWFUL SOUNDS COME FROM A HUGE HOLE IN THE TOP. NO BEAST WILL SET FOOT ON IT, AND NO BIRD WILL FLY OVER IT.
IT SEEMS THAT FISH WILL SWIM NEAR IT, THOUGH. SO THAT'S WHERE WE'RE GOING.
SINCE YOU KNOW WHERE IT IS, WHY DON'T YOU COME HELP US FIND THE FISH?
WELL...

YOU MAY BE THE *COWARDLY LION*, BUT YOU'RE NOT *AFRAID*, ARE YOU?

*AFRAID?* I'M AFRAID OF *EVERYTHING...* BUT I NEVER LET THAT STOP ME. OF COURSE I'LL GO, DOROTHY. BESIDES, IT'LL GIVE ME A CHANCE TO CHECK ON MY KINGDOM.

I'D GO TOO, BUT ONE OF MY *CHICKS* HAS THE FLU, AND I'VE GOT TO STAY NEARBY.

THAT'S TOO BAD, BILLINA.

WHY, THIS WOULD BE A GOOD *FIELD TEST* FOR MY MOST RECENT INVENTION-- THE *TRAVELLING EMERGENCY MAGIC KIT.*

IT'S DESIGNED FOR TRAVELLERS IN TROUBLE, BUT IT'S ONLY BEEN TESTED IN MY LABORATORY.

IT CONTAINS *MAGIC POWDER,* BUT THERE ARE ALSO SEVERAL *MAGIC INSTRUMENTS*-- SUCH AS THIS MAGIC *WAYFINDER* FOR TRAVELLERS WHO LOSE THEIR WAY.

IT WILL POINT TO WHATEVER YOU ASK IT TO FIND-- THE PERFECT THING TO HELP YOU FIND YOUR FISH.

OF COURSE WE'LL TEST IT FOR YOU, WIZARD.

COME ON, YOU TWO, I'LL PACK SOME FOOD. THEN WE'RE OFF TO FIND OUR FISH.

ALL THIS TALK ABOUT *FISH*-- HMMM. SOUNDS *TASTY!*

GOOD-BYE!

GOOD LUCK, DOROTHY.

64

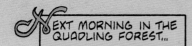

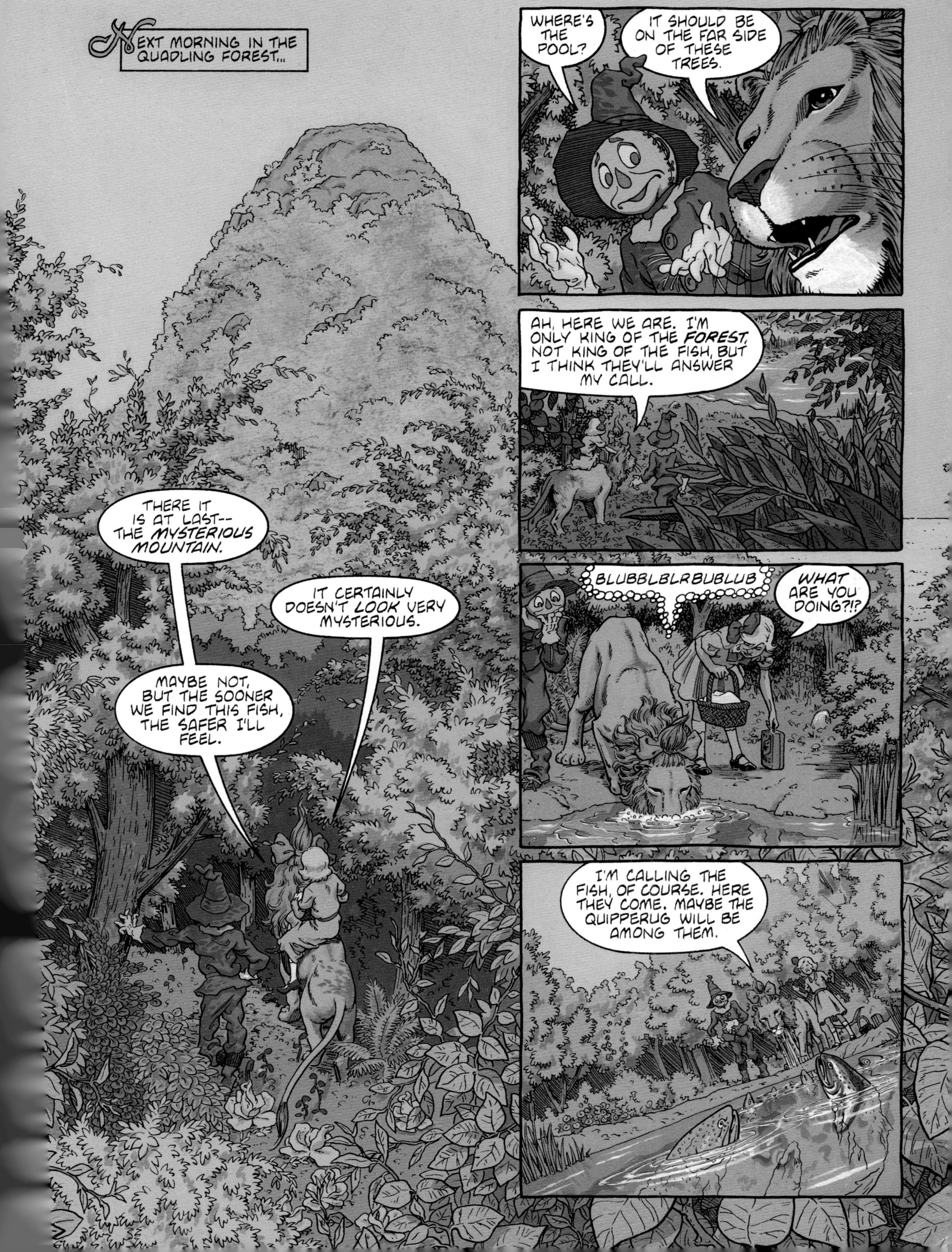
NEXT MORNING IN THE QUADLING FOREST...
THERE IT IS AT LAST-- THE *MYSTERIOUS MOUNTAIN*.
IT CERTAINLY DOESN'T *LOOK* VERY MYSTERIOUS.
MAYBE NOT, BUT THE SOONER WE FIND THIS FISH, THE SAFER I'LL FEEL.
WHERE'S THE POOL?
IT SHOULD BE ON THE FAR SIDE OF THESE TREES.
AH, HERE WE ARE. I'M ONLY KING OF THE *FOREST*, NOT KING OF THE FISH, BUT I THINK THEY'LL ANSWER MY CALL.
BLUBBLBLRBUBLUB
*WHAT* ARE YOU DOING?!?
I'M CALLING THE FISH, OF COURSE. HERE THEY COME. MAYBE THE QUIPPERUG WILL BE AMONG THEM.

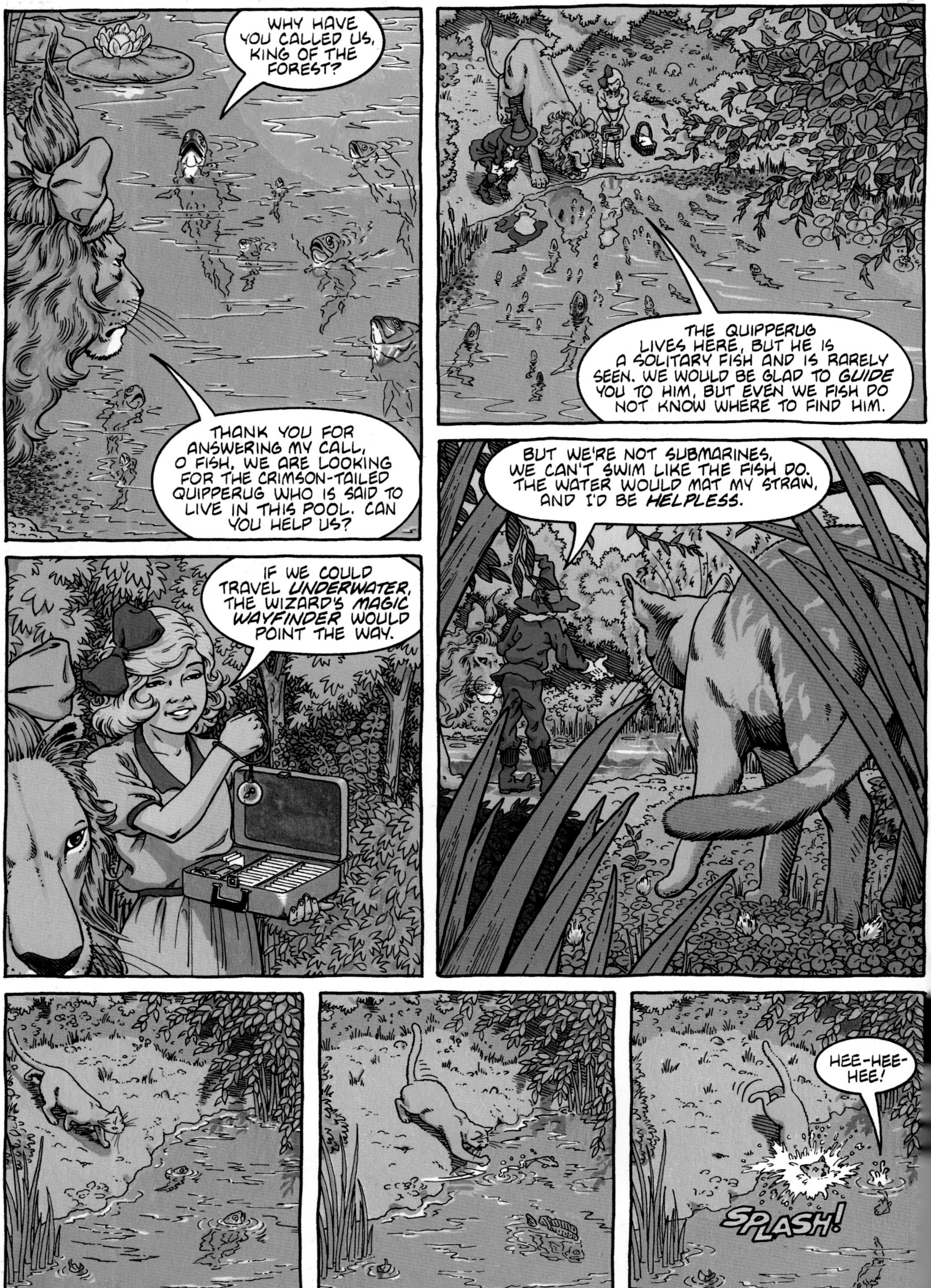
WHY HAVE YOU CALLED US, KING OF THE FOREST?
THANK YOU FOR ANSWERING MY CALL, O FISH. WE ARE LOOKING FOR THE CRIMSON-TAILED QUIPPERUG WHO IS SAID TO LIVE IN THIS POOL. CAN YOU HELP US?
THE QUIPPERUG LIVES HERE, BUT HE IS A SOLITARY FISH AND IS RARELY SEEN. WE WOULD BE GLAD TO *GUIDE* YOU TO HIM, BUT EVEN WE FISH DO NOT KNOW WHERE TO FIND HIM.
IF WE COULD TRAVEL *UNDERWATER*, THE WIZARD'S *MAGIC WAYFINDER* WOULD POINT THE WAY.
BUT WE'RE NOT SUBMARINES, WE CAN'T SWIM LIKE THE FISH DO. THE WATER WOULD MAT MY STRAW, AND I'D BE *HELPLESS*.
HEE-HEE-HEE!
SPLASH!

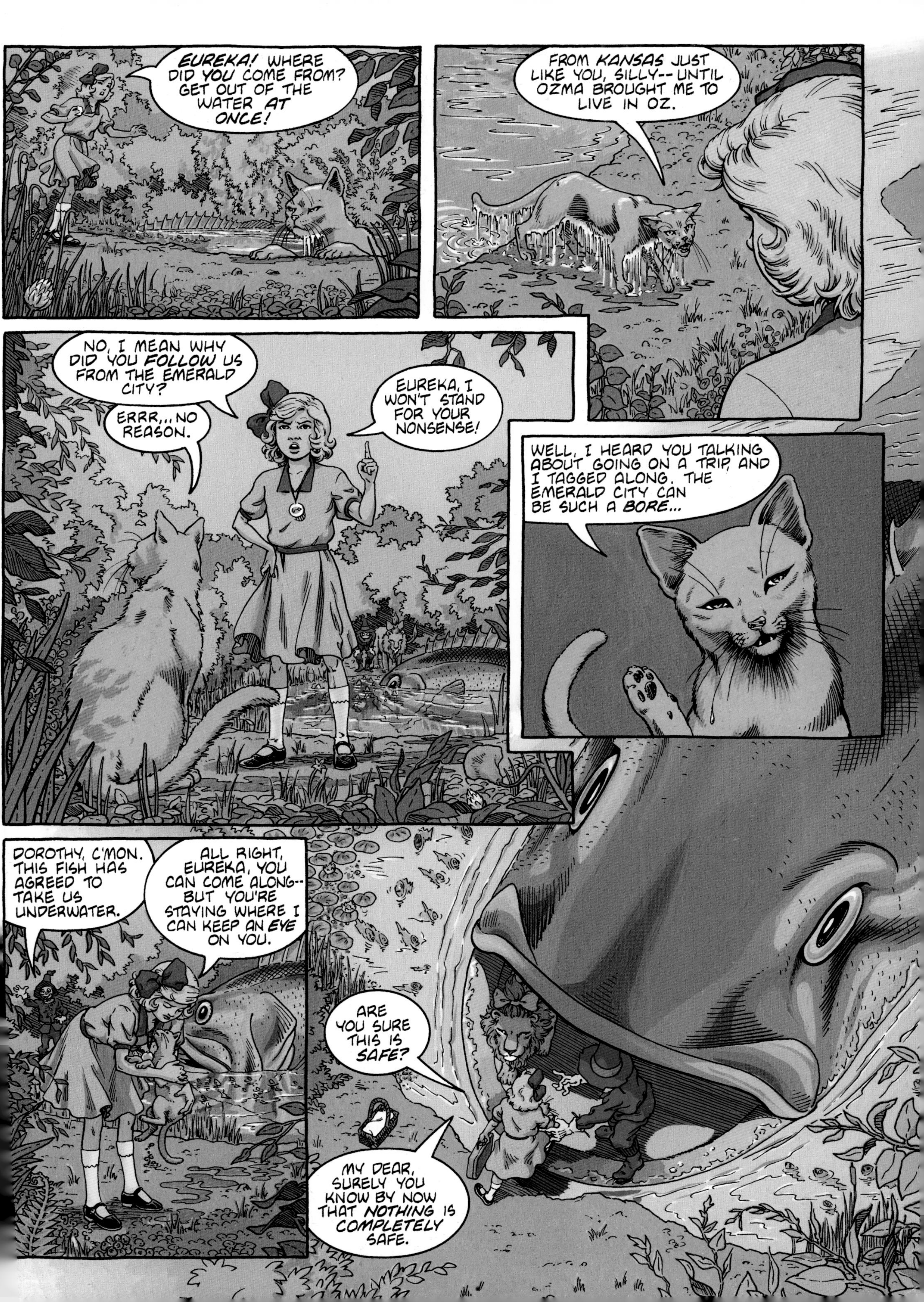
EUREKA! WHERE DID YOU COME FROM? GET OUT OF THE WATER AT ONCE!
FROM KANSAS JUST LIKE YOU, SILLY-- UNTIL OZMA BROUGHT ME TO LIVE IN OZ.
NO, I MEAN WHY DID YOU FOLLOW US FROM THE EMERALD CITY?
ERRR,.. NO REASON.
EUREKA, I WON'T STAND FOR YOUR NONSENSE!
WELL, I HEARD YOU TALKING ABOUT GOING ON A TRIP, AND I TAGGED ALONG. THE EMERALD CITY CAN BE SUCH A BORE...
DOROTHY, C'MON. THIS FISH HAS AGREED TO TAKE US UNDERWATER.
ALL RIGHT, EUREKA, YOU CAN COME ALONG-- BUT YOU'RE STAYING WHERE I CAN KEEP AN EYE ON YOU.
ARE YOU SURE THIS IS SAFE?
MY DEAR, SURELY YOU KNOW BY NOW THAT NOTHING IS COMPLETELY SAFE.

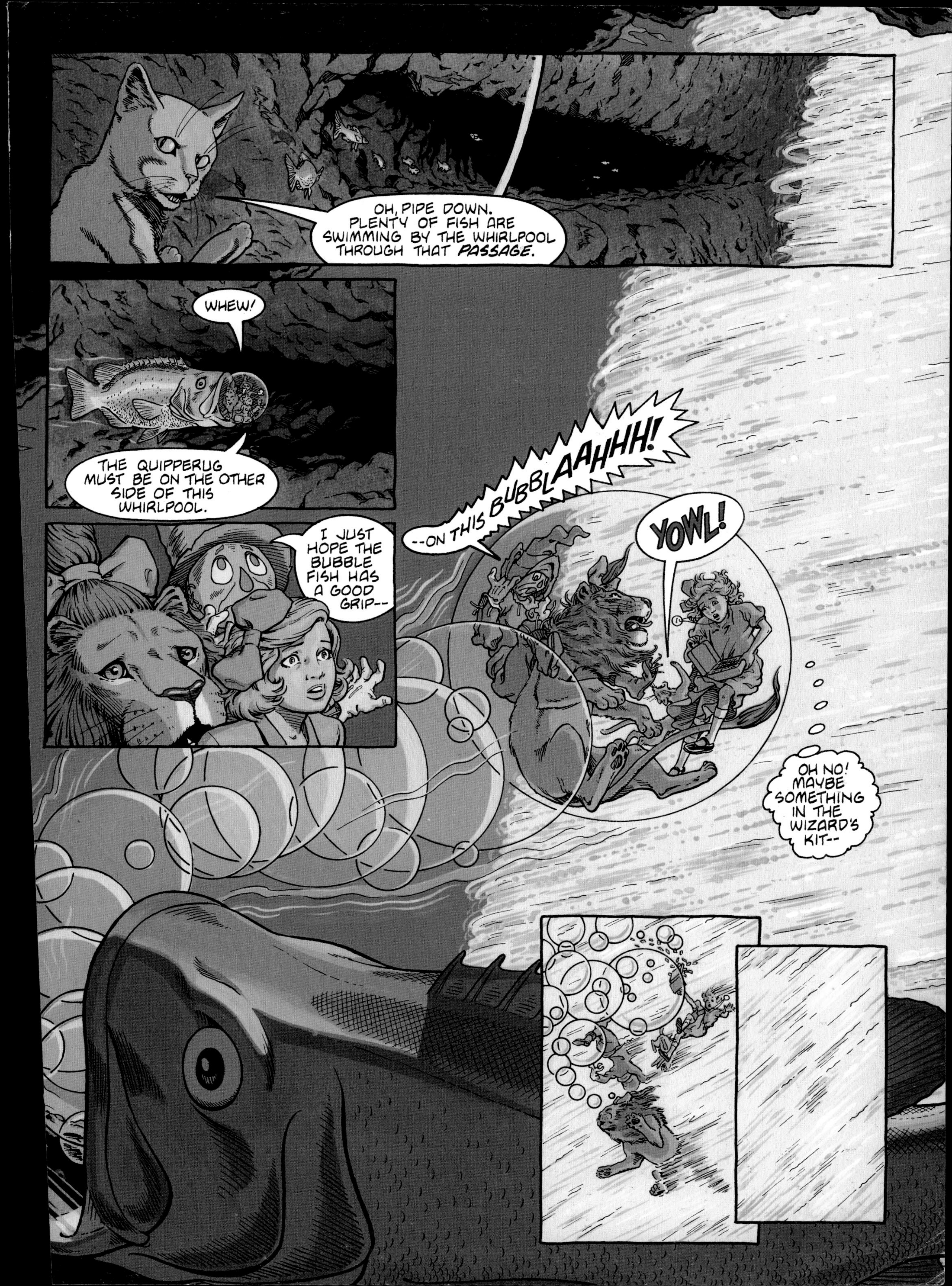
OH, PIPE DOWN. PLENTY OF FISH ARE SWIMMING BY THE WHIRLPOOL THROUGH THAT PASSAGE.
WHEW!
THE QUIPPERUG MUST BE ON THE OTHER SIDE OF THIS WHIRLPOOL.
I JUST HOPE THE BUBBLE FISH HAS A GOOD GRIP--
--ON THIS BUBBLAAHHH!
YOWL!
OH NO! MAYBE SOMETHING IN THE WIZARD'S KIT--

# Chapter 2 Knotboy

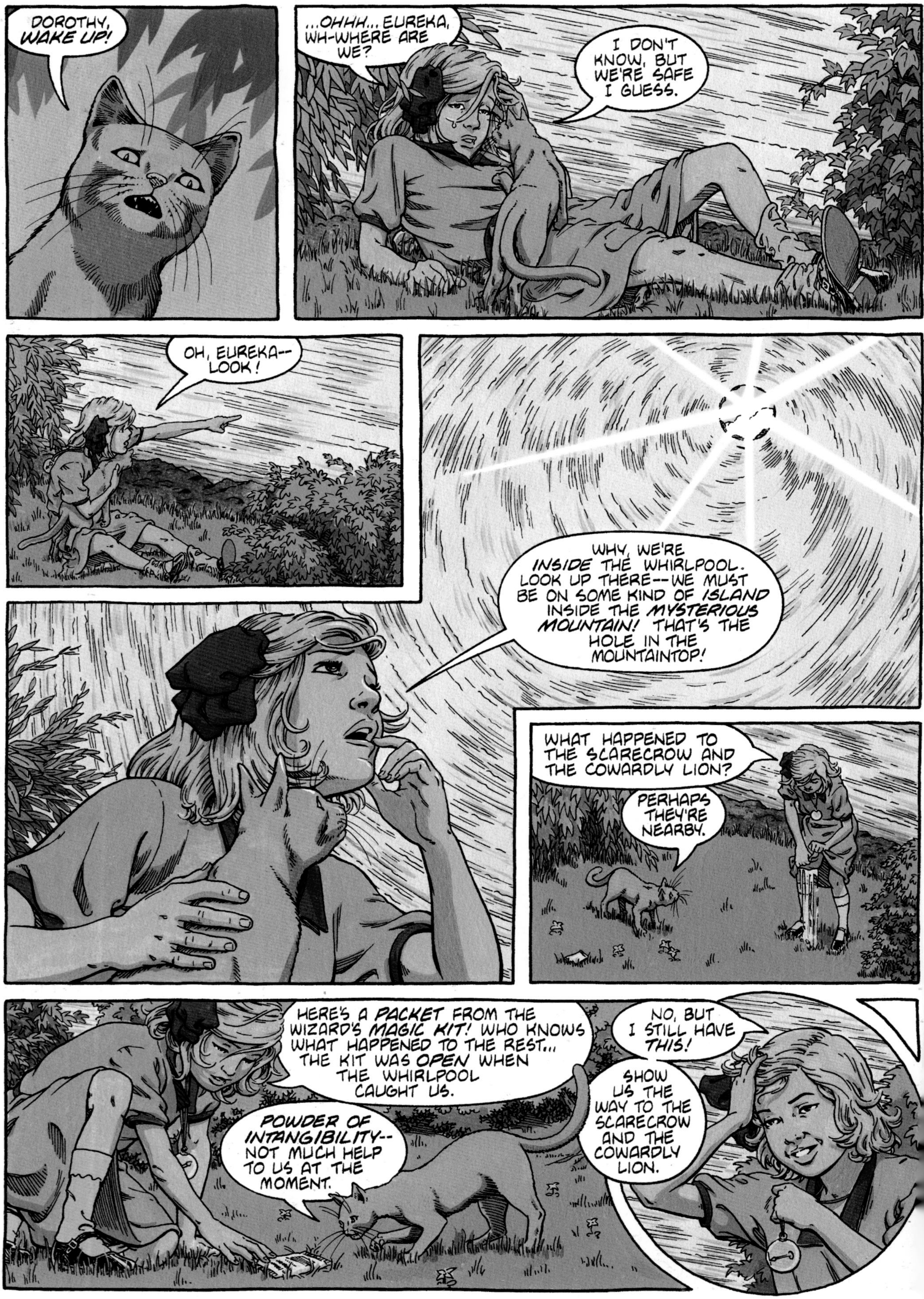
DOROTHY, WAKE UP!
...OHHH... EUREKA, WH-WHERE ARE WE?
I DON'T KNOW, BUT WE'RE SAFE I GUESS.
OH, EUREKA-- LOOK!
WHY, WE'RE INSIDE THE WHIRLPOOL. LOOK UP THERE--WE MUST BE ON SOME KIND OF ISLAND INSIDE THE MYSTERIOUS MOUNTAIN! THAT'S THE HOLE IN THE MOUNTAINTOP!
WHAT HAPPENED TO THE SCARECROW AND THE COWARDLY LION?
PERHAPS THEY'RE NEARBY.
HERE'S A PACKET FROM THE WIZARD'S MAGIC KIT! WHO KNOWS WHAT HAPPENED TO THE REST... THE KIT WAS OPEN WHEN THE WHIRLPOOL CAUGHT US.
POWDER OF INTANGIBILITY-- NOT MUCH HELP TO US AT THE MOMENT.
NO, BUT I STILL HAVE THIS!
SHOW US THE WAY TO THE SCARECROW AND THE COWARDLY LION.

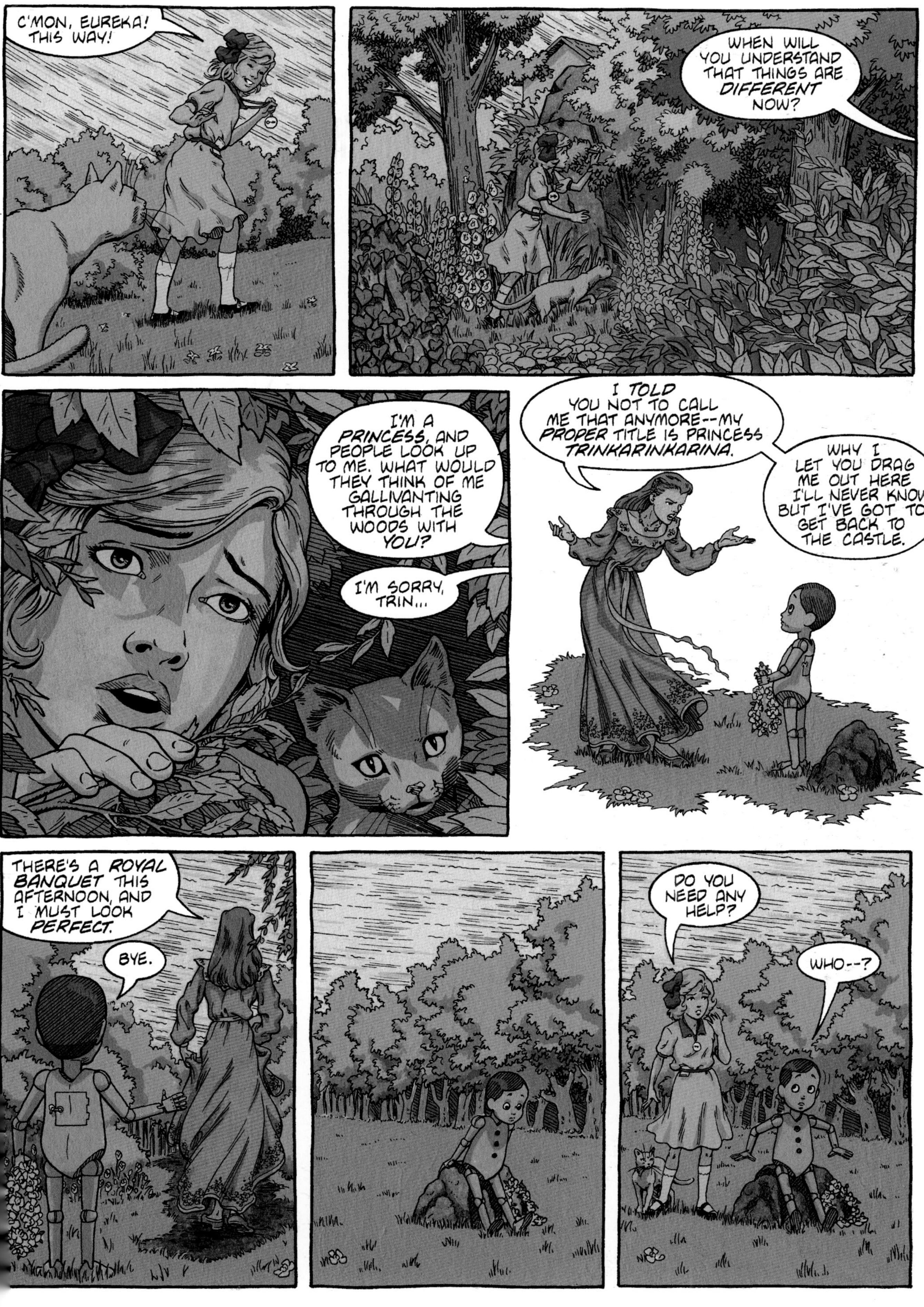
C'MON, EUREKA! THIS WAY!
WHEN WILL YOU UNDERSTAND THAT THINGS ARE *DIFFERENT* NOW?
I'M A *PRINCESS*, AND PEOPLE LOOK UP TO ME. WHAT WOULD THEY THINK OF ME GALLIVANTING THROUGH THE WOODS WITH *YOU*?
I'M SORRY, TRIN...
I *TOLD* YOU NOT TO CALL ME THAT ANYMORE--MY *PROPER* TITLE IS PRINCESS *TRINKARINKARINA*.
WHY I LET YOU DRAG ME OUT HERE I'LL NEVER KNOW, BUT I'VE GOT TO GET BACK TO THE CASTLE.
THERE'S A *ROYAL BANQUET* THIS AFTERNOON, AND I MUST LOOK *PERFECT*.
BYE.
DO YOU NEED ANY HELP?
WHO--?

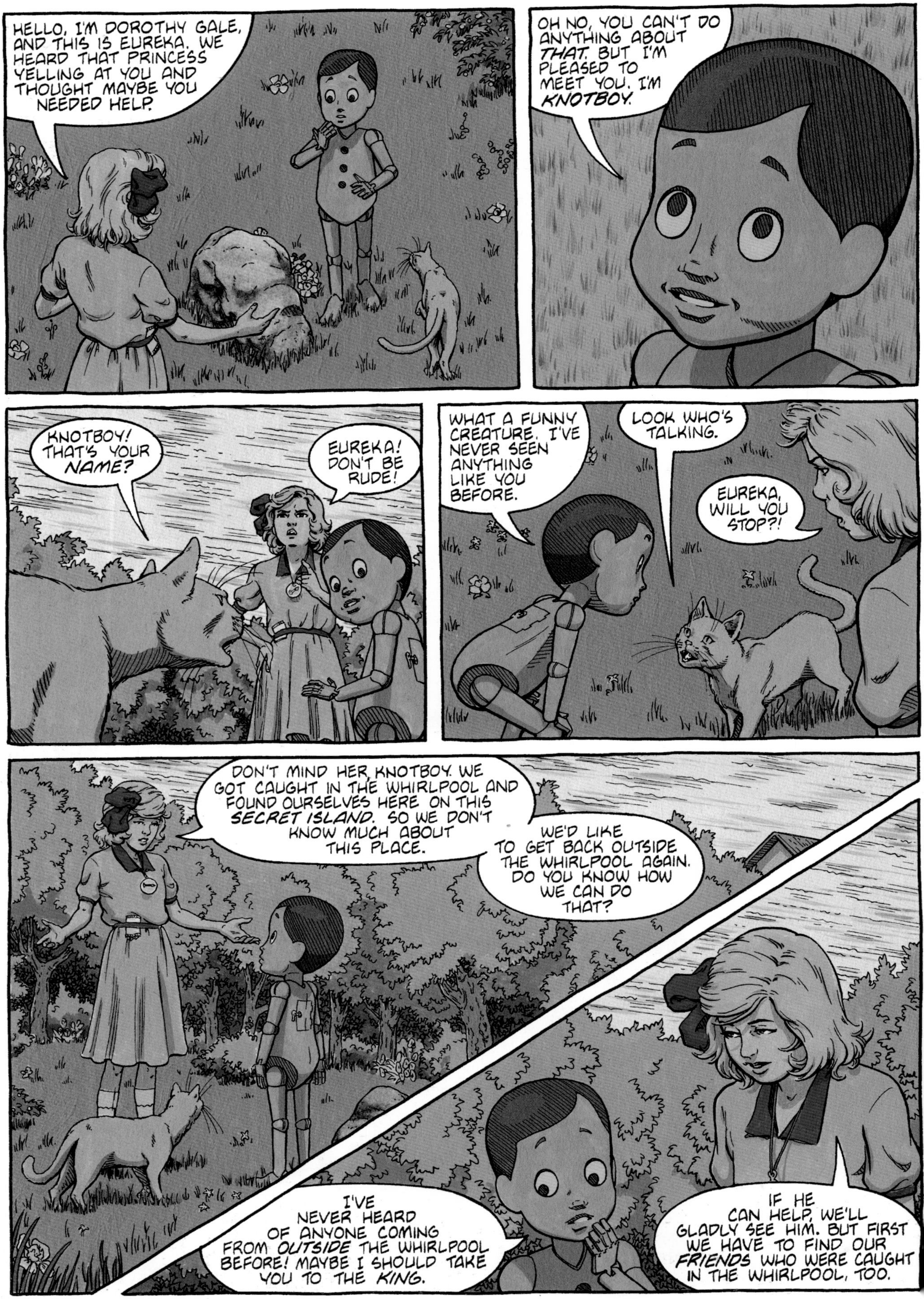
HELLO, I'M DOROTHY GALE, AND THIS IS EUREKA. WE HEARD THAT PRINCESS YELLING AT YOU AND THOUGHT MAYBE YOU NEEDED HELP.
OH NO, YOU CAN'T DO ANYTHING ABOUT *THAT*. BUT I'M PLEASED TO MEET YOU. I'M *KNOTBOY*.
KNOTBOY! THAT'S YOUR *NAME*?
EUREKA! DON'T BE RUDE!
WHAT A FUNNY CREATURE. I'VE NEVER SEEN ANYTHING LIKE YOU BEFORE.
LOOK WHO'S TALKING.
EUREKA, WILL YOU STOP?!
DON'T MIND HER, KNOTBOY. WE GOT CAUGHT IN THE WHIRLPOOL AND FOUND OURSELVES HERE ON THIS *SECRET ISLAND*. SO WE DON'T KNOW MUCH ABOUT THIS PLACE.
WE'D LIKE TO GET BACK OUTSIDE THE WHIRLPOOL AGAIN. DO YOU KNOW HOW WE CAN DO THAT?
I'VE NEVER HEARD OF ANYONE COMING FROM *OUTSIDE* THE WHIRLPOOL BEFORE! MAYBE I SHOULD TAKE YOU TO THE *KING*.
IF HE CAN HELP, WE'LL GLADLY SEE HIM. BUT FIRST WE HAVE TO FIND OUR *FRIENDS* WHO WERE CAUGHT IN THE WHIRLPOOL, TOO.

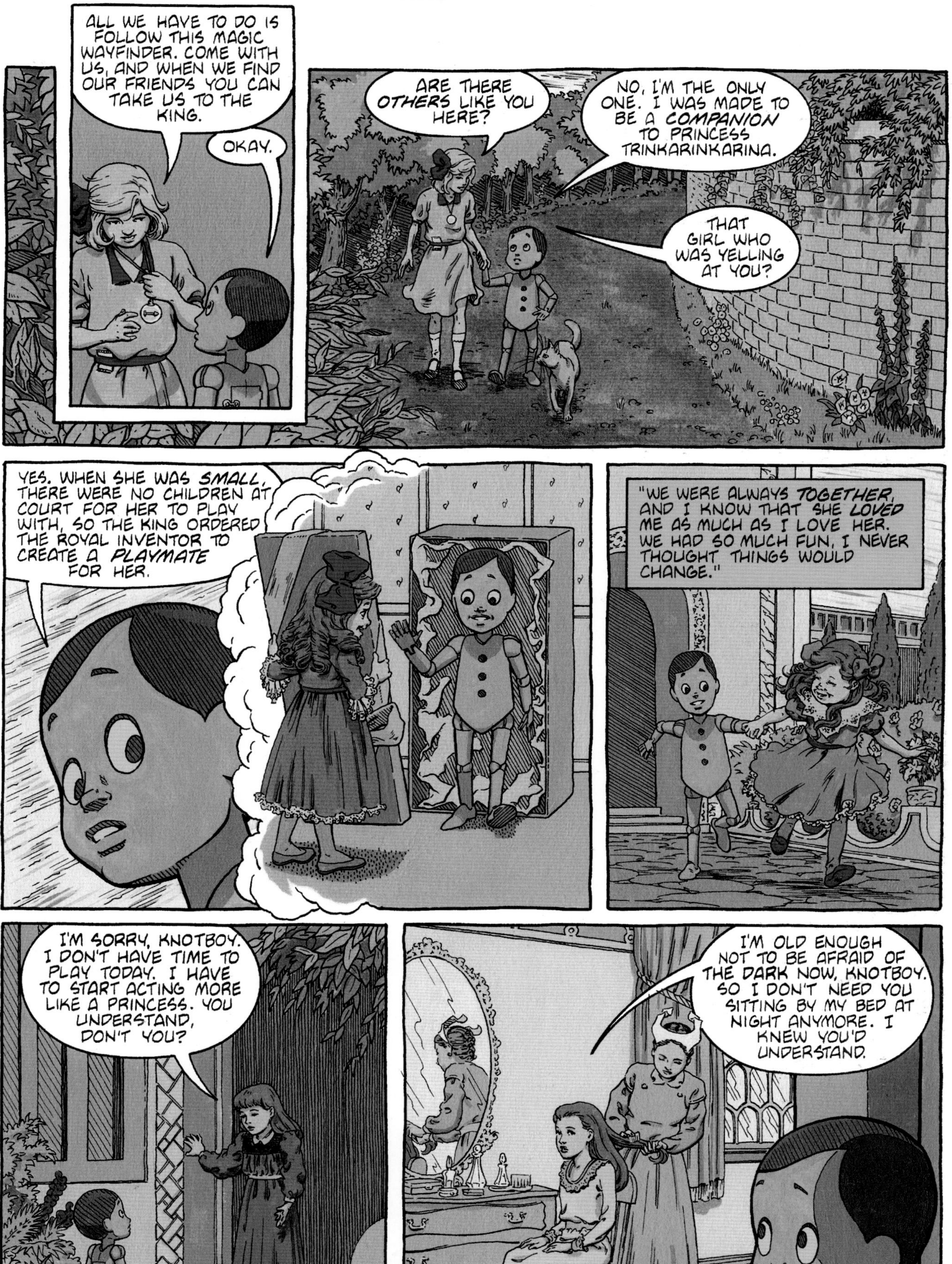
ALL WE HAVE TO DO IS FOLLOW THIS MAGIC WAYFINDER. COME WITH US, AND WHEN WE FIND OUR FRIENDS YOU CAN TAKE US TO THE KING.
OKAY.
ARE THERE OTHERS LIKE YOU HERE?
NO, I'M THE ONLY ONE. I WAS MADE TO BE A COMPANION TO PRINCESS TRINKARINKARINA.
THAT GIRL WHO WAS YELLING AT YOU?
YES. WHEN SHE WAS SMALL, THERE WERE NO CHILDREN AT COURT FOR HER TO PLAY WITH, SO THE KING ORDERED THE ROYAL INVENTOR TO CREATE A PLAYMATE FOR HER.
"WE WERE ALWAYS TOGETHER, AND I KNOW THAT SHE LOVED ME AS MUCH AS I LOVE HER. WE HAD SO MUCH FUN, I NEVER THOUGHT THINGS WOULD CHANGE."
I'M SORRY, KNOTBOY. I DON'T HAVE TIME TO PLAY TODAY. I HAVE TO START ACTING MORE LIKE A PRINCESS. YOU UNDERSTAND, DON'T YOU?
I'M OLD ENOUGH NOT TO BE AFRAID OF THE DARK NOW, KNOTBOY. SO I DON'T NEED YOU SITTING BY MY BED AT NIGHT ANYMORE. I KNEW YOU'D UNDERSTAND.

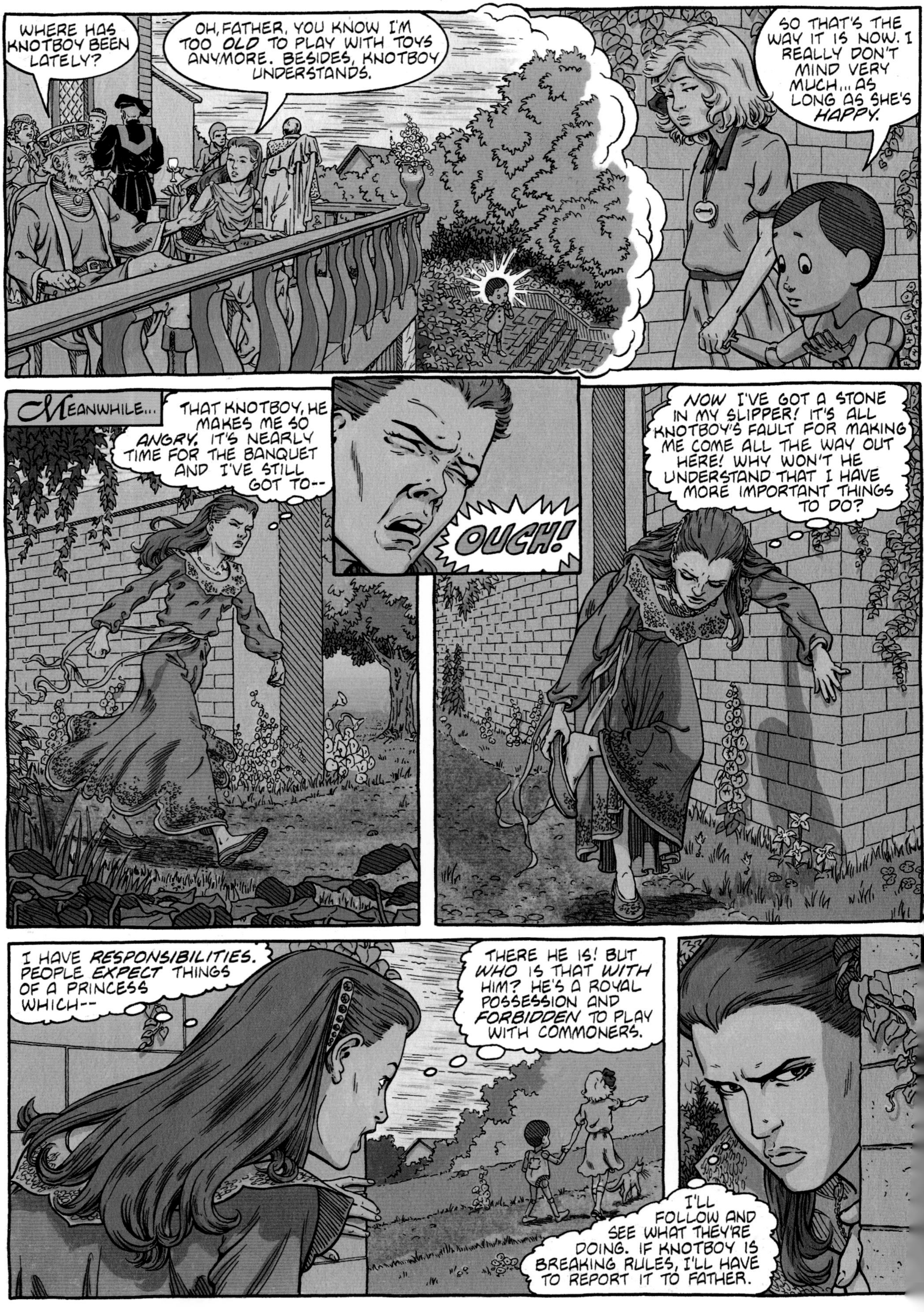
WHERE HAS KNOTBOY BEEN LATELY?
OH, FATHER, YOU KNOW I'M TOO OLD TO PLAY WITH TOYS ANYMORE. BESIDES, KNOTBOY UNDERSTANDS.
SO THAT'S THE WAY IT IS NOW. I REALLY DON'T MIND VERY MUCH... AS LONG AS SHE'S HAPPY.
MEANWHILE...
THAT KNOTBOY, HE MAKES ME SO ANGRY. IT'S NEARLY TIME FOR THE BANQUET AND I'VE STILL GOT TO--
OUCH!
NOW I'VE GOT A STONE IN MY SLIPPER! IT'S ALL KNOTBOY'S FAULT FOR MAKING ME COME ALL THE WAY OUT HERE! WHY WON'T HE UNDERSTAND THAT I HAVE MORE IMPORTANT THINGS TO DO?
I HAVE RESPONSIBILITIES. PEOPLE EXPECT THINGS OF A PRINCESS WHICH--
THERE HE IS! BUT WHO IS THAT WITH HIM? HE'S A ROYAL POSSESSION AND FORBIDDEN TO PLAY WITH COMMONERS.
I'LL FOLLOW AND SEE WHAT THEY'RE DOING. IF KNOTBOY IS BREAKING RULES, I'LL HAVE TO REPORT IT TO FATHER.

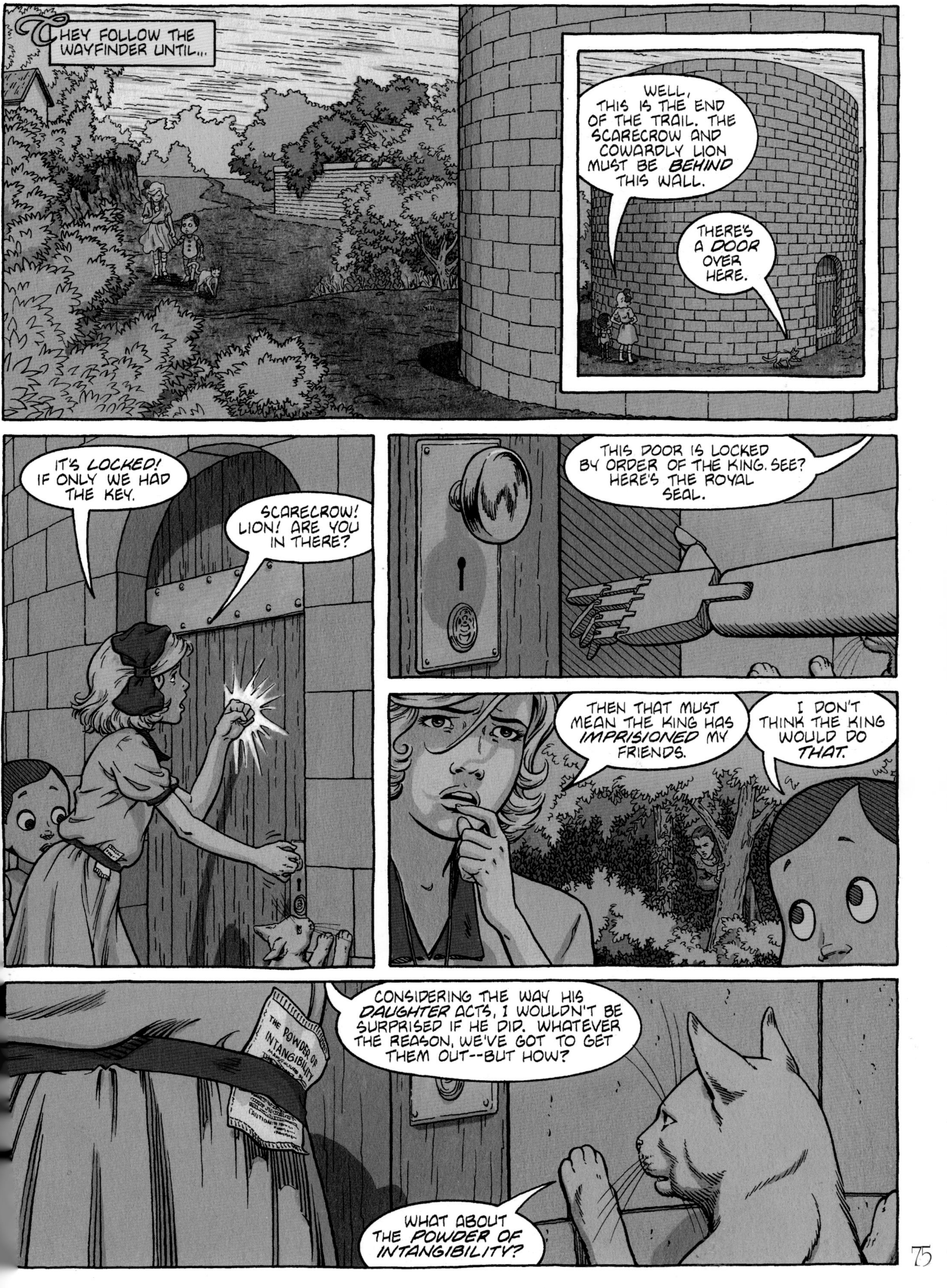
THEY FOLLOW THE WAYFINDER UNTIL...
WELL, THIS IS THE END OF THE TRAIL. THE SCARECROW AND COWARDLY LION MUST BE *BEHIND* THIS WALL.
THERE'S A *DOOR* OVER HERE.
IT'S *LOCKED!* IF ONLY WE HAD THE KEY.
SCARECROW! LION! ARE YOU IN THERE?
THIS DOOR IS LOCKED BY ORDER OF THE KING. SEE? HERE'S THE ROYAL SEAL.
THEN THAT MUST MEAN THE KING HAS *IMPRISIONED* MY FRIENDS.
I DON'T THINK THE KING WOULD DO *THAT.*
THE POWDER OF INTANGIBILITY
CONSIDERING THE WAY HIS *DAUGHTER* ACTS, I WOULDN'T BE SURPRISED IF HE DID. WHATEVER THE REASON, WE'VE GOT TO GET THEM OUT--BUT HOW?
WHAT ABOUT THE *POWDER OF INTANGIBILITY?*

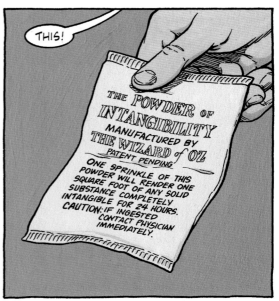

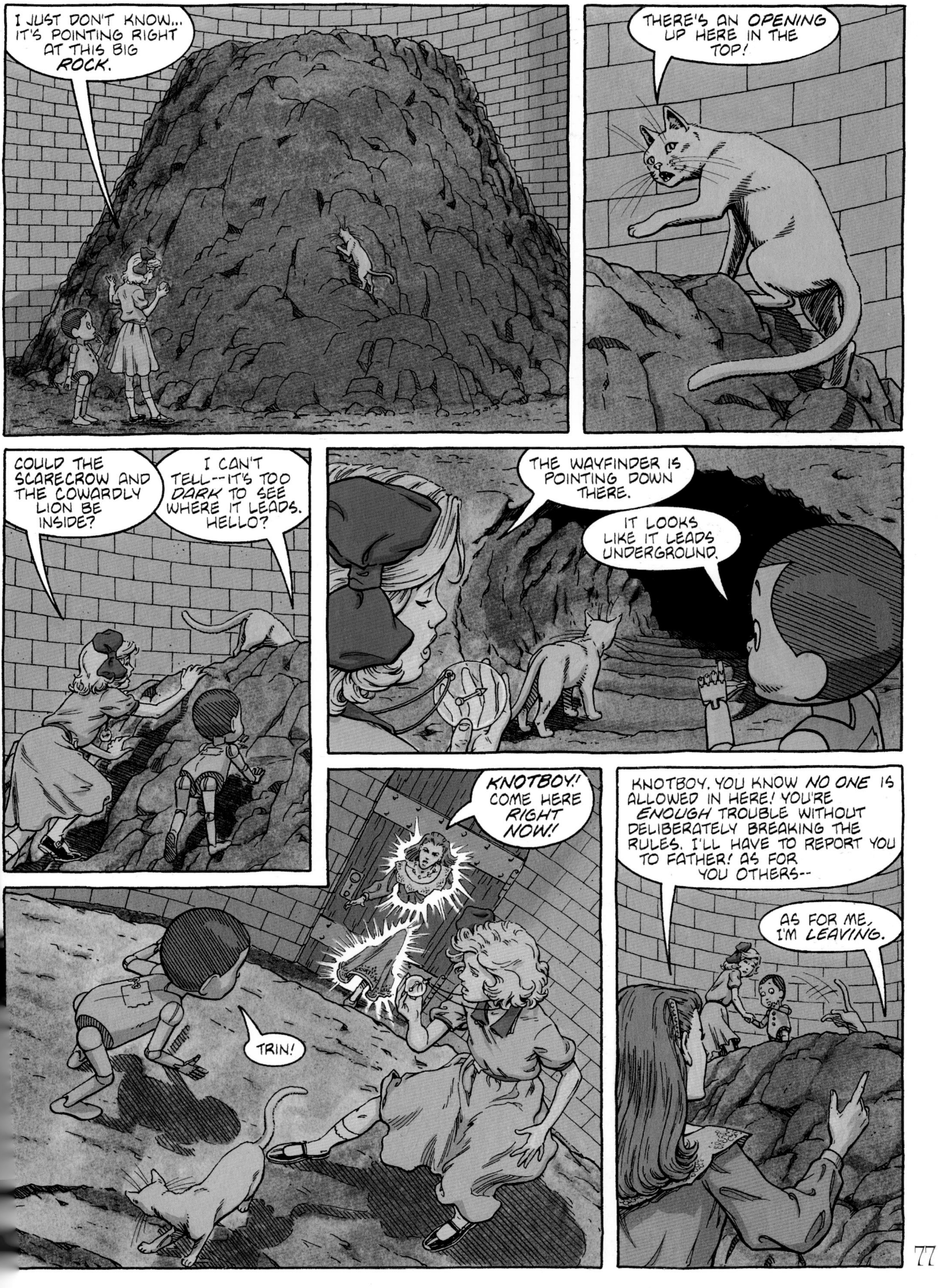
I JUST DON'T KNOW... IT'S POINTING RIGHT AT THIS BIG ROCK.
THERE'S AN OPENING UP HERE IN THE TOP!
COULD THE SCARECROW AND THE COWARDLY LION BE INSIDE?
I CAN'T TELL--IT'S TOO DARK TO SEE WHERE IT LEADS. HELLO?
THE WAYFINDER IS POINTING DOWN THERE.
IT LOOKS LIKE IT LEADS UNDERGROUND.
KNOTBOY! COME HERE RIGHT NOW!
TRIN!
KNOTBOY. YOU KNOW NO ONE IS ALLOWED IN HERE! YOU'RE ENOUGH TROUBLE WITHOUT DELIBERATELY BREAKING THE RULES. I'LL HAVE TO REPORT YOU TO FATHER! AS FOR YOU OTHERS--
AS FOR ME, I'M LEAVING.

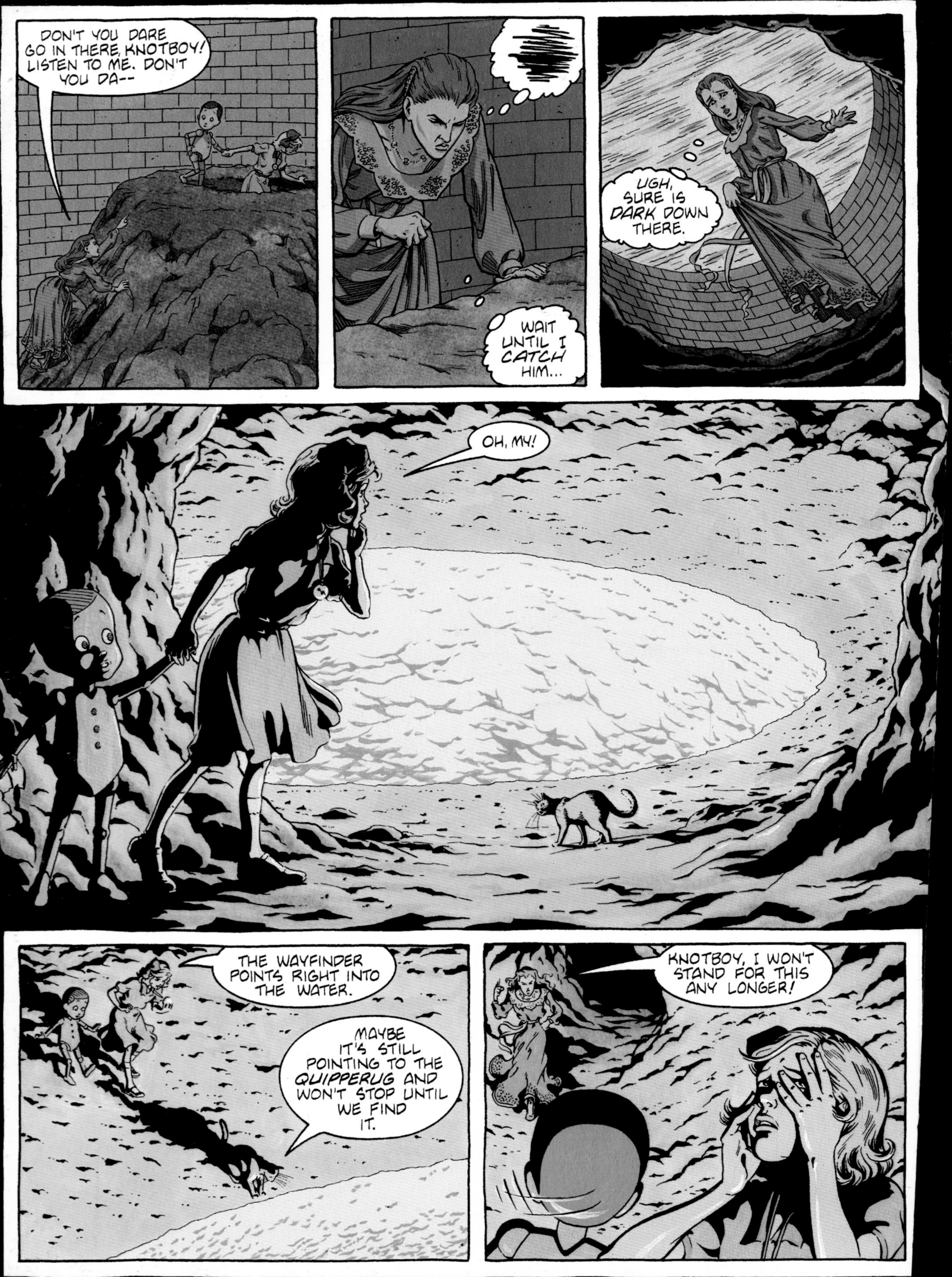
DON'T YOU DARE GO IN THERE, KNOTBOY! LISTEN TO ME. DON'T YOU DA--
WAIT UNTIL I CATCH HIM...
UGH, SURE IS DARK DOWN THERE.
OH, MY!
THE WAYFINDER POINTS RIGHT INTO THE WATER.
MAYBE IT'S STILL POINTING TO THE QUIPPERUG AND WON'T STOP UNTIL WE FIND IT.
KNOTBOY, I WON'T STAND FOR THIS ANY LONGER!

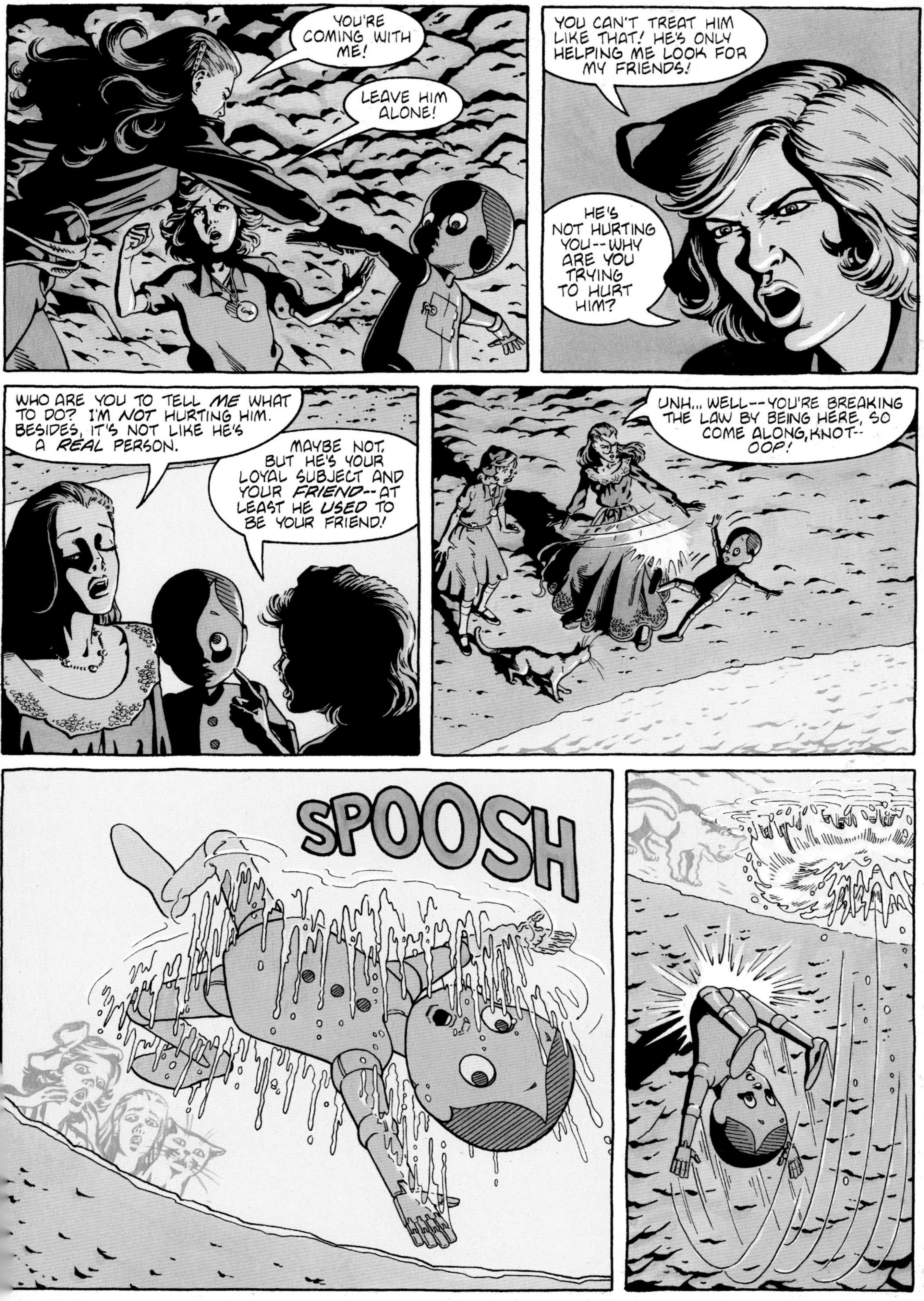
YOU'RE COMING WITH ME!
LEAVE HIM ALONE!
YOU CAN'T TREAT HIM LIKE THAT! HE'S ONLY HELPING ME LOOK FOR MY FRIENDS!
HE'S NOT HURTING YOU--WHY ARE YOU TRYING TO HURT HIM?
WHO ARE YOU TO TELL *ME* WHAT TO DO? I'M *NOT* HURTING HIM. BESIDES, IT'S NOT LIKE HE'S A *REAL* PERSON.
MAYBE NOT. BUT HE'S YOUR LOYAL SUBJECT AND YOUR *FRIEND*--AT LEAST HE *USED* TO BE YOUR FRIEND!
UNH... WELL--YOU'RE BREAKING THE LAW BY BEING HERE, SO COME ALONG, KNOT--OOP!
SPOOSH

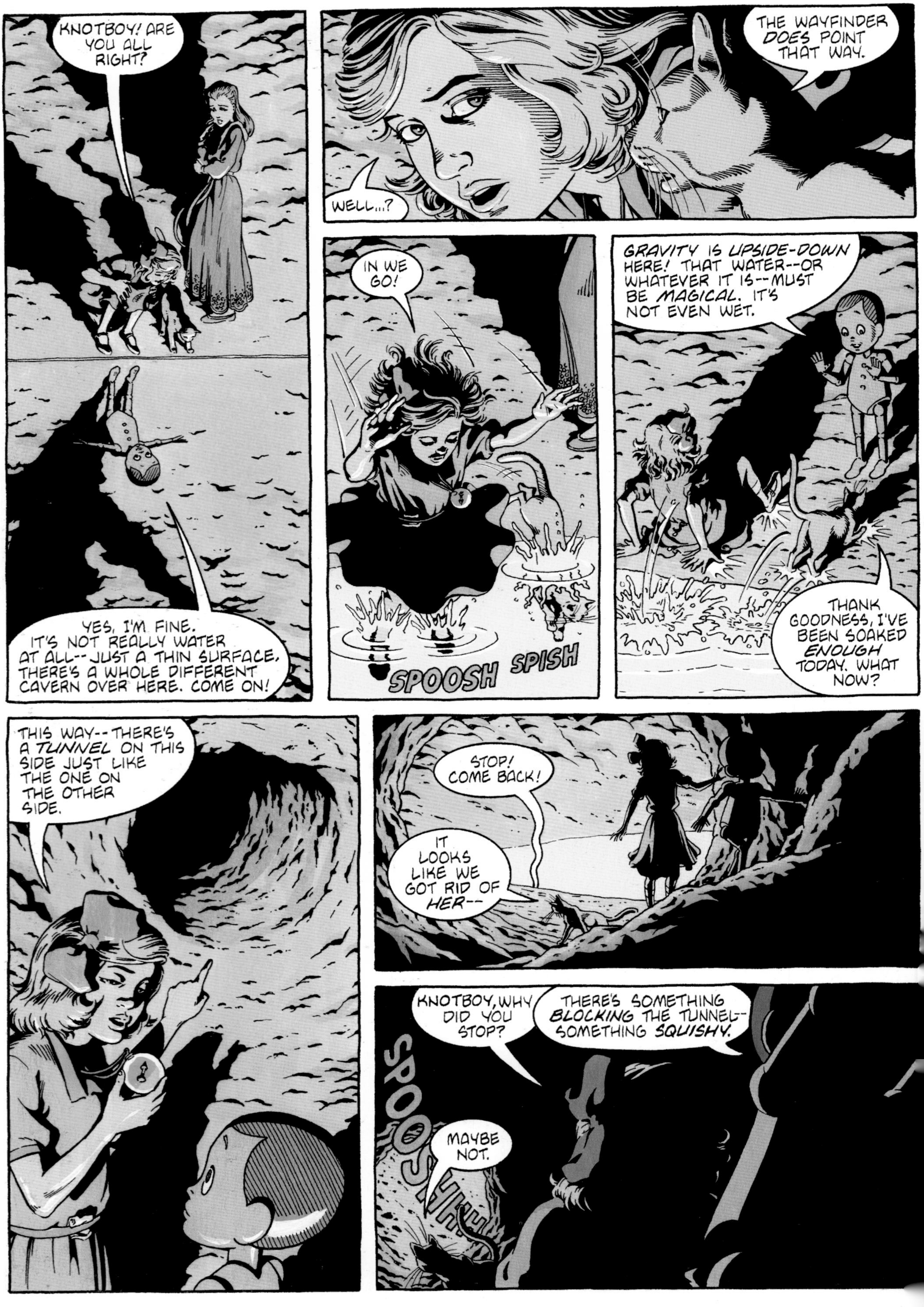
KNOTBOY! ARE YOU ALL RIGHT?
YES, I'M FINE. IT'S NOT REALLY WATER AT ALL--JUST A THIN SURFACE. THERE'S A WHOLE DIFFERENT CAVERN OVER HERE. COME ON!
THE WAYFINDER *DOES* POINT THAT WAY.
WELL...?
IN WE GO!
SPOOSH
SPISH
*GRAVITY* IS *UPSIDE-DOWN* HERE! THAT WATER--OR WHATEVER IT IS--MUST BE *MAGICAL*. IT'S NOT EVEN WET.
THANK GOODNESS, I'VE BEEN SOAKED *ENOUGH* TODAY. WHAT NOW?
THIS WAY--THERE'S A *TUNNEL* ON THIS SIDE JUST LIKE THE ONE ON THE OTHER SIDE.
STOP! COME BACK!
IT LOOKS LIKE WE GOT RID OF *HER*--
KNOTBOY, WHY DID YOU STOP?
THERE'S SOMETHING *BLOCKING* THE TUNNEL--SOMETHING *SQUISHY*.
SPOOSHH
MAYBE NOT.

## Chapter 3 The Contest

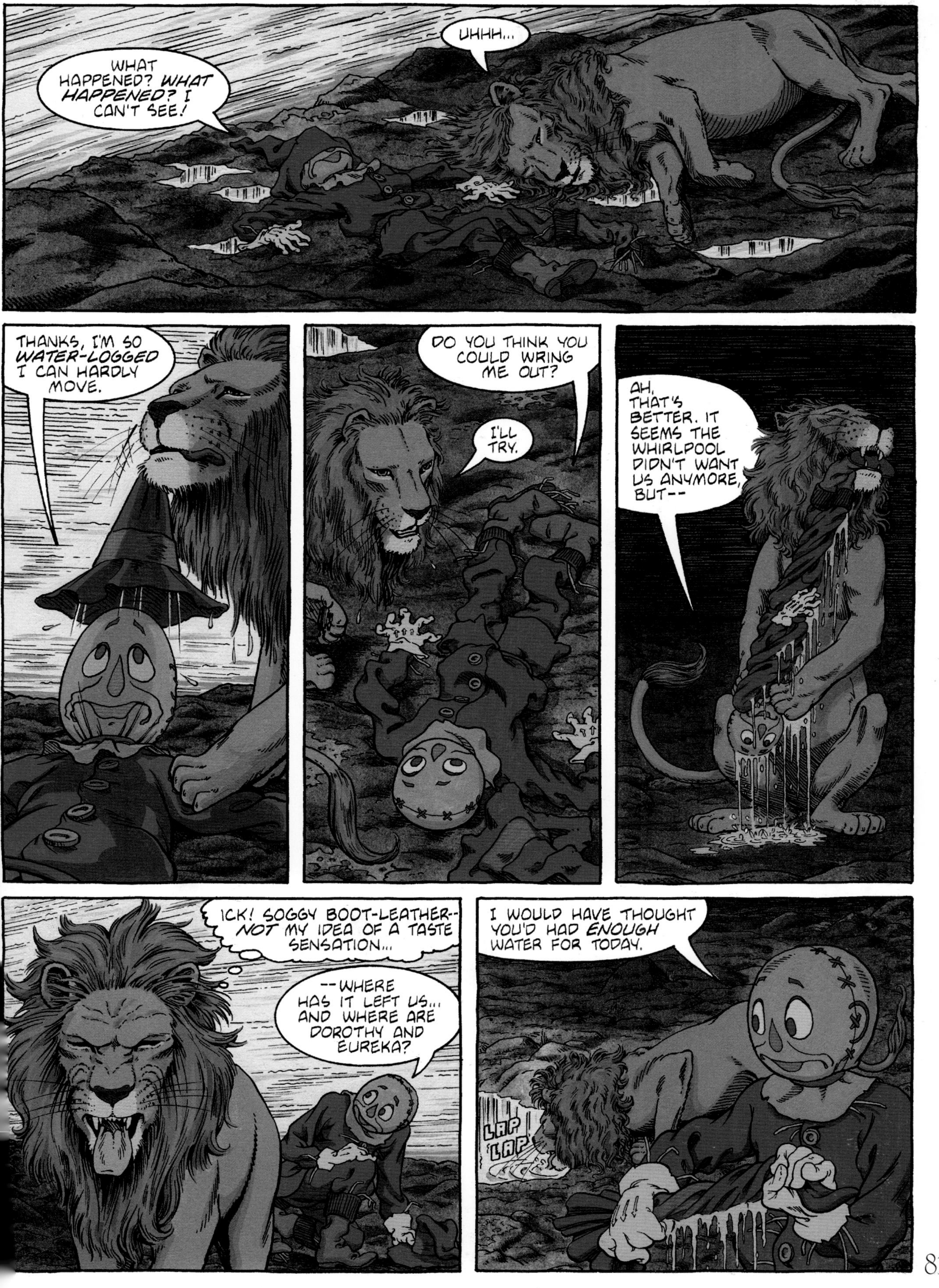
UHHH...
WHAT HAPPENED? WHAT HAPPENED? I CAN'T SEE!
THANKS, I'M SO WATER-LOGGED I CAN HARDLY MOVE.
DO YOU THINK YOU COULD WRING ME OUT?
I'LL TRY.
AH, THAT'S BETTER. IT SEEMS THE WHIRLPOOL DIDN'T WANT US ANYMORE, BUT--
ICK! SOGGY BOOT-LEATHER-- NOT MY IDEA OF A TASTE SENSATION...
--WHERE HAS IT LEFT US... AND WHERE ARE DOROTHY AND EUREKA?
I WOULD HAVE THOUGHT YOU'D HAD ENOUGH WATER FOR TODAY.
LAP LAP

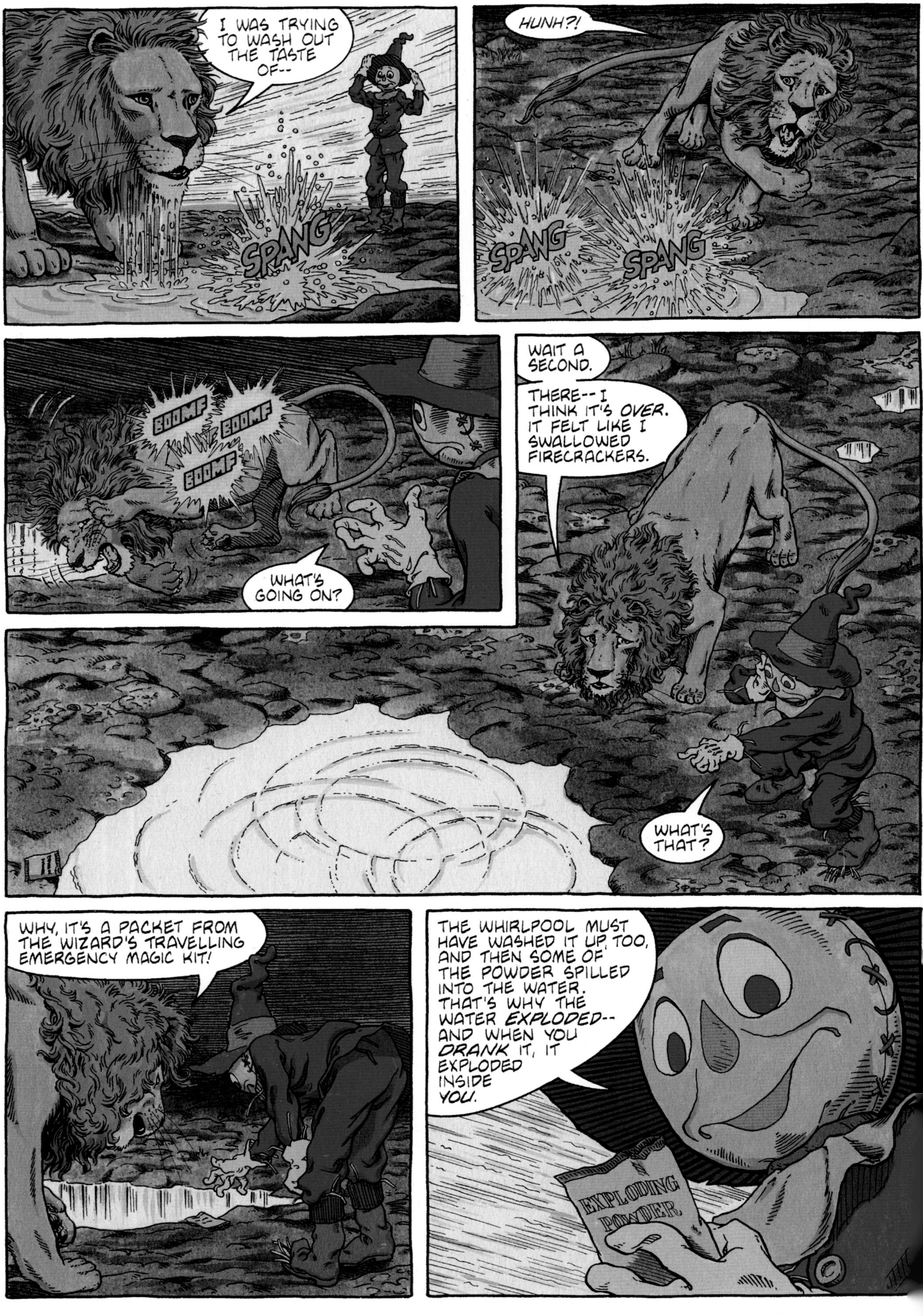
I WAS TRYING TO WASH OUT THE TASTE OF--
SPANG
HUNH?!
SPANG
SPANG
BOOMF
BOOMF
BOOMF
WHAT'S GOING ON?
WAIT A SECOND.
THERE--I THINK IT'S *OVER*. IT FELT LIKE I SWALLOWED FIRECRACKERS.
WHAT'S THAT?
WHY, IT'S A PACKET FROM THE WIZARD'S TRAVELLING EMERGENCY MAGIC KIT!
THE WHIRLPOOL MUST HAVE WASHED IT UP, TOO, AND THEN SOME OF THE POWDER SPILLED INTO THE WATER. THAT'S WHY THE WATER *EXPLODED*-- AND WHEN YOU *DRANK* IT, IT EXPLODED INSIDE *YOU*.
EXPLODING POWDER

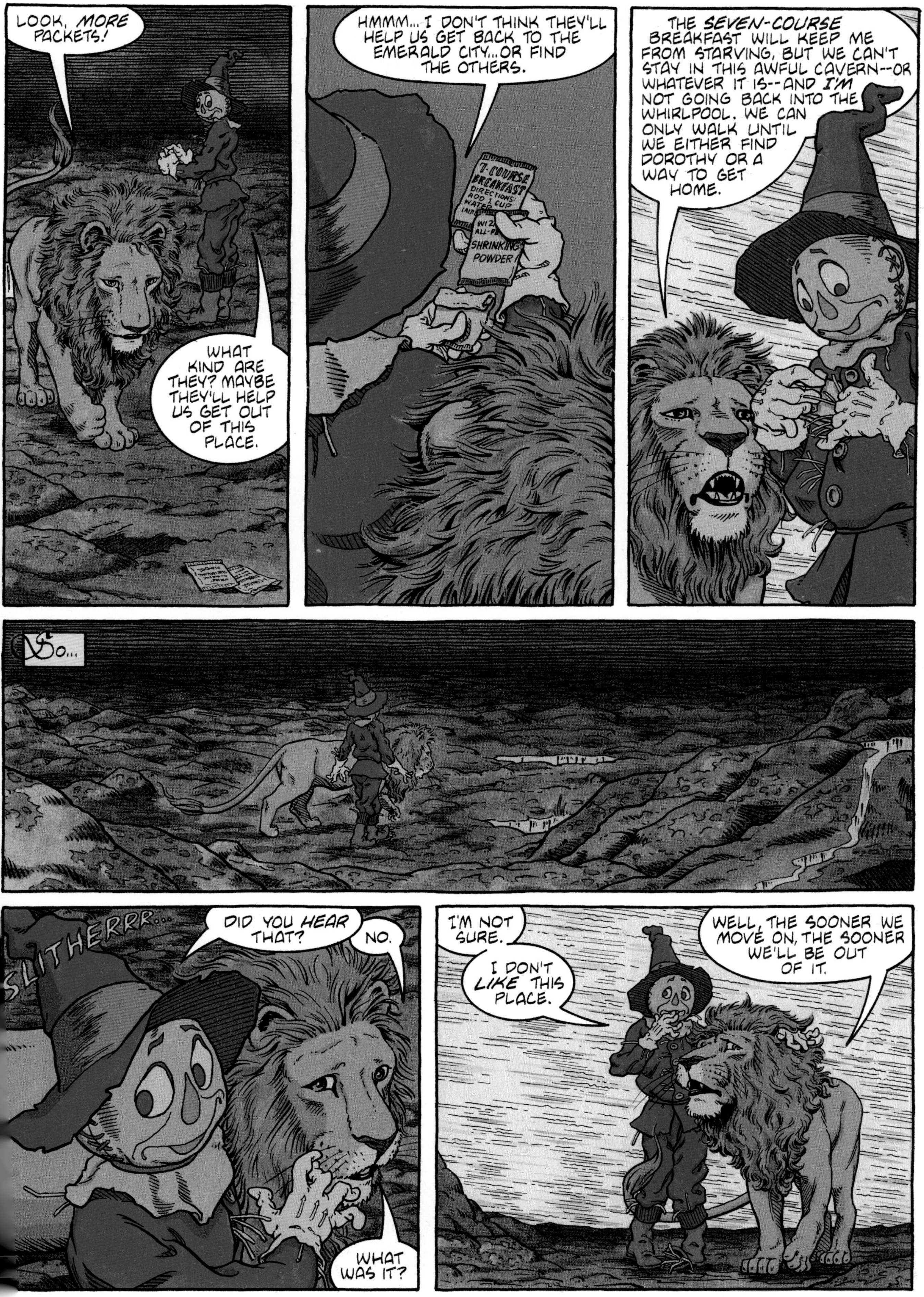
LOOK, MORE PACKETS!
WHAT KIND ARE THEY? MAYBE THEY'LL HELP US GET OUT OF THIS PLACE.
HMMM... I DON'T THINK THEY'LL HELP US GET BACK TO THE EMERALD CITY...OR FIND THE OTHERS.
7-COURSE BREAKFAST DIRECTIONS: ADD 1 CUP WATER
SHRINKING POWDER
THE SEVEN-COURSE BREAKFAST WILL KEEP ME FROM STARVING, BUT WE CAN'T STAY IN THIS AWFUL CAVERN--OR WHATEVER IT IS--AND I'M NOT GOING BACK INTO THE WHIRLPOOL. WE CAN ONLY WALK UNTIL WE EITHER FIND DOROTHY OR A WAY TO GET HOME.
SO...
SLITHERRR...
DID YOU HEAR THAT?
NO.
WHAT WAS IT?
I'M NOT SURE.
I DON'T LIKE THIS PLACE.
WELL, THE SOONER WE MOVE ON, THE SOONER WE'LL BE OUT OF IT.

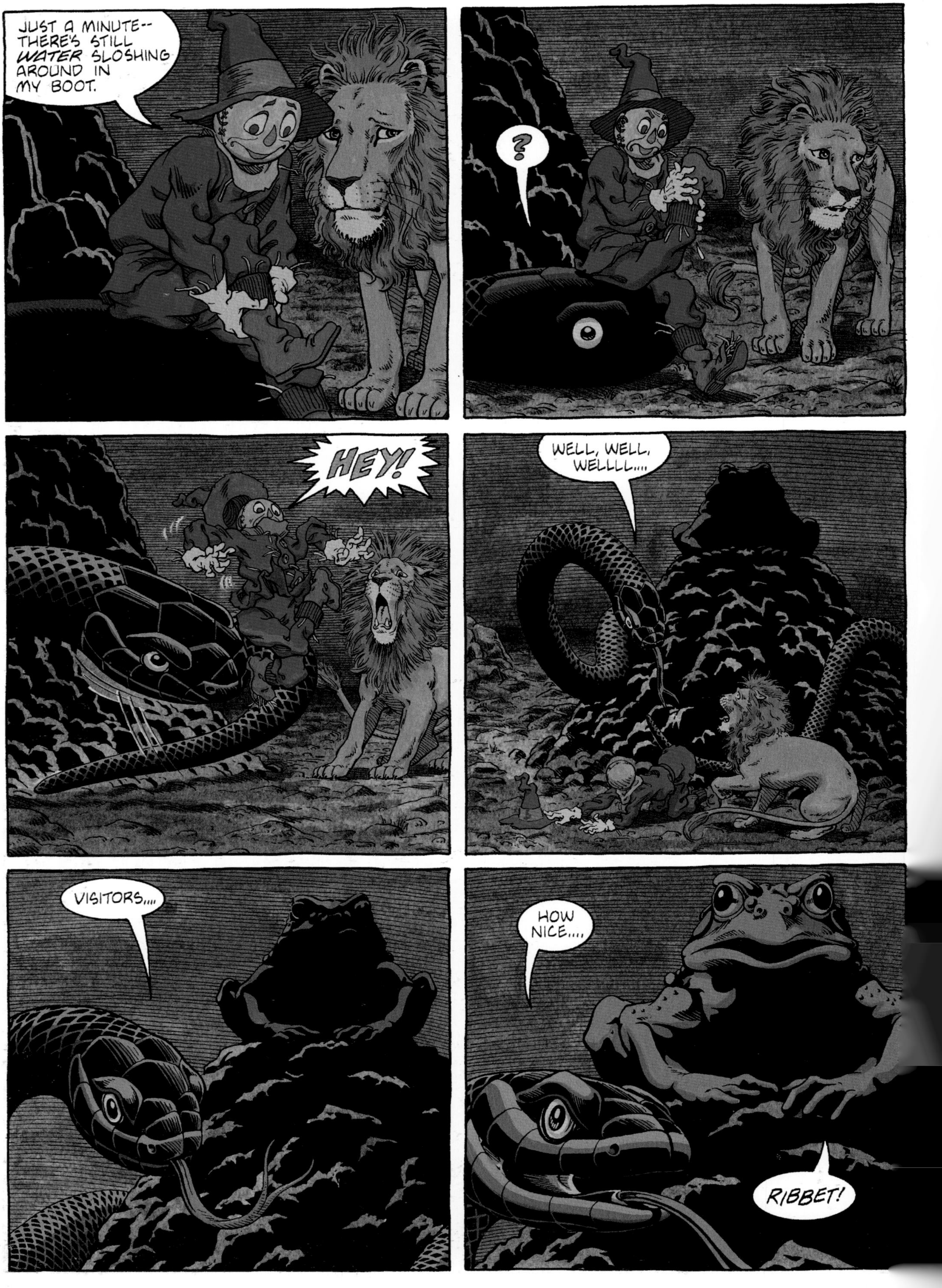
JUST A MINUTE-- THERE'S STILL WATER SLOSHING AROUND IN MY BOOT.
?
HEY!
WELL, WELL, WELLLL....
VISITORS....
HOW NICE....
RIBBET!

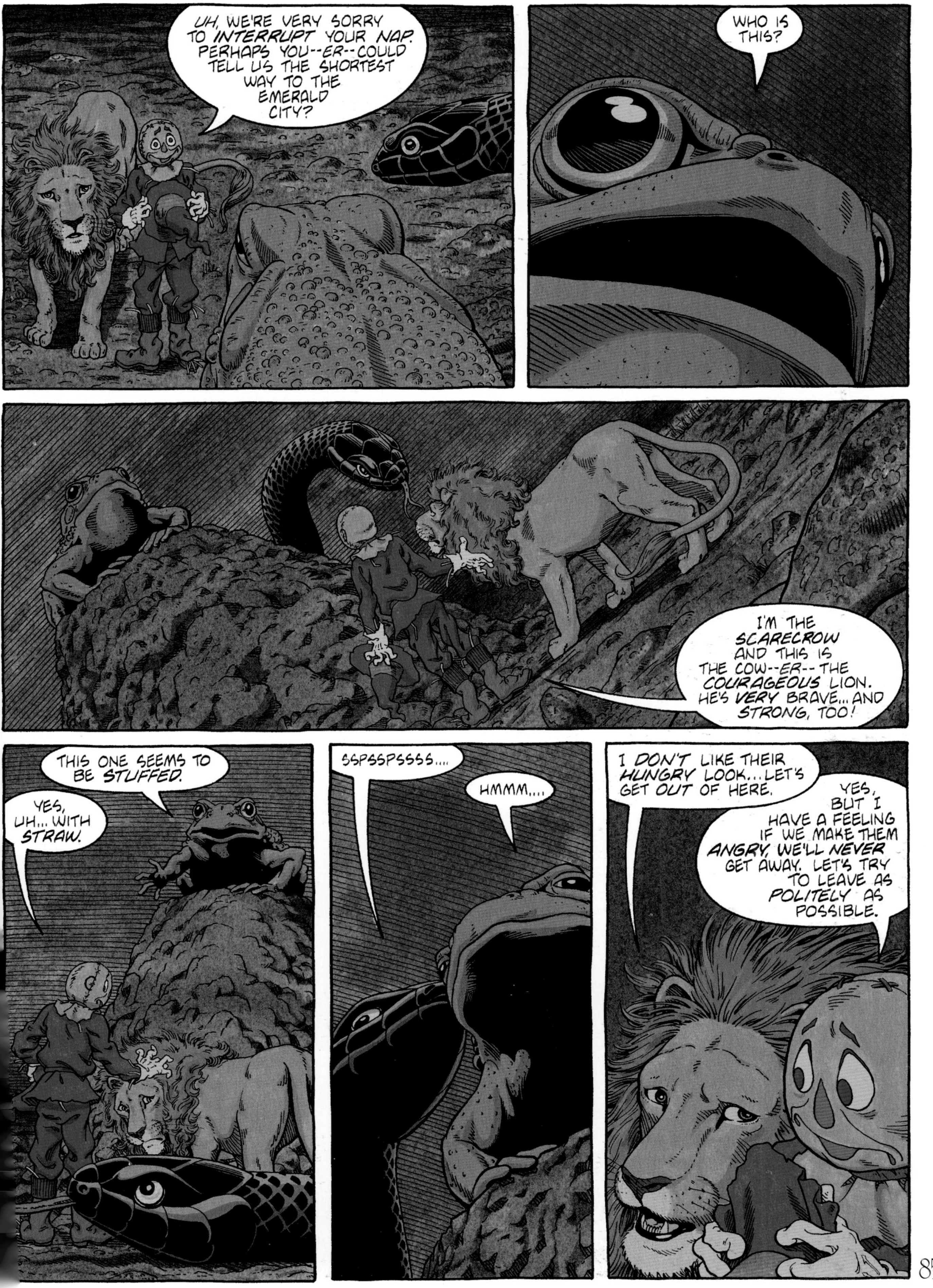

UH, WE'RE VERY SORRY TO INTERRUPT YOUR NAP. PERHAPS YOU--ER--COULD TELL US THE SHORTEST WAY TO THE EMERALD CITY?
WHO IS THIS?
I'M THE SCARECROW AND THIS IS THE COW--ER-- THE COURAGEOUS LION. HE'S VERY BRAVE... AND STRONG, TOO!
THIS ONE SEEMS TO BE STUFFED.
YES, UH... WITH STRAW.
SSPSSPSSSS....
HMMM,...
I DON'T LIKE THEIR HUNGRY LOOK... LET'S GET OUT OF HERE.
YES, BUT I HAVE A FEELING IF WE MAKE THEM ANGRY, WE'LL NEVER GET AWAY. LET'S TRY TO LEAVE AS POLITELY AS POSSIBLE.

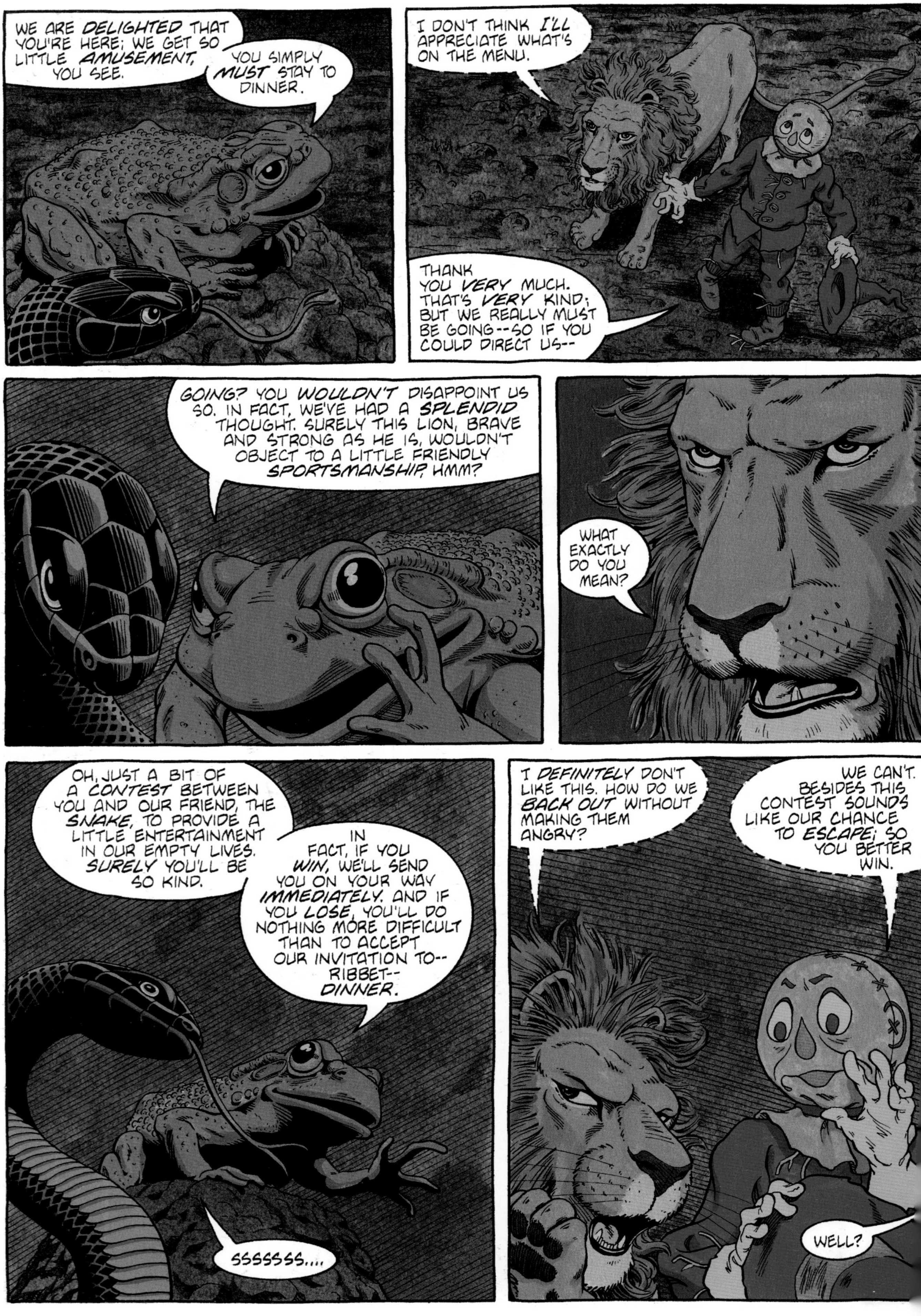

WE ARE DELIGHTED THAT YOU'RE HERE; WE GET SO LITTLE AMUSEMENT, YOU SEE.
YOU SIMPLY MUST STAY TO DINNER.
I DON'T THINK I'LL APPRECIATE WHAT'S ON THE MENU.
THANK YOU VERY MUCH. THAT'S VERY KIND; BUT WE REALLY MUST BE GOING--SO IF YOU COULD DIRECT US--
GOING? YOU WOULDN'T DISAPPOINT US SO. IN FACT, WE'VE HAD A SPLENDID THOUGHT. SURELY THIS LION, BRAVE AND STRONG AS HE IS, WOULDN'T OBJECT TO A LITTLE FRIENDLY SPORTSMANSHIP, HMM?
WHAT EXACTLY DO YOU MEAN?
OH, JUST A BIT OF A CONTEST BETWEEN YOU AND OUR FRIEND, THE SNAKE, TO PROVIDE A LITTLE ENTERTAINMENT IN OUR EMPTY LIVES. SURELY YOU'LL BE SO KIND.
IN FACT, IF YOU WIN, WE'LL SEND YOU ON YOUR WAY IMMEDIATELY. AND IF YOU LOSE, YOU'LL DO NOTHING MORE DIFFICULT THAN TO ACCEPT OUR INVITATION TO-- RIBBET-- DINNER.
SSSSSSS....
I DEFINITELY DON'T LIKE THIS. HOW DO WE BACK OUT WITHOUT MAKING THEM ANGRY?
WE CAN'T. BESIDES THIS CONTEST SOUNDS LIKE OUR CHANCE TO ESCAPE; SO YOU BETTER WIN.
WELL?

WE ACCEPT.

HEY--!

SPLENDID! SPLENDID! VERY WELL, THE FIRST PART OF THE CONTEST IS A *RACE*. THE SNAKE AND THE LION WILL RACE FROM THIS ROCK TO THE EDGE OF THAT *MARSH* AND BACK. WHOEVER FINISHES FIRST WILL WIN.

NOW, PLEASE, ON YOUR MARKS.

SILENCE PLEASE. GET SET.

I'M GLAD *YOU'RE* SURE ABOUT THIS.

IT'S TOO LATE TO BACK OUT NOW.

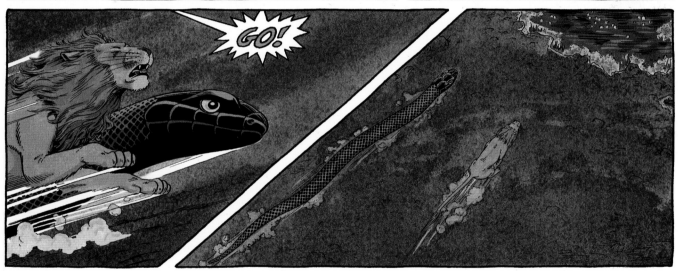

GO!

WHAK!

SS-SS-SS-SS-SS-SS-SSS....

AND THE SNAKE WINS. I SUPPOSE STRONG, BRAVE, *COURAGEOUS* LIONS AREN'T *QUITE* ACCUSTOMED TO RUNNING RACES NEAR MARSHES. PERHAPS HE'LL DO BETTER IN THE *SECOND* PART OF THE CONTEST.

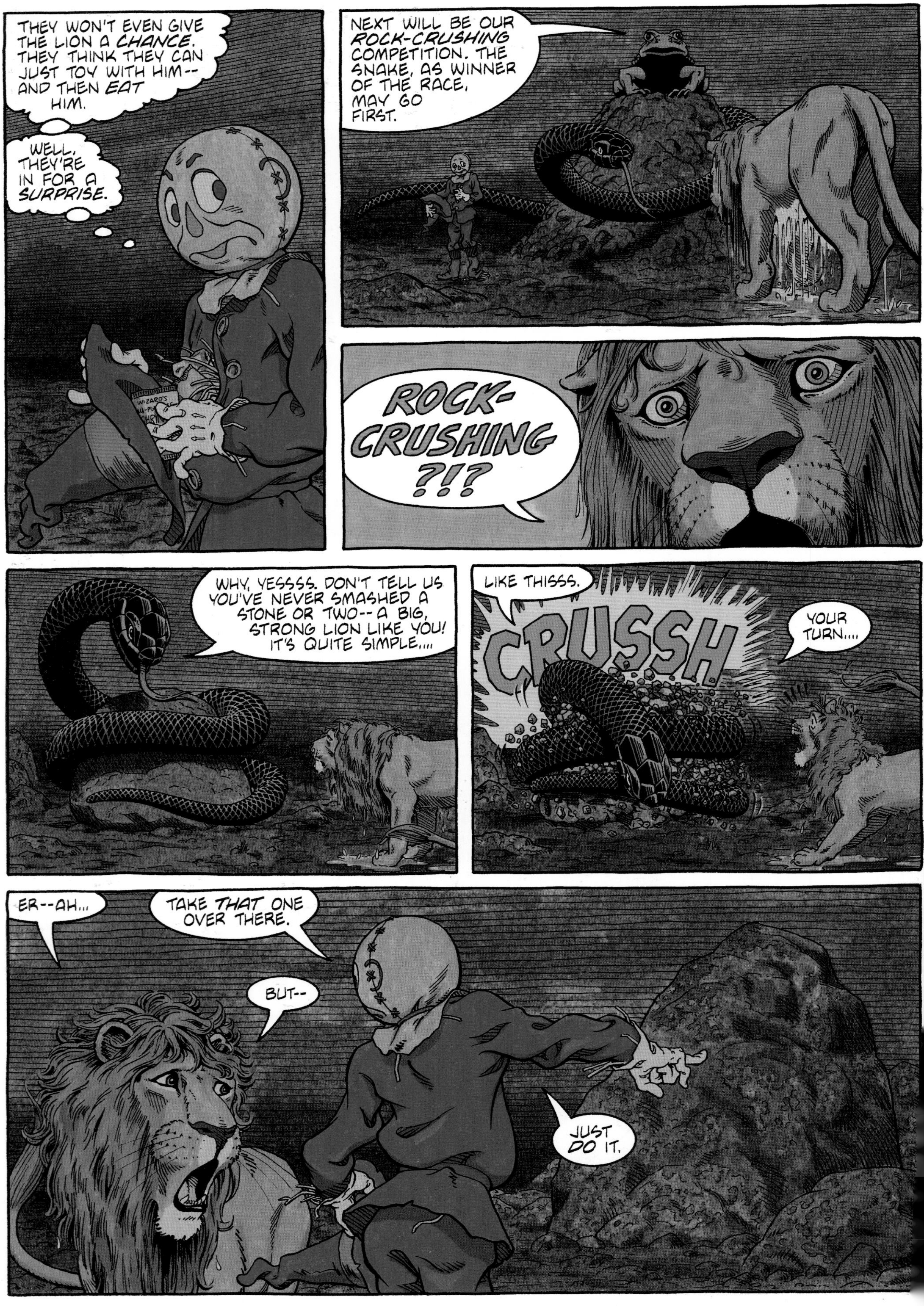
THEY WON'T EVEN GIVE THE LION A CHANCE. THEY THINK THEY CAN JUST TOY WITH HIM-- AND THEN EAT HIM.
WELL, THEY'RE IN FOR A SURPRISE.
WIZARD'S
NEXT WILL BE OUR ROCK-CRUSHING COMPETITION. THE SNAKE, AS WINNER OF THE RACE, MAY GO FIRST.
ROCK-CRUSHING ?!?
WHY, YESSSS. DON'T TELL US YOU'VE NEVER SMASHED A STONE OR TWO-- A BIG, STRONG LION LIKE YOU! IT'S QUITE SIMPLE....
LIKE THISSS.
CRUSSH
YOUR TURN....
ER--AH...
TAKE THAT ONE OVER THERE.
BUT--
JUST DO IT.

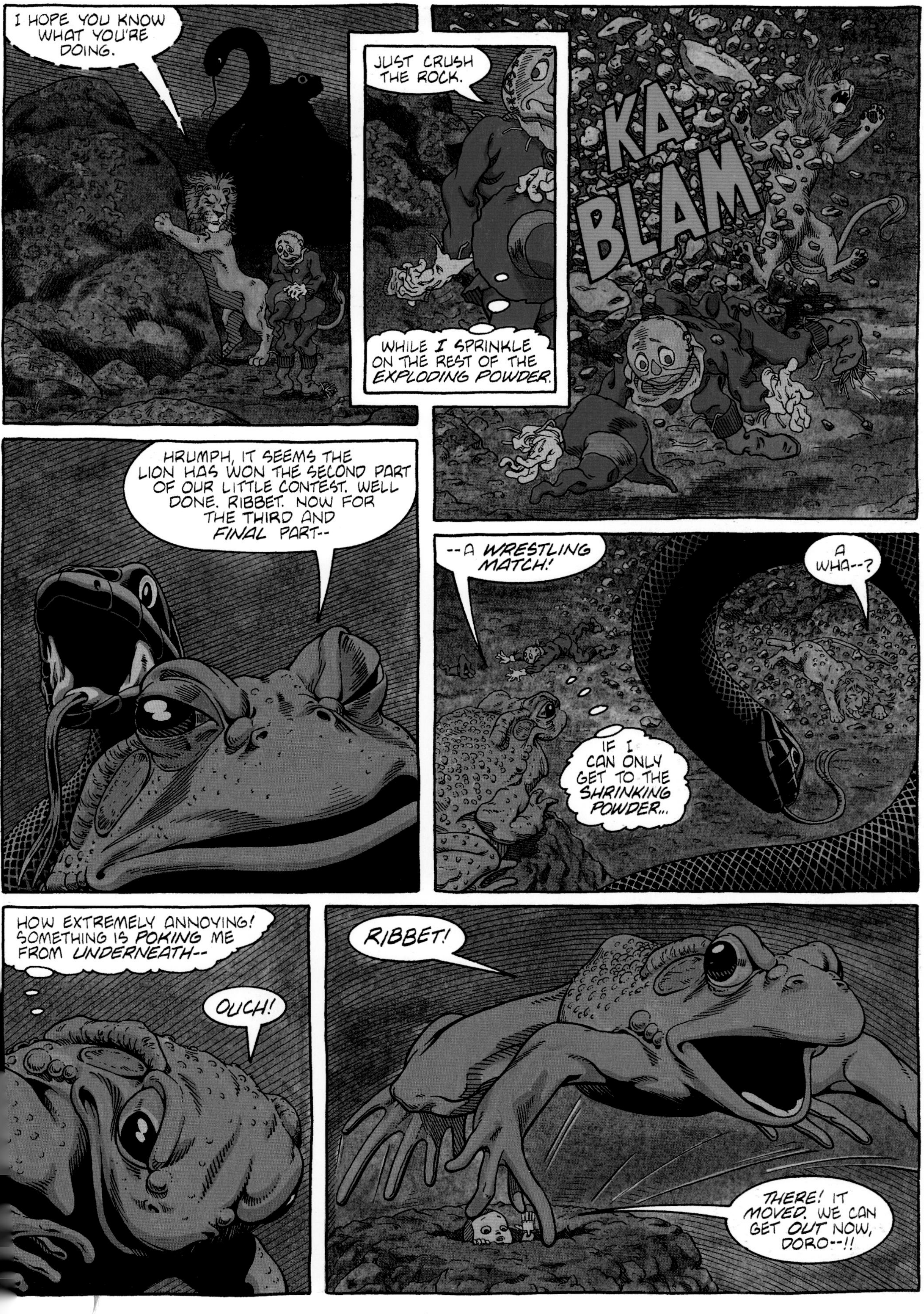
I HOPE YOU KNOW WHAT YOU'RE DOING.
JUST CRUSH THE ROCK.
WHILE *I* SPRINKLE ON THE REST OF THE *EXPLODING POWDER*.
KA-BLAM
HRUMPH, IT SEEMS THE LION HAS WON THE SECOND PART OF OUR LITTLE CONTEST. WELL DONE. RIBBET. NOW FOR THE THIRD AND *FINAL* PART--
--A *WRESTLING MATCH!*
A WHA--?
IF I CAN ONLY GET TO THE *SHRINKING POWDER*...
HOW EXTREMELY ANNOYING! SOMETHING IS *POKING* ME FROM *UNDERNEATH*--
OUCH!
RIBBET!
*THERE!* IT *MOVED*. WE CAN GET *OUT* NOW, DORO--!!

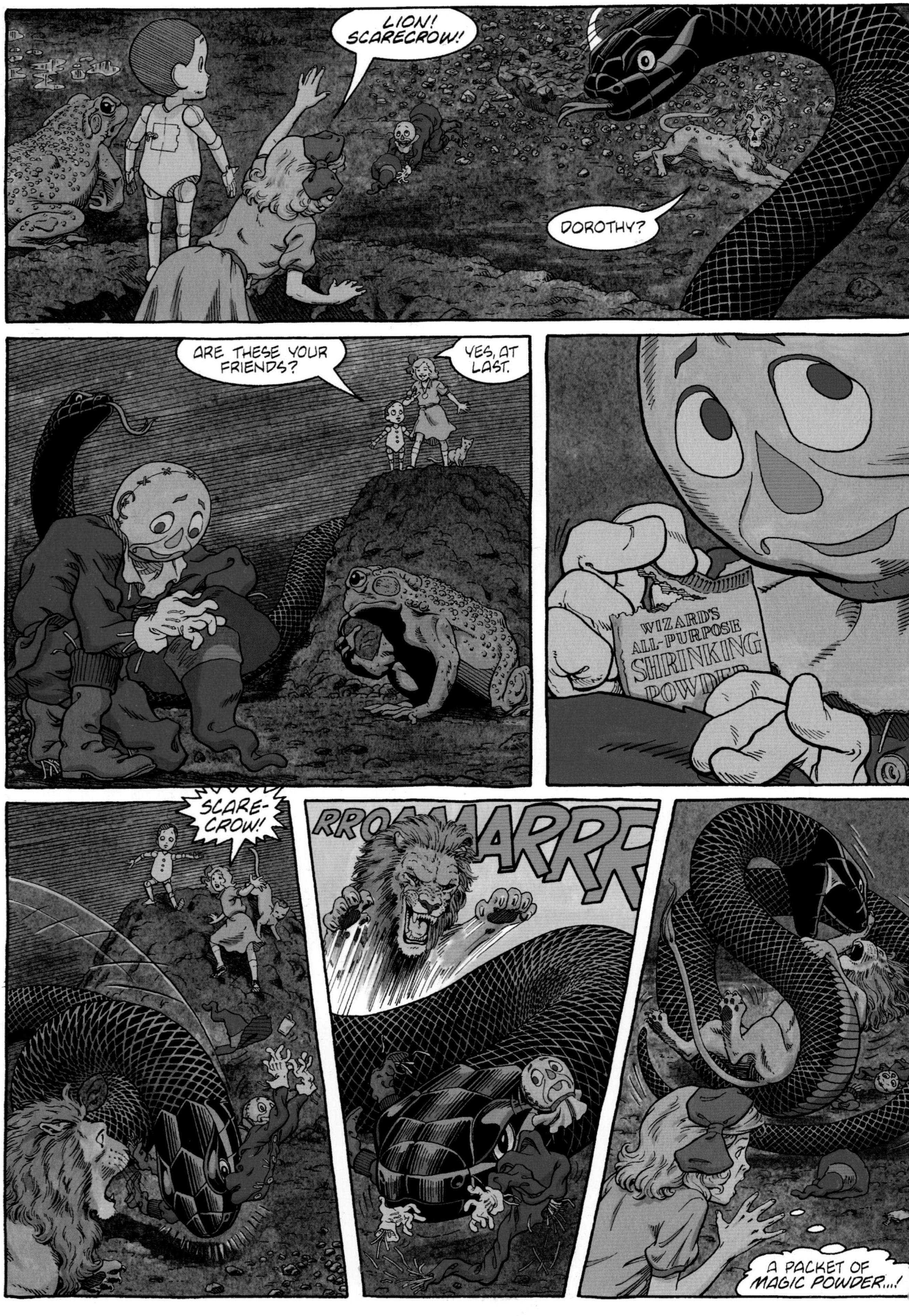
LION! SCARECROW!
DOROTHY?
ARE THESE YOUR FRIENDS?
YES, AT LAST.
WIZARD'S ALL-PURPOSE SHRINKING POWDER
SCARE-CROW!
RROAAARRR
A PACKET OF MAGIC POWDER...!

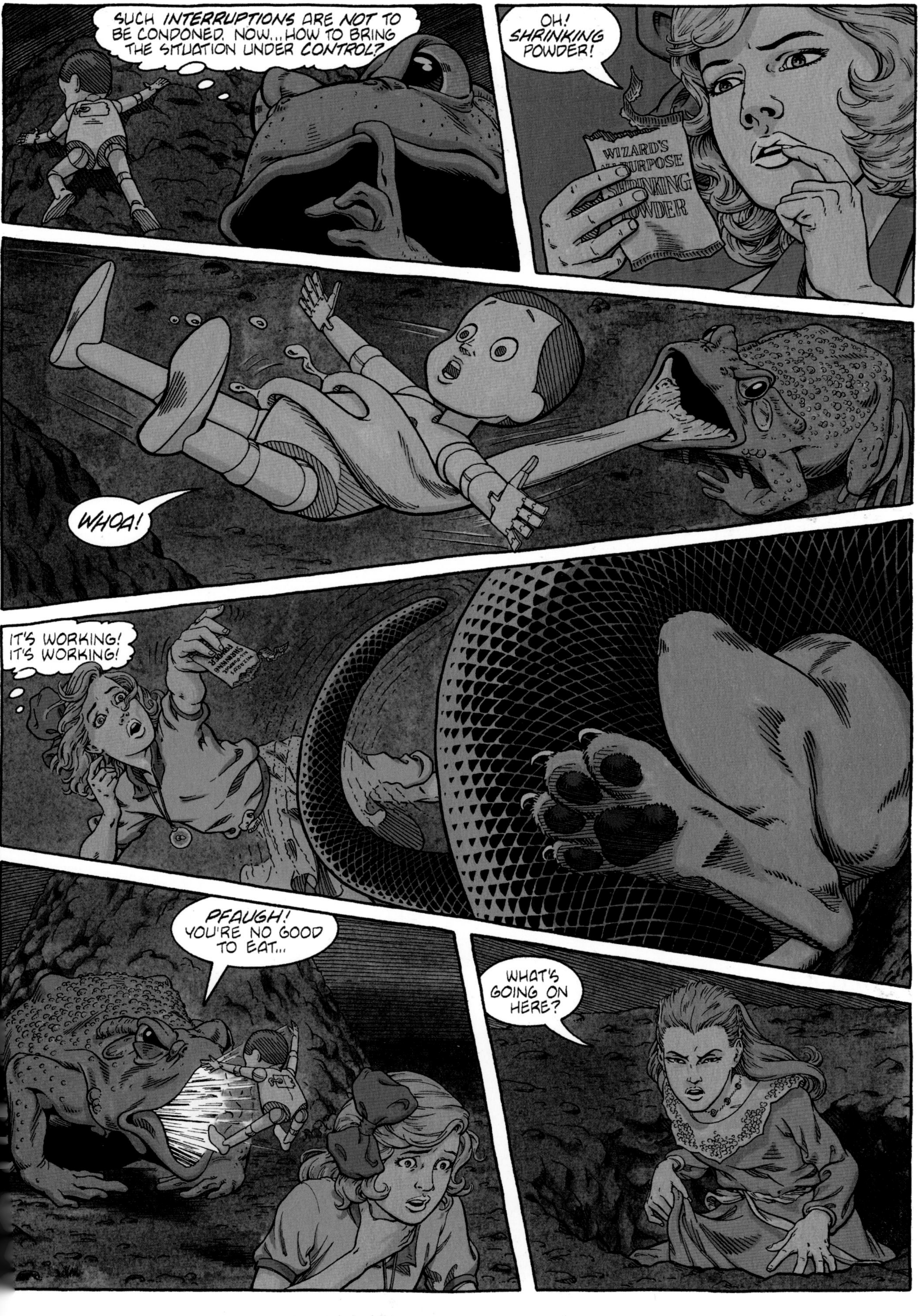
SUCH INTERRUPTIONS ARE NOT TO BE CONDONED. NOW... HOW TO BRING THE SITUATION UNDER CONTROL?
OH! SHRINKING POWDER!
WIZARD'S
WHOA!
IT'S WORKING! IT'S WORKING!
PFAUGH! YOU'RE NO GOOD TO EAT...
WHAT'S GOING ON HERE?

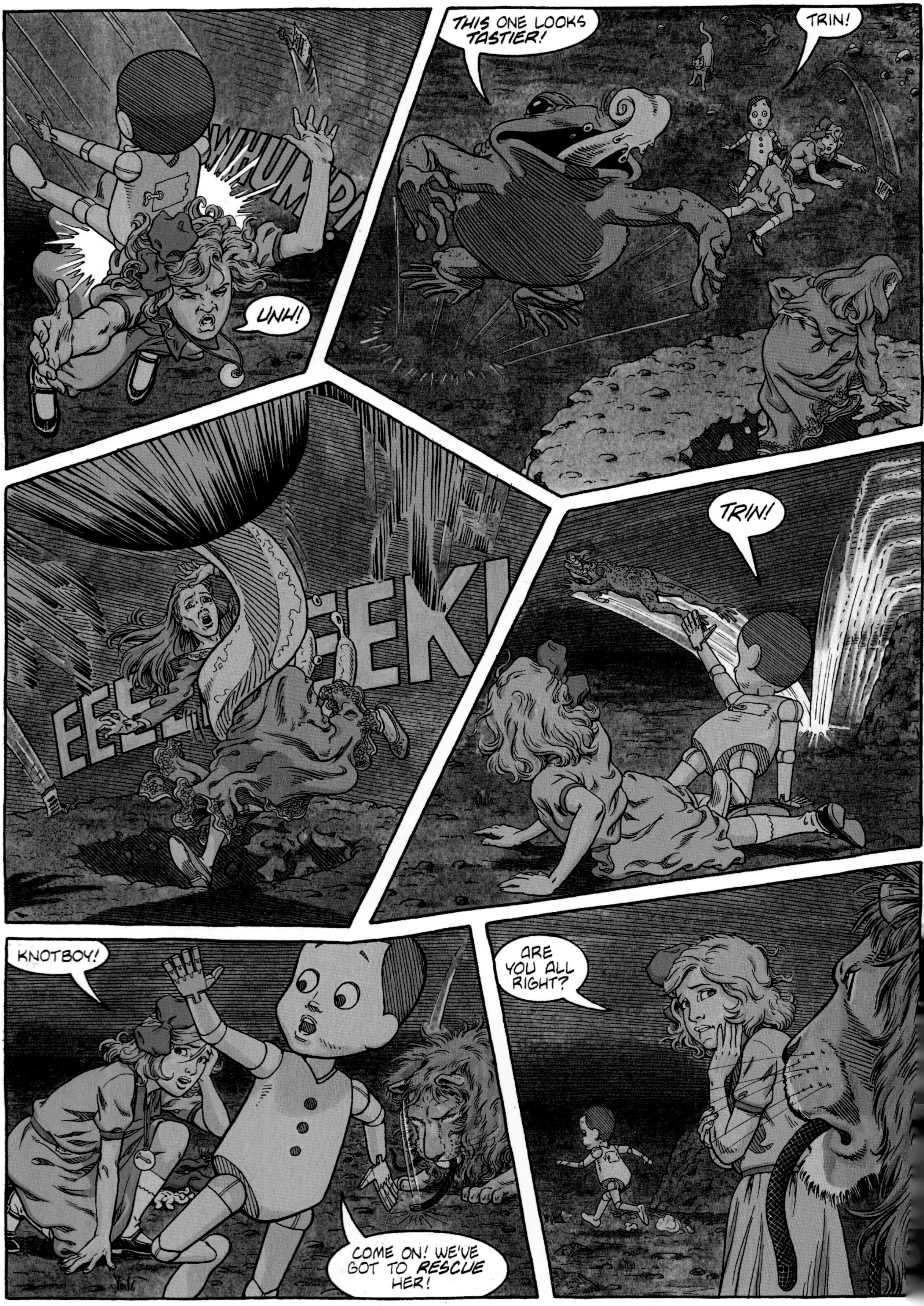
WHUMP!
UNH!
THIS ONE LOOKS TASTIER!
TRIN!
EEEEEK!
TRIN!
KNOTBOY!
COME ON! WE'VE GOT TO RESCUE HER!
ARE YOU ALL RIGHT?

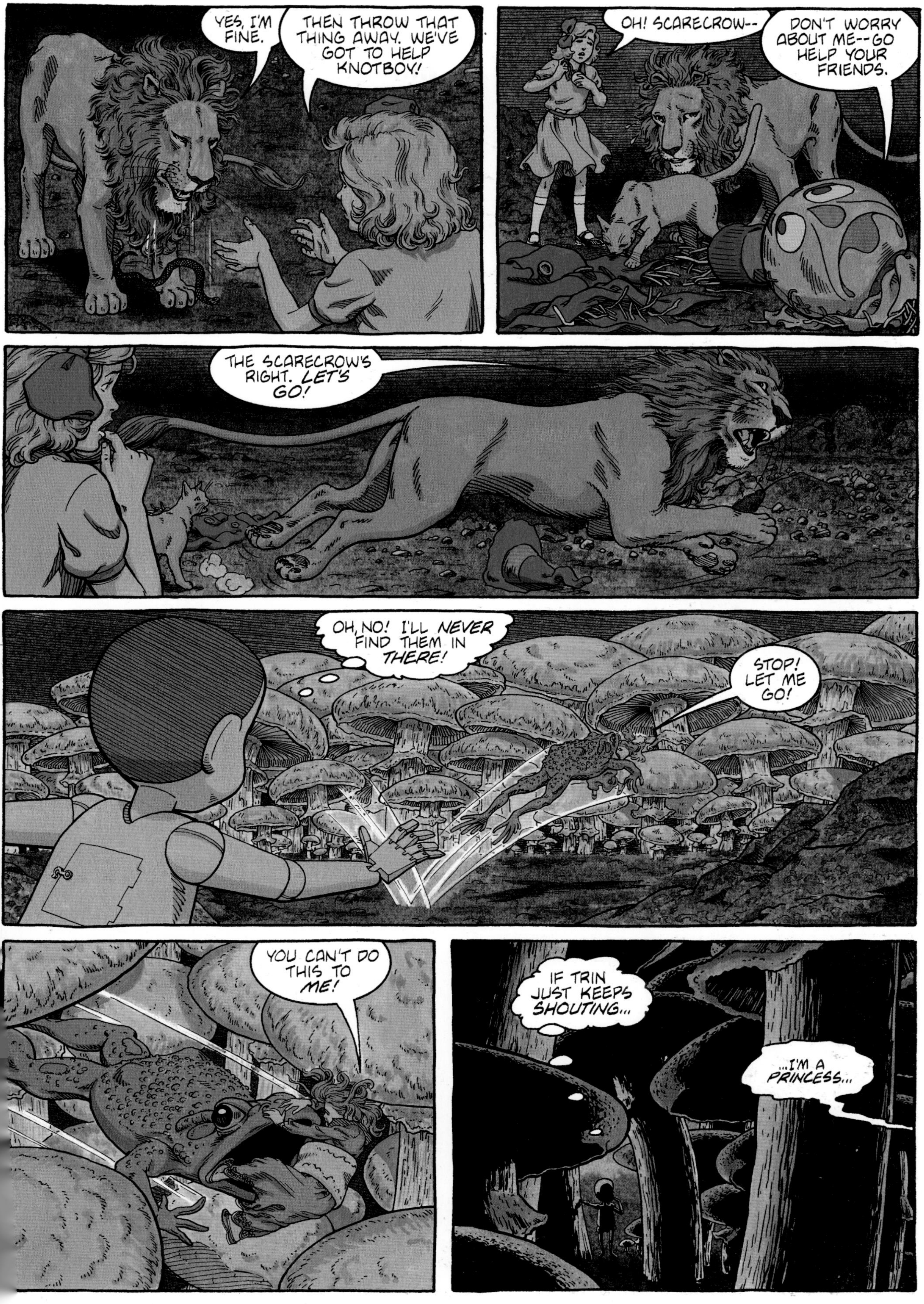
YES, I'M FINE.
THEN THROW THAT THING AWAY. WE'VE GOT TO HELP KNOTBOY!
OH! SCARECROW--
DON'T WORRY ABOUT ME--GO HELP YOUR FRIENDS.
THE SCARECROW'S RIGHT. *LET'S GO!*
OH, NO! I'LL *NEVER* FIND THEM IN *THERE!*
STOP! LET ME GO!
YOU CAN'T DO THIS TO *ME!*
IF TRIN JUST KEEPS *SHOUTING...*
...I'M A *PRINCESS...*

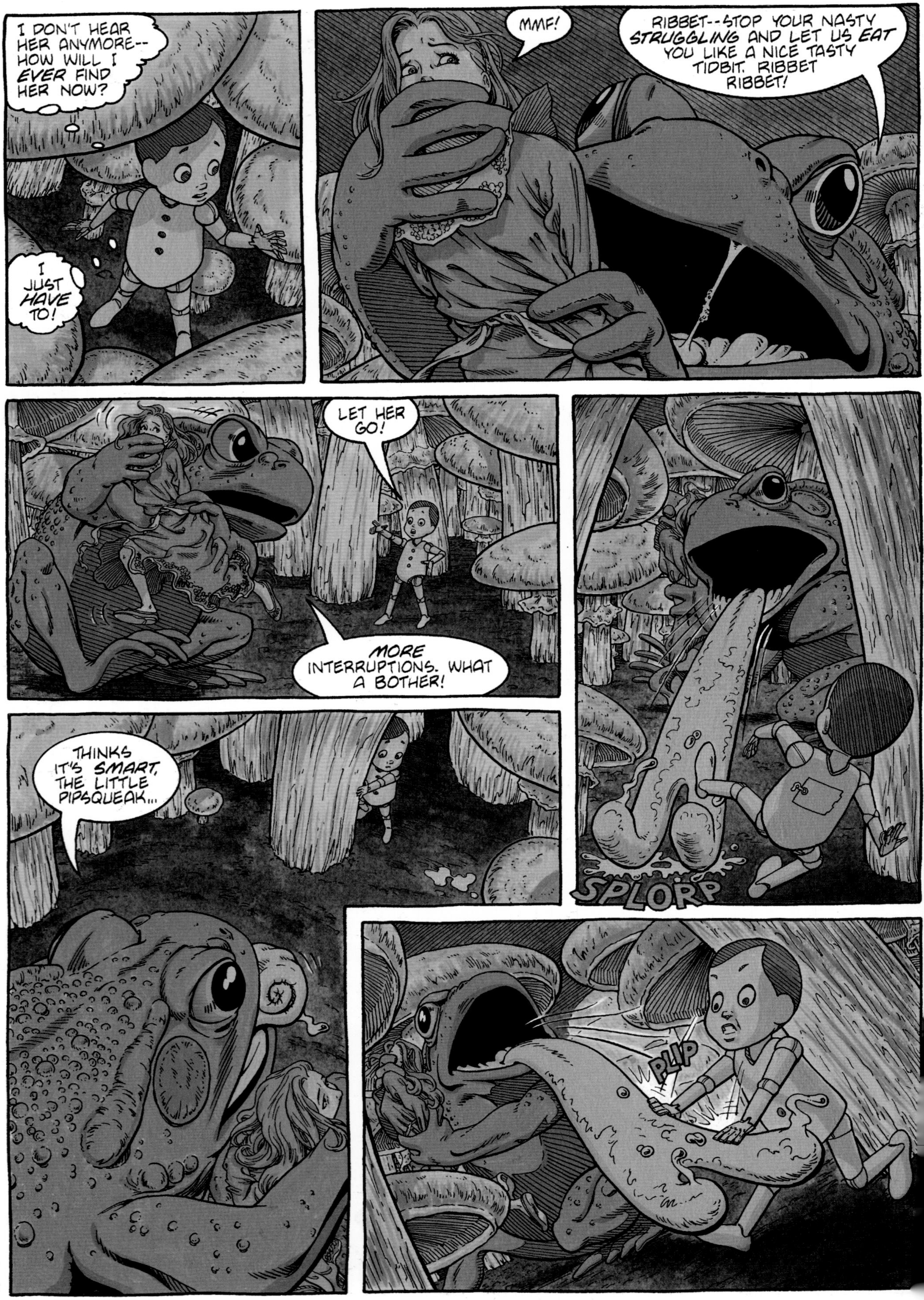
I DON'T HEAR HER ANYMORE-- HOW WILL I EVER FIND HER NOW?
I JUST HAVE TO!
MMF!
RIBBET--STOP YOUR NASTY STRUGGLING AND LET US EAT YOU LIKE A NICE TASTY TIDBIT. RIBBET RIBBET!
LET HER GO!
MORE INTERRUPTIONS. WHAT A BOTHER!
SPLORP
THINKS IT'S SMART, THE LITTLE PIPSQUEAK...
PLIP

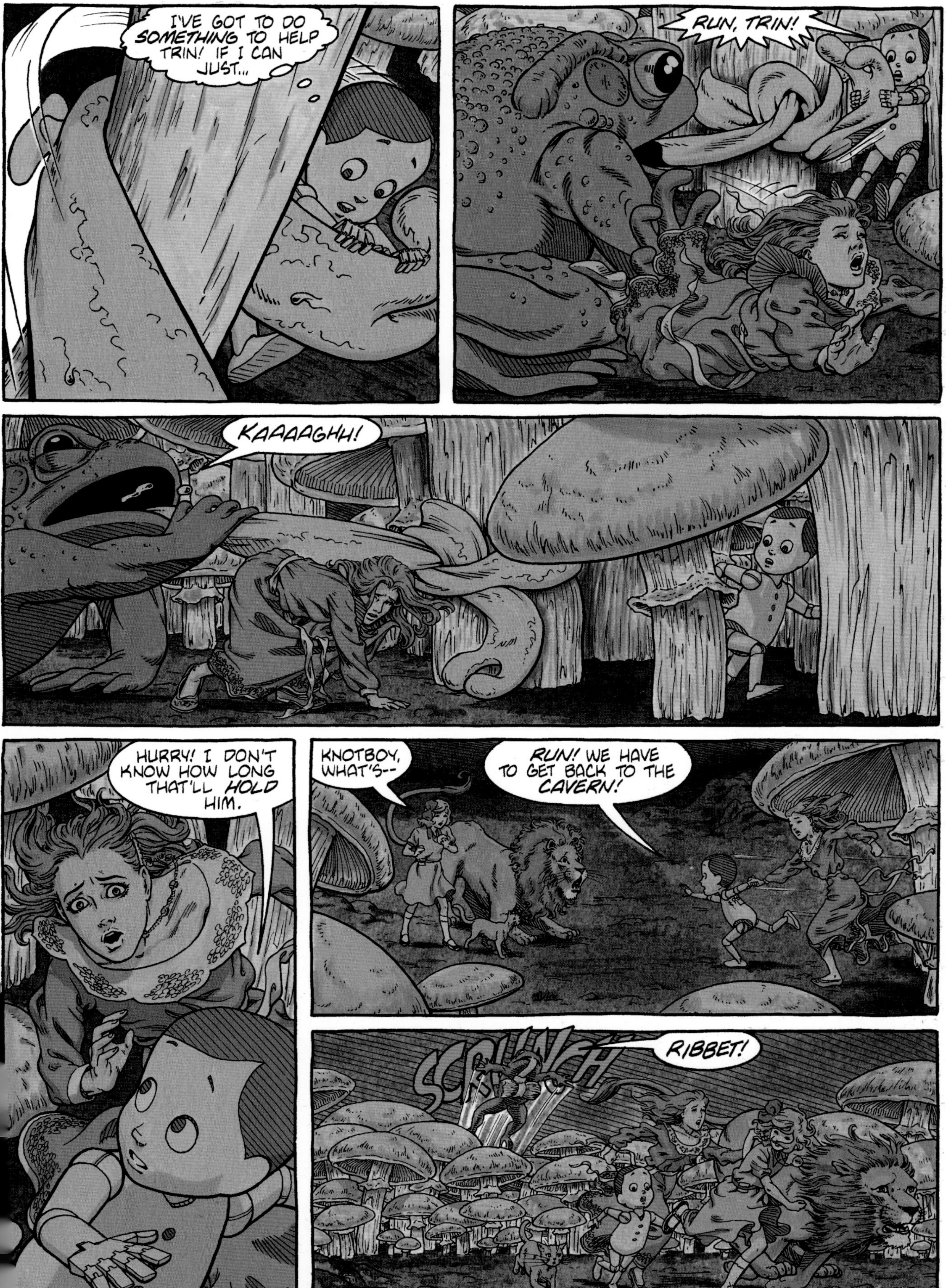
I'VE GOT TO DO SOMETHING TO HELP TRIN! IF I CAN JUST...
RUN, TRIN!
KAAAAGHH!
HURRY! I DON'T KNOW HOW LONG THAT'LL HOLD HIM.
KNOTBOY, WHAT'S--
RUN! WE HAVE TO GET BACK TO THE CAVERN!
SCRUNCH
RIBBET!

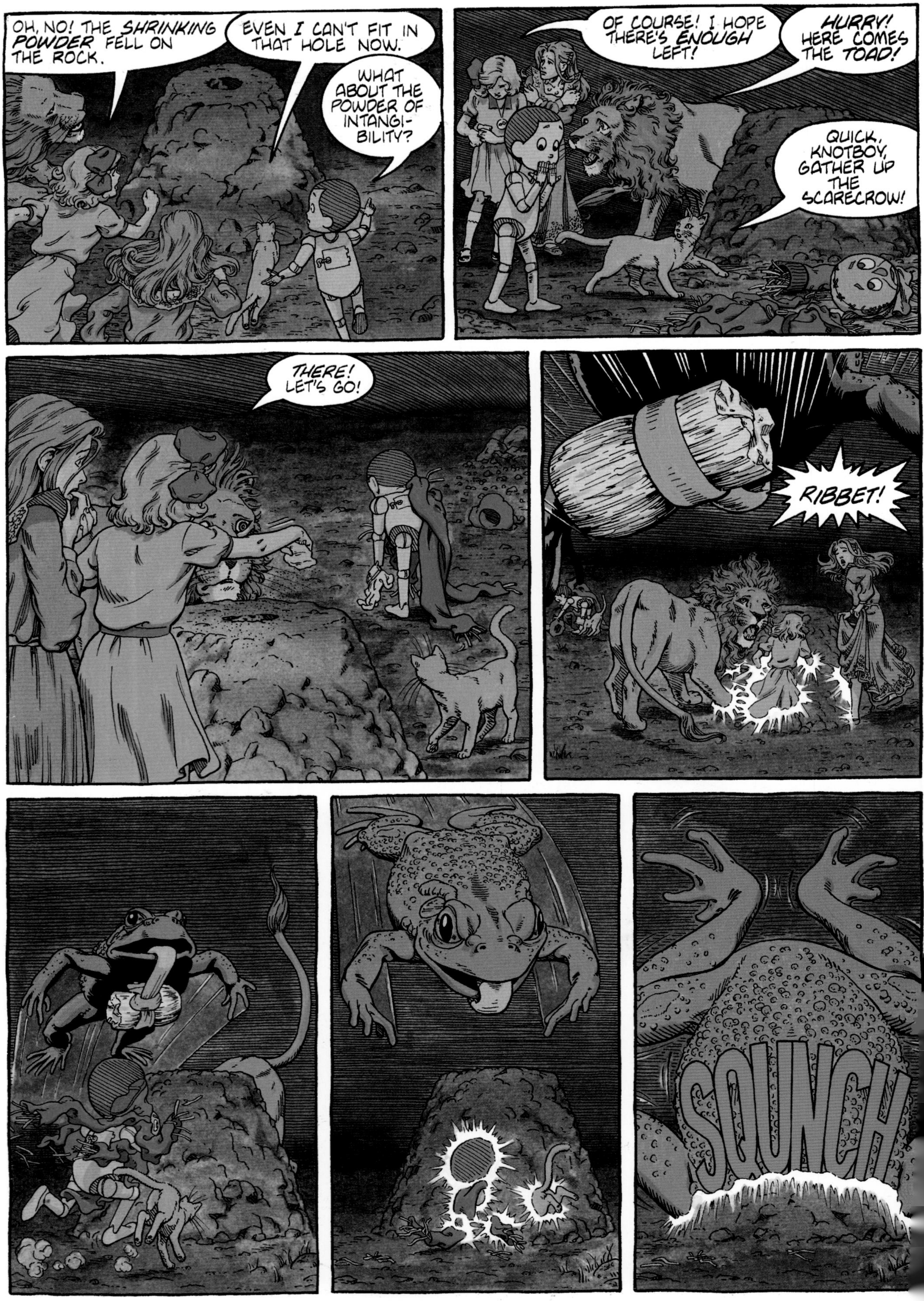

OH, NO! THE SHRINKING POWDER FELL ON THE ROCK.
EVEN I CAN'T FIT IN THAT HOLE NOW.
WHAT ABOUT THE POWDER OF INTANGI-BILITY?
OF COURSE! I HOPE THERE'S ENOUGH LEFT!
HURRY! HERE COMES THE TOAD!
QUICK, KNOTBOY, GATHER UP THE SCARECROW!
THERE! LET'S GO!
RIBBET!
SQUNCH!

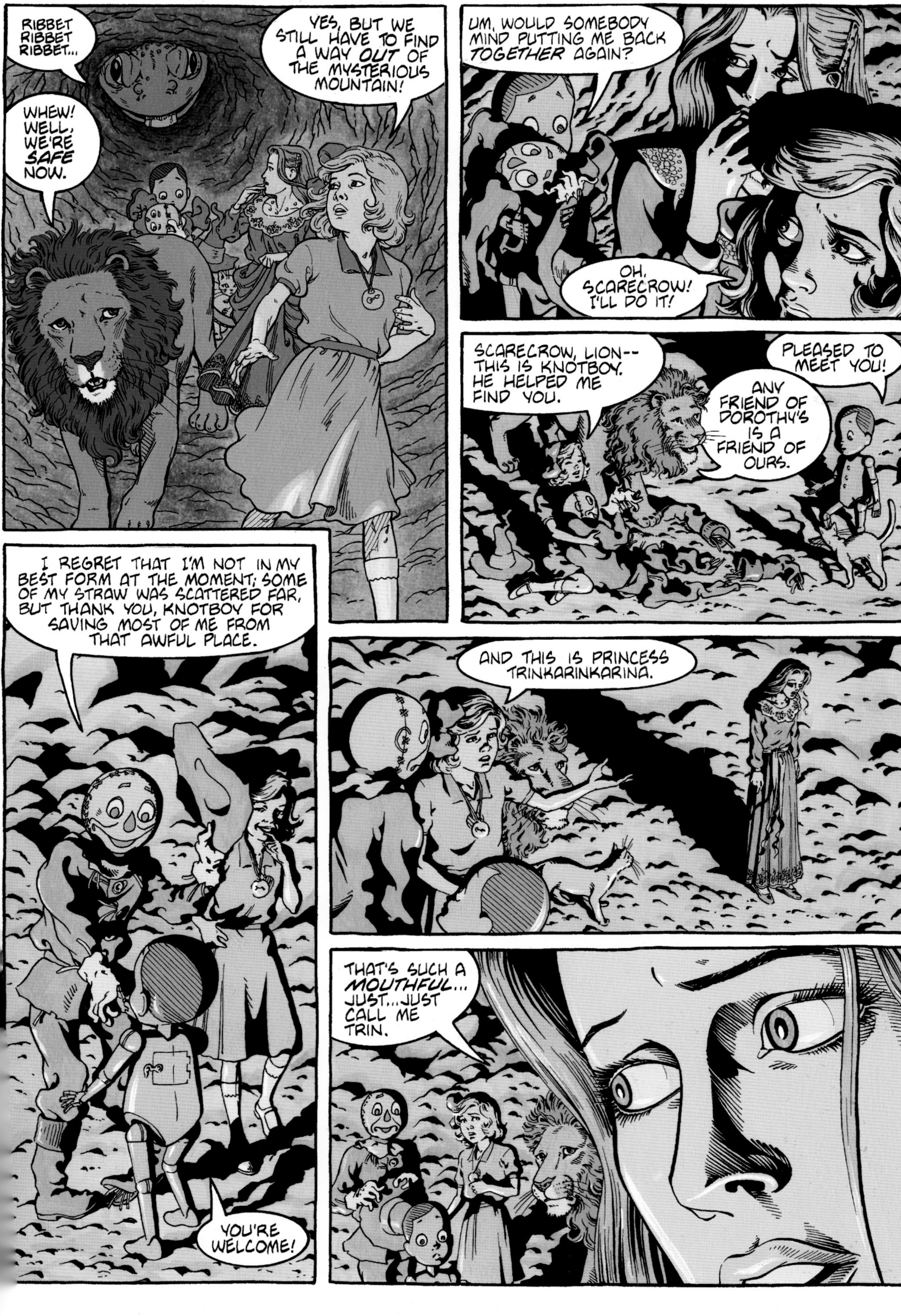
RIBBET RIBBET RIBBET...
WHEW! WELL, WE'RE **SAFE** NOW.
YES, BUT WE STILL HAVE TO FIND A WAY **OUT** OF THE MYSTERIOUS MOUNTAIN!
UM, WOULD SOMEBODY MIND PUTTING ME BACK *TOGETHER* AGAIN?
OH, SCARECROW! I'LL DO IT!
SCARECROW, LION-- THIS IS KNOTBOY. HE HELPED ME FIND YOU.
PLEASED TO MEET YOU!
ANY FRIEND OF DOROTHY'S IS A FRIEND OF OURS.
I REGRET THAT I'M NOT IN MY BEST FORM AT THE MOMENT; SOME OF MY STRAW WAS SCATTERED FAR, BUT THANK YOU, KNOTBOY FOR SAVING MOST OF ME FROM THAT AWFUL PLACE.
YOU'RE WELCOME!
AND THIS IS PRINCESS TRINKARINKARINA.
THAT'S SUCH A **MOUTHFUL**... JUST... JUST CALL ME TRIN.

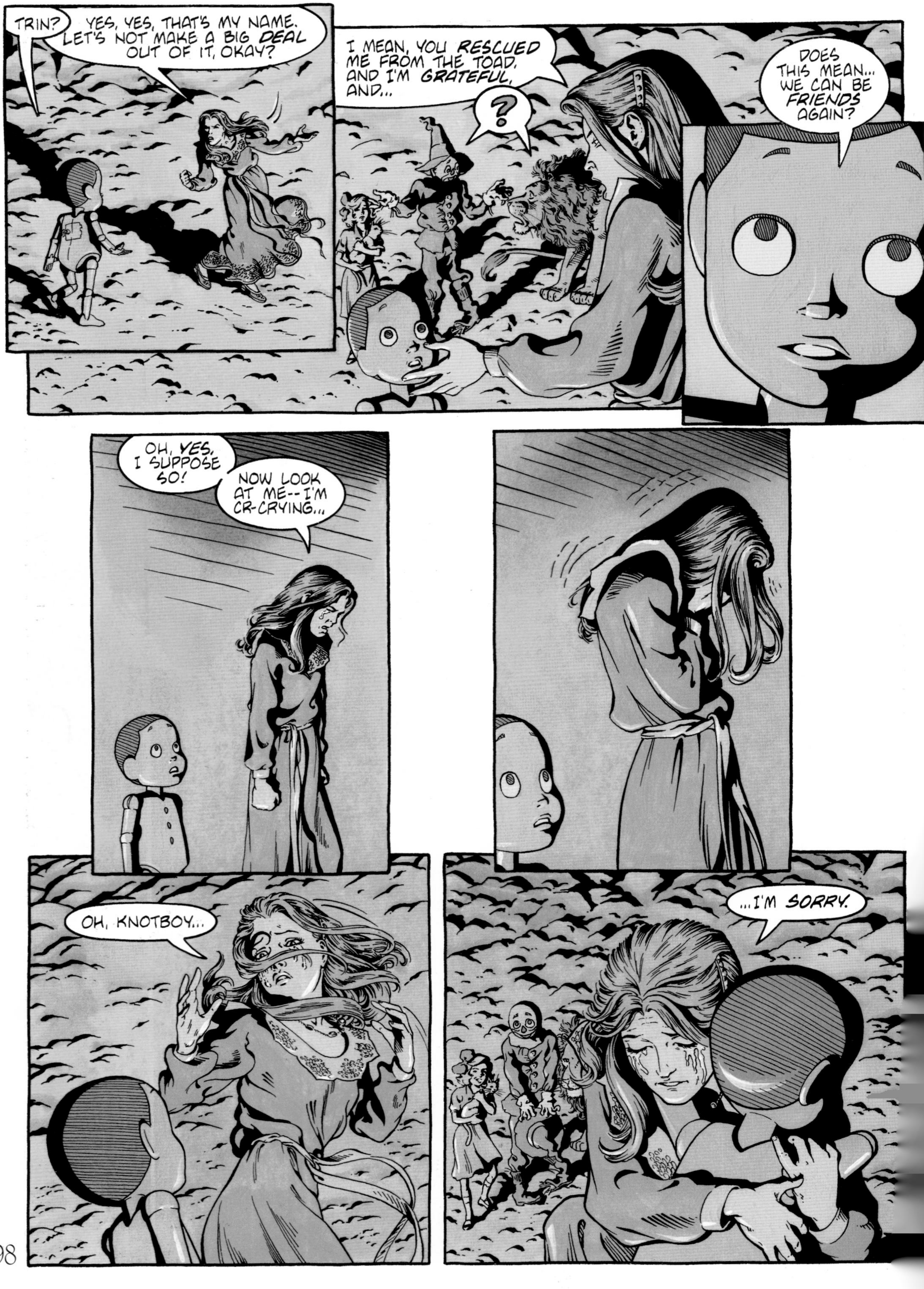
TRIN?
YES, YES, THAT'S MY NAME. LET'S NOT MAKE A BIG DEAL OUT OF IT, OKAY?
I MEAN, YOU RESCUED ME FROM THE TOAD, AND I'M GRATEFUL, AND...
?
DOES THIS MEAN... WE CAN BE FRIENDS AGAIN?
OH, YES, I SUPPOSE SO!
NOW LOOK AT ME--I'M CR-CRYING...
OH, KNOTBOY...
...I'M SORRY.

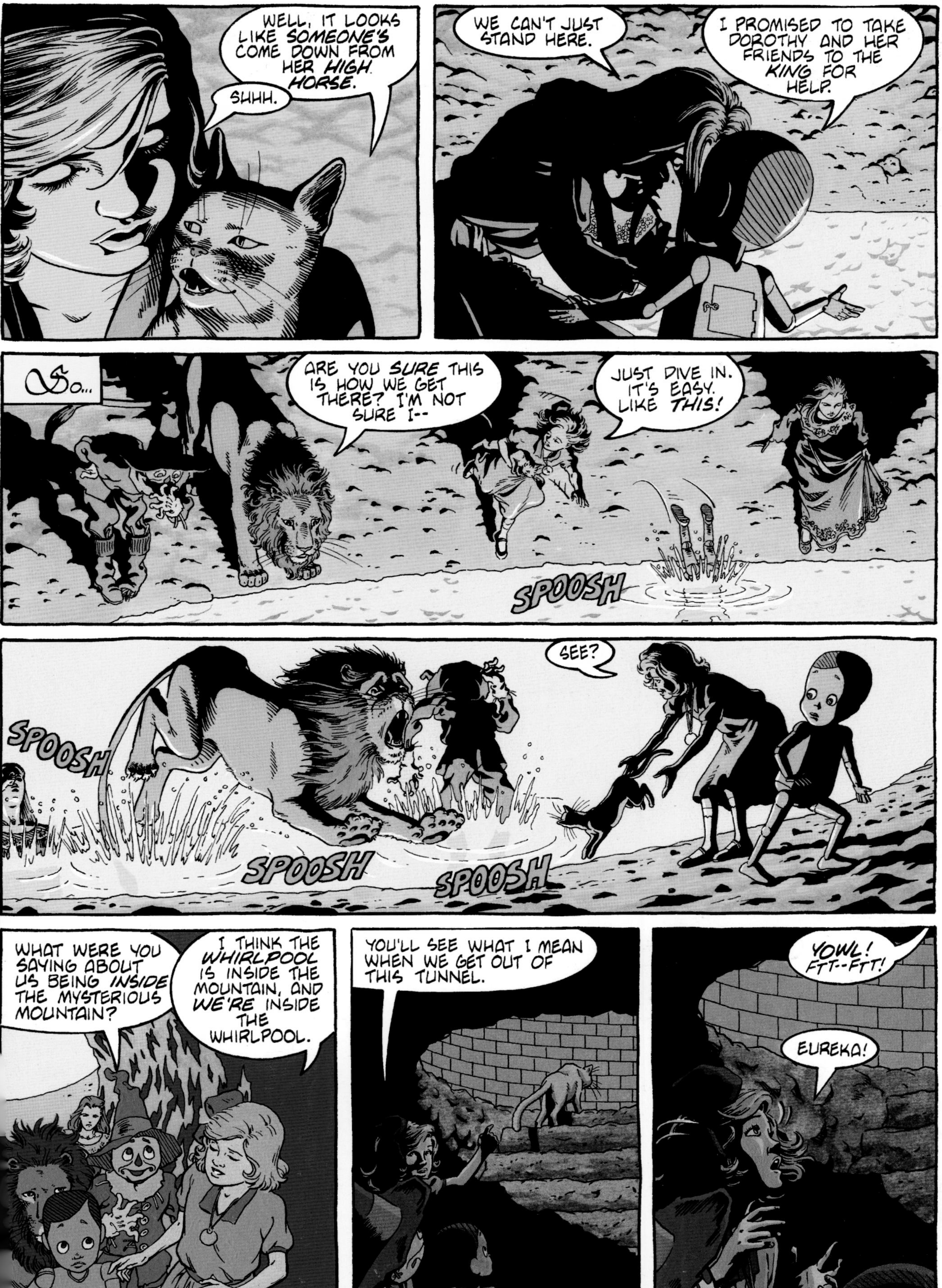
WELL, IT LOOKS LIKE SOMEONE'S COME DOWN FROM HER HIGH HORSE.
SHHH.
WE CAN'T JUST STAND HERE.
I PROMISED TO TAKE DOROTHY AND HER FRIENDS TO THE KING FOR HELP.
So...
ARE YOU SURE THIS IS HOW WE GET THERE? I'M NOT SURE I--
JUST DIVE IN. IT'S EASY. LIKE THIS!
SPOOSH
SEE?
SPOOSH
SPOOSH
SPOOSH
WHAT WERE YOU SAYING ABOUT US BEING INSIDE THE MYSTERIOUS MOUNTAIN?
I THINK THE WHIRLPOOL IS INSIDE THE MOUNTAIN, AND WE'RE INSIDE THE WHIRLPOOL.
YOU'LL SEE WHAT I MEAN WHEN WE GET OUT OF THIS TUNNEL.
YOWL! FTT--FTT!
EUREKA!

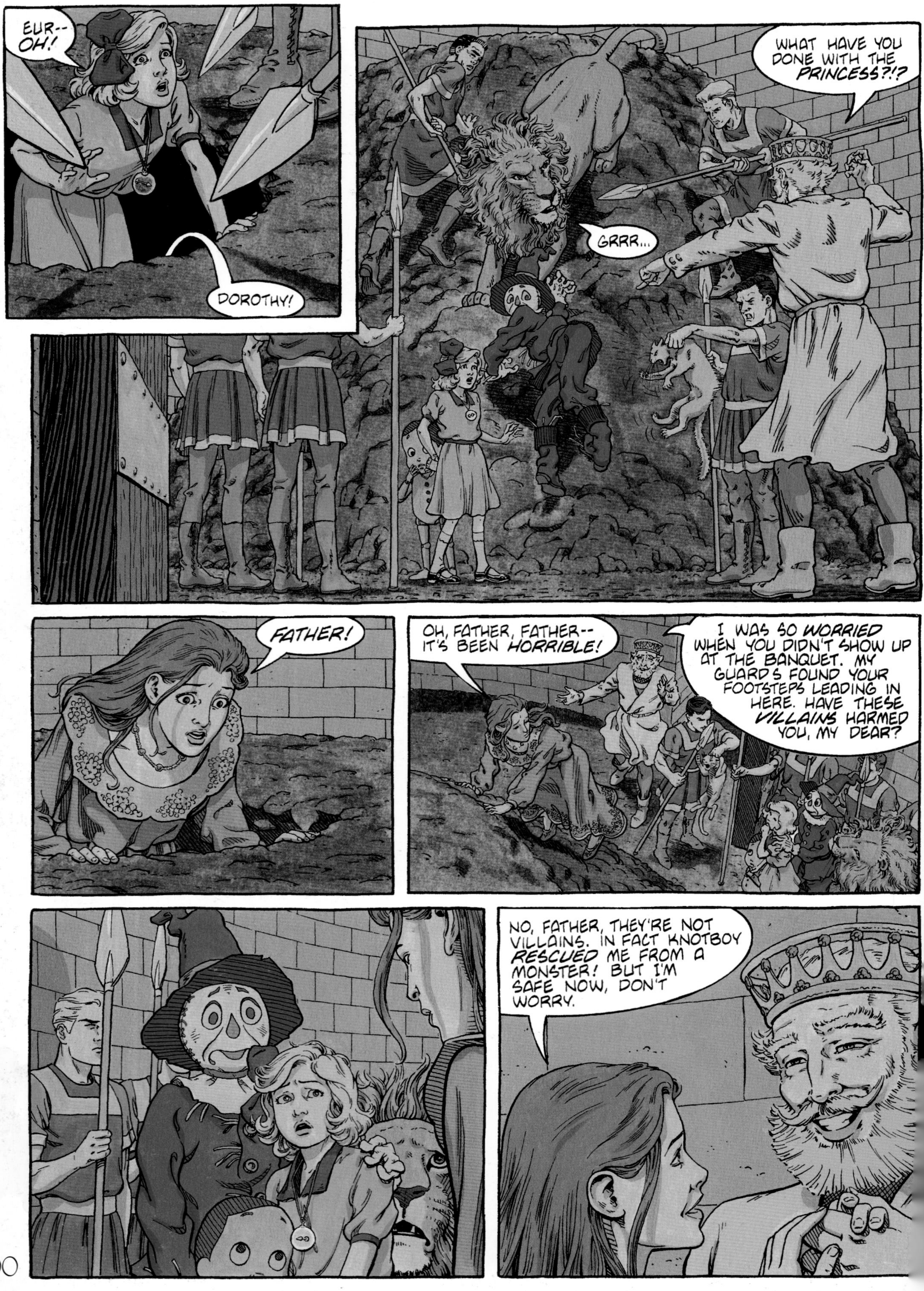
EUR--OH!
DOROTHY!
WHAT HAVE YOU DONE WITH THE PRINCESS?!?
GRRR...
FATHER!
OH, FATHER, FATHER-- IT'S BEEN HORRIBLE!
I WAS SO WORRIED WHEN YOU DIDN'T SHOW UP AT THE BANQUET. MY GUARDS FOUND YOUR FOOTSTEPS LEADING IN HERE. HAVE THESE VILLAINS HARMED YOU, MY DEAR?
NO, FATHER, THEY'RE NOT VILLAINS. IN FACT KNOTBOY RESCUED ME FROM A MONSTER! BUT I'M SAFE NOW, DON'T WORRY.

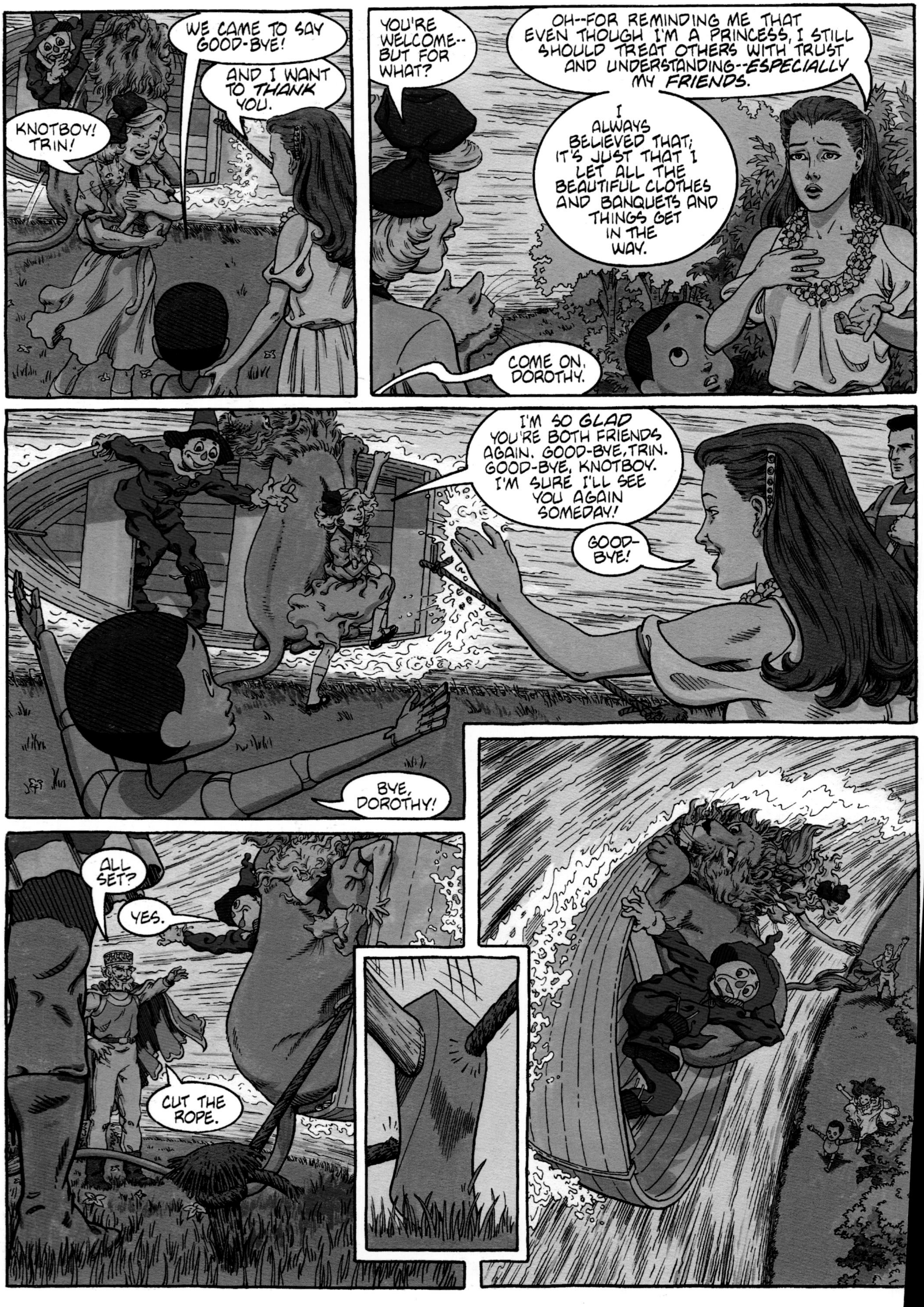
WE CAME TO SAY GOOD-BYE!
KNOTBOY! TRIN!
AND I WANT TO THANK YOU.
YOU'RE WELCOME-- BUT FOR WHAT?
OH--FOR REMINDING ME THAT EVEN THOUGH I'M A PRINCESS, I STILL SHOULD TREAT OTHERS WITH TRUST AND UNDERSTANDING--ESPECIALLY MY FRIENDS.
I ALWAYS BELIEVED THAT; IT'S JUST THAT I LET ALL THE BEAUTIFUL CLOTHES AND BANQUETS AND THINGS GET IN THE WAY.
COME ON, DOROTHY.
I'M SO GLAD YOU'RE BOTH FRIENDS AGAIN. GOOD-BYE, TRIN. GOOD-BYE, KNOTBOY. I'M SURE I'LL SEE YOU AGAIN SOMEDAY!
GOOD-BYE!
BYE, DOROTHY!
ALL SET?
YES.
CUT THE ROPE.

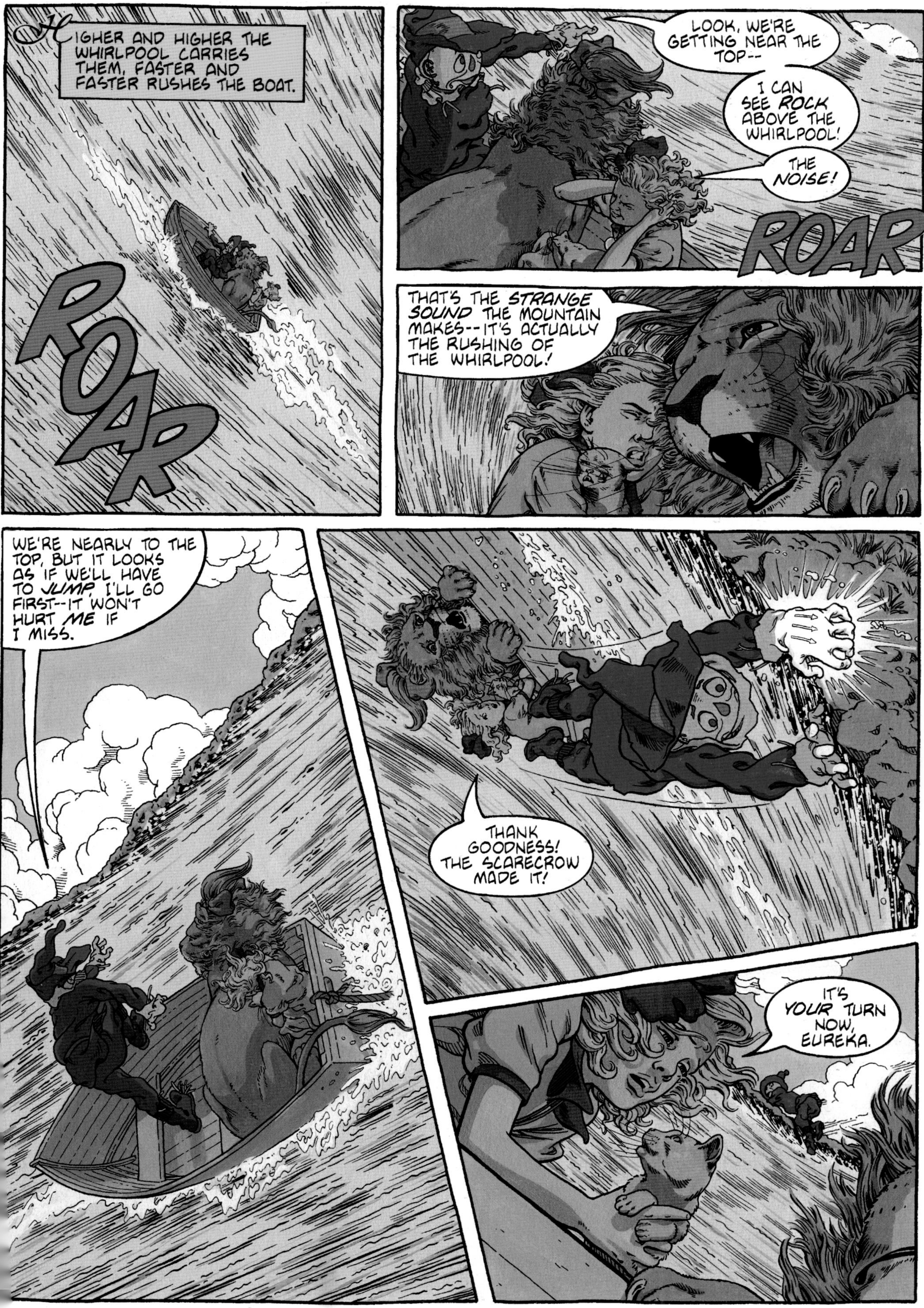
HIGHER AND HIGHER THE WHIRLPOOL CARRIES THEM, FASTER AND FASTER RUSHES THE BOAT.
ROAR
LOOK, WE'RE GETTING NEAR THE TOP--
I CAN SEE ROCK ABOVE THE WHIRLPOOL!
THE NOISE!
ROAR
THAT'S THE STRANGE SOUND THE MOUNTAIN MAKES--IT'S ACTUALLY THE RUSHING OF THE WHIRLPOOL!
WE'RE NEARLY TO THE TOP, BUT IT LOOKS AS IF WE'LL HAVE TO JUMP. I'LL GO FIRST--IT WON'T HURT ME IF I MISS.
THANK GOODNESS! THE SCARECROW MADE IT!
IT'S YOUR TURN NOW, EUREKA.

QUICK, LION, BEFORE THE BOAT GOES *OVER* THE *EDGE* OF THE WHIRLPOOL!

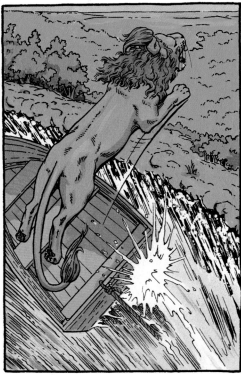

CRASH

SPLINTER

YIKES!

YOU DON'T HAVE TO BE *SCARED* ANYMORE, WE'RE *SAFE!*

LET'S START FOR HOME.

BUT I *DO* HAVE TO BE SCARED NOW-- I DIDN'T HAVE A *CHANCE* BEFORE.

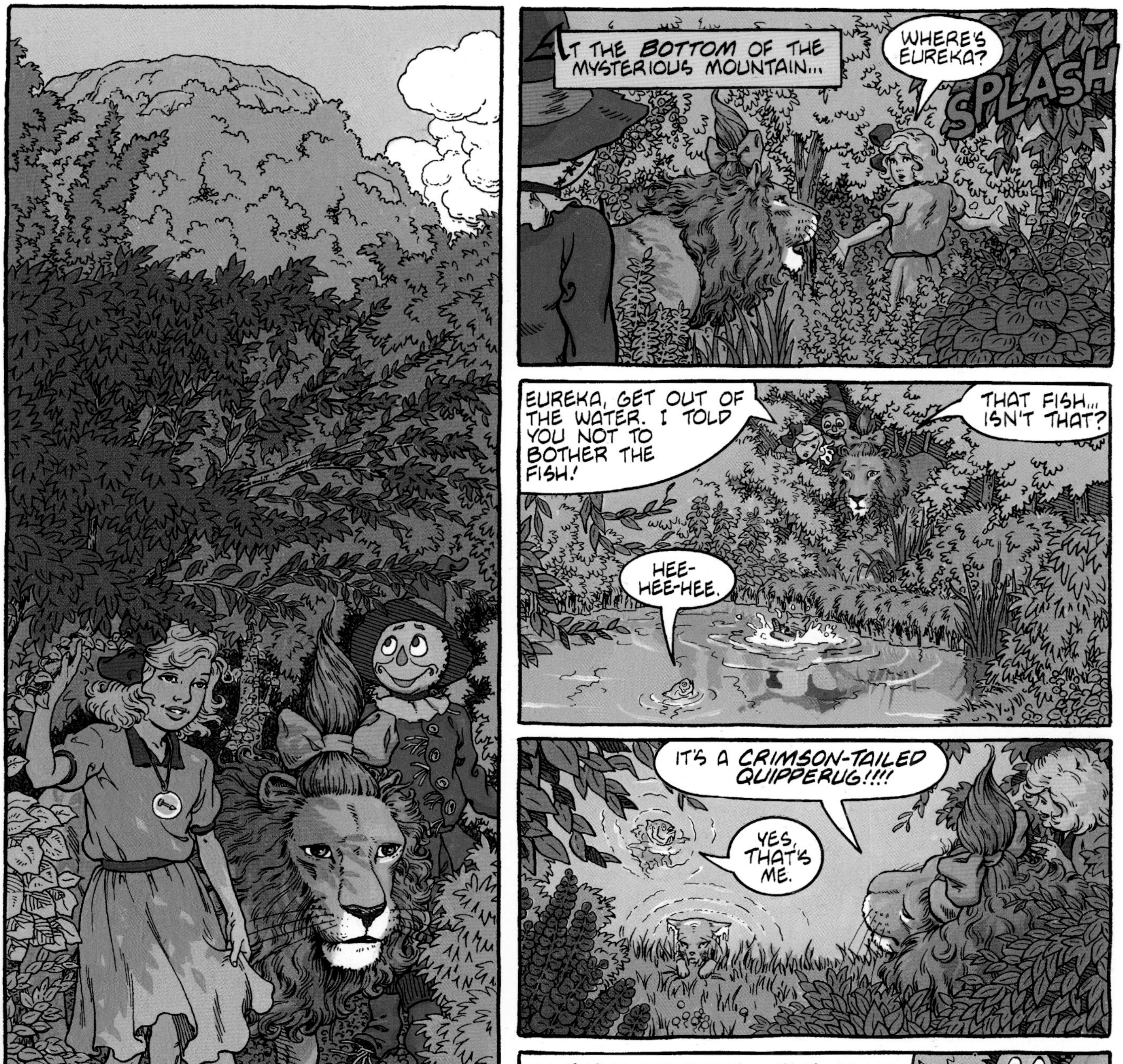
AT THE *BOTTOM* OF THE MYSTERIOUS MOUNTAIN...
WHERE'S EUREKA?
SPLASH
EUREKA, GET OUT OF THE WATER. I TOLD YOU NOT TO BOTHER THE FISH!
THAT FISH... ISN'T THAT?
HEE-HEE-HEE.
IT'S A *CRIMSON-TAILED QUIPPERUG!!!!*
YES, THAT'S ME.
OH, THANK GOODNESS WE'VE FOUND YOU AT LAST. THE *ROYAL GARDENER* WILL BE SO HAPPY! WE'VE COME TO TAKE YOU TO THE *ROYAL FISHPOND* IN THE EMERALD CITY WHERE YOU'LL LIVE IN THE MOST *LUXURIOUS POOL* IN THE WORLD, AND EVERYONE WILL *ADMIRE* YOUR *BEAUTY.*

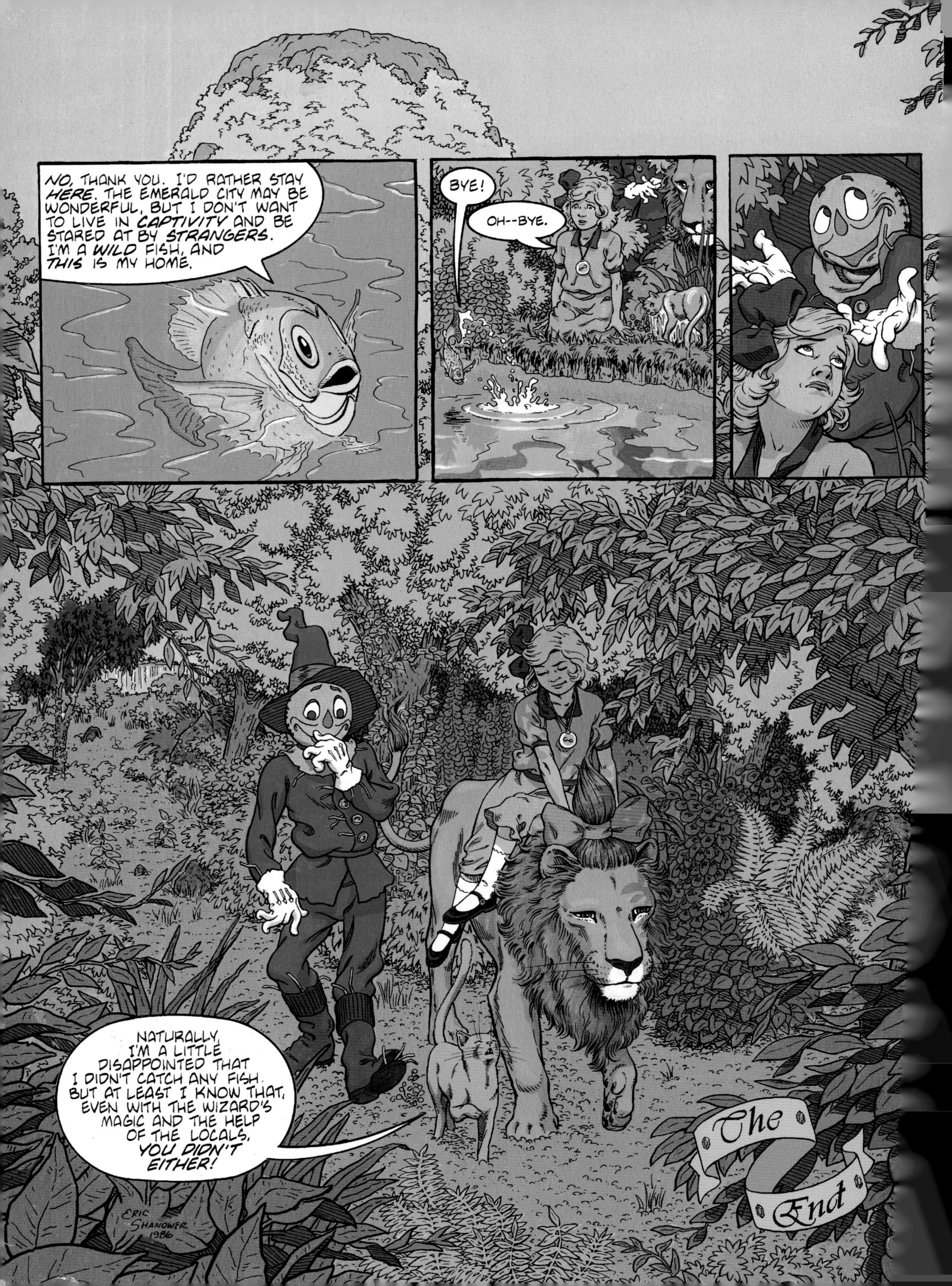
NO, THANK YOU. I'D RATHER STAY HERE. THE EMERALD CITY MAY BE WONDERFUL, BUT I DON'T WANT TO LIVE IN CAPTIVITY AND BE STARED AT BY STRANGERS. I'M A WILD FISH, AND THIS IS MY HOME.
BYE!
OH--BYE.
NATURALLY, I'M A LITTLE DISAPPOINTED THAT I DIDN'T CATCH ANY FISH. BUT AT LEAST I KNOW THAT, EVEN WITH THE WIZARD'S MAGIC AND THE HELP OF THE LOCALS, YOU DIDN'T EITHER!
ERIC SHANOWER 1986
The End

# The ICE KING of OZ

To the Olsons:
Mary, Rick, Jimmy, and Amy
with gratitude

# Chapter One The Proposal

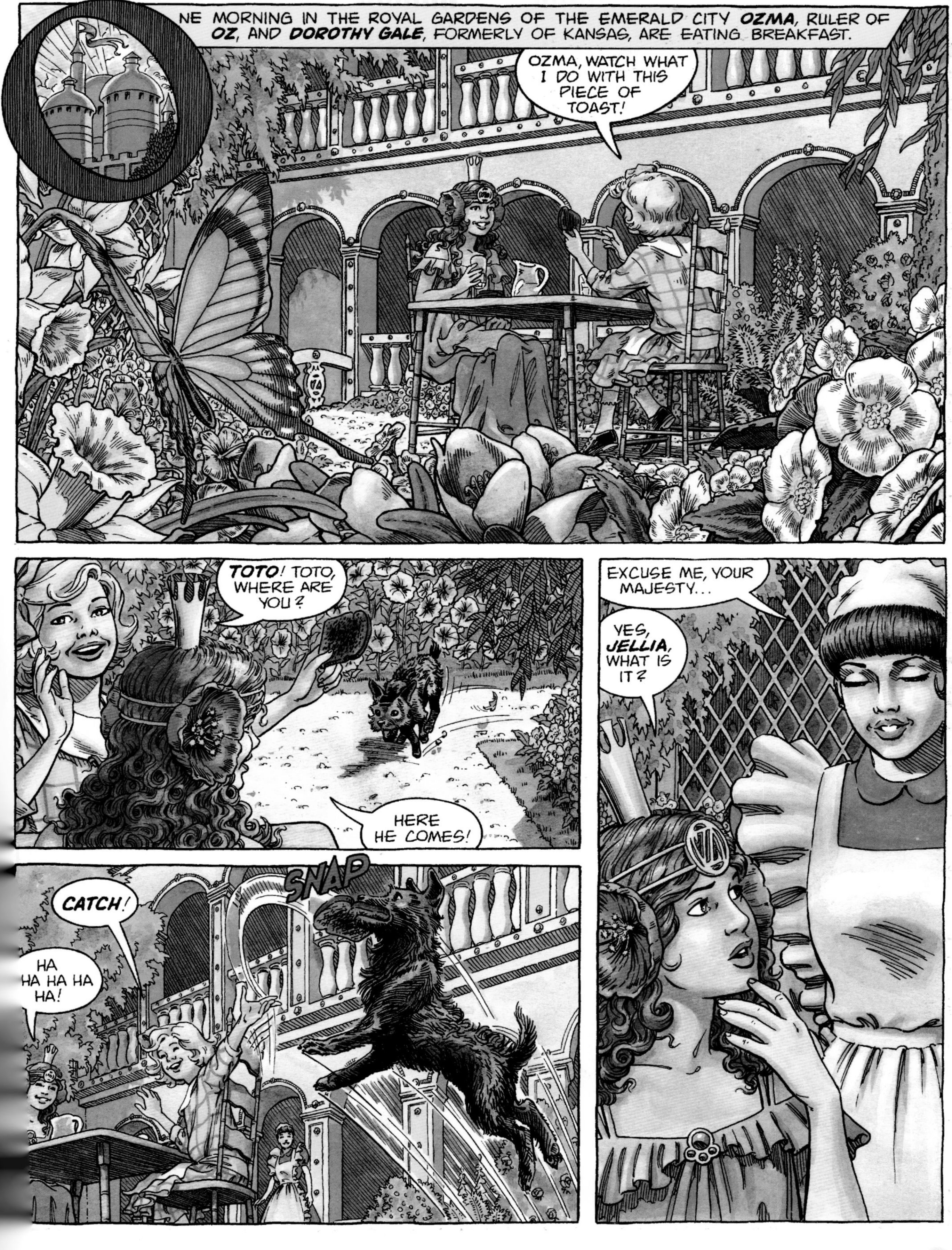
ONE MORNING IN THE ROYAL GARDENS OF THE EMERALD CITY OZMA, RULER OF OZ, AND DOROTHY GALE, FORMERLY OF KANSAS, ARE EATING BREAKFAST.
OZMA, WATCH WHAT I DO WITH THIS PIECE OF TOAST!
TOTO! TOTO, WHERE ARE YOU?
HERE HE COMES!
CATCH!
HA HA HA HA HA!
SNAP
EXCUSE ME, YOUR MAJESTY...
YES, JELLIA, WHAT IS IT?

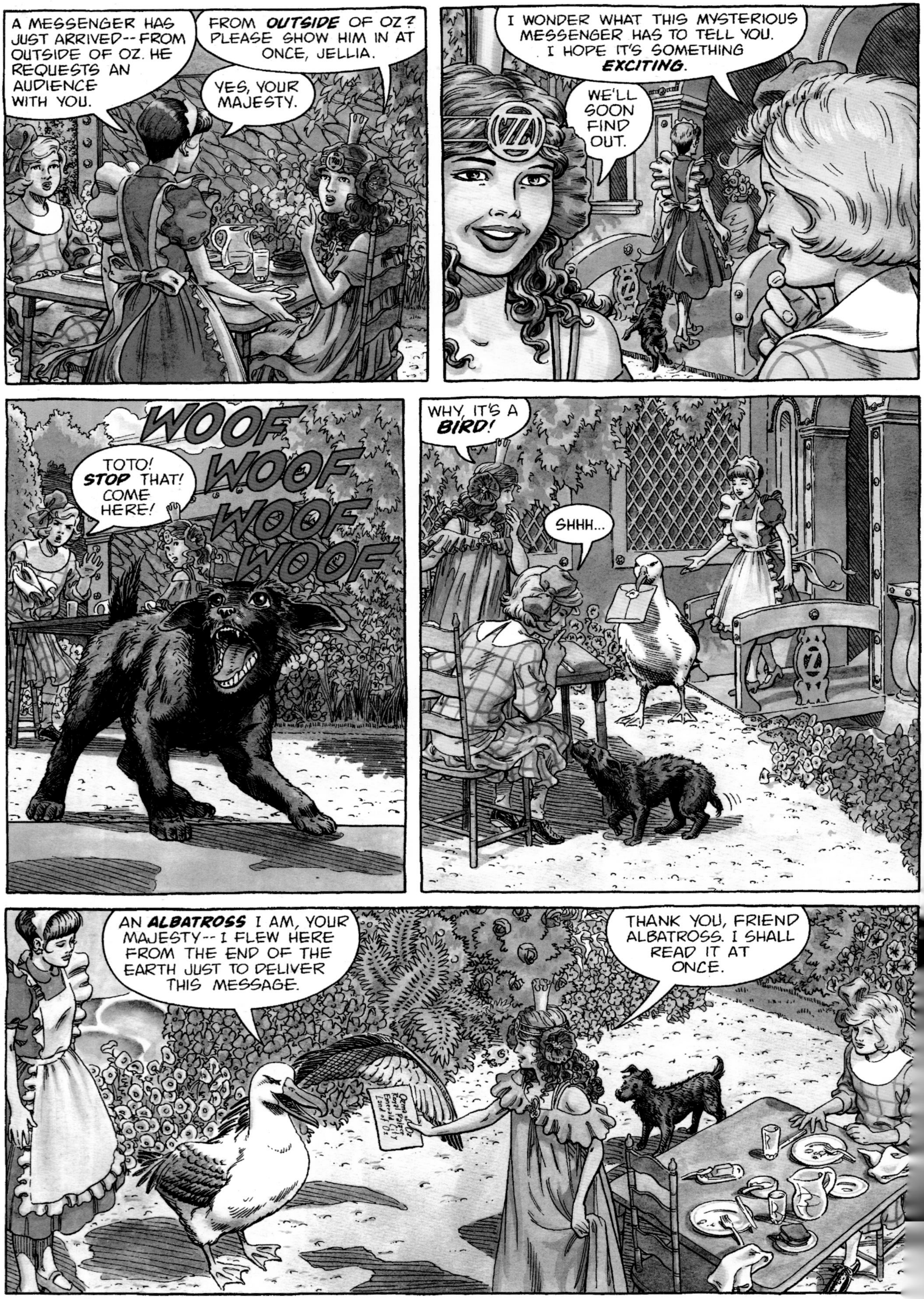
A MESSENGER HAS JUST ARRIVED-- FROM OUTSIDE OF OZ. HE REQUESTS AN AUDIENCE WITH YOU.
FROM OUTSIDE OF OZ? PLEASE SHOW HIM IN AT ONCE, JELLIA.
YES, YOUR MAJESTY.
I WONDER WHAT THIS MYSTERIOUS MESSENGER HAS TO TELL YOU. I HOPE IT'S SOMETHING EXCITING.
WE'LL SOON FIND OUT.
WOOF WOOF WOOF WOOF
TOTO! STOP THAT! COME HERE!
WHY, IT'S A BIRD!
SHHH...
AN ALBATROSS I AM, YOUR MAJESTY-- I FLEW HERE FROM THE END OF THE EARTH JUST TO DELIVER THIS MESSAGE.
THANK YOU, FRIEND ALBATROSS. I SHALL READ IT AT ONCE.

HMM.

WHAT **IS** IT, OZMA?

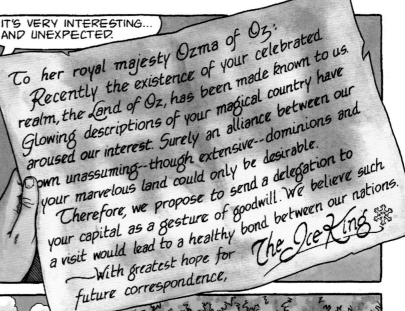

IT'S VERY INTERESTING... AND UNEXPECTED.

To her royal majesty Ozma of Oz:

Recently the existence of your celebrated realm, the Land of Oz, has been made known to us. Glowing descriptions of your magical country have aroused our interest. Surely an alliance between our own unassuming--though extensive--dominions and your marvelous land could only be desirable.

Therefore, we propose to send a delegation to your capital as a gesture of goodwill. We believe such a visit would lead to a healthy bond between our nations.

--With greatest hope for future correspondence,

The Ice King

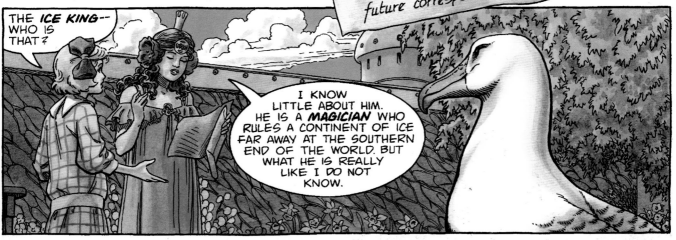

THE **ICE KING**-- WHO IS THAT?

I KNOW LITTLE ABOUT HIM. HE IS A **MAGICIAN** WHO RULES A CONTINENT OF ICE FAR AWAY AT THE SOUTHERN END OF THE WORLD. BUT WHAT HE IS REALLY LIKE I DO NOT KNOW.

WELL, I CAN HARDLY WAIT TO FIND OUT!

YOU **WILL** ACCEPT THE DELEGATION FROM THE ICE KING... WON'T YOU?

I THINK SO. THOUGH OZ IS CUT OFF FROM THE REST OF THE WORLD BY THE **DEADLY DESERT**, WE **HAVE** HAD WELCOME RELATIONS WITH OTHER COUNTRIES.

TO **REFUSE** THIS OFFER OF FRIENDSHIP WOULD BE UNKIND. IN ANY CASE, LEARNING MORE ABOUT THE ICE KING WILL BE INTERESTING.

OH, **GOOD!**

I'LL WRITE A REPLY IMMEDIATELY. YOU WILL DELIVER THE RETURN MESSAGE, WON'T YOU, FRIEND ALBATROSS?

CERTAINLY, YOUR MAJESTY. GLAD TO BE OF USE TO ROYALTY, I ALWAYS SAY.

113

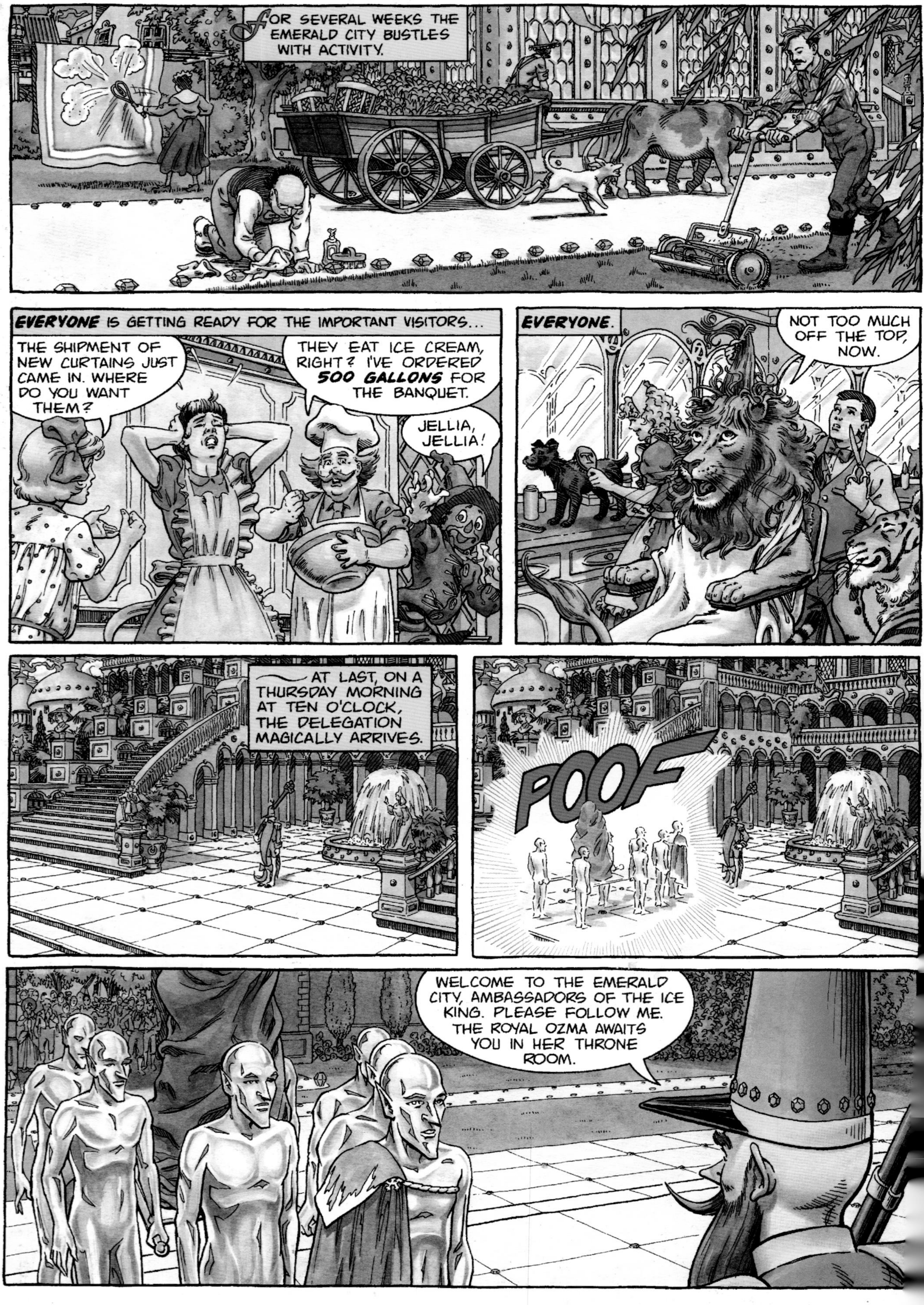

FOR SEVERAL WEEKS THE EMERALD CITY BUSTLES WITH ACTIVITY.
EVERYONE IS GETTING READY FOR THE IMPORTANT VISITORS...
THE SHIPMENT OF NEW CURTAINS JUST CAME IN. WHERE DO YOU WANT THEM?
THEY EAT ICE CREAM, RIGHT? I'VE ORDERED 500 GALLONS FOR THE BANQUET.
JELLIA, JELLIA!
EVERYONE.
NOT TOO MUCH OFF THE TOP, NOW.
—AT LAST, ON A THURSDAY MORNING AT TEN O'CLOCK, THE DELEGATION MAGICALLY ARRIVES.
POOF
WELCOME TO THE EMERALD CITY, AMBASSADORS OF THE ICE KING. PLEASE FOLLOW ME. THE ROYAL OZMA AWAITS YOU IN HER THRONE ROOM.

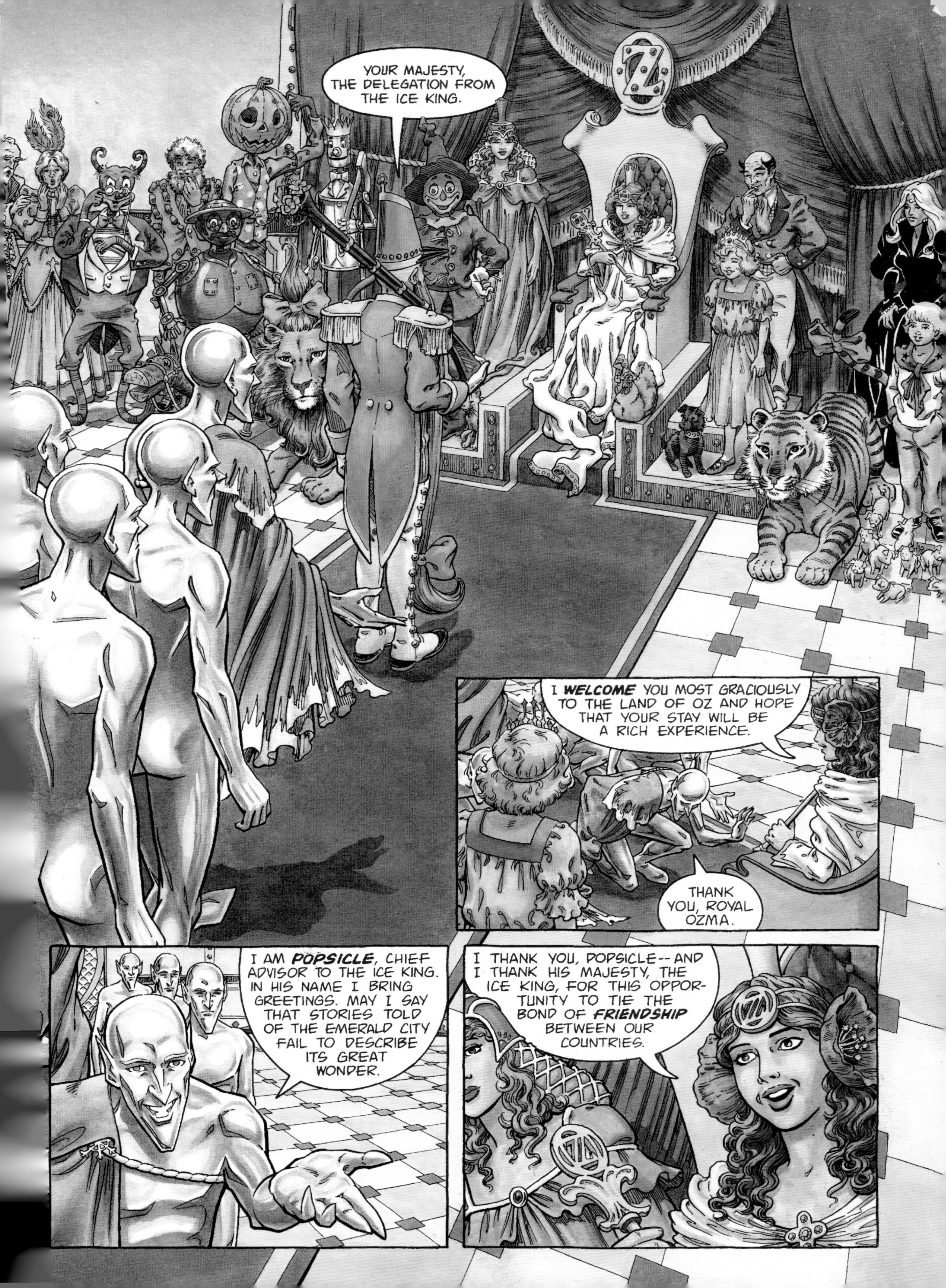
YOUR MAJESTY, THE DELEGATION FROM THE ICE KING.
I **WELCOME** YOU MOST GRACIOUSLY TO THE LAND OF OZ AND HOPE THAT YOUR STAY WILL BE A RICH EXPERIENCE.
THANK YOU, ROYAL OZMA.
I AM **POPSICLE**, CHIEF ADVISOR TO THE ICE KING. IN HIS NAME I BRING GREETINGS. MAY I SAY THAT STORIES TOLD OF THE EMERALD CITY FAIL TO DESCRIBE ITS GREAT WONDER.
I THANK YOU, POPSICLE-- AND I THANK HIS MAJESTY, THE ICE KING, FOR THIS OPPOR-TUNITY TO TIE THE BOND OF **FRIENDSHIP** BETWEEN OUR COUNTRIES.

THE ICE KING FEELS THE SAME WAY. AND TO **SHOW** HIS GRATITUDE, HE HAS SENT TWO **GIFTS** TO THE PEOPLE OF OZ.

UNVEIL THE FIRST GIFT!

OH!

OH, LOOK!

IT'S MAGNIFICENT!

HIS MAJESTY IS VERY GENEROUS. I SHALL INSTALL THIS WONDERFUL **ICE SCULPTURE** IN THE ROYAL GARDENS FOR EVERYONE TO ENJOY.

BUT WON'T IT **MELT**?

NO, FOR IT WAS CREATED WITH **MAGIC** -- THE SAME MAGIC THAT ALLOWS US **ICE IMPS** TO SURVIVE IN YOUR WARM COUNTRY. FORTUNATELY, OZ IS A **MAGICAL** LAND. WERE WE TO VISIT A LAND WHERE MAGIC DID **NOT** EXIST, WE WOULD SOON BECOME PUDDLES OF WATER.

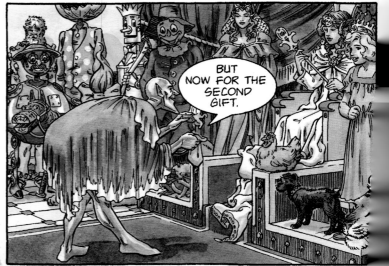

BUT NOW FOR THE SECOND GIFT.

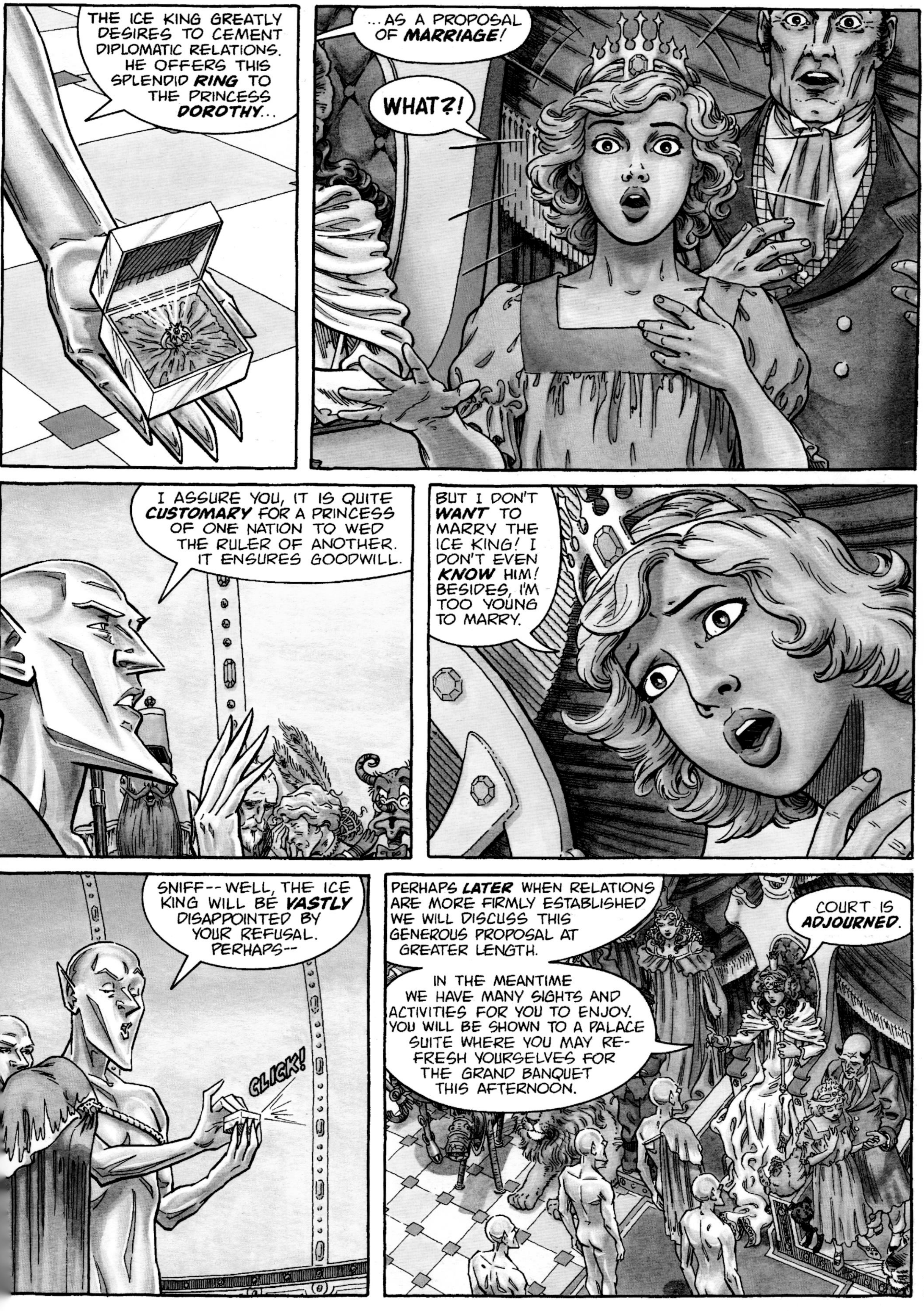

THE ICE KING GREATLY DESIRES TO CEMENT DIPLOMATIC RELATIONS. HE OFFERS THIS SPLENDID RING TO THE PRINCESS DOROTHY...
...AS A PROPOSAL OF MARRIAGE!
WHAT?!
I ASSURE YOU, IT IS QUITE CUSTOMARY FOR A PRINCESS OF ONE NATION TO WED THE RULER OF ANOTHER. IT ENSURES GOODWILL.
BUT I DON'T WANT TO MARRY THE ICE KING! I DON'T EVEN KNOW HIM! BESIDES, I'M TOO YOUNG TO MARRY.
SNIFF-- WELL, THE ICE KING WILL BE VASTLY DISAPPOINTED BY YOUR REFUSAL. PERHAPS--
CLICK!
PERHAPS LATER WHEN RELATIONS ARE MORE FIRMLY ESTABLISHED WE WILL DISCUSS THIS GENEROUS PROPOSAL AT GREATER LENGTH.
IN THE MEANTIME WE HAVE MANY SIGHTS AND ACTIVITIES FOR YOU TO ENJOY. YOU WILL BE SHOWN TO A PALACE SUITE WHERE YOU MAY RE-FRESH YOURSELVES FOR THE GRAND BANQUET THIS AFTERNOON.
COURT IS ADJOURNED.

# Chapter Two Treachery

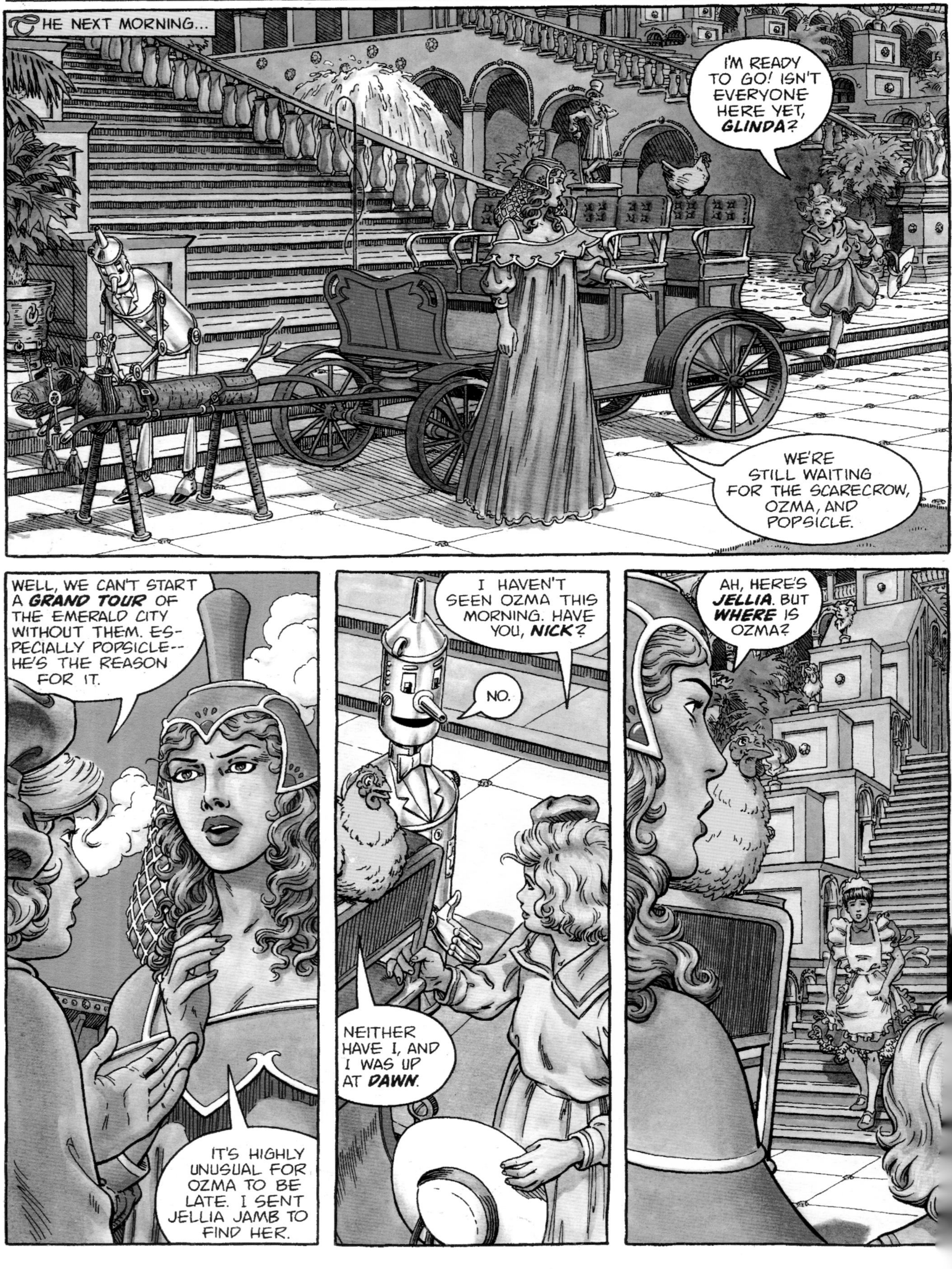
THE NEXT MORNING...
I'M READY TO GO! ISN'T EVERYONE HERE YET, GLINDA?
WE'RE STILL WAITING FOR THE SCARECROW, OZMA, AND POPSICLE.
WELL, WE CAN'T START A GRAND TOUR OF THE EMERALD CITY WITHOUT THEM. ES-PECIALLY POPSICLE-- HE'S THE REASON FOR IT.
IT'S HIGHLY UNUSUAL FOR OZMA TO BE LATE. I SENT JELLIA JAMB TO FIND HER.
I HAVEN'T SEEN OZMA THIS MORNING. HAVE YOU, NICK?
NO.
NEITHER HAVE I, AND I WAS UP AT DAWN.
AH, HERE'S JELLIA. BUT WHERE IS OZMA?

I CAN'T FIND HER. SHE'S NOT IN HER ROOM, AND NO ONE IN THE PALACE HAS SEEN HER.

DOROTHY! GLINDA!

WHAT'S WRONG, SCARECROW?

LAST NIGHT I WAS PLAYING CARDS WITH SOME OF THE ICE IMPS, AND I LEFT MY HAT IN THEIR SUITE. THIS MORNING WHEN I WENT BACK, MY HAT WAS THERE, BUT THE ENTIRE DELEGATION WAS *GONE!*

WHAT'S GOING ON?

IS ANYONE *ELSE* MISSING?

I DON'T LIKE IT.

FOLLOW ME. WE MUST LOOK INTO THE *MAGIC PICTURE.*

WILL SOMEONE *UNHITCH* ME, PLEASE?

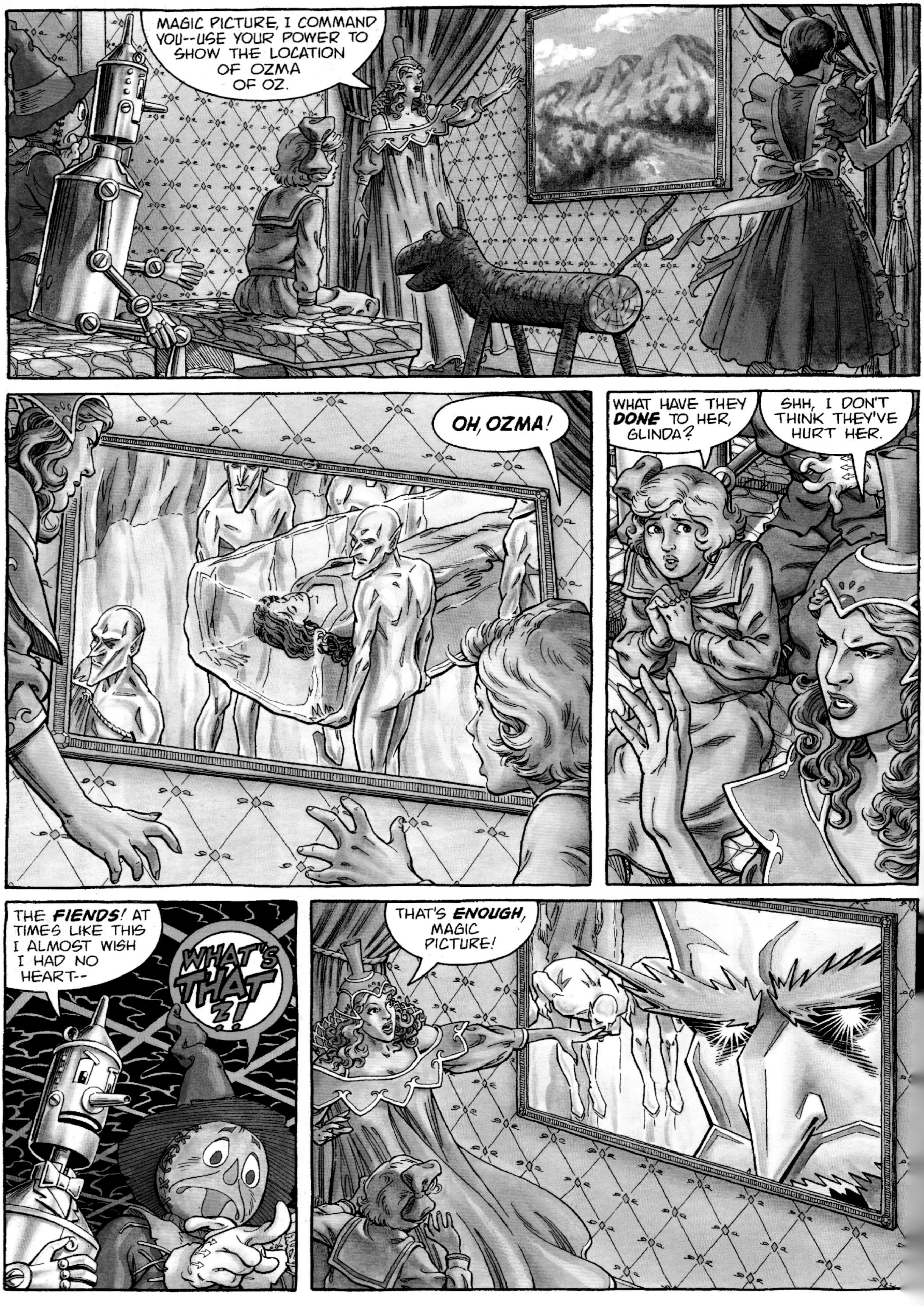
MAGIC PICTURE, I COMMAND YOU--USE YOUR POWER TO SHOW THE LOCATION OF OZMA OF OZ.
OH, OZMA!
WHAT HAVE THEY DONE TO HER, GLINDA?
SHH, I DON'T THINK THEY'VE HURT HER.
THE FIENDS! AT TIMES LIKE THIS I ALMOST WISH I HAD NO HEART--
WHAT'S THAT?!
THAT'S ENOUGH, MAGIC PICTURE!

MY FRIENDS, OUR BELOVED OZMA IS IN THE GRASP OF THE *ICE KING*--BUT BE *BRAVE*. THE *WIZARD* OF OZ AND I WILL EXPERIMENT MAGICALLY TO DISCOVER A WAY TO CHALLENGE THE ICE KING'S POWER.

THIS EVENING I WILL CALL A COUNCIL TO PLAN THE RESCUE OF OZMA. FEAR NOT-- WE WILL FIND A WAY.

THAT EVENING IN THE COUNCIL CHAMBER...

I'M AFRAID THAT OVERCOMING THE ICE KING WILL BE *MORE* DIF- FICULT THAN I FIRST THOUGHT. I NEED SUPPORT FROM *ALL* OF YOU-- SO LISTEN CAREFULLY.

WHETHER THE ICE KING IS COMPLETELY EVIL OR MERELY *MISGUIDED*, AND *WHY* HE HAS KIDNAPPED OZMA I DO NOT KNOW. NO ONE KNOWS MUCH ABOUT THE ICE KING FOR ONLY HE AND HIS IMPS CAN EXIST FOR LONG IN THE *BITTER SNOW* AND *ICY WIND* OF HIS FARAWAY LAND.

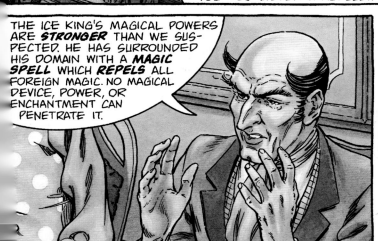

THE ICE KING'S MAGICAL POWERS ARE *STRONGER* THAN WE SUS- PECTED. HE HAS SURROUNDED HIS DOMAIN WITH A *MAGIC SPELL* WHICH *REPELS* ALL FOREIGN MAGIC. NO MAGICAL DEVICE, POWER, OR ENCHANTMENT CAN PENETRATE IT.

GLIN-DA, YOU ARE THE MOST POW-ER-FUL SOR-CER-ESS IN OZ. SURE-LY YOUR MAG-IC IS STRONG-ER THAN THE ICE KING'S.

UNFORTUNATELY THE ICE KING HAS INVENTED HIS OWN TYPE OF MAGIC--**ICE MAGIC**. THE WIZARD AND I ARE NOT FAMILIAR WITH ITS PRINCIPLES--SO WE CANNOT **CHALLENGE** IT.

THEN **HOW** CAN WE RESCUE OZMA?

WE MUST SEND A GROUP OF RESCUERS TO THE ICE KING'S DOMAIN. NO MEMBER OF THE GROUP MAY CARRY ANY MAGICAL DEVICE.

ONCE THESE RESCUERS **CROSS** THE BORDER INTO THE ICE KING'S POWER, THEY ARE ON THEIR **OWN** TO FIND AND RESCUE OZMA.

I KNOW ALL OF YOU WOULD RISK YOUR LIVES FOR OZMA--BUT **DOROTHY**, THE **SCARECROW** AND THE **TIN WOODMAN** HAVE THE ABILITIES BEST SUITED FOR THIS TASK.

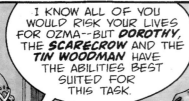

ME?

PROBABLY CHOSE ME FOR MY EXCELLENT **BRAINS!**

THANK YOU, GREAT SORCERESS.

THE ONLY QUESTION LEFT IS HOW TO **REACH** THE ICE KING'S DOMAIN. I WILL PONDER THIS PROBLEM TONIGHT. IN THE MORNING THE RESCUE PARTY WILL LEAVE.

LET US RETIRE, BUT REMEMBER--WHILE OZMA REMAINS A PRISONER, WE WILL **NOT GIVE UP!**

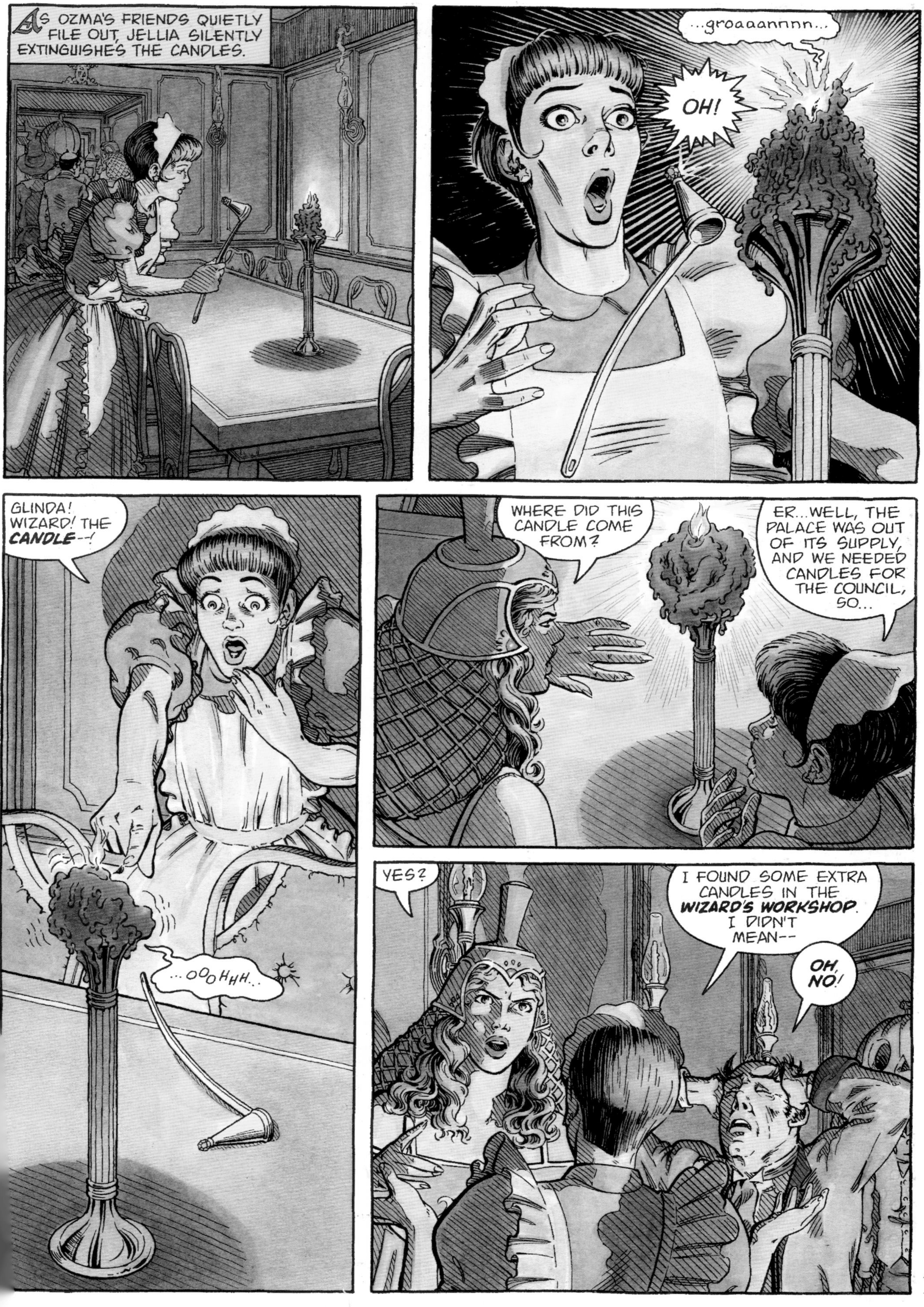
AS OZMA'S FRIENDS QUIETLY FILE OUT, JELLIA SILENTLY EXTINGUISHES THE CANDLES.
...groaaannnn...
OH!
GLINDA! WIZARD! THE CANDLE--!
...OOOHHH...
WHERE DID THIS CANDLE COME FROM?
ER...WELL, THE PALACE WAS OUT OF ITS SUPPLY, AND WE NEEDED CANDLES FOR THE COUNCIL, SO...
YES?
I FOUND SOME EXTRA CANDLES IN THE WIZARD'S WORKSHOP. I DIDN'T MEAN--
OH, NO!

I WAS **SAVING** THOSE CANDLES FOR **STUDY**! THEY ONCE BELONGED TO THE **WICKED WITCH** OF THE **WEST**!

LOOK!

WHERE IS SHE?!?

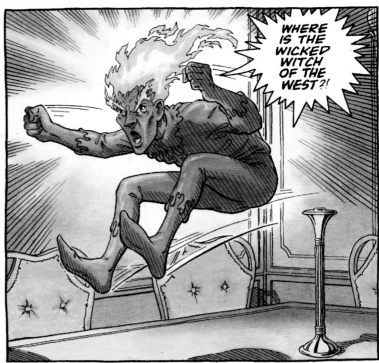

WHERE IS THE WICKED WITCH OF THE WEST?!

PEACE, FRIEND. THE WITCH WAS DESTROYED LONG AGO.

WHAT! HOW?

DOROTHY **MELTED** HER-- WITH A BUCKET OF WATER.

WHO'S DOROTHY?

I AM.

DEAR GIRL, YOU HAVE DESTROYED MY **BITTEREST** ENEMY. I AM IN YOUR **DEBT**.

BUT I--

NO, DON'T PROTEST--**FLICKER**, THE **CANDLE-MAKER**, AT YOUR SERVICE.

THANK YOU, FLICKER. PARDON ME, BUT YOU SEEM TO BE MORE **CANDLE** THAN CANDLE-**MAKER.**

EH? MY SKIN AND CLOTHES-- THEY'RE **WAX!** AND WHAT HAPPENED TO MY **HAIR**?! IT'S THAT DREADFUL WITCH'S FAULT!

THE WICKED WITCH OF THE WEST? WHAT DID SHE DO?

SHE PUT A SPELL ON ME. I WAS ONCE AS **HUMAN** AS YOU--THOUGH NOT NEARLY AS CHARMING. I LIVED IN THE WESTERN PART OF THE LAND OF OZ AND MANUFACTURED CANDLES FOR A LIVING-- CANDLES FAMED THROUGHOUT THE **ENTIRE WINKIE COUNTRY** FOR THEIR BRIGHT-BURNING LIGHT.

"THEN ONE DAY THE SKY DARKENED-- AND THE WICKED WITCH OF THE WEST **ENSLAVED** THE WINKIE PEOPLE.

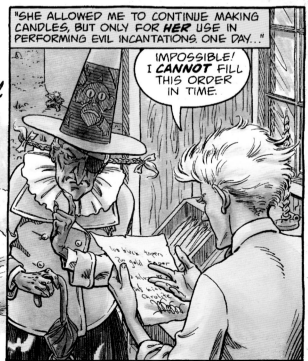

"SHE ALLOWED ME TO CONTINUE MAKING CANDLES, BUT ONLY FOR **HER** USE IN PERFORMING EVIL INCANTATIONS. ONE DAY..."

IMPOSSIBLE! I **CANNOT** FILL THIS ORDER IN TIME.

126

# Chapter Three The Land of Ice

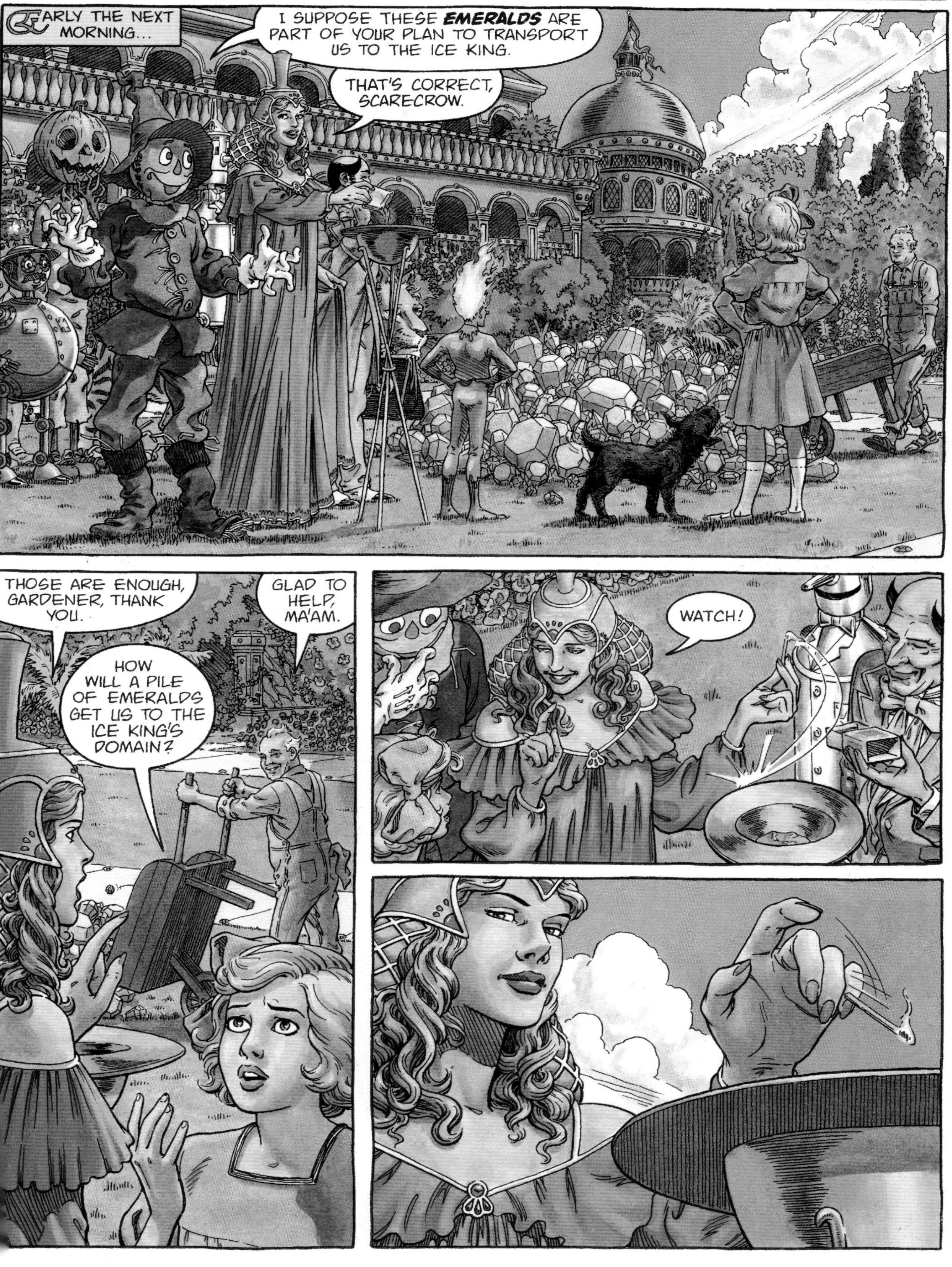
EARLY THE NEXT MORNING...
I SUPPOSE THESE EMERALDS ARE PART OF YOUR PLAN TO TRANSPORT US TO THE ICE KING.
THAT'S CORRECT, SCARECROW.
THOSE ARE ENOUGH, GARDENER, THANK YOU.
GLAD TO HELP, MA'AM.
HOW WILL A PILE OF EMERALDS GET US TO THE ICE KING'S DOMAIN?
WATCH!

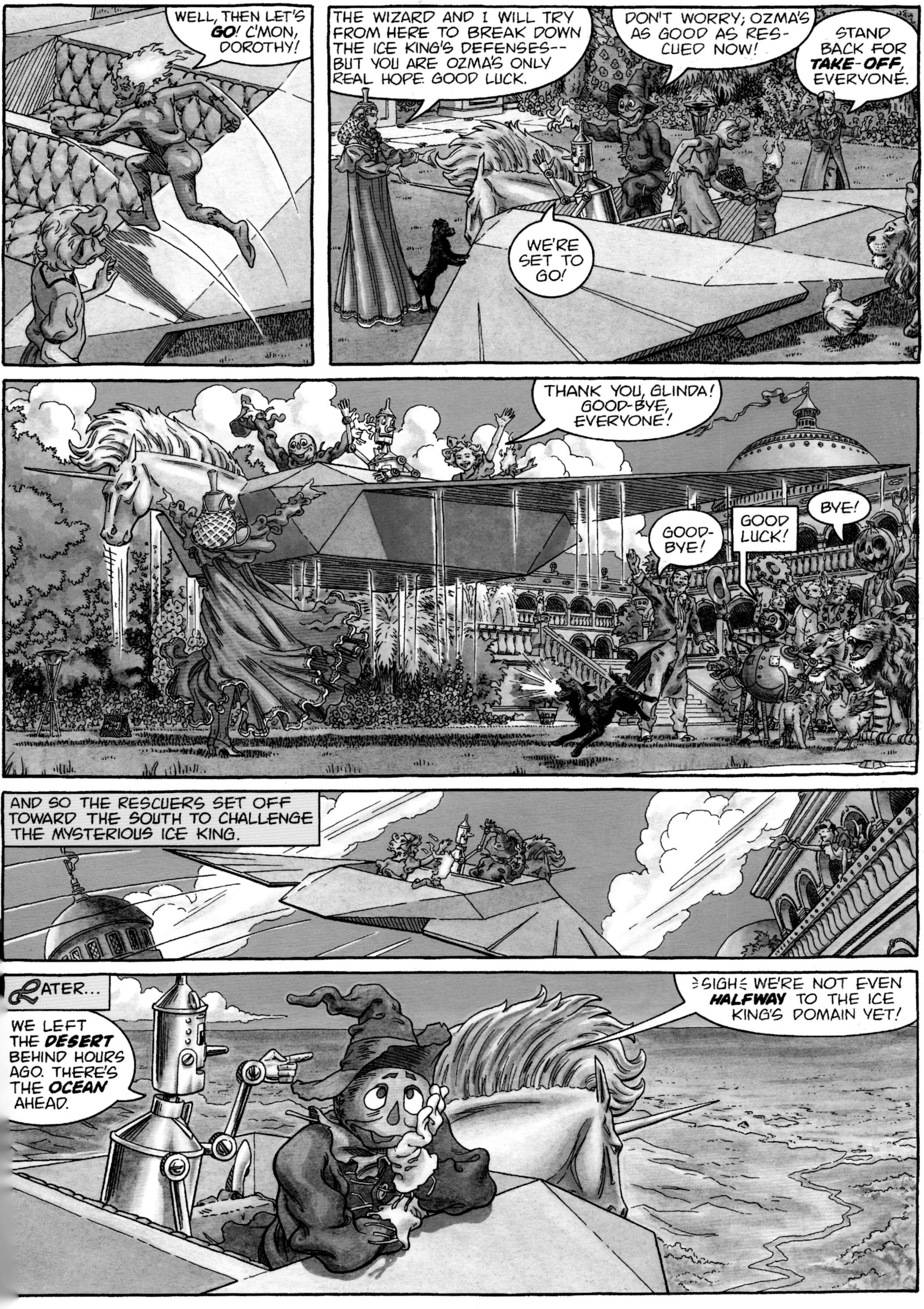

WELL, THEN LET'S **GO**! C'MON, DOROTHY!
THE WIZARD AND I WILL TRY FROM HERE TO BREAK DOWN THE ICE KING'S DEFENSES-- BUT YOU ARE OZMA'S ONLY REAL HOPE. GOOD LUCK.
DON'T WORRY; OZMA'S AS GOOD AS RES-CUED NOW!
STAND BACK FOR **TAKE-OFF**, EVERYONE.
WE'RE SET TO GO!
THANK YOU, GLINDA! GOOD-BYE, EVERYONE!
GOOD-BYE!
GOOD LUCK!
BYE!
AND SO THE RESCUERS SET OFF TOWARD THE SOUTH TO CHALLENGE THE MYSTERIOUS ICE KING.
LATER...
WE LEFT THE **DESERT** BEHIND HOURS AGO. THERE'S THE **OCEAN** AHEAD.
⋽SIGH⋲ WE'RE NOT EVEN **HALFWAY** TO THE ICE KING'S DOMAIN YET!

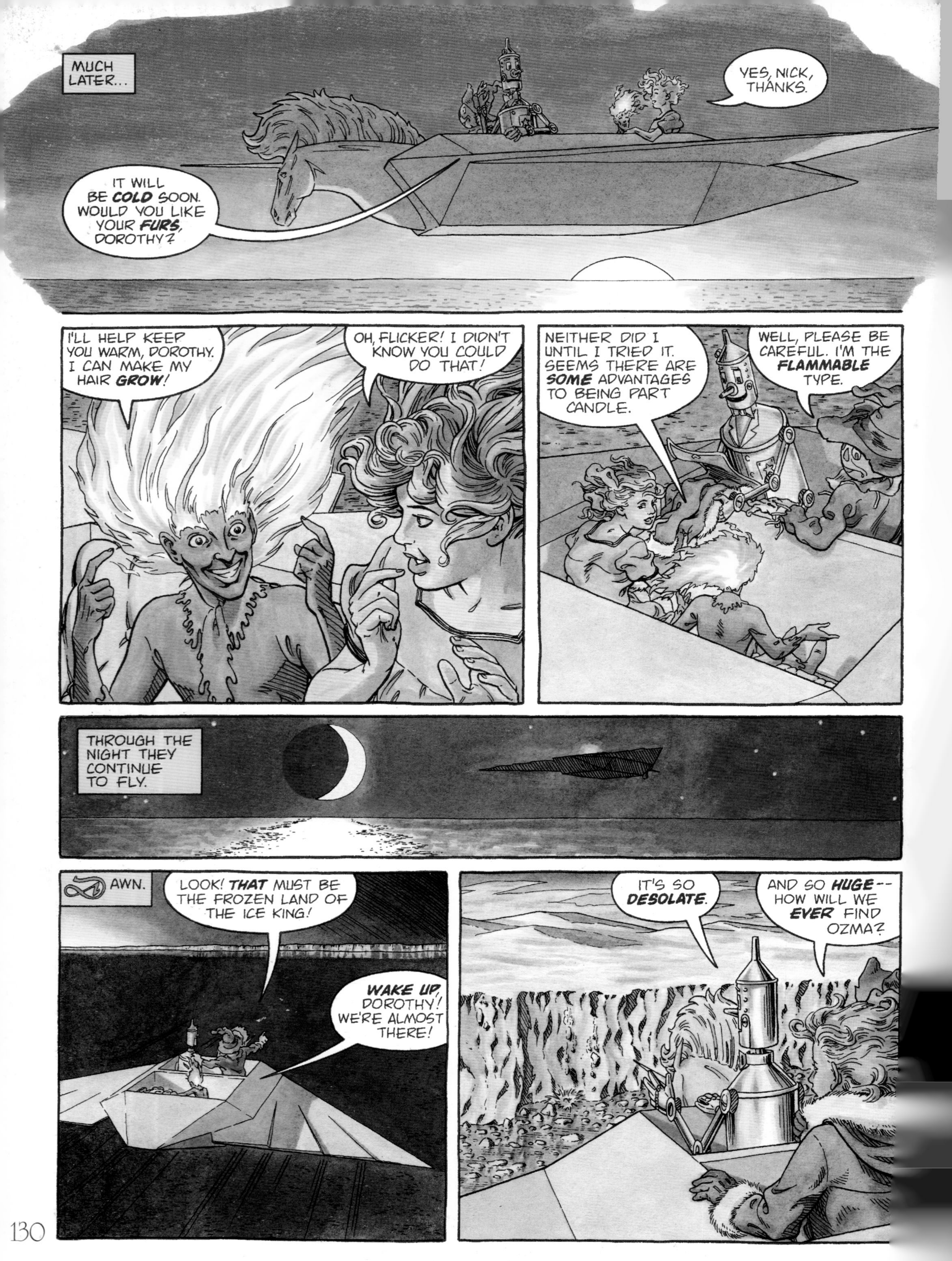
MUCH LATER...
YES, NICK, THANKS.
IT WILL BE COLD SOON. WOULD YOU LIKE YOUR FURS, DOROTHY?
I'LL HELP KEEP YOU WARM, DOROTHY. I CAN MAKE MY HAIR GROW!
OH, FLICKER! I DIDN'T KNOW YOU COULD DO THAT!
NEITHER DID I UNTIL I TRIED IT. SEEMS THERE ARE SOME ADVANTAGES TO BEING PART CANDLE.
WELL, PLEASE BE CAREFUL. I'M THE FLAMMABLE TYPE.
THROUGH THE NIGHT THEY CONTINUE TO FLY.
AWN.
LOOK! THAT MUST BE THE FROZEN LAND OF THE ICE KING!
WAKE UP, DOROTHY! WE'RE ALMOST THERE!
IT'S SO DESOLATE.
AND SO HUGE-- HOW WILL WE EVER FIND OZMA?

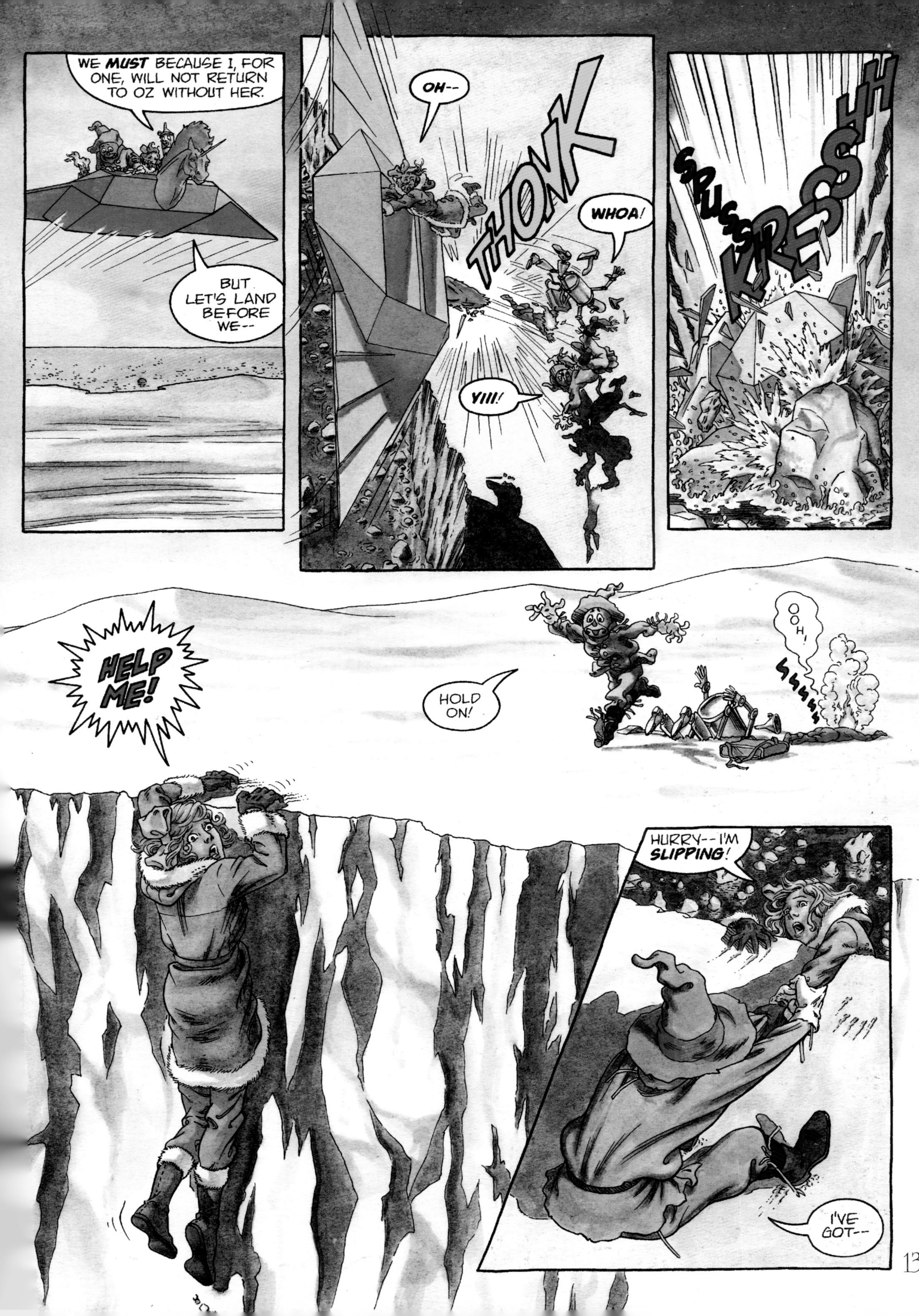

WE MUST BECAUSE I, FOR ONE, WILL NOT RETURN TO OZ WITHOUT HER.
BUT LET'S LAND BEFORE WE--
OH--
THONK
WHOA!
YIII!
SPLUSSSH
KRESSSHH
HELP ME!
HOLD ON!
OOH!
HURRY--I'M SLIPPING!
I'VE GOT--

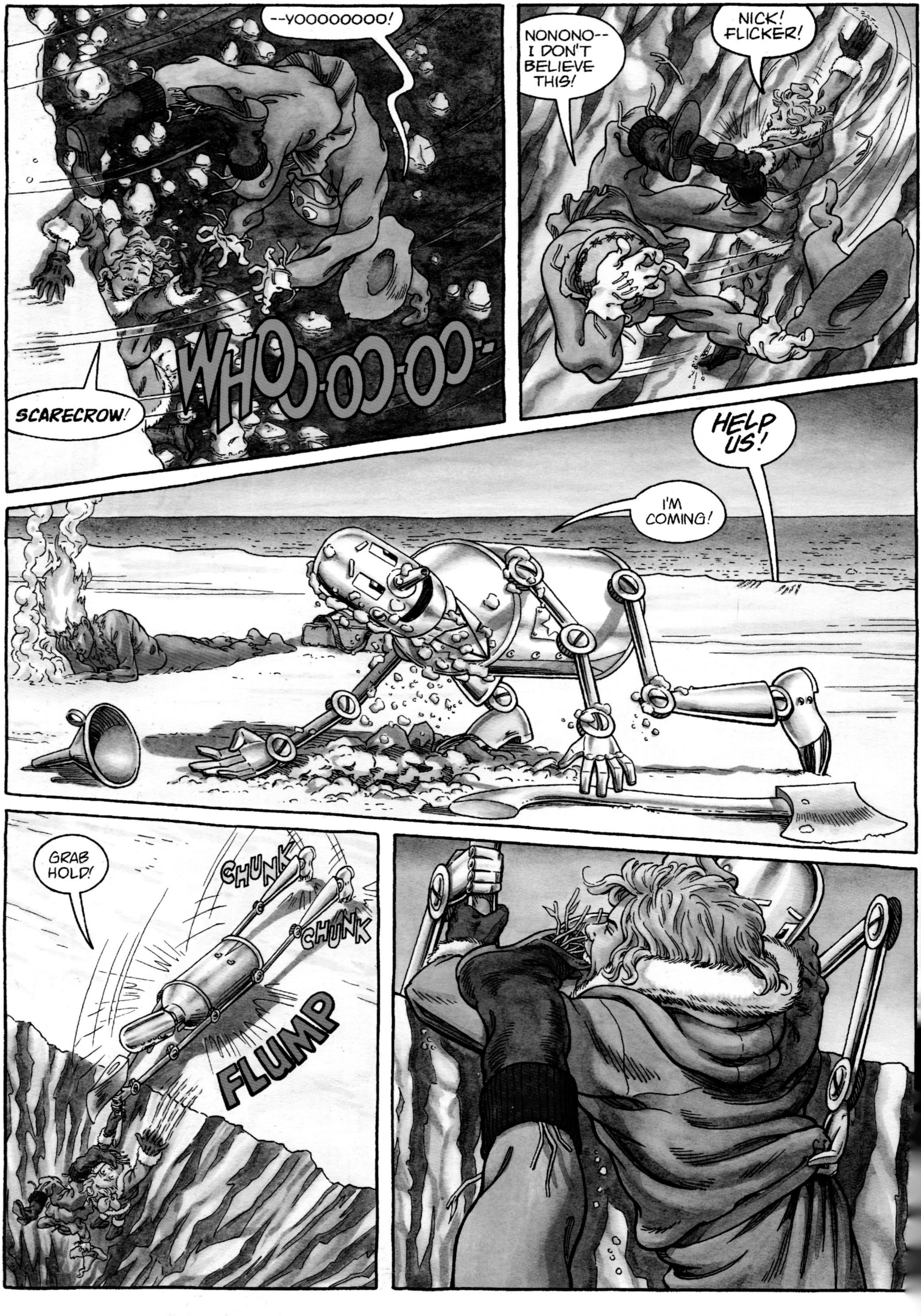
--YOOOOOOOO!
WHOO-OO-OO-OO-
SCARECROW!
NONONO-- I DON'T BELIEVE THIS!
NICK! FLICKER!
HELP US!
I'M COMING!
GRAB HOLD!
CHUNK
CHUNK
FLUMP

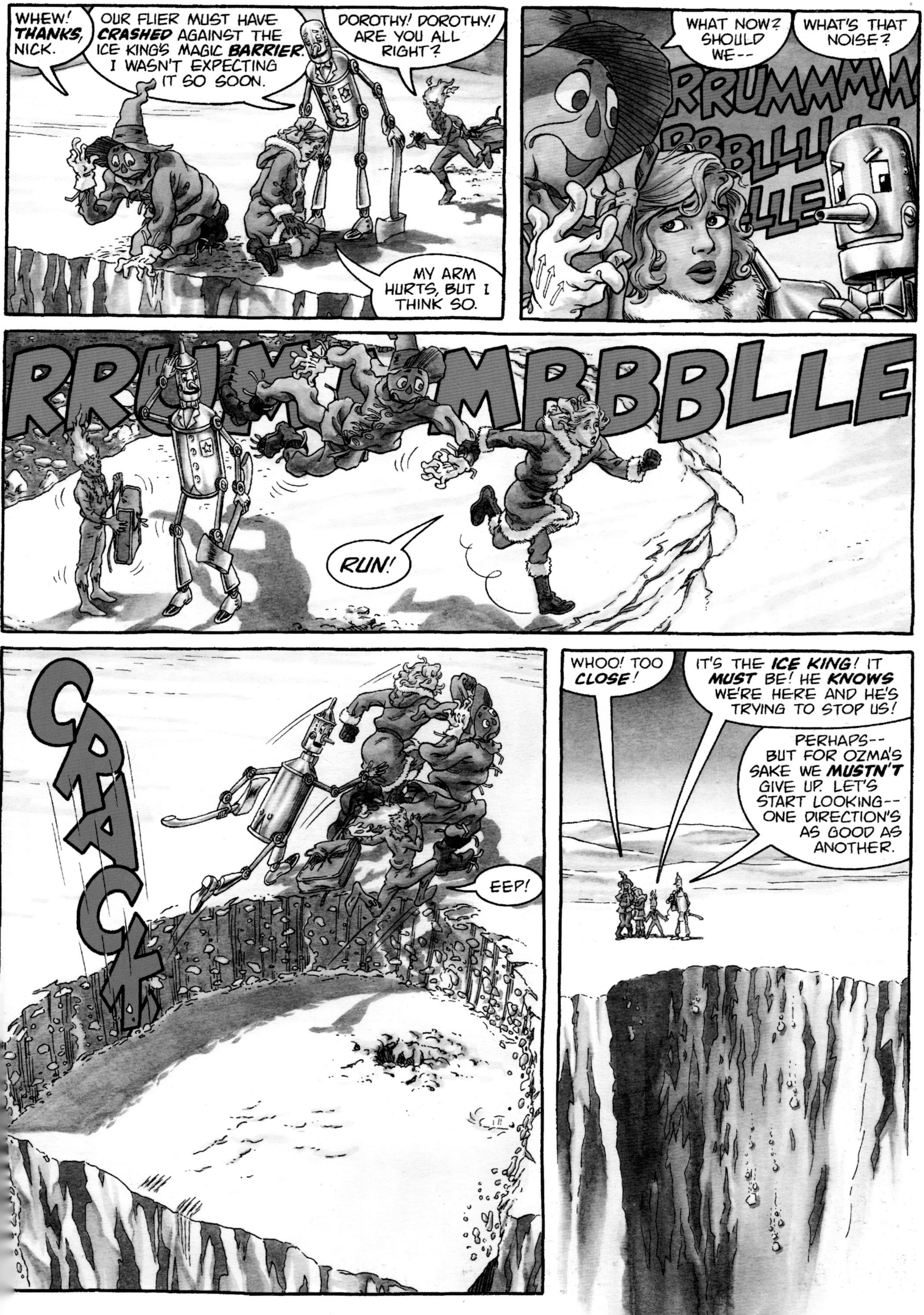
WHEW! **THANKS**, NICK.
OUR FLIER MUST HAVE **CRASHED** AGAINST THE ICE KING'S MAGIC **BARRIER**. I WASN'T EXPECTING IT SO SOON.
DOROTHY! DOROTHY! ARE YOU ALL RIGHT?
MY ARM HURTS, BUT I THINK SO.
WHAT NOW? SHOULD WE--
WHAT'S THAT NOISE?
RUN!
CRACK
EEP!
WHOO! TOO **CLOSE**!
IT'S THE **ICE KING**! IT **MUST** BE! HE **KNOWS** WE'RE HERE AND HE'S TRYING TO STOP US!
PERHAPS-- BUT FOR OZMA'S SAKE WE **MUSTN'T** GIVE UP. LET'S START LOOKING-- ONE DIRECTION'S AS GOOD AS ANOTHER.

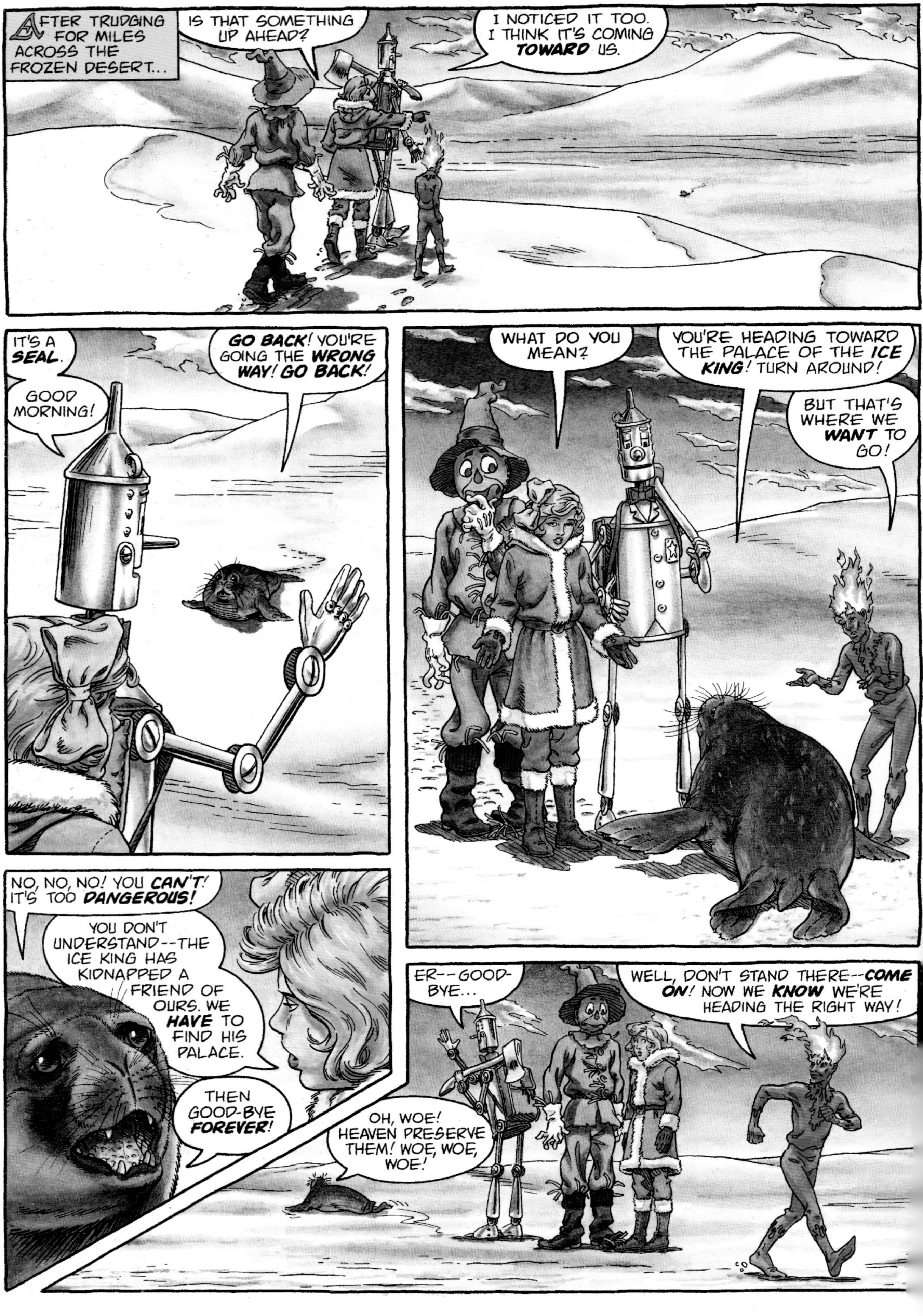
AFTER TRUDGING FOR MILES ACROSS THE FROZEN DESERT...
IS THAT SOMETHING UP AHEAD?
I NOTICED IT TOO. I THINK IT'S COMING TOWARD US.
IT'S A SEAL.
GOOD MORNING!
GO BACK! YOU'RE GOING THE WRONG WAY! GO BACK!
WHAT DO YOU MEAN?
YOU'RE HEADING TOWARD THE PALACE OF THE ICE KING! TURN AROUND!
BUT THAT'S WHERE WE WANT TO GO!
NO, NO, NO! YOU CAN'T! IT'S TOO DANGEROUS!
YOU DON'T UNDERSTAND--THE ICE KING HAS KIDNAPPED A FRIEND OF OURS. WE HAVE TO FIND HIS PALACE.
THEN GOOD-BYE FOREVER!
ER--GOOD-BYE...
OH, WOE! HEAVEN PRESERVE THEM! WOE, WOE, WOE!
WELL, DON'T STAND THERE--COME ON! NOW WE KNOW WE'RE HEADING THE RIGHT WAY!

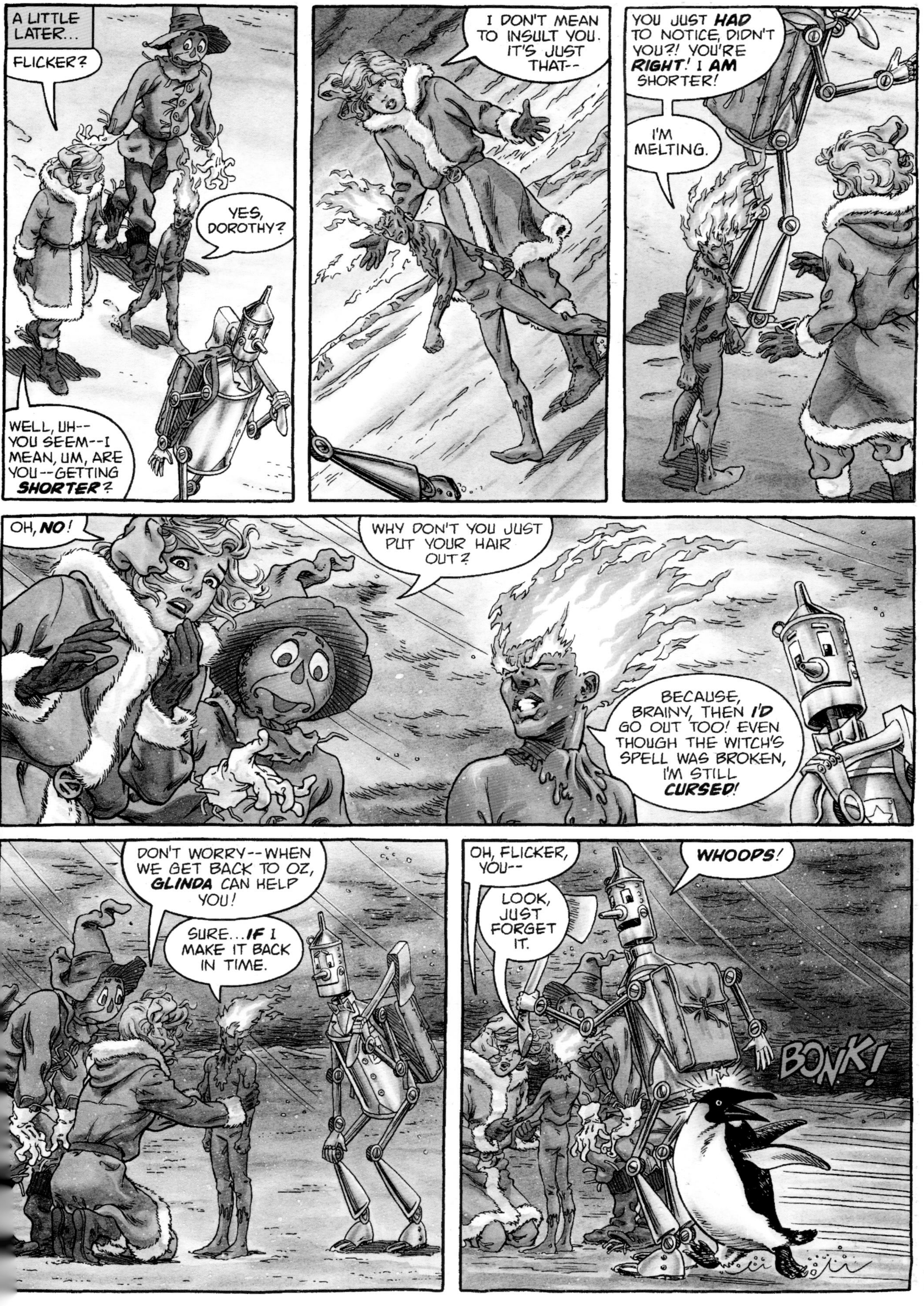
A LITTLE LATER...
FLICKER?
YES, DOROTHY?
WELL, UH-- YOU SEEM--I MEAN, UM, ARE YOU--GETTING SHORTER?
I DON'T MEAN TO INSULT YOU. IT'S JUST THAT--
YOU JUST HAD TO NOTICE, DIDN'T YOU?! YOU'RE RIGHT! I AM SHORTER!
I'M MELTING.
OH, NO!
WHY DON'T YOU JUST PUT YOUR HAIR OUT?
BECAUSE, BRAINY, THEN I'D GO OUT TOO! EVEN THOUGH THE WITCH'S SPELL WAS BROKEN, I'M STILL CURSED!
DON'T WORRY--WHEN WE GET BACK TO OZ, GLINDA CAN HELP YOU!
SURE...IF I MAKE IT BACK IN TIME.
OH, FLICKER, YOU--
LOOK, JUST FORGET IT.
WHOOPS!
BONK!

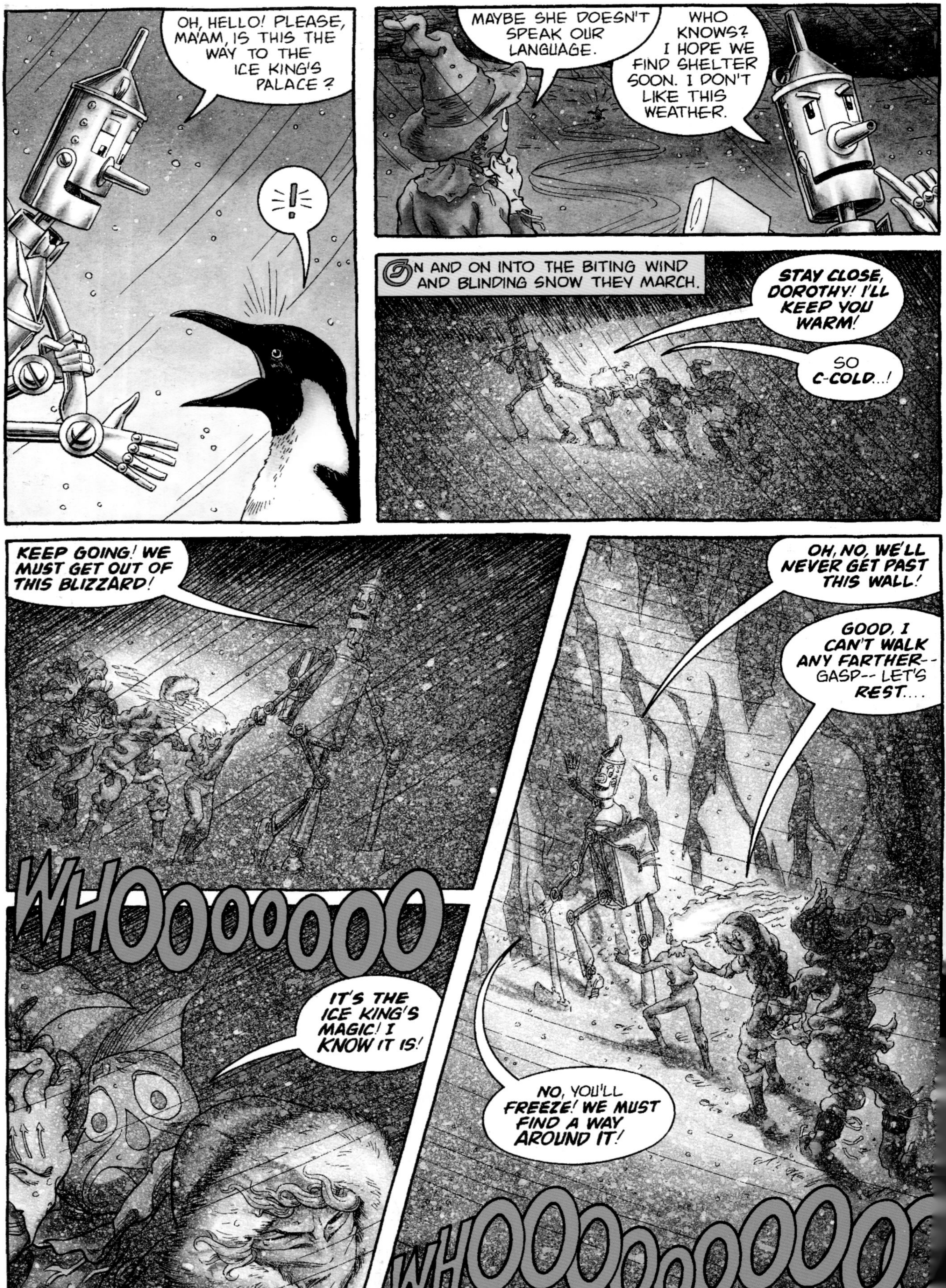
OH, HELLO! PLEASE, MA'AM, IS THIS THE WAY TO THE ICE KING'S PALACE?
!
MAYBE SHE DOESN'T SPEAK OUR LANGUAGE.
WHO KNOWS? I HOPE WE FIND SHELTER SOON. I DON'T LIKE THIS WEATHER.
ON AND ON INTO THE BITING WIND AND BLINDING SNOW THEY MARCH.
STAY CLOSE, DOROTHY! I'LL KEEP YOU WARM!
SO C-COLD...!
KEEP GOING! WE MUST GET OUT OF THIS BLIZZARD!
WHOOOOOOOO
IT'S THE ICE KING'S MAGIC! I KNOW IT IS!
OH, NO, WE'LL NEVER GET PAST THIS WALL!
GOOD, I CAN'T WALK ANY FARTHER-- GASP-- LET'S REST....
NO, YOU'LL FREEZE! WE MUST FIND A WAY AROUND IT!
WHOOOOOOOOOOO

# Chapter Four In the Ice Palace

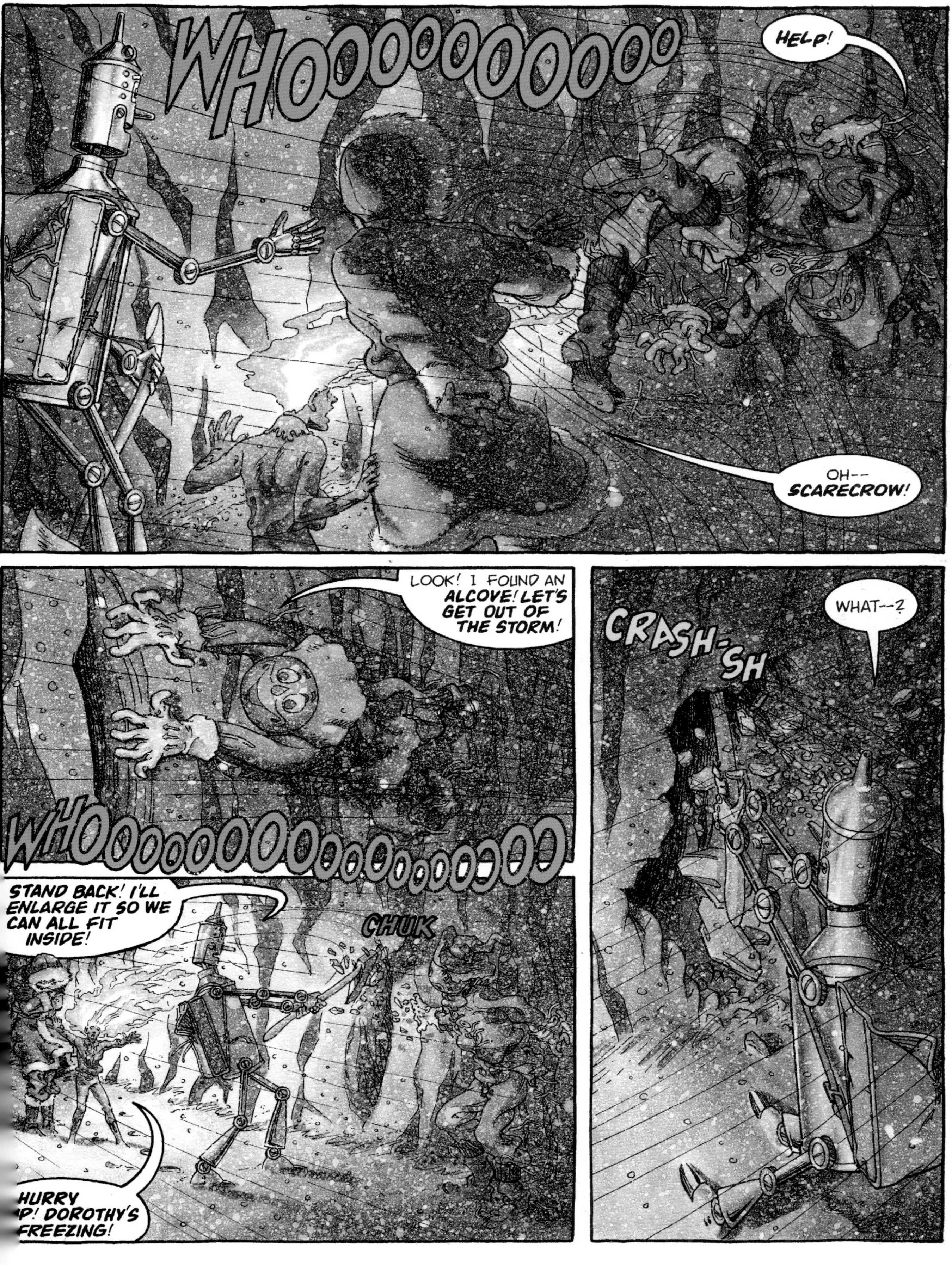
WHOOOOOOOOOO
HELP!
OH-- SCARECROW!
LOOK! I FOUND AN ALCOVE! LET'S GET OUT OF THE STORM!
WHOOOOOOOOOOOOOOOOOO
STAND BACK! I'LL ENLARGE IT SO WE CAN ALL FIT INSIDE!
CHUK
HURRY P! DOROTHY'S FREEZING!
CRASH-SH
WHAT--?

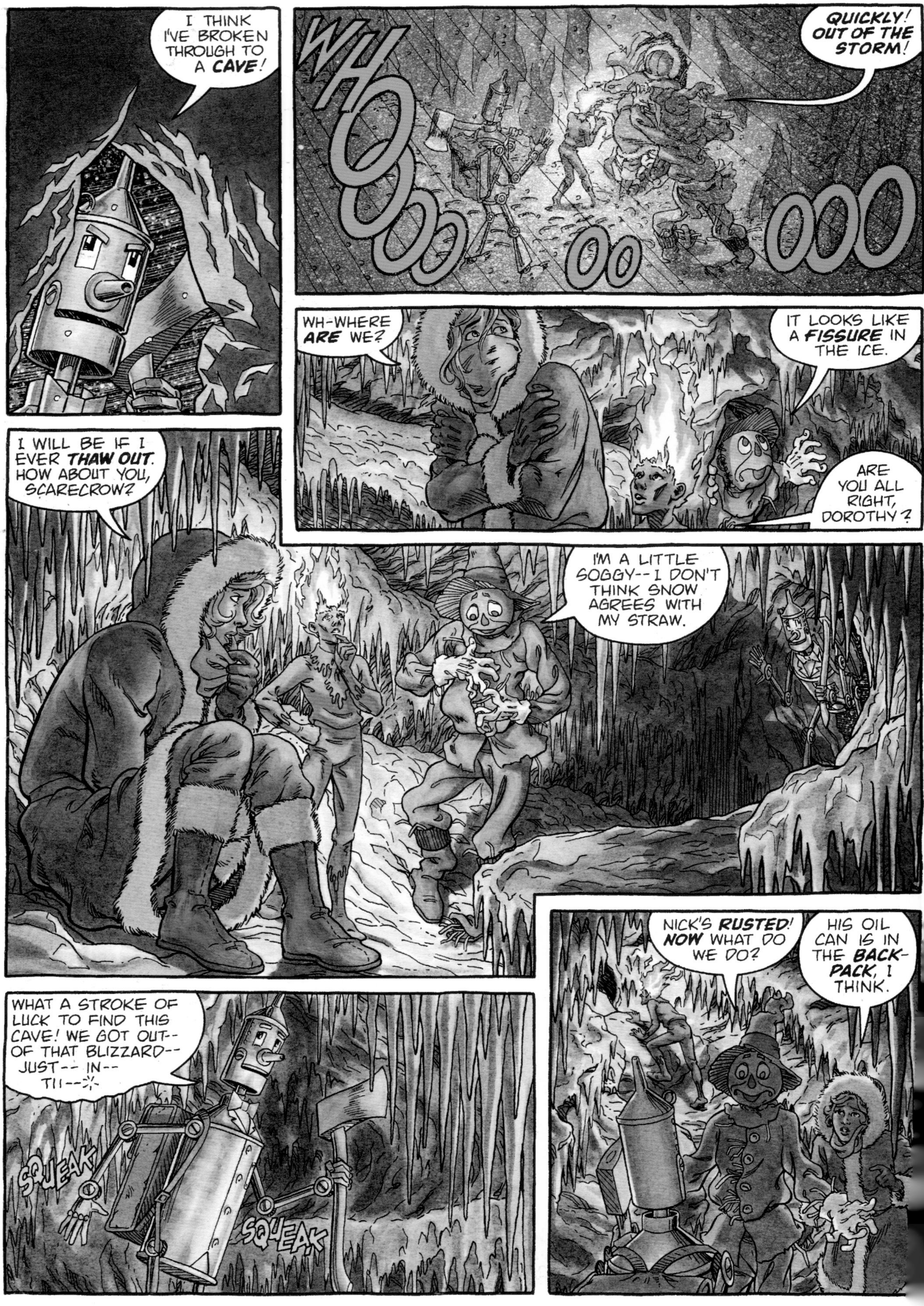
I THINK I'VE BROKEN THROUGH TO A **CAVE**!
WHOOOOO OO OOO
***QUICKLY! OUT OF THE STORM!***
WH-WHERE **ARE** WE?
IT LOOKS LIKE A **FISSURE** IN THE ICE.
ARE YOU ALL RIGHT, DOROTHY?
I WILL BE IF I EVER **THAW OUT**. HOW ABOUT YOU, SCARECROW?
I'M A LITTLE SOGGY-- I DON'T THINK SNOW AGREES WITH MY STRAW.
WHAT A STROKE OF LUCK TO FIND THIS CAVE! WE GOT OUT-- OF THAT BLIZZARD-- JUST-- IN-- TII--
SQUEAK
SQUEAK
NICK'S **RUSTED**! **NOW** WHAT DO WE DO?
HIS OIL CAN IS IN THE **BACK-PACK**, I THINK.

YES, HERE IT IS!

I CAN HARDLY **SEE** TO OIL HIM.

WHERE'S FLICKER? **FLICKER!** WE NEED YOUR **LIGHT!**

GLUGALUG GLUGALUG GLUG

AH, THANK YOU, DOROTHY.

LISTEN, EVERYONE! I SAW A **LIGHT** AT THE OTHER END OF THE CAVE!

WHAT COULD IT **BE?**

I'M NOT EAGER TO MARCH BACK INTO THAT **BLIZZARD**. WE MIGHT AS WELL EXPLORE.

COME ON! IT'S NOT FAR.

SEE?

PERHAPS IT'S THE OTHER SIDE OF THE WALL OF ICE.

OH!

SHH!

WHAT DO YOU SEE?

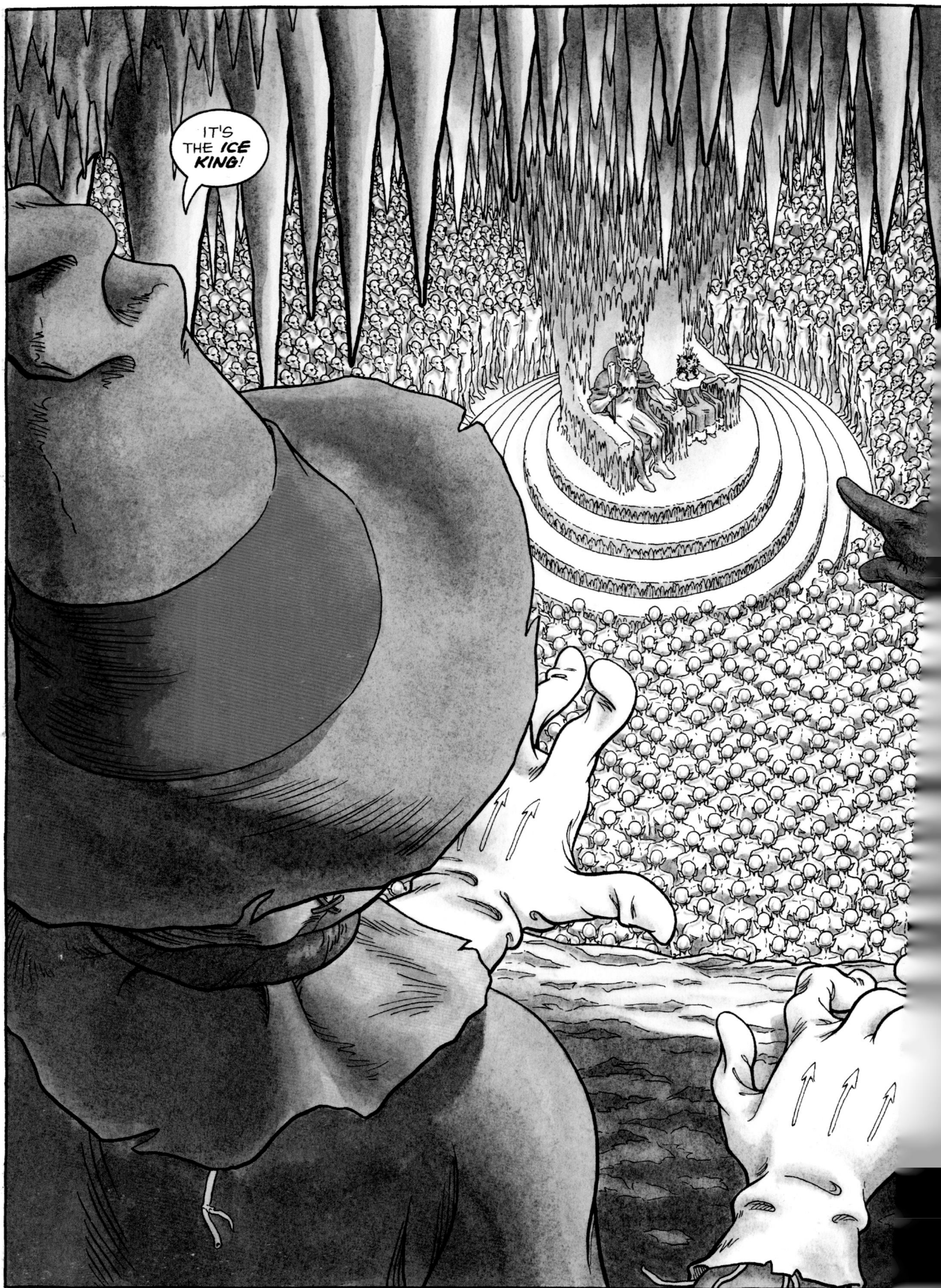
IT'S THE ICE KING!

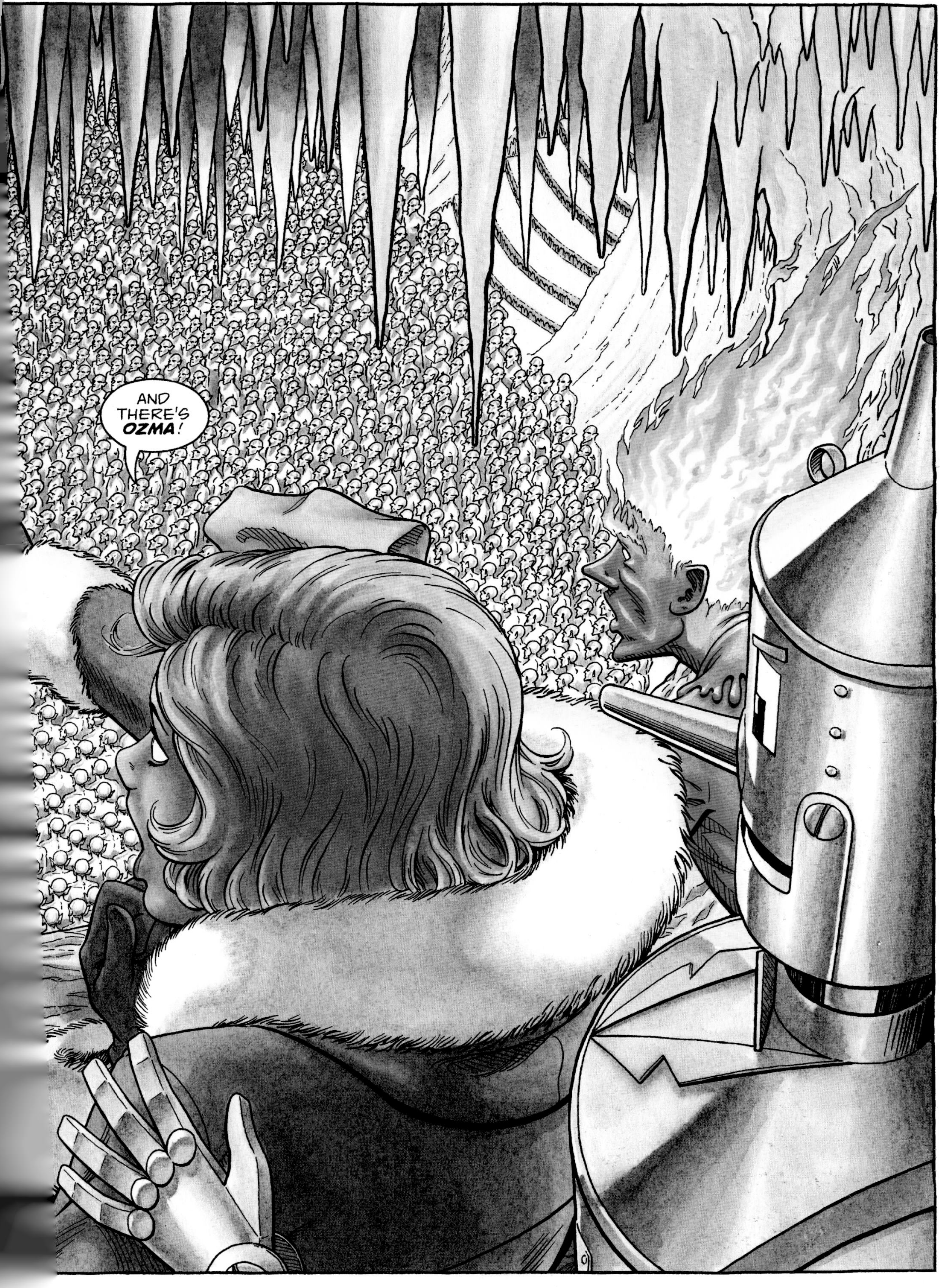
AND THERE'S **OZMA**!

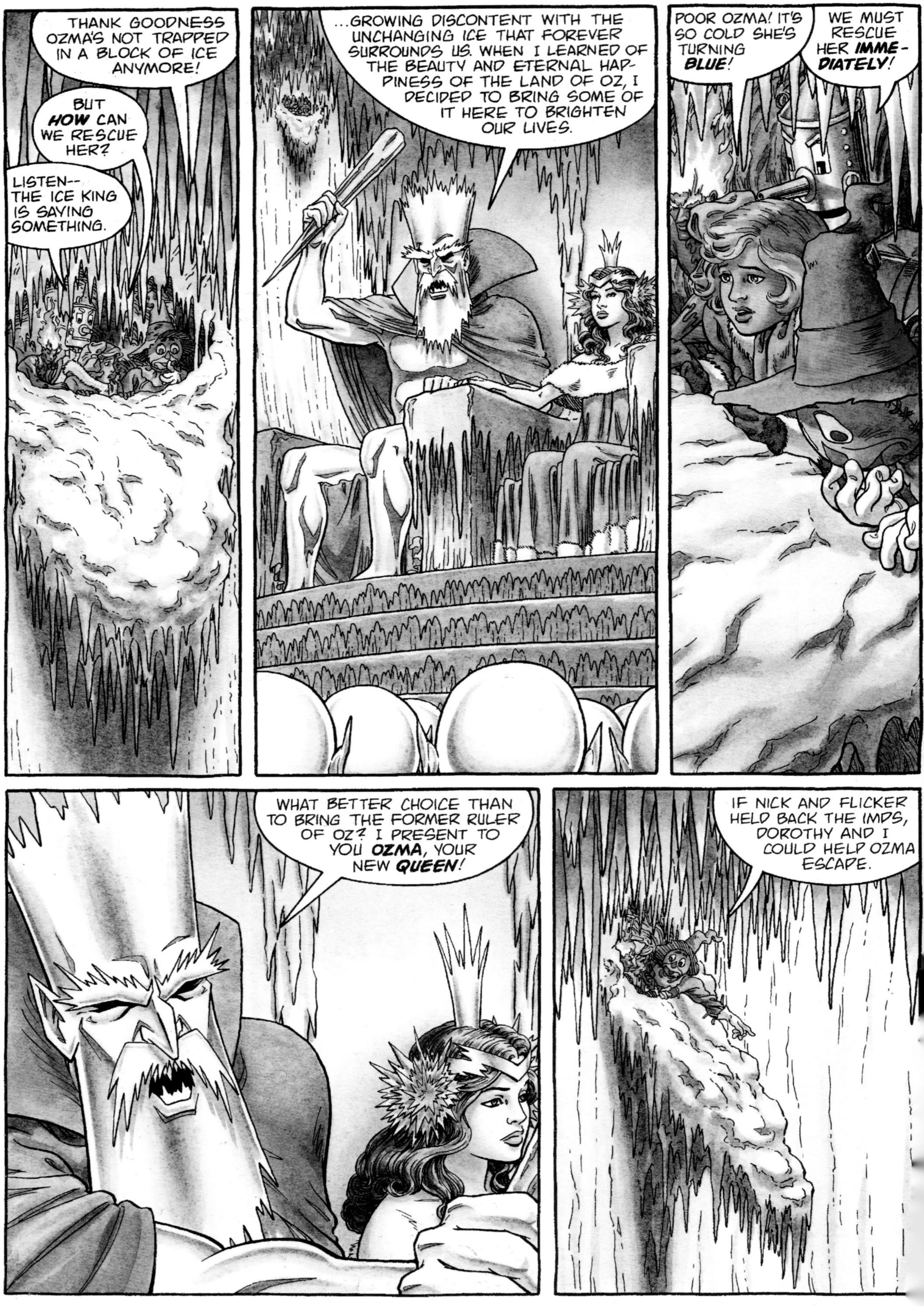
THANK GOODNESS OZMA'S NOT TRAPPED IN A BLOCK OF ICE ANYMORE!
BUT **HOW** CAN WE RESCUE HER?
LISTEN-- THE ICE KING IS SAYING SOMETHING.
...GROWING DISCONTENT WITH THE UNCHANGING ICE THAT FOREVER SURROUNDS US. WHEN I LEARNED OF THE BEAUTY AND ETERNAL HAPPINESS OF THE LAND OF OZ, I DECIDED TO BRING SOME OF IT HERE TO BRIGHTEN OUR LIVES.
POOR OZMA! IT'S SO COLD SHE'S TURNING **BLUE**!
WE MUST RESCUE HER **IMMEDIATELY**!
WHAT BETTER CHOICE THAN TO BRING THE FORMER RULER OF OZ? I PRESENT TO YOU **OZMA**, YOUR NEW **QUEEN**!
IF NICK AND FLICKER HELD BACK THE IMPS, DOROTHY AND I COULD HELP OZMA ESCAPE.

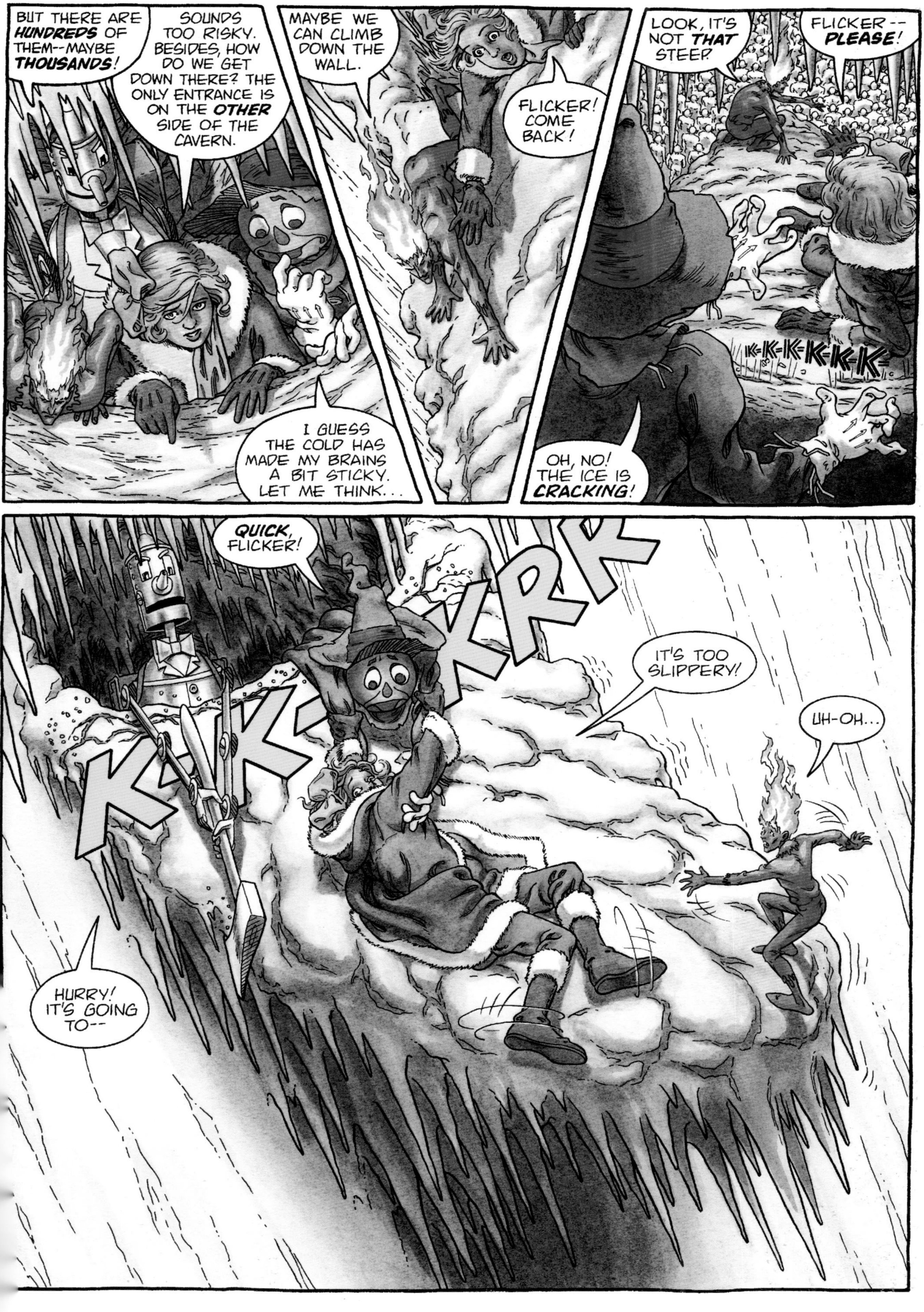
BUT THERE ARE HUNDREDS OF THEM--MAYBE THOUSANDS!
SOUNDS TOO RISKY. BESIDES, HOW DO WE GET DOWN THERE? THE ONLY ENTRANCE IS ON THE OTHER SIDE OF THE CAVERN.
I GUESS THE COLD HAS MADE MY BRAINS A BIT STICKY. LET ME THINK...
MAYBE WE CAN CLIMB DOWN THE WALL.
FLICKER! COME BACK!
LOOK, IT'S NOT THAT STEEP.
FLICKER-- PLEASE!
K-K-K-K-K-K-K
OH, NO! THE ICE IS CRACKING!
QUICK, FLICKER!
K-K-K-KRR
IT'S TOO SLIPPERY!
UH-OH...
HURRY! IT'S GOING TO--

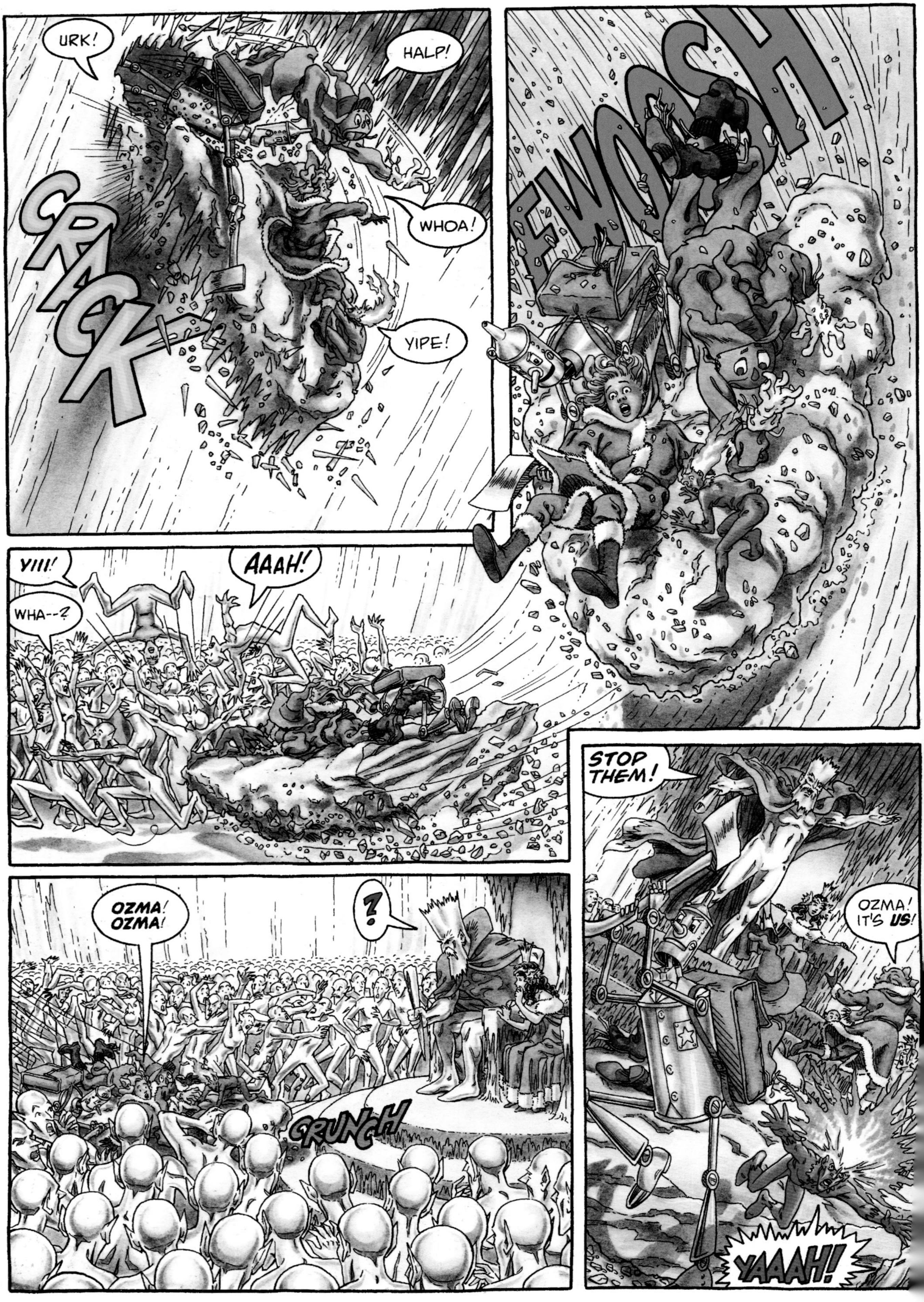
URK!
HALP!
CRACK
WHOA!
YIPE!
FWOOSH
YIII!
WHA--?
AAAH!
OZMA! OZMA!
?
CRUNCH
STOP THEM!
OZMA! IT'S US!
YAAAH!

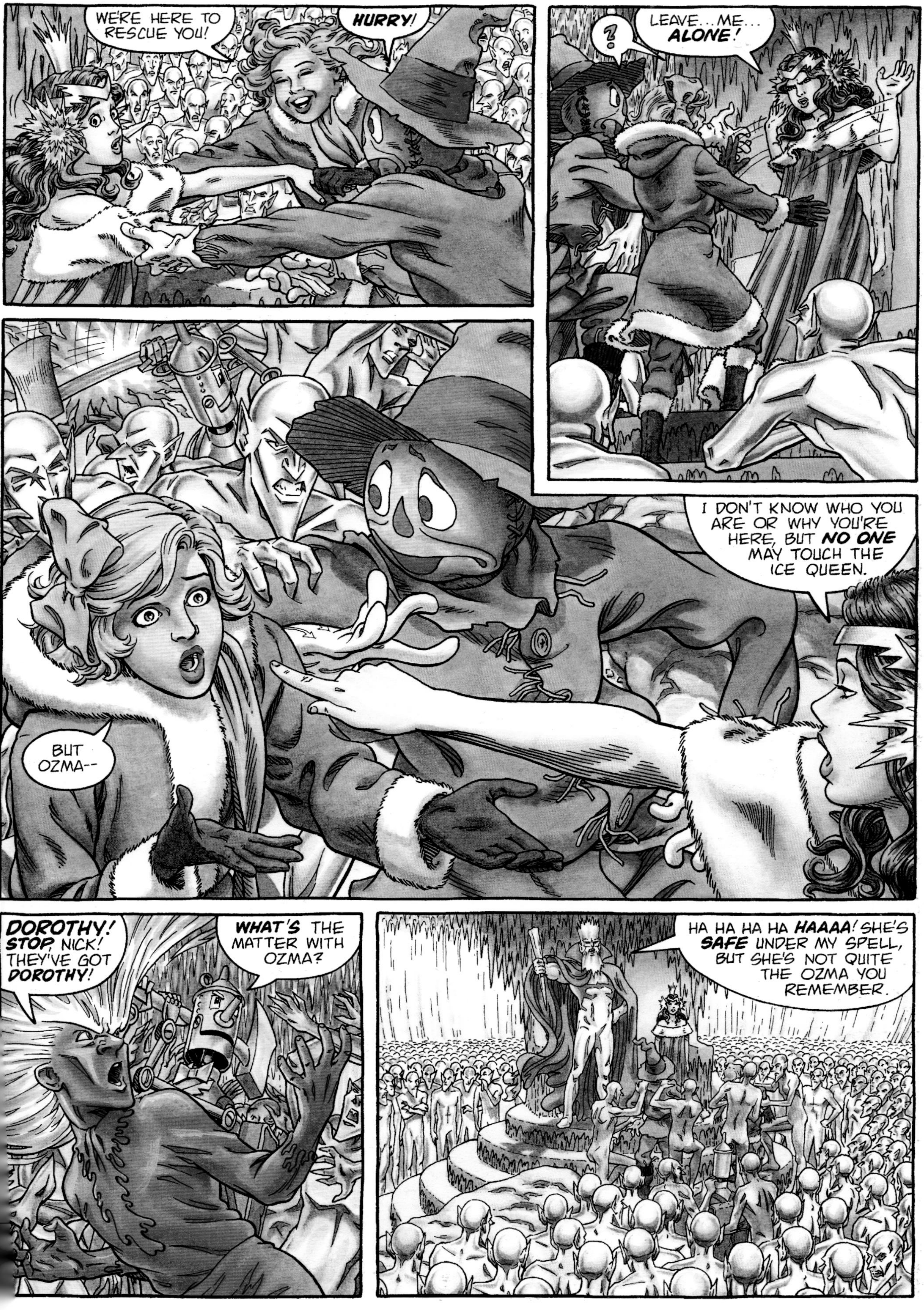
WE'RE HERE TO RESCUE YOU!
HURRY!
?
LEAVE... ME... ALONE!
I DON'T KNOW WHO YOU ARE OR WHY YOU'RE HERE, BUT NO ONE MAY TOUCH THE ICE QUEEN.
BUT OZMA--
DOROTHY! STOP NICK! THEY'VE GOT DOROTHY!
WHAT'S THE MATTER WITH OZMA?
HA HA HA HA HAAAA! SHE'S SAFE UNDER MY SPELL, BUT SHE'S NOT QUITE THE OZMA YOU REMEMBER.

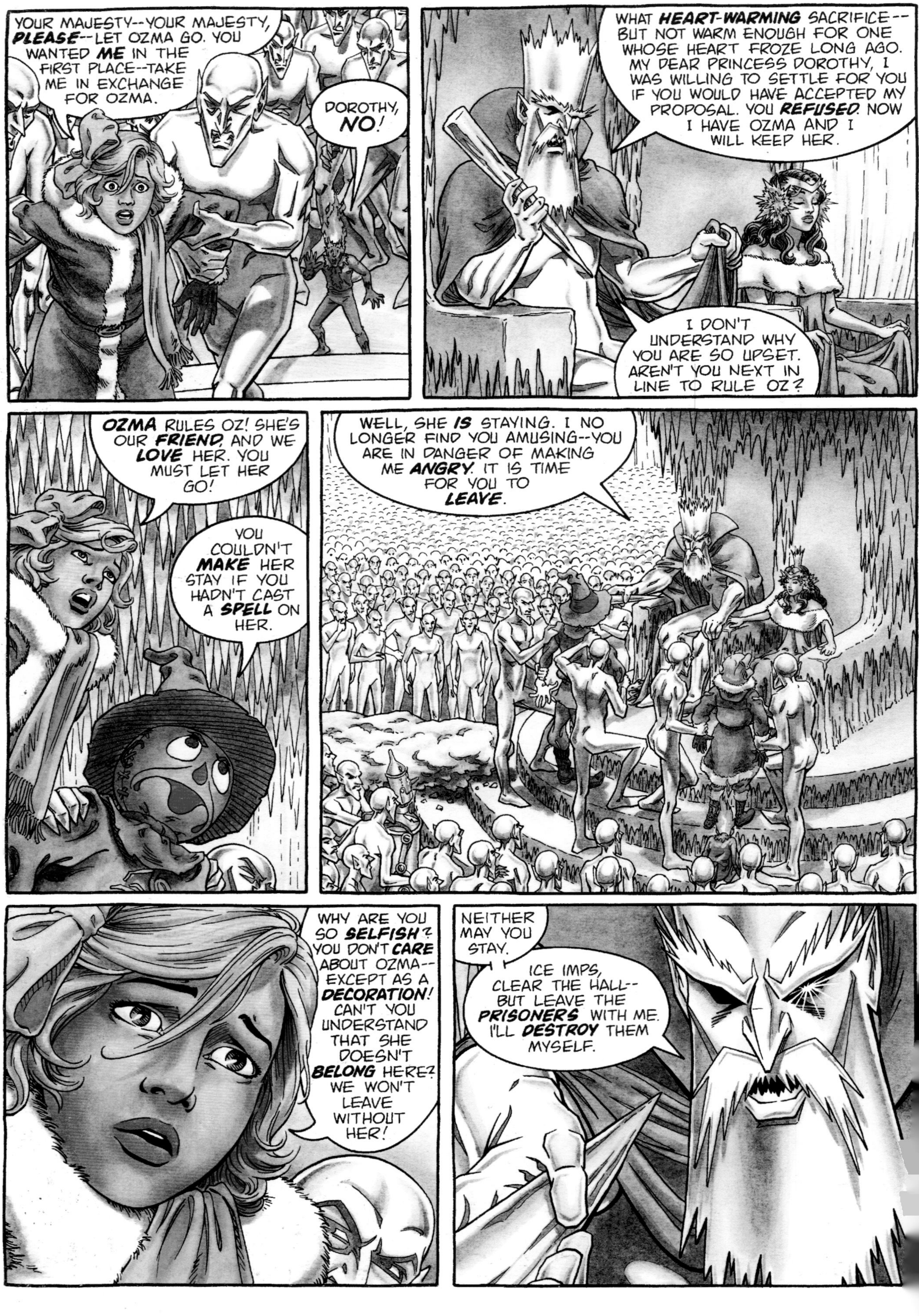
YOUR MAJESTY--YOUR MAJESTY, PLEASE--LET OZMA GO. YOU WANTED ME IN THE FIRST PLACE--TAKE ME IN EXCHANGE FOR OZMA.
DOROTHY, NO!
WHAT HEART-WARMING SACRIFICE--BUT NOT WARM ENOUGH FOR ONE WHOSE HEART FROZE LONG AGO. MY DEAR PRINCESS DOROTHY, I WAS WILLING TO SETTLE FOR YOU IF YOU WOULD HAVE ACCEPTED MY PROPOSAL. YOU REFUSED. NOW I HAVE OZMA AND I WILL KEEP HER.
I DON'T UNDERSTAND WHY YOU ARE SO UPSET. AREN'T YOU NEXT IN LINE TO RULE OZ?
OZMA RULES OZ! SHE'S OUR FRIEND, AND WE LOVE HER. YOU MUST LET HER GO!
YOU COULDN'T MAKE HER STAY IF YOU HADN'T CAST A SPELL ON HER.
WELL, SHE IS STAYING. I NO LONGER FIND YOU AMUSING--YOU ARE IN DANGER OF MAKING ME ANGRY. IT IS TIME FOR YOU TO LEAVE.
WHY ARE YOU SO SELFISH? YOU DON'T CARE ABOUT OZMA--EXCEPT AS A DECORATION! CAN'T YOU UNDERSTAND THAT SHE DOESN'T BELONG HERE? WE WON'T LEAVE WITHOUT HER!
NEITHER MAY YOU STAY.
ICE IMPS, CLEAR THE HALL--BUT LEAVE THE PRISONERS WITH ME. I'LL DESTROY THEM MYSELF.

# Chapter Five The Ice King's Power

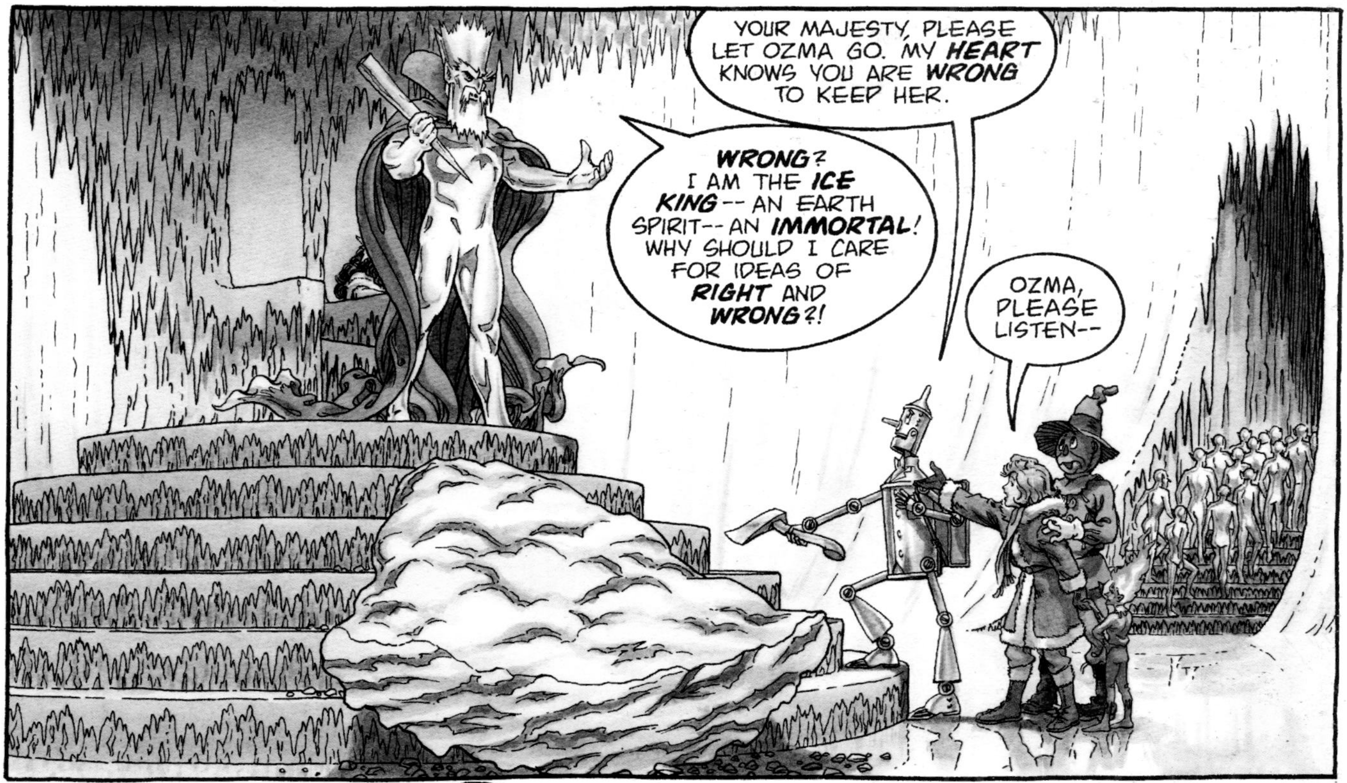
YOUR MAJESTY, PLEASE LET OZMA GO. MY HEART KNOWS YOU ARE WRONG TO KEEP HER.
WRONG? I AM THE ICE KING-- AN EARTH SPIRIT-- AN IMMORTAL! WHY SHOULD I CARE FOR IDEAS OF RIGHT AND WRONG?!
OZMA, PLEASE LISTEN--

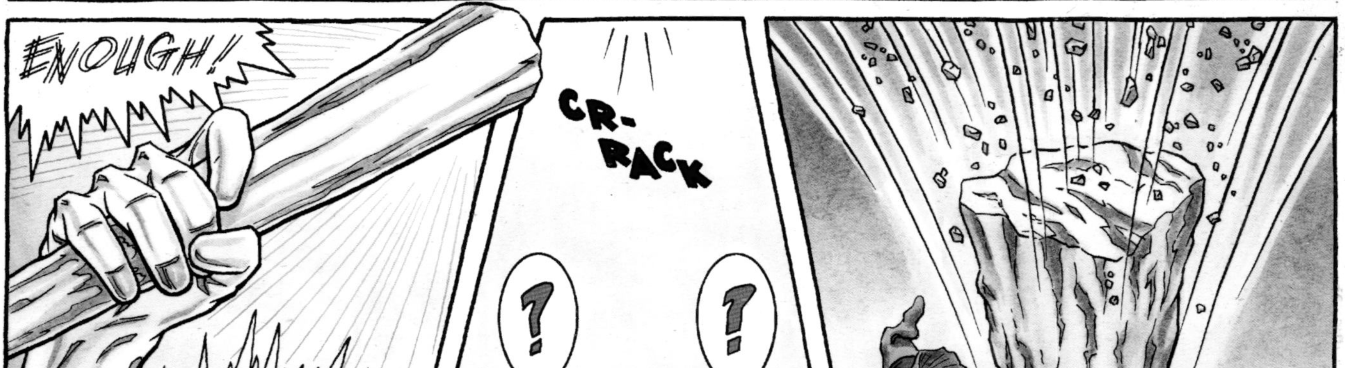
ENOUGH!
CR-RACK
?
?
WHUNK

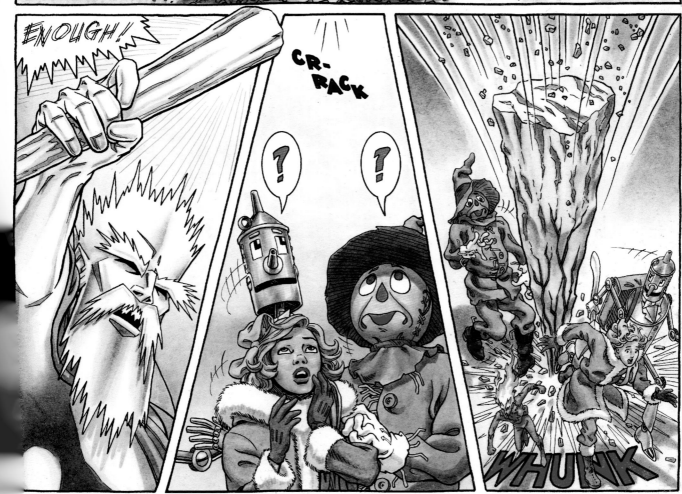

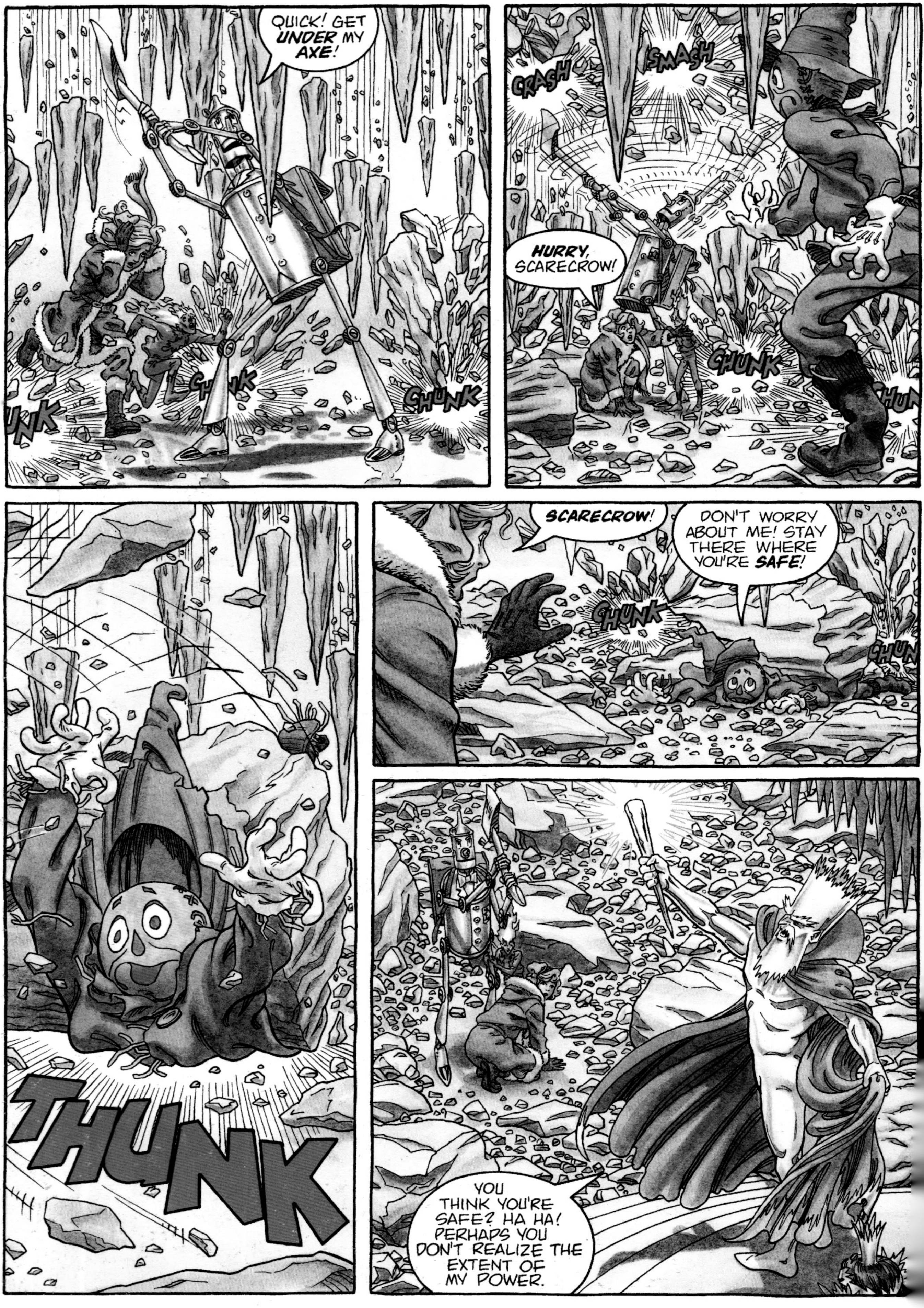

QUICK! GET **UNDER** MY **AXE**!
CHUNK
CHUNK
CRASH
SMASH
**HURRY**, SCARECROW!
CHUNK
THUNK
**SCARECROW**!
DON'T WORRY ABOUT ME! STAY THERE WHERE YOU'RE **SAFE**!
CHUNK
YOU THINK YOU'RE SAFE? HA HA! PERHAPS YOU DON'T REALIZE THE EXTENT OF MY POWER.

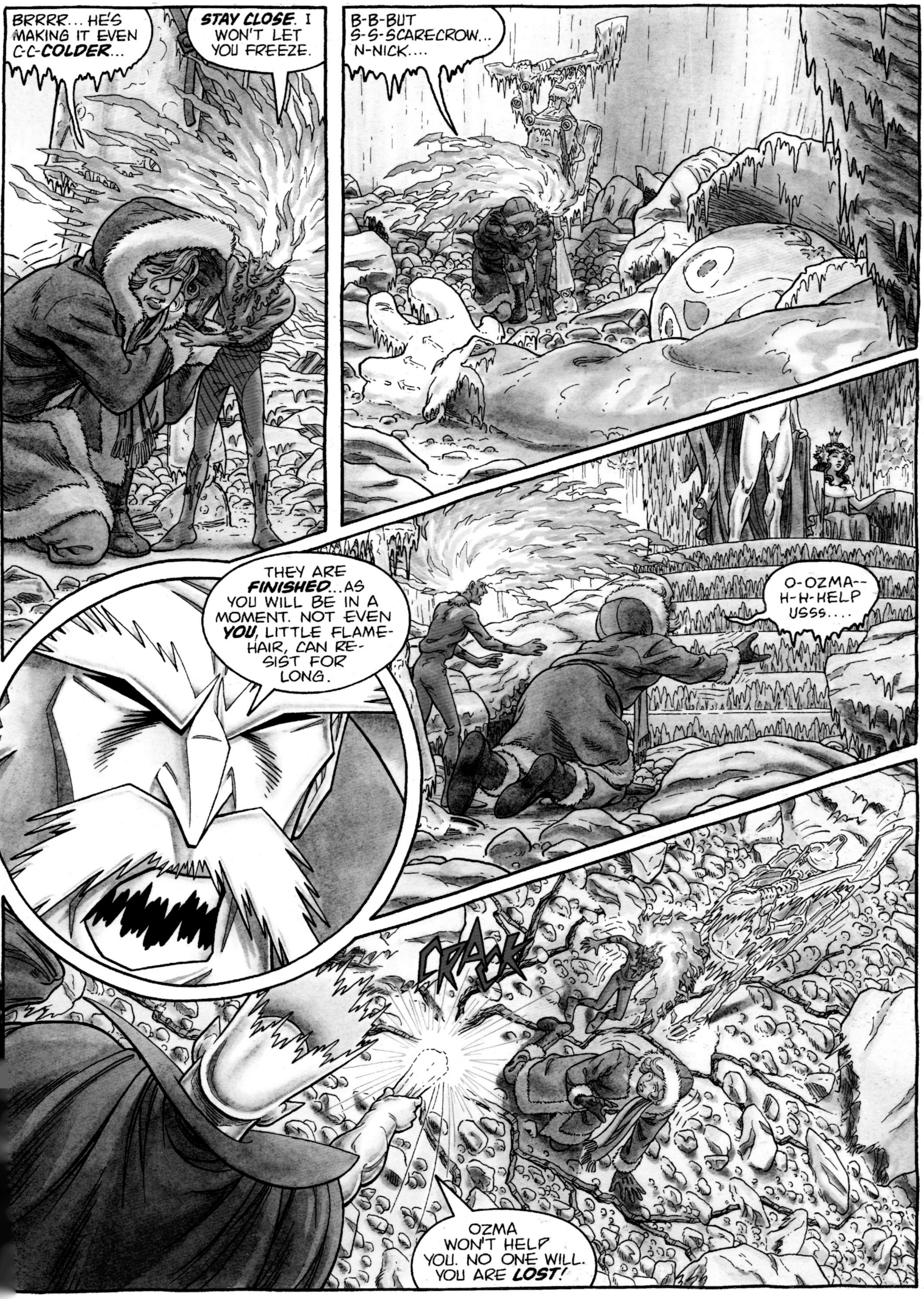
BRRRR... HE'S MAKING IT EVEN C-C-COLDER...
STAY CLOSE. I WON'T LET YOU FREEZE.
B-B-BUT S-S-SCARECROW... N-NICK....
THEY ARE FINISHED...AS YOU WILL BE IN A MOMENT. NOT EVEN YOU, LITTLE FLAME-HAIR, CAN RESIST FOR LONG.
O-OZMA-- H-H-HELP USSS....
CRAAK
OZMA WON'T HELP YOU. NO ONE WILL. YOU ARE LOST!

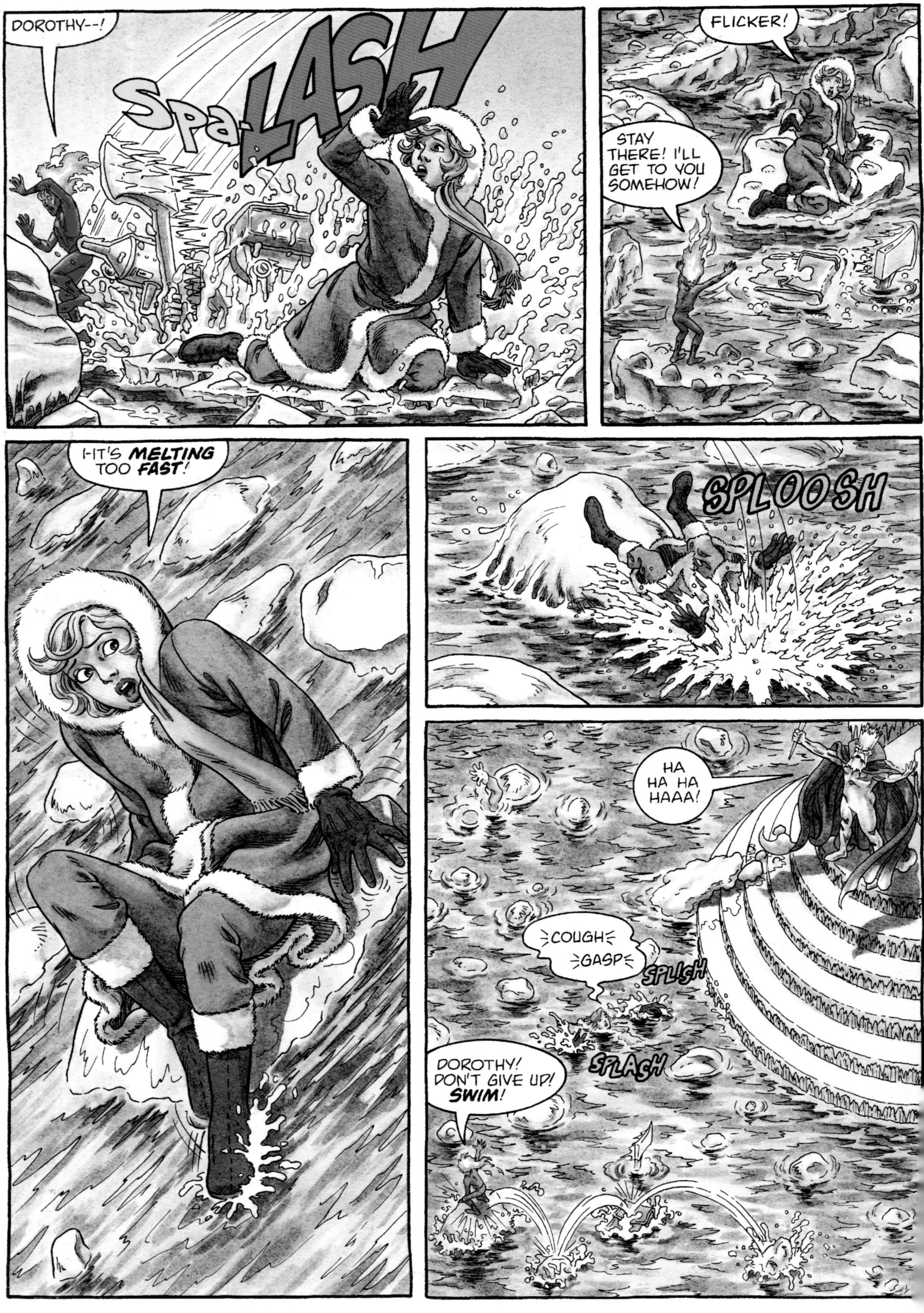
DOROTHY--!
Spa-LASH
FLICKER!
STAY THERE! I'LL GET TO YOU SOMEHOW!
I-IT'S MELTING TOO FAST!
SPLOOSH
HA HA HA HAAA!
COUGH
GASP
SPLISH
SPLASH
DOROTHY! DON'T GIVE UP! SWIM!

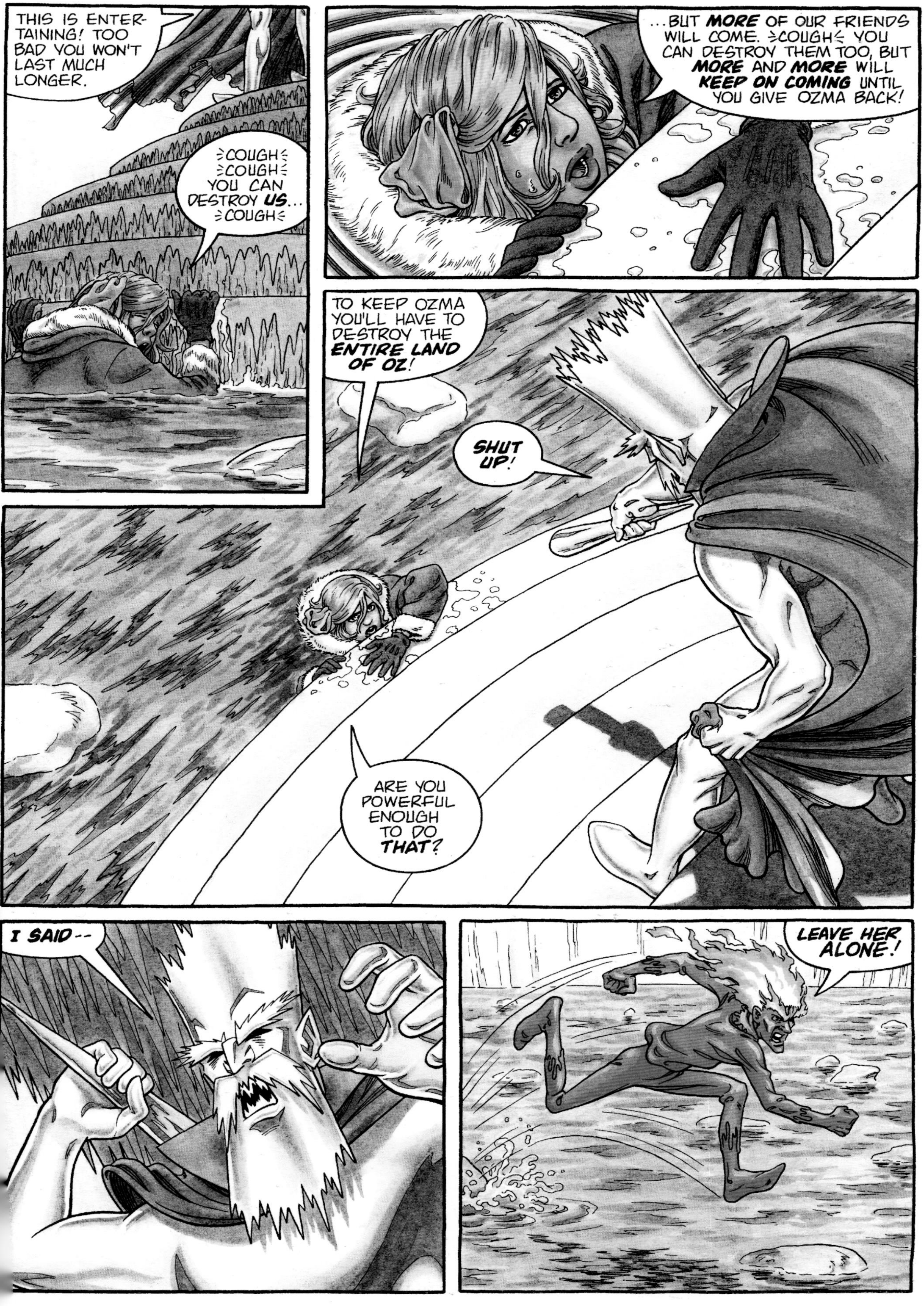
THIS IS ENTERTAINING! TOO BAD YOU WON'T LAST MUCH LONGER.
≥COUGH≤ ≥COUGH≤ YOU CAN DESTROY **US**... ≥COUGH≤
...BUT **MORE** OF OUR FRIENDS WILL COME. ≥COUGH≤ YOU CAN DESTROY THEM TOO, BUT **MORE** AND **MORE** WILL **KEEP ON COMING** UNTIL YOU GIVE OZMA BACK!
TO KEEP OZMA YOU'LL HAVE TO DESTROY THE **ENTIRE LAND OF OZ**!
**SHUT UP**!
ARE YOU POWERFUL ENOUGH TO DO **THAT**?
**I SAID--**
**LEAVE HER ALONE**!

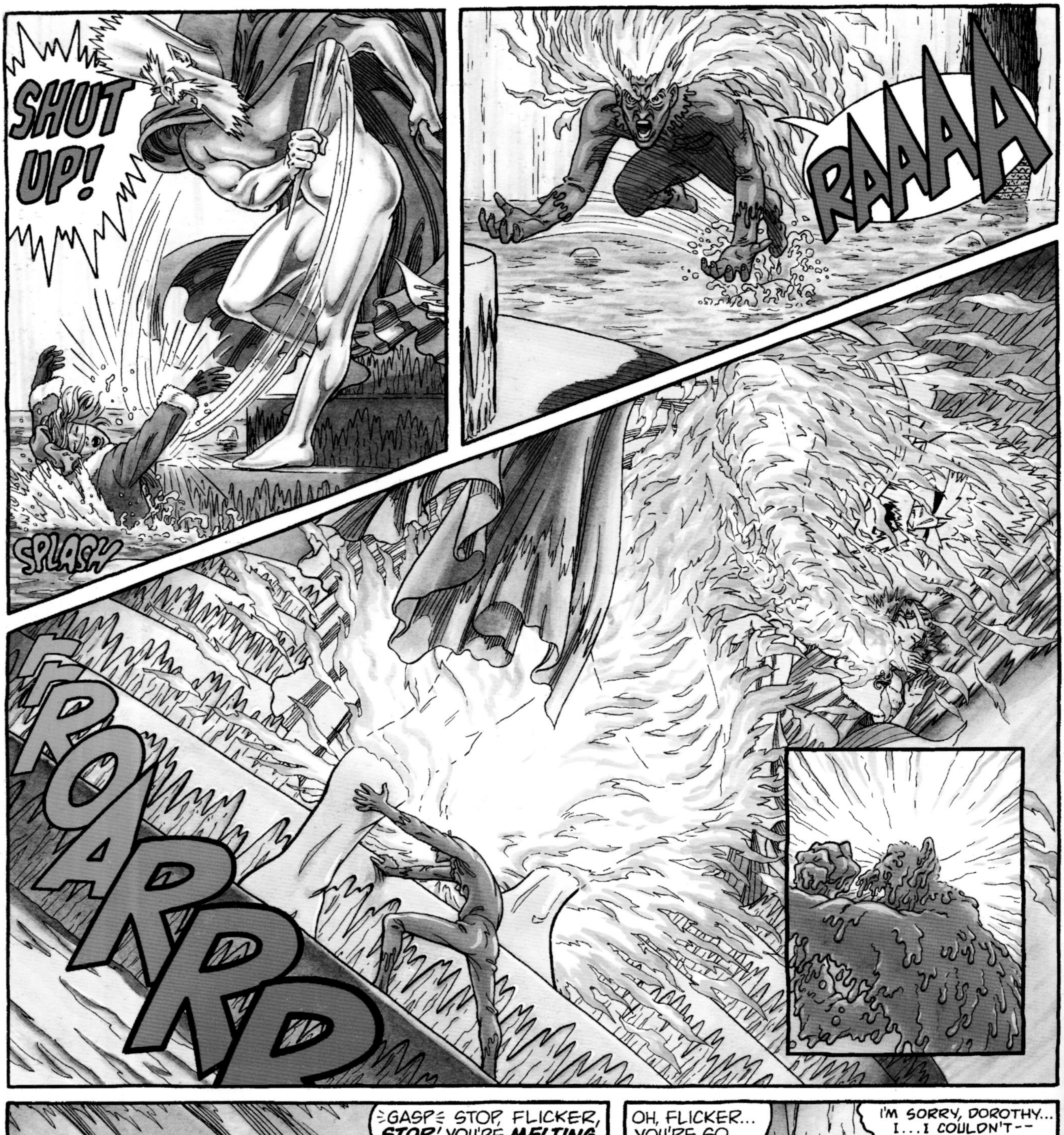

SHUT UP!
SPLASH
RAAAA
rrROARRRD
GASP STOP, FLICKER, STOP! YOU'RE MELTING AWAY! STOP!
AAAHHRRRR...
OH, FLICKER... YOU'RE SO SMALL!
I'M SORRY, DOROTHY... I... I COULDN'T-- MELT HIM....

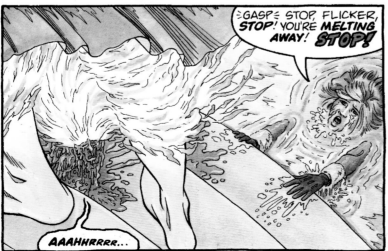

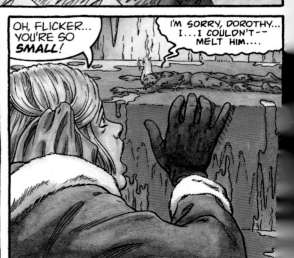

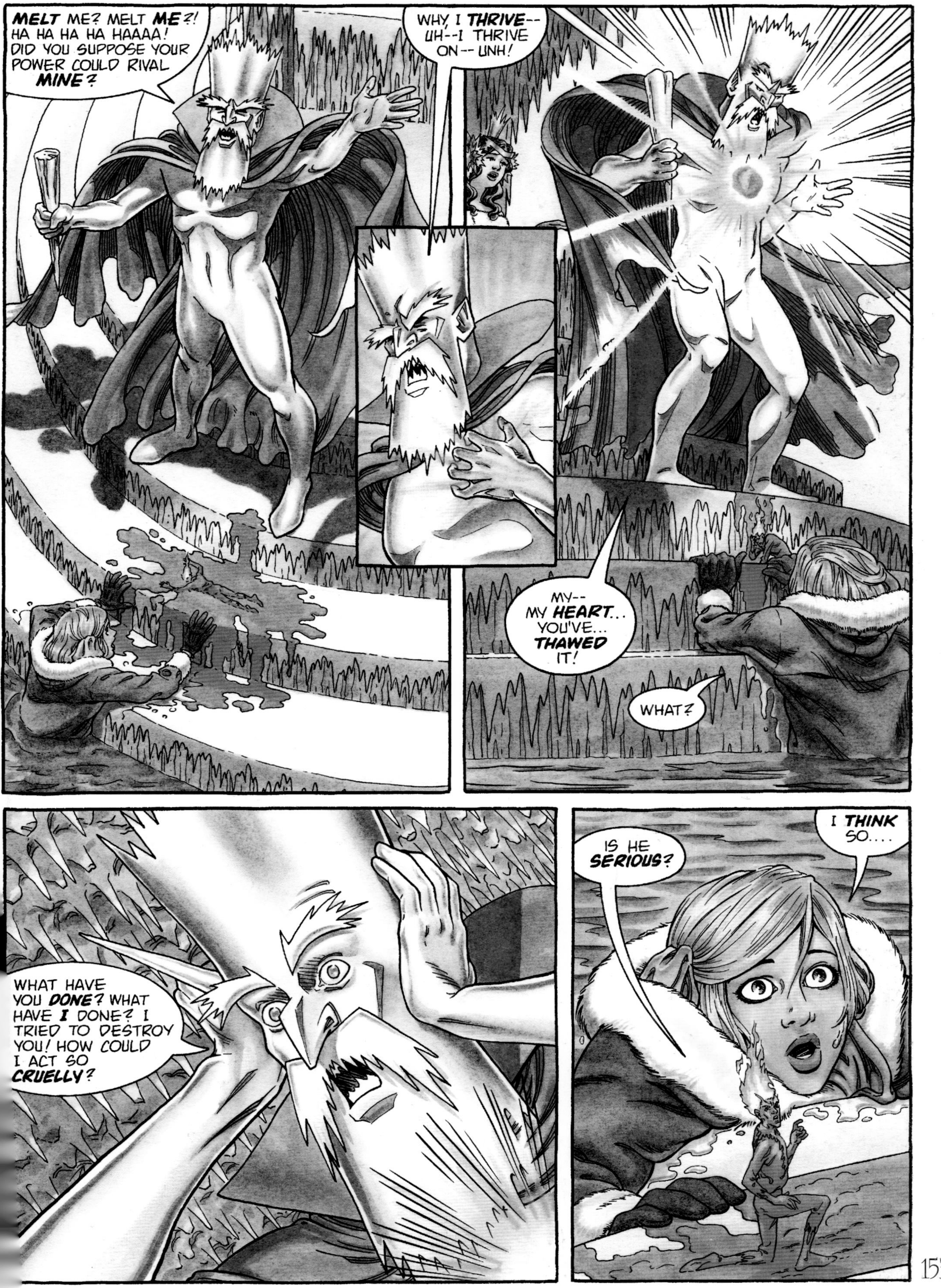
MELT ME? MELT ME?! HA HA HA HA HAAAA! DID YOU SUPPOSE YOUR POWER COULD RIVAL MINE?
WHY, I THRIVE-- UH--I THRIVE ON-- UNH!
MY-- MY HEART... YOU'VE... THAWED IT!
WHAT?
WHAT HAVE YOU DONE? WHAT HAVE I DONE? I TRIED TO DESTROY YOU! HOW COULD I ACT SO CRUELLY?
IS HE SERIOUS?
I THINK SO....

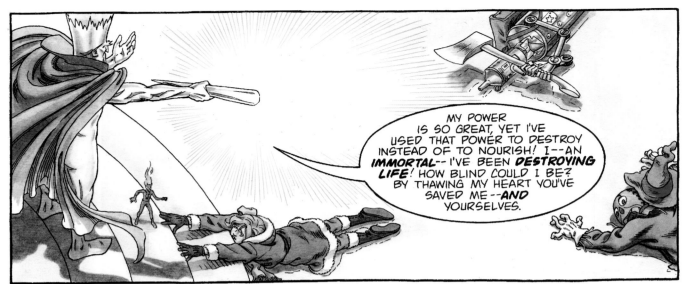

MY POWER IS SO GREAT, YET I'VE USED THAT POWER TO DESTROY INSTEAD OF TO NOURISH! I--AN *IMMORTAL*-- I'VE BEEN *DESTROYING LIFE!* HOW BLIND COULD I BE? BY THAWING MY HEART YOU'VE SAVED ME--*AND* YOURSELVES.

DOROTHY! FUNNY, YOU DON'T *LOOK* DESTROYED!

SCARECROW! ARE YOU ALL RIGHT?

YES, BUT LOOK AT THE TIN WOODMAN. HE'S *RUSTED* AGAIN.

YOU HAVE NOTHING MORE TO FEAR FROM ME. GO, LEAVE MY KINGDOM IN *SAFETY.*

GLUG A LUG

BUT, YOUR MAJESTY, HAVE YOU *FORGOTTEN?* WE WON'T LEAVE WITHOUT *OZMA.*

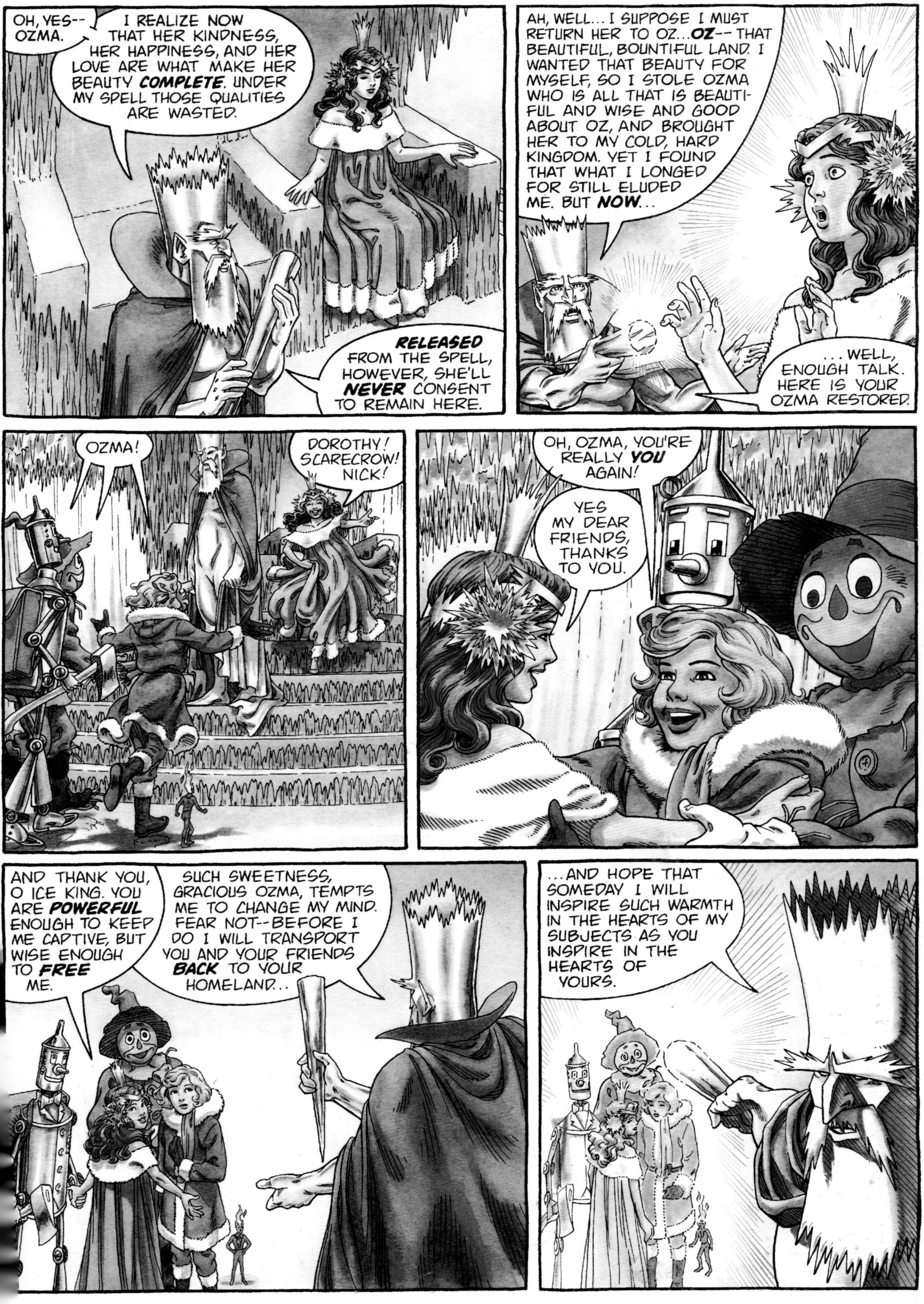
OH, YES-- OZMA.
I REALIZE NOW THAT HER KINDNESS, HER HAPPINESS, AND HER LOVE ARE WHAT MAKE HER BEAUTY **COMPLETE**. UNDER MY SPELL THOSE QUALITIES ARE WASTED.
**RELEASED** FROM THE SPELL, HOWEVER, SHE'LL **NEVER** CONSENT TO REMAIN HERE.
AH, WELL... I SUPPOSE I MUST RETURN HER TO OZ...**OZ**-- THAT BEAUTIFUL, BOUNTIFUL LAND. I WANTED THAT BEAUTY FOR MYSELF, SO I STOLE OZMA WHO IS ALL THAT IS BEAUTIFUL AND WISE AND GOOD ABOUT OZ, AND BROUGHT HER TO MY COLD, HARD KINGDOM. YET I FOUND THAT WHAT I LONGED FOR STILL ELUDED ME. BUT **NOW**...
...WELL, ENOUGH TALK. HERE IS YOUR OZMA RESTORED.
OZMA!
DOROTHY! SCARECROW! NICK!
OH, OZMA, YOU'RE REALLY **YOU** AGAIN!
YES MY DEAR FRIENDS, THANKS TO YOU.
AND THANK YOU, O ICE KING. YOU ARE **POWERFUL** ENOUGH TO KEEP ME CAPTIVE, BUT WISE ENOUGH TO **FREE** ME.
SUCH SWEETNESS, GRACIOUS OZMA, TEMPTS ME TO CHANGE MY MIND. FEAR NOT--BEFORE I DO I WILL TRANSPORT YOU AND YOUR FRIENDS **BACK** TO YOUR HOMELAND...
...AND HOPE THAT SOMEDAY I WILL INSPIRE SUCH WARMTH IN THE HEARTS OF MY SUBJECTS AS YOU INSPIRE IN THE HEARTS OF YOURS.

# Oz

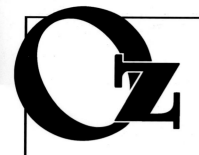

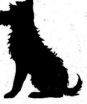

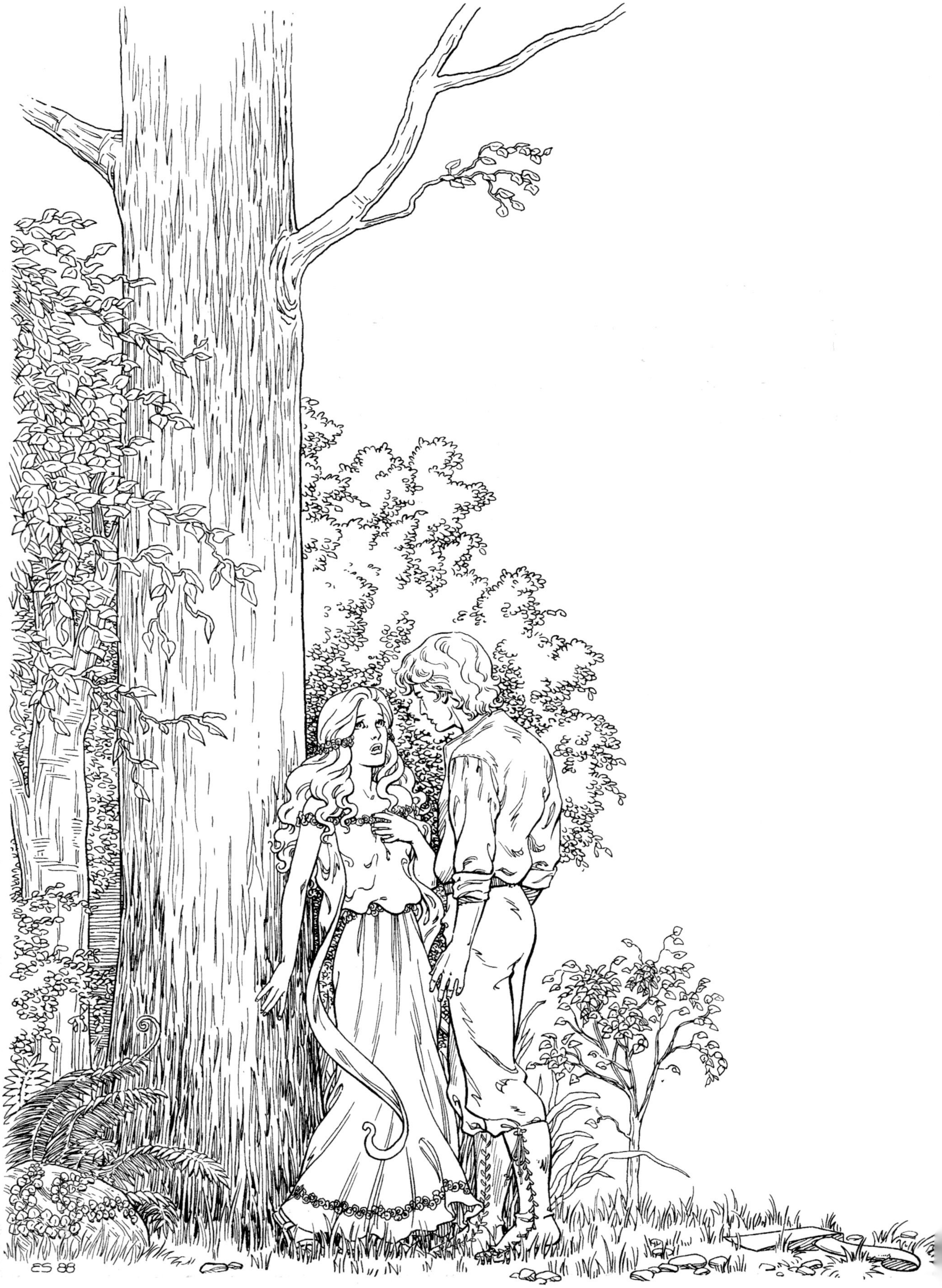
ES 88

# The Forgotten Forest of Oz

For David

ACROSS THE DEADLY DESERT FROM THE LAND OF OZ LIES THE FOREST OF **BURZEE**. IN THIS ANCIENT FOREST THE TRUNKS GROW TALL, THICK, AND STURDY, NEVER KNOWING THE SHARP CHOP OF AN AXE. TREE LIMBS SPRING FORTH MIGHTILY, BRANCHING AGAIN AND AGAIN TO FORM A LEAFY ROOF OVER THE TWILIGHT WORLD.

IF YOU WERE TO STAND IN THE FOREST OF BURZEE, STAND AS STILL AND AS QUIET AS THE GREAT TREES THEMSELVES, YOU WOULD BEGIN TO **HEAR** THINGS...

Snap

TO **SEE** THINGS...

AND IF YOU STOOD, BARELY BREATHING, AS NIGHT CREPT UPON THE FOREST, YOU WOULD BEGIN TO **FEEL** SOMETHING TOO-- SOMETHING **MAGICAL**!

FOR THE FOREST OF BURZEE IS NO ORDINARY FOREST. THERE IS A REASON IT HAS GROWN SO PROUDLY FOR SO LONG.

IT HAS **CARETAKERS**...

161

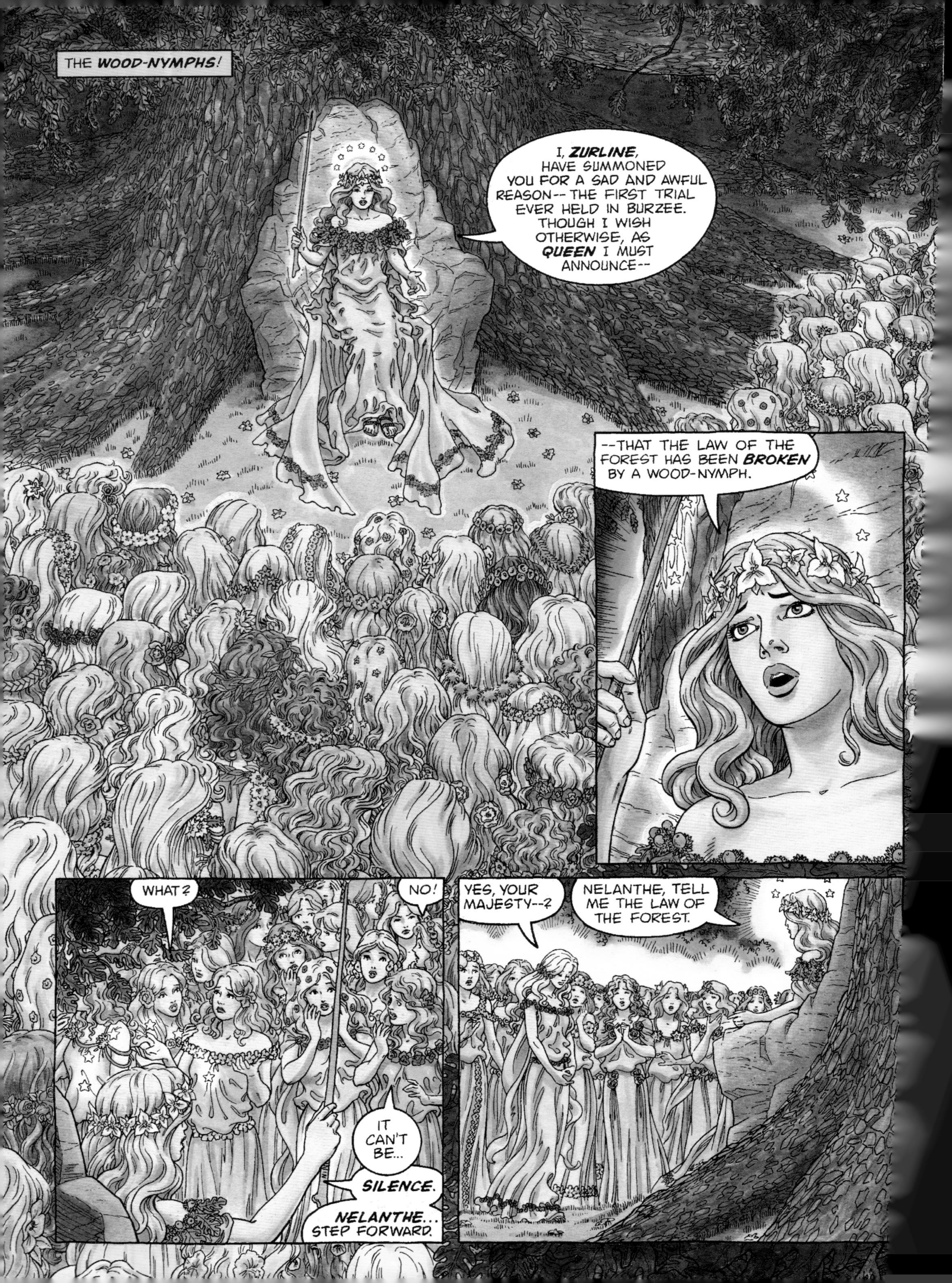
THE WOOD-NYMPHS!
I, ZURLINE, HAVE SUMMONED YOU FOR A SAD AND AWFUL REASON-- THE FIRST TRIAL EVER HELD IN BURZEE. THOUGH I WISH OTHERWISE, AS QUEEN I MUST ANNOUNCE--
--THAT THE LAW OF THE FOREST HAS BEEN BROKEN BY A WOOD-NYMPH.
WHAT?
NO!
IT CAN'T BE...
SILENCE.
NELANTHE... STEP FORWARD.
YES, YOUR MAJESTY--?
NELANTHE, TELL ME THE LAW OF THE FOREST.

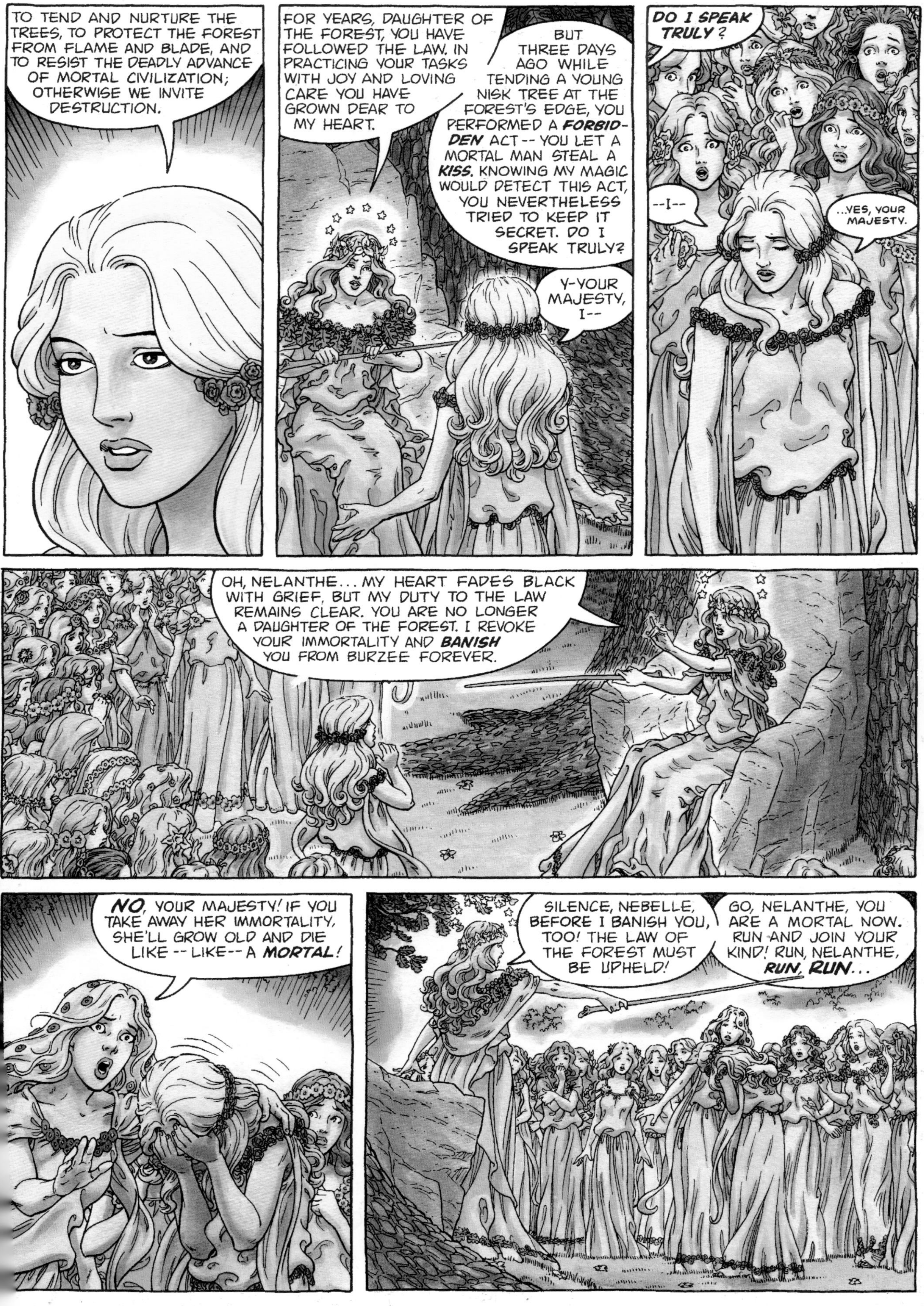
TO TEND AND NURTURE THE TREES, TO PROTECT THE FOREST FROM FLAME AND BLADE, AND TO RESIST THE DEADLY ADVANCE OF MORTAL CIVILIZATION; OTHERWISE WE INVITE DESTRUCTION.
FOR YEARS, DAUGHTER OF THE FOREST, YOU HAVE FOLLOWED THE LAW. IN PRACTICING YOUR TASKS WITH JOY AND LOVING CARE YOU HAVE GROWN DEAR TO MY HEART.
BUT THREE DAYS AGO WHILE TENDING A YOUNG NISK TREE AT THE FOREST'S EDGE, YOU PERFORMED A FORBIDDEN ACT -- YOU LET A MORTAL MAN STEAL A KISS. KNOWING MY MAGIC WOULD DETECT THIS ACT, YOU NEVERTHELESS TRIED TO KEEP IT SECRET. DO I SPEAK TRULY?
Y-YOUR MAJESTY, I--
DO I SPEAK TRULY?
--I--
...YES, YOUR MAJESTY.
OH, NELANTHE... MY HEART FADES BLACK WITH GRIEF, BUT MY DUTY TO THE LAW REMAINS CLEAR. YOU ARE NO LONGER A DAUGHTER OF THE FOREST. I REVOKE YOUR IMMORTALITY AND BANISH YOU FROM BURZEE FOREVER.
NO, YOUR MAJESTY! IF YOU TAKE AWAY HER IMMORTALITY, SHE'LL GROW OLD AND DIE LIKE -- LIKE -- A MORTAL!
SILENCE, NEBELLE, BEFORE I BANISH YOU, TOO! THE LAW OF THE FOREST MUST BE UPHELD!
GO, NELANTHE, YOU ARE A MORTAL NOW. RUN AND JOIN YOUR KIND! RUN, NELANTHE, RUN, RUN...

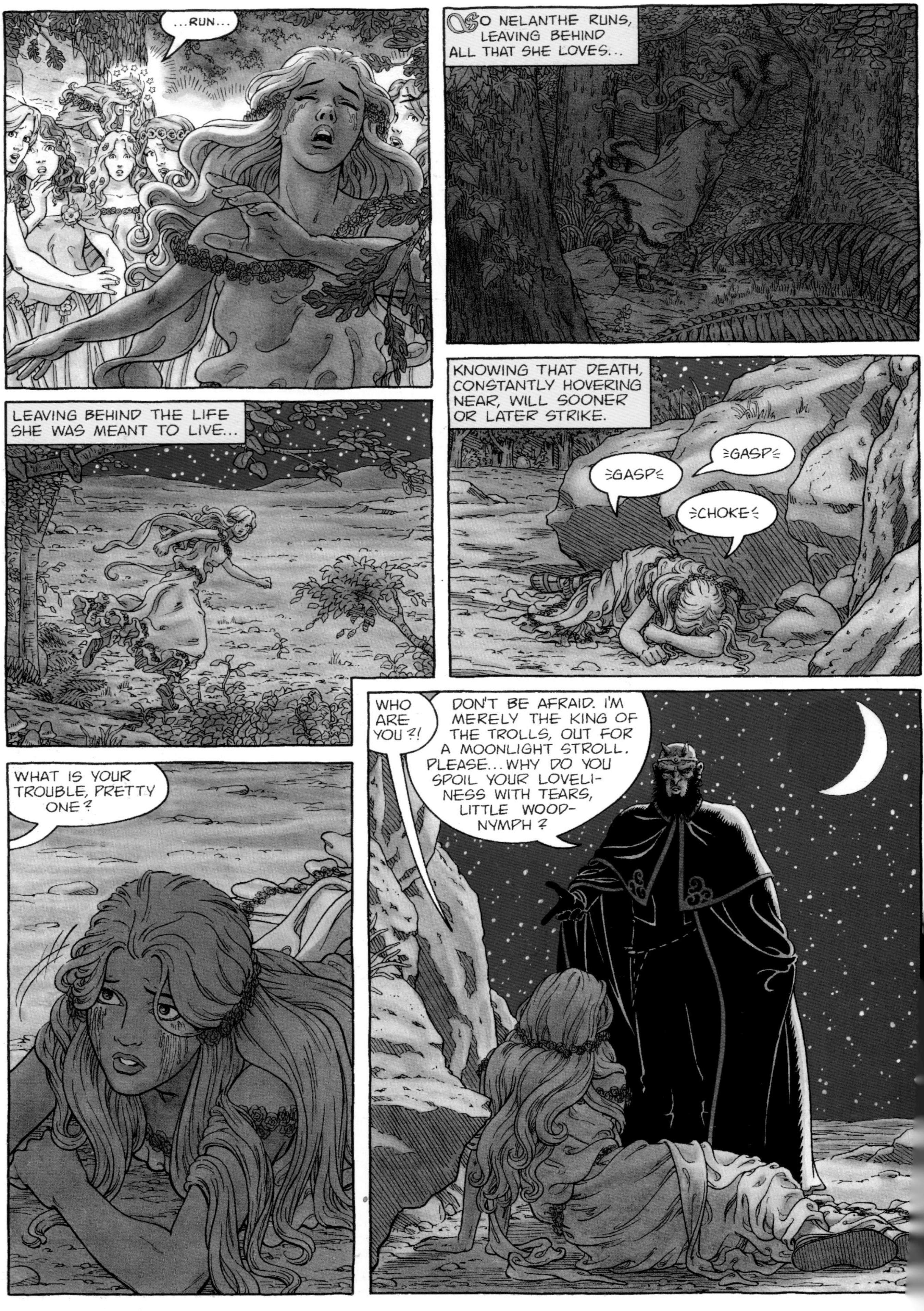
...RUN...
SO NELANTHE RUNS, LEAVING BEHIND ALL THAT SHE LOVES...
LEAVING BEHIND THE LIFE SHE WAS MEANT TO LIVE...
KNOWING THAT DEATH, CONSTANTLY HOVERING NEAR, WILL SOONER OR LATER STRIKE.
GASP
GASP
CHOKE
WHAT IS YOUR TROUBLE, PRETTY ONE?
WHO ARE YOU?!
DON'T BE AFRAID. I'M MERELY THE KING OF THE TROLLS, OUT FOR A MOONLIGHT STROLL. PLEASE... WHY DO YOU SPOIL YOUR LOVELI-NESS WITH TEARS, LITTLE WOOD-NYMPH?

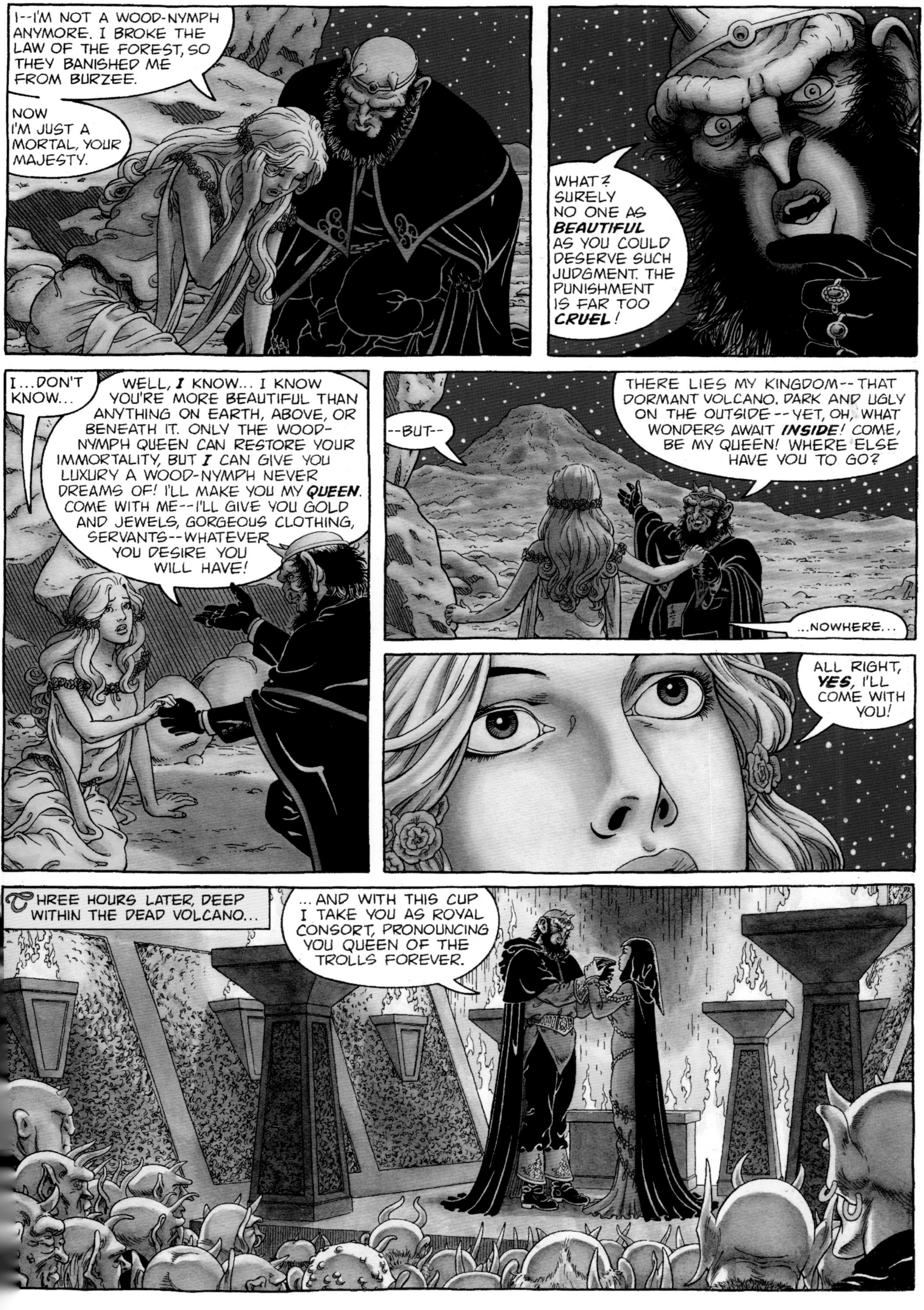
I--I'M NOT A WOOD-NYMPH ANYMORE. I BROKE THE LAW OF THE FOREST, SO THEY BANISHED ME FROM BURZEE.
NOW I'M JUST A MORTAL, YOUR MAJESTY.
WHAT? SURELY NO ONE AS BEAUTIFUL AS YOU COULD DESERVE SUCH JUDGMENT. THE PUNISHMENT IS FAR TOO CRUEL!
I...DON'T KNOW...
WELL, I KNOW... I KNOW YOU'RE MORE BEAUTIFUL THAN ANYTHING ON EARTH, ABOVE, OR BENEATH IT. ONLY THE WOOD-NYMPH QUEEN CAN RESTORE YOUR IMMORTALITY, BUT I CAN GIVE YOU LUXURY A WOOD-NYMPH NEVER DREAMS OF! I'LL MAKE YOU MY QUEEN. COME WITH ME--I'LL GIVE YOU GOLD AND JEWELS, GORGEOUS CLOTHING, SERVANTS--WHATEVER YOU DESIRE YOU WILL HAVE!
--BUT--
THERE LIES MY KINGDOM--THAT DORMANT VOLCANO. DARK AND UGLY ON THE OUTSIDE--YET, OH, WHAT WONDERS AWAIT INSIDE! COME, BE MY QUEEN! WHERE ELSE HAVE YOU TO GO?
...NOWHERE...
ALL RIGHT, YES, I'LL COME WITH YOU!
THREE HOURS LATER, DEEP WITHIN THE DEAD VOLCANO...
...AND WITH THIS CUP I TAKE YOU AS ROYAL CONSORT, PRONOUNCING YOU QUEEN OF THE TROLLS FOREVER.

THE TROLL KING'S PROMISES ALL COME TRUE -- BUT, AS THE MONTHS PASS, NELANTHE BROODS.

THE KING IS RIGHT. TAKING AWAY MY IMMORTALITY WASN'T JUSTICE--IT WAS *CRUELTY!* I KISSED A MORTAL MAN--*ONCE*--SO WHAT? I ONLY WANTED TO KNOW WHAT IT WAS LIKE. *HE* DID MOST OF THE KISSING ANYWAY--NOT ME.

BUT THOSE STUPID WOOD-NYMPHS WOULDN'T LISTEN. THEY WERE *JEALOUS*-- YES, THAT'S IT. WELL, IF THEY SAW ME NOW, I'D SHOW THEM *REASON* TO BE JEALOUS! AND THAT PUSHY, SMIRKING ZURLINE--HOW I *HATE* HER AND HER SILLY LAW OF THE FOREST. THE FOREST HAS LIVED FOR CENTURIES. IT WILL *GO ON* LIVING--UNLESS...

I MUST SUMMON A COUNCIL IMMEDIATELY!

YOUR MAJESTY, HONORED COUNCILLORS, I HAVE CALLED YOU TONIGHT BECAUSE I WISH TO PROPOSE AN *IDEA*, ONE I URGENTLY HOPE YOU'LL SUPPORT.

TELL US YOUR PROPOSAL.

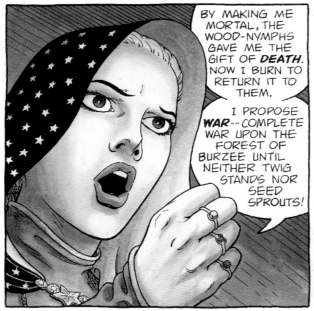

BY MAKING ME MORTAL, THE WOOD-NYMPHS GAVE ME THE GIFT OF *DEATH*. NOW I BURN TO RETURN IT TO THEM.

I PROPOSE *WAR*--COMPLETE WAR UPON THE FOREST OF BURZEE UNTIL NEITHER TWIG STANDS NOR SEED SPROUTS!

YOUR HIGHNESS, THE WOOD-NYMPHS ARE OUR NATURAL *ENEMIES*. WE'VE LONG DESIRED TO DESTROY THEM, BUT THE CHANCE OF SUCCESS IS SO SLIGHT THAT--

HEH HEH...

THAT'S RIGHT, ≥SNORT≥ OUR TROLL ARMY COULD NEVER DEFEAT THEIR *MAGIC*.

166

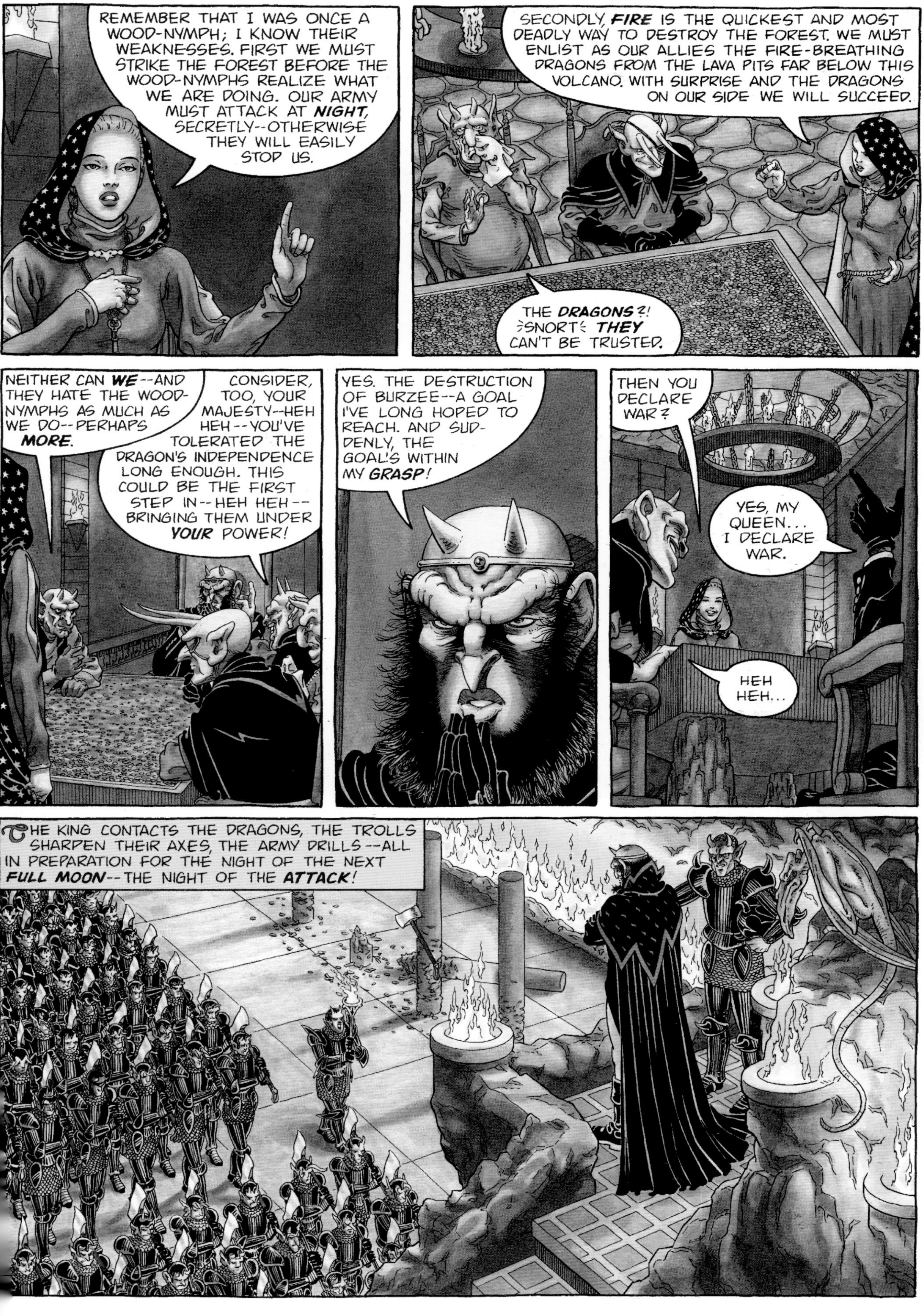
REMEMBER THAT I WAS ONCE A WOOD-NYMPH; I KNOW THEIR WEAKNESSES. FIRST WE MUST STRIKE THE FOREST BEFORE THE WOOD-NYMPHS REALIZE WHAT WE ARE DOING. OUR ARMY MUST ATTACK AT **NIGHT**, SECRETLY--OTHERWISE THEY WILL EASILY STOP US.
SECONDLY, **FIRE** IS THE QUICKEST AND MOST DEADLY WAY TO DESTROY THE FOREST. WE MUST ENLIST AS OUR ALLIES THE FIRE-BREATHING DRAGONS FROM THE LAVA PITS FAR BELOW THIS VOLCANO. WITH SURPRISE AND THE DRAGONS ON OUR SIDE WE WILL SUCCEED.
THE **DRAGONS**?! *SNORT* **THEY** CAN'T BE TRUSTED.
NEITHER CAN **WE**--AND THEY HATE THE WOOD-NYMPHS AS MUCH AS WE DO--PERHAPS **MORE**.
CONSIDER, TOO, YOUR MAJESTY--HEH HEH--YOU'VE TOLERATED THE DRAGON'S INDEPENDENCE LONG ENOUGH. THIS COULD BE THE FIRST STEP IN--HEH HEH--BRINGING THEM UNDER **YOUR** POWER!
YES. THE DESTRUCTION OF BURZEE--A GOAL I'VE LONG HOPED TO REACH. AND SUDDENLY, THE GOAL'S WITHIN MY **GRASP**!
THEN YOU DECLARE WAR?
YES, MY QUEEN... I DECLARE WAR.
HEH HEH...
THE KING CONTACTS THE DRAGONS, THE TROLLS SHARPEN THEIR AXES, THE ARMY DRILLS--ALL IN PREPARATION FOR THE NIGHT OF THE NEXT **FULL MOON**--THE NIGHT OF THE **ATTACK**!

THE NIGHT ARRIVES.

OH, WHAT'S THE MATTER WITH ME? EVER SINCE THE KING DECLARED WAR, I'VE BEEN HAVING SECOND THOUGHTS.

WHY?

WHY?

SOMETIMES I ALMOST WISH TO RETURN TO BURZEE... TO LAUGH WITH THE OTHERS BY CRYSTAL SPRINGS...

...TO DANCE UPON THE SUNBEAMS THAT SPLIT THE LAYERS OF GLOWING LEAVES... AND, AH, TO TEND THE MAGNIFICENT TREES...

THE CURSED TREES! SLAVING OVER THEM DAY AFTER DAY-- AND FOR WHAT? USELESS, USELESS, USELESS!

rrrip

YAAAA!

IF ONLY I COULD FORGET! I NEED TO FORGET! BUT HOW?

CRASH

HOW? I CAN'T GO-- OH!

WHAT'S THIS?

...PEDIA of...
...and of A-Ramose.
...owerful spell.
...f Velkemin
...lden Valley of
...Sea of Sighs
...race of wasps
...nagical stings.
...sting of a wasp
...painful, though
...granted to the
...the stinger is
...he wasp dies.

ENCYCLOPÆDIA of MAGIC
The Water of Oblivion
In the royal gardens of the Emerald City is the Forbidden Fountain containing the potent Water of Oblivion. This water is capable of completely erasing the memory of any being who drinks it. For this reason Ozma, ruler of Oz, has decreed the water forbidden to all.

Long ago Glinda, Good Sorceress of the South, placed the fountain in 1043

# Chapter Two Sounds in the Night

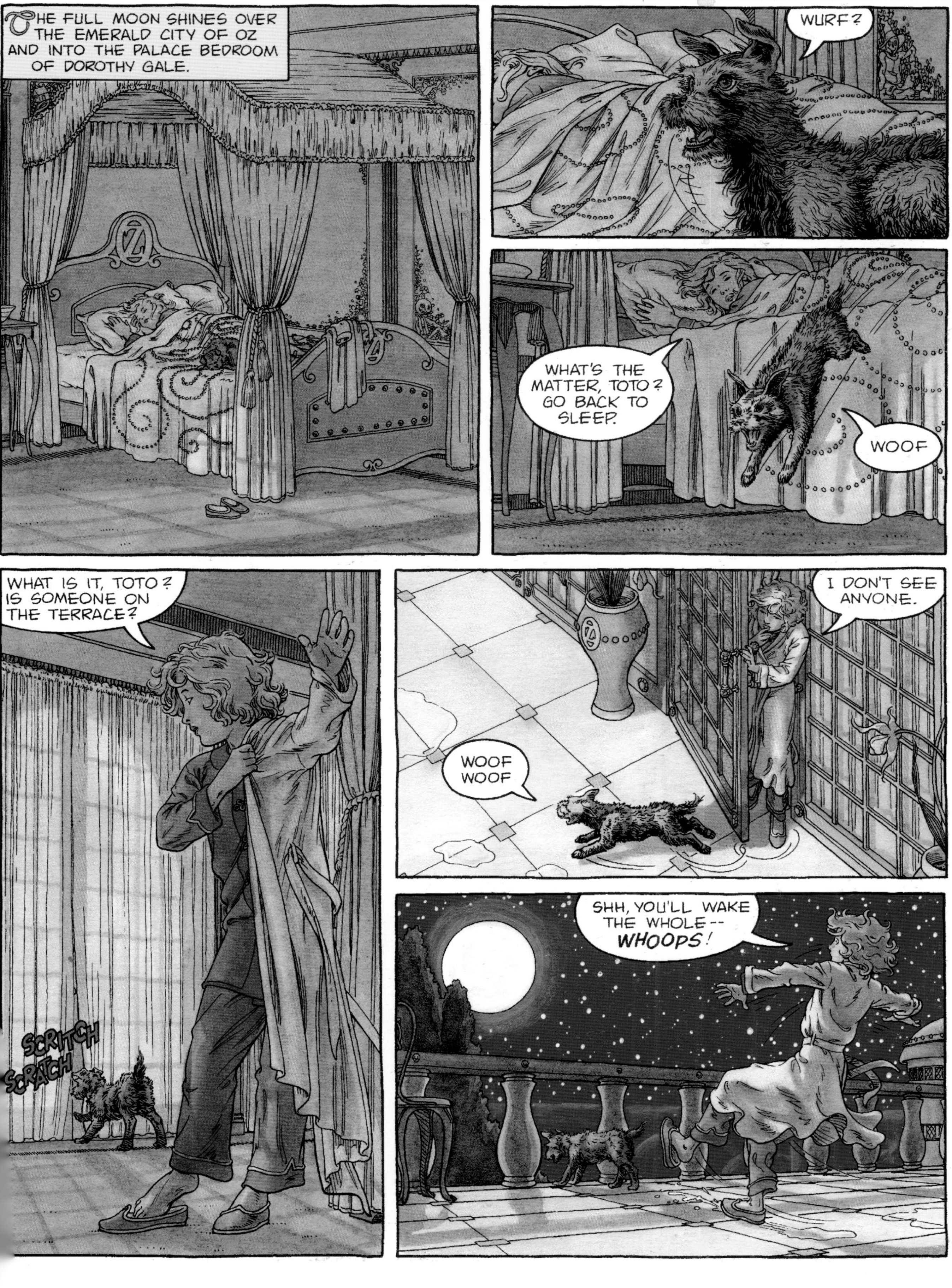
THE FULL MOON SHINES OVER THE EMERALD CITY OF OZ AND INTO THE PALACE BEDROOM OF DOROTHY GALE.
WURF?
WHAT'S THE MATTER, TOTO? GO BACK TO SLEEP.
WOOF
WHAT IS IT, TOTO? IS SOMEONE ON THE TERRACE?
SCRITCH
SCRATCH
I DON'T SEE ANYONE.
WOOF WOOF
SHH, YOU'LL WAKE THE WHOLE-- WHOOPS!

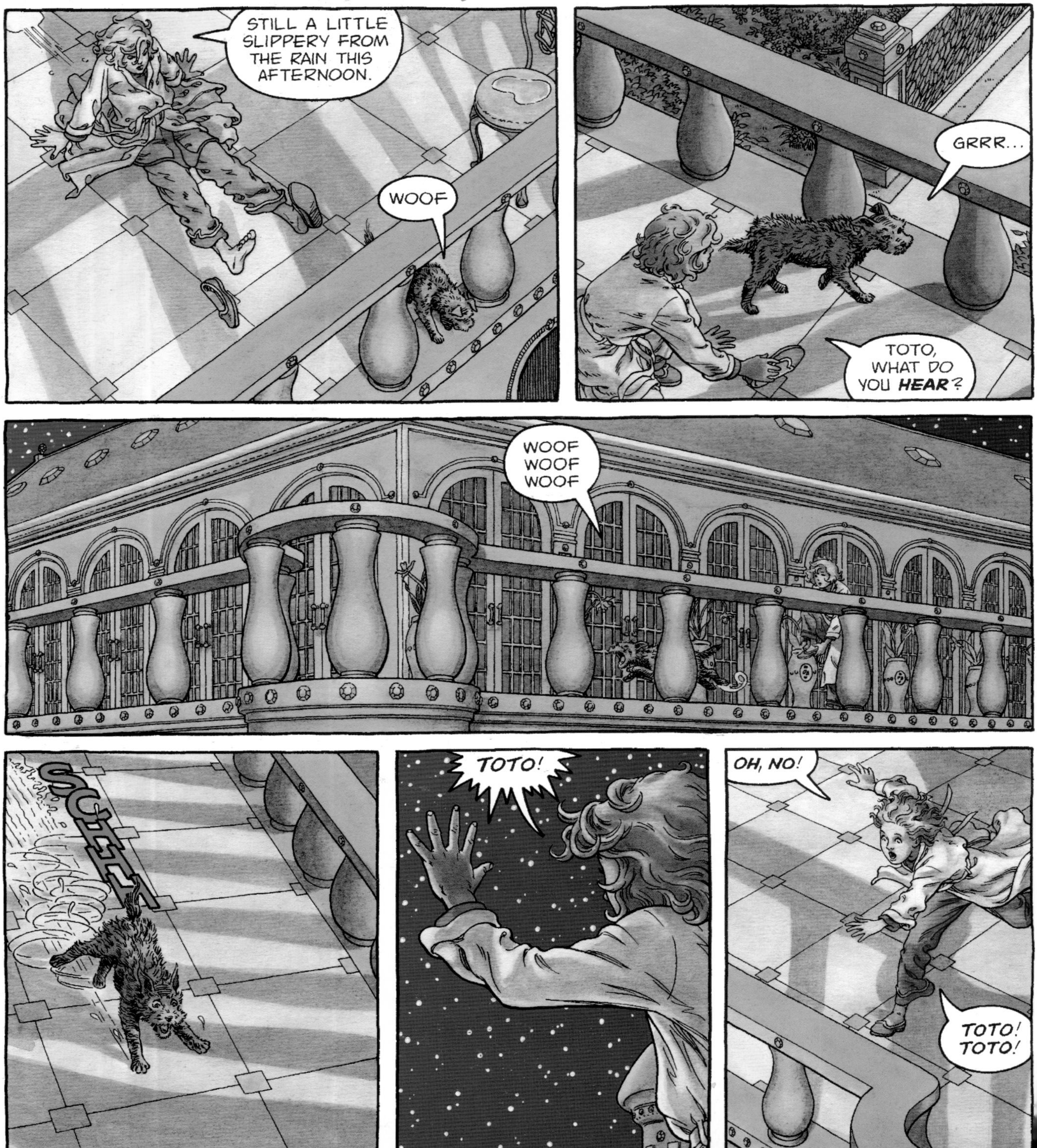
STILL A LITTLE SLIPPERY FROM THE RAIN THIS AFTERNOON.
WOOF
GRRR...
TOTO, WHAT DO YOU **HEAR**?
WOOF WOOF WOOF
SCHH
TOTO!
OH, NO!
TOTO! TOTO!

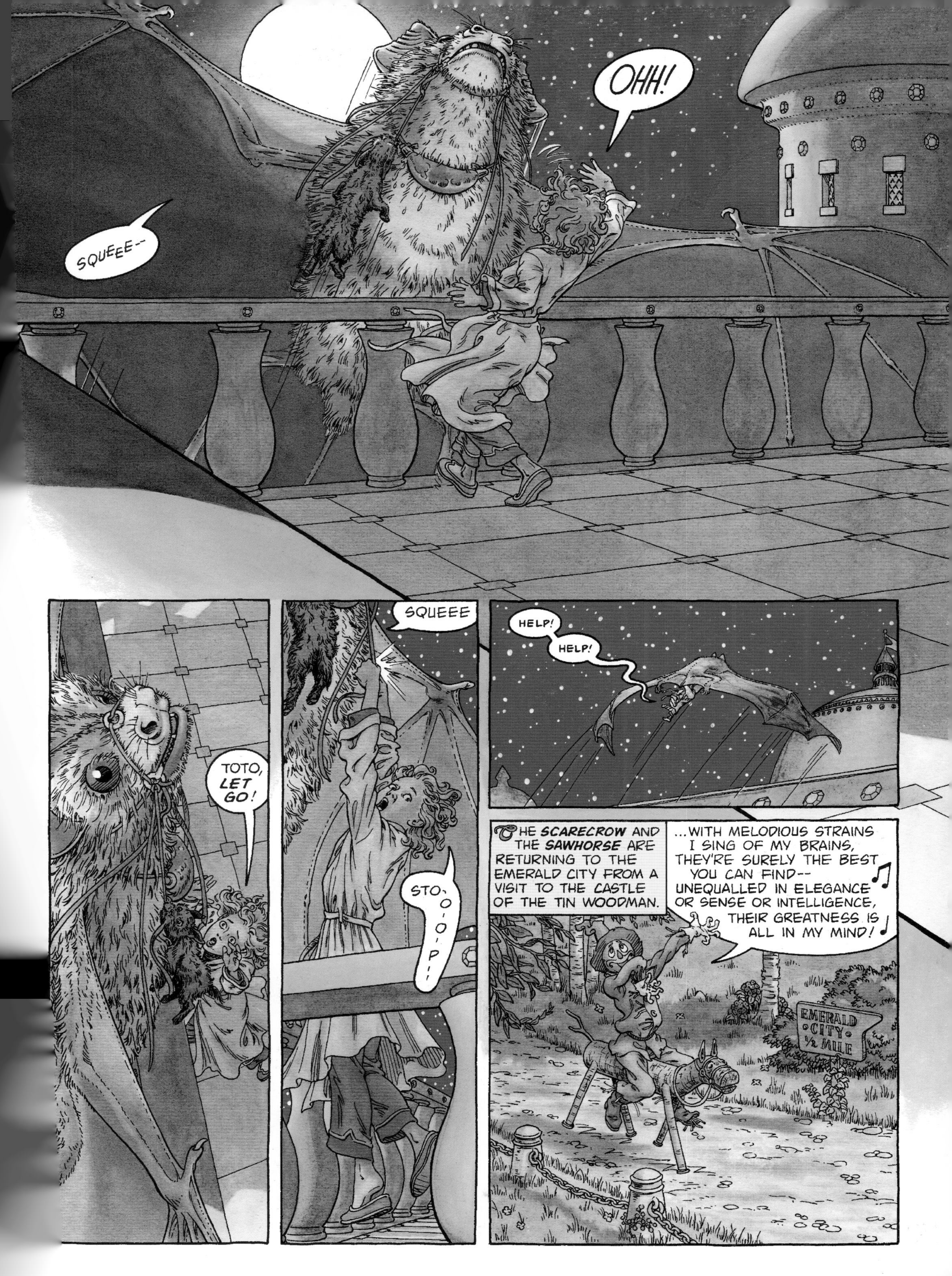
SQUEEE--
OHH!
TOTO, LET GO!
SQUEEE
STO-O-O-P!
HELP!
HELP!
THE SCARECROW AND THE SAWHORSE ARE RETURNING TO THE EMERALD CITY FROM A VISIT TO THE CASTLE OF THE TIN WOODMAN.
...WITH MELODIOUS STRAINS I SING OF MY BRAINS, THEY'RE SURELY THE BEST YOU CAN FIND-- UNEQUALLED IN ELEGANCE OR SENSE OR INTELLIGENCE, THEIR GREATNESS IS ALL IN MY MIND!
EMERALD CITY ½ MILE

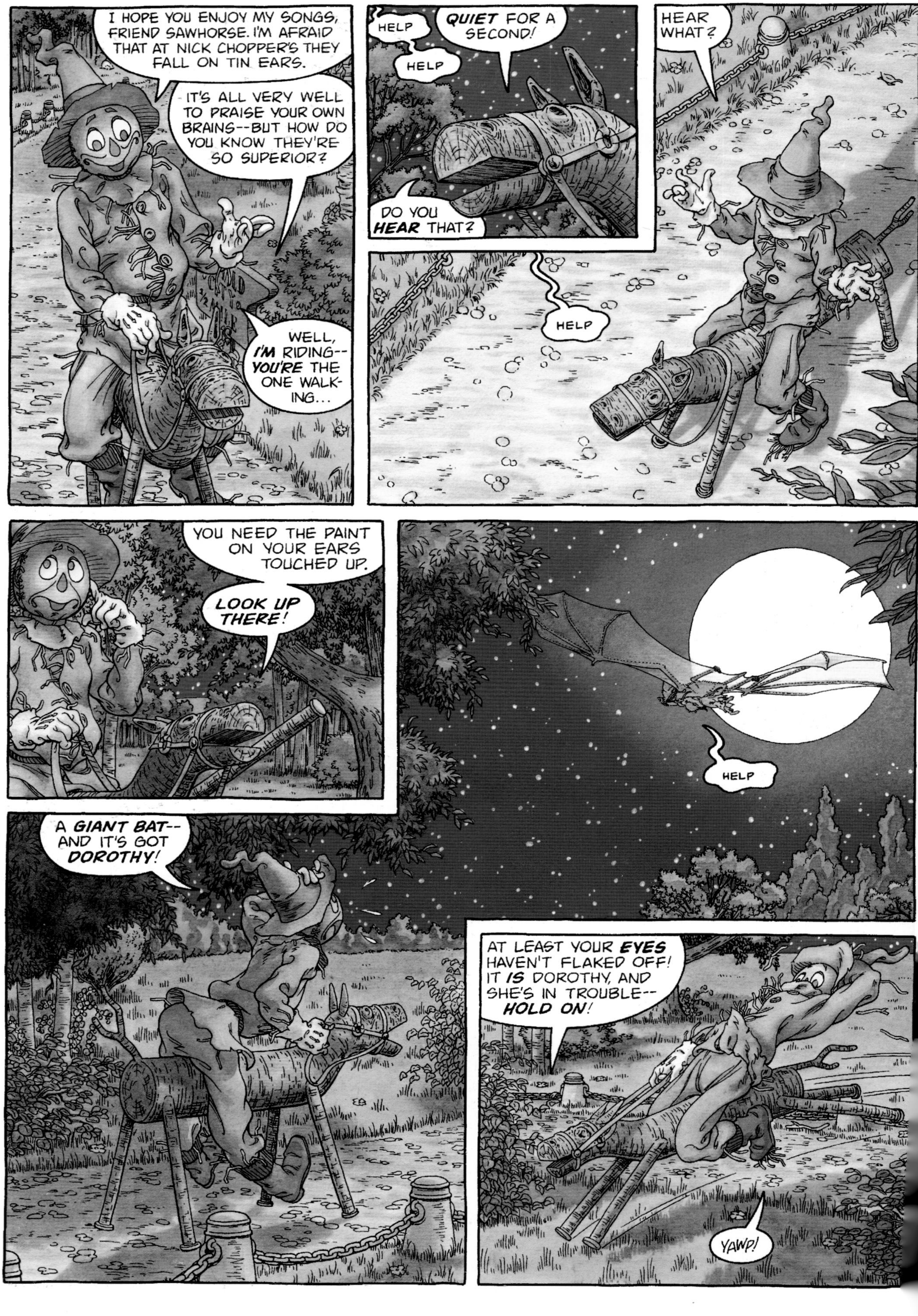

I HOPE YOU ENJOY MY SONGS, FRIEND SAWHORSE. I'M AFRAID THAT AT NICK CHOPPER'S THEY FALL ON TIN EARS.
IT'S ALL VERY WELL TO PRAISE YOUR OWN BRAINS--BUT HOW DO YOU KNOW THEY'RE SO SUPERIOR?
WELL, *I'M* RIDING-- *YOU'RE* THE ONE WALKING...
HELP
HELP
*QUIET* FOR A SECOND!
DO YOU *HEAR* THAT?
HEAR WHAT?
HELP
YOU NEED THE PAINT ON YOUR EARS TOUCHED UP.
*LOOK UP THERE!*
HELP
A *GIANT BAT*-- AND IT'S GOT *DOROTHY*!
AT LEAST YOUR *EYES* HAVEN'T FLAKED OFF! IT *IS* DOROTHY, AND SHE'S IN TROUBLE-- *HOLD ON*!
YAWP!

OVER THE FERTILE FIELDS OF OZ FLASH THE TIRELESS LEGS OF THE SAWHORSE.

MU-MU-MUST YOU RU-RUN S-SO BU-BU-*BUMPILY*?

CAN'T HELP IT--BESIDES, NO ONE ELSE IN OZ COULD KEEP UP WITH THAT BAT.

KEEP YOUR EYE ON IT. WE CAN'T AFFORD TO LOSE IT BEFORE IT LANDS!

BU-BUT WHAT I-IF IT FLIES O-O-OVER THE...

...*DESERT*?

WHAT NOW?

DOROTHY NEEDS HELP-- *LET'S GO!*

DANGER! TURN BACK!
YOU HAVE REACHED THE
DEADLY DESERT
WHICH COMPLETELY SURROUNDS THE
MARVELOUS LAND *of* OZ.
ONE TOUCH OF THESE DANGEROUS SANDS WILL TURN ANY LIVING FLESH TO DUST IN AN INSTANT. ALL PERSONS ARE WARNED TO STAND WELL AWAY FROM THE EDGE TO AVOID BEING OVERCOME BY DESERT'S NOXIOUS FUMES.

BUT--

LOOK, *I'M* NOT MADE OF FLESH, AND MY FEET ARE SHOD WITH GOLD AS WELL. IF *YOU'RE* SCARED, JUST DON'T FALL OFF.

BUT THE *NOXIOUS FUMES*--!

YOU'RE STUFFED WITH *STRAW*! YOU DON'T BREATHE AND NEITHER DO I -- STOP WORRYING!

YOU'RE RIGHT.

I WONDER WHY MY BRAINS NEVER THOUGHT OF THIS BEFORE...

173

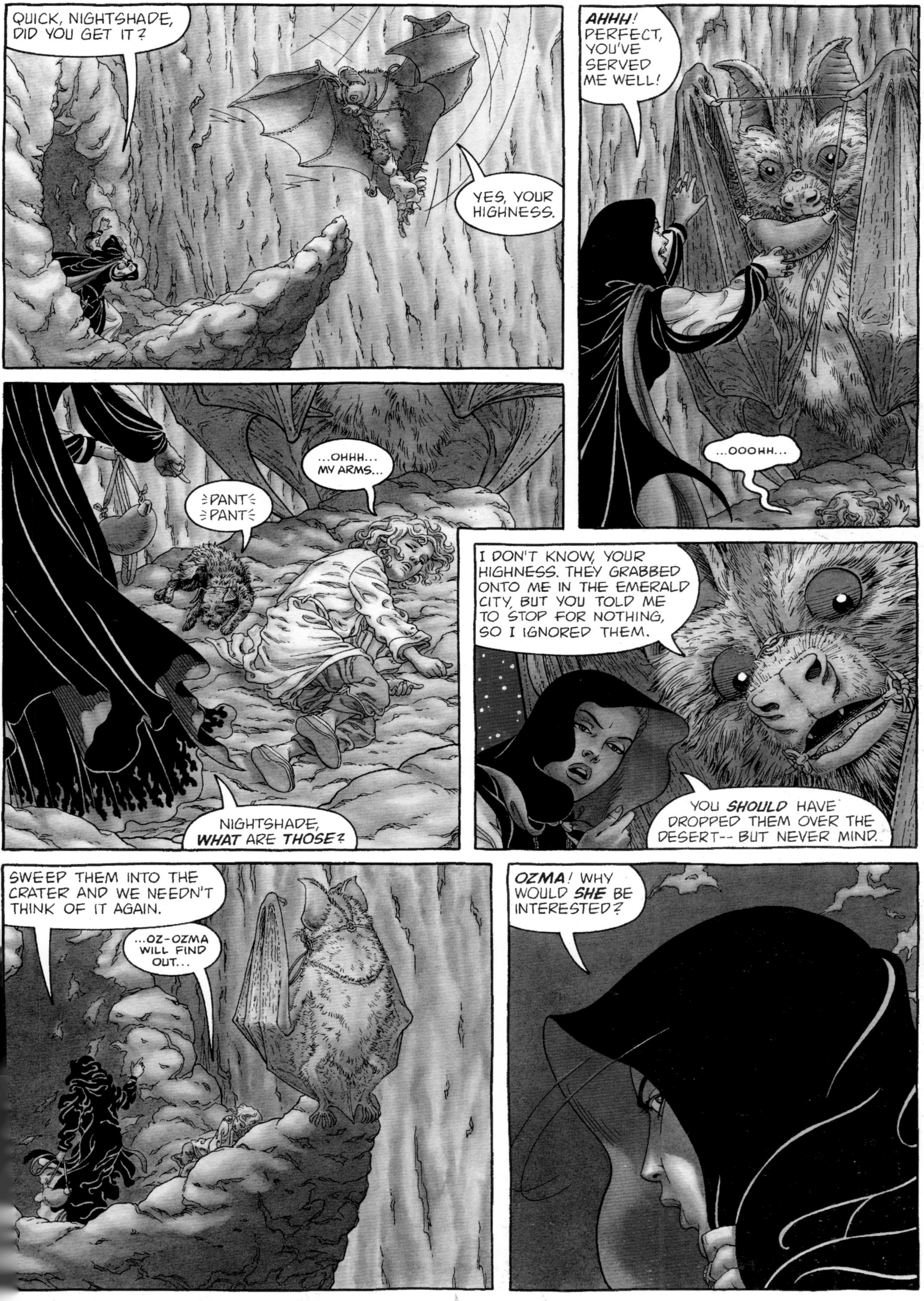
QUICK, NIGHTSHADE, DID YOU GET IT?
YES, YOUR HIGHNESS.
AHHH! PERFECT, YOU'VE SERVED ME WELL!
...OOOHH...
...OHHH... MY ARMS...
PANT PANT
NIGHTSHADE, WHAT ARE THOSE?
I DON'T KNOW, YOUR HIGHNESS. THEY GRABBED ONTO ME IN THE EMERALD CITY, BUT YOU TOLD ME TO STOP FOR NOTHING, SO I IGNORED THEM.
YOU SHOULD HAVE DROPPED THEM OVER THE DESERT-- BUT NEVER MIND.
SWEEP THEM INTO THE CRATER AND WE NEEDN'T THINK OF IT AGAIN.
...OZ-OZMA WILL FIND OUT...
OZMA! WHY WOULD SHE BE INTERESTED?

OZMA IS MY **BEST FRIEND.** I'M PRINCESS DOROTHY AND THIS IS TOTO. I WARN YOU--IF YOU HURT US, OZMA WILL *PUNISH* YOU.

VERY WELL.

BOTH OF YOU, FOLLOW ME.

NIGHTSHADE, WAIT FOR MY RETURN. SOON WE SHALL HELP LEAD THE ARMY TO THE ATTACK.

WHO ARE YOU? WHAT'LL YOU DO WITH US?

I AM THE QUEEN OF THE TROLLS. DON'T WORRY-- YOU WON'T BE HURT.

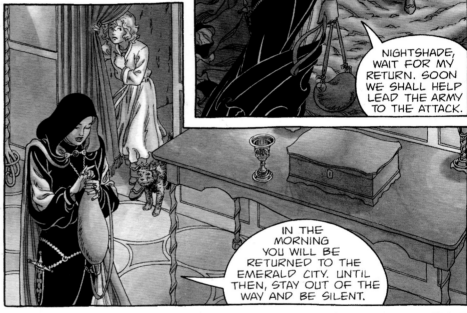

IN THE MORNING YOU WILL BE RETURNED TO THE EMERALD CITY. UNTIL THEN, STAY OUT OF THE WAY AND BE SILENT.

glup·glup·glup

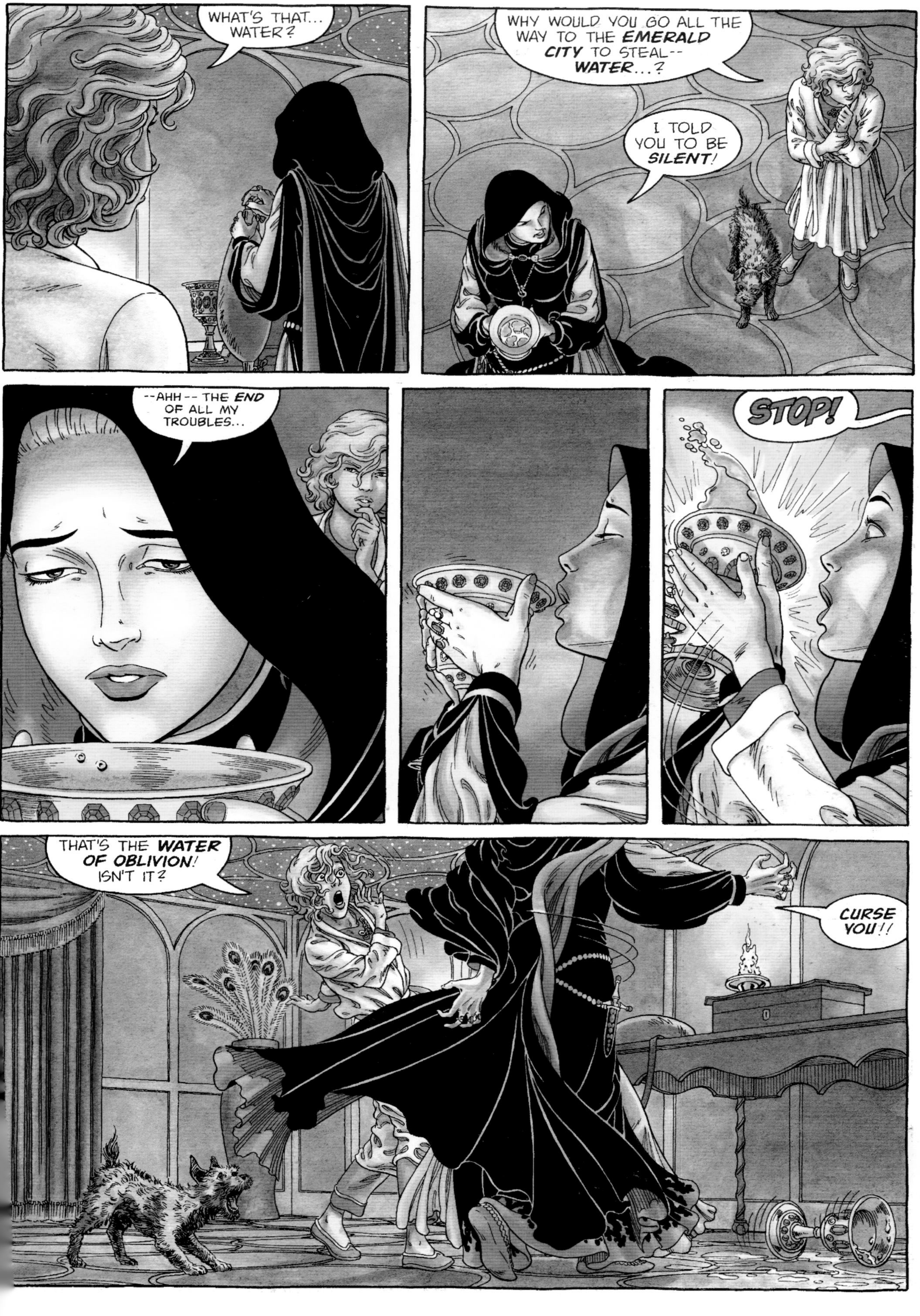
WHAT'S THAT... WATER?
WHY WOULD YOU GO ALL THE WAY TO THE EMERALD CITY TO STEAL-- WATER...?
I TOLD YOU TO BE SILENT!
--AHH-- THE END OF ALL MY TROUBLES...
STOP!
THAT'S THE WATER OF OBLIVION! ISN'T IT?
CURSE YOU!!

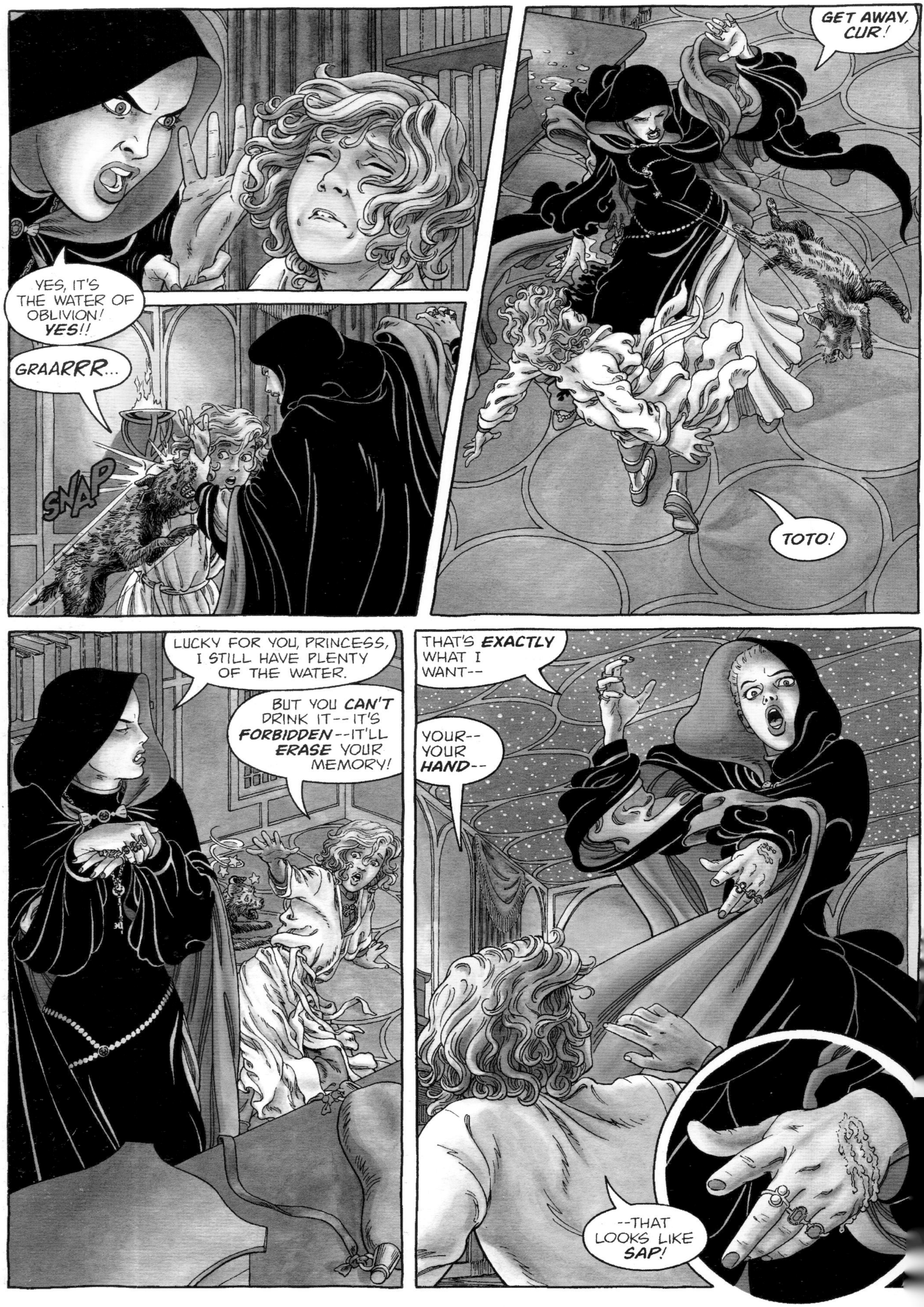
YES, IT'S THE WATER OF OBLIVION! YES!!
GET AWAY, CUR!
GRAARRR...
SNAP
TOTO!
LUCKY FOR YOU, PRINCESS, I STILL HAVE PLENTY OF THE WATER.
BUT YOU CAN'T DRINK IT--IT'S FORBIDDEN--IT'LL ERASE YOUR MEMORY!
THAT'S EXACTLY WHAT I WANT--
YOUR--YOUR HAND--
--THAT LOOKS LIKE SAP!

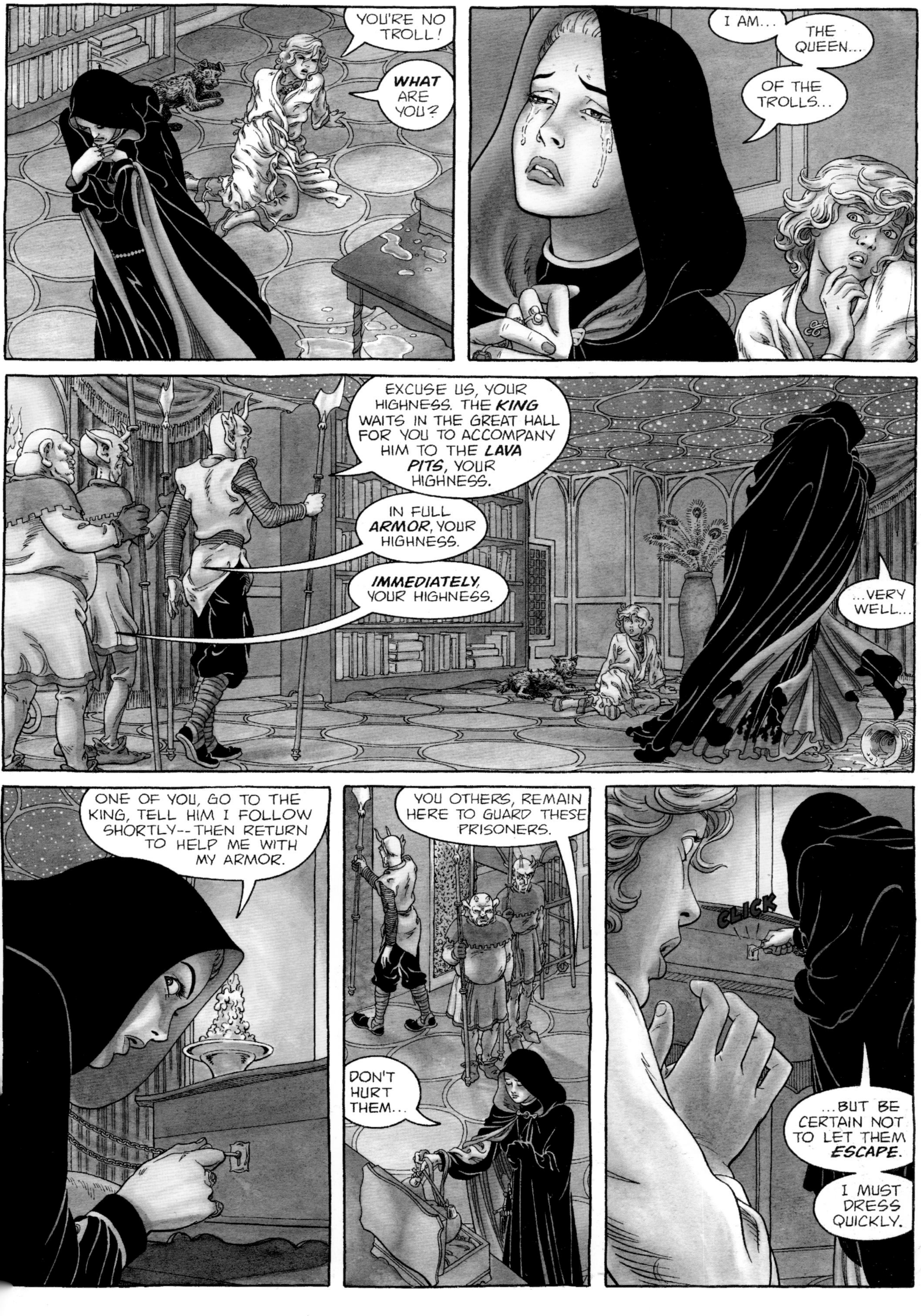
YOU'RE NO TROLL!
WHAT ARE YOU?
I AM...
THE QUEEN...
OF THE TROLLS...
EXCUSE US, YOUR HIGHNESS. THE KING WAITS IN THE GREAT HALL FOR YOU TO ACCOMPANY HIM TO THE LAVA PITS, YOUR HIGHNESS.
IN FULL ARMOR, YOUR HIGHNESS.
IMMEDIATELY, YOUR HIGHNESS.
...VERY WELL...
ONE OF YOU, GO TO THE KING, TELL HIM I FOLLOW SHORTLY--THEN RETURN TO HELP ME WITH MY ARMOR.
YOU OTHERS, REMAIN HERE TO GUARD THESE PRISONERS.
DON'T HURT THEM...
CLICK
...BUT BE CERTAIN NOT TO LET THEM ESCAPE.
I MUST DRESS QUICKLY.

# Chapter Four — In the Troll Tunnels

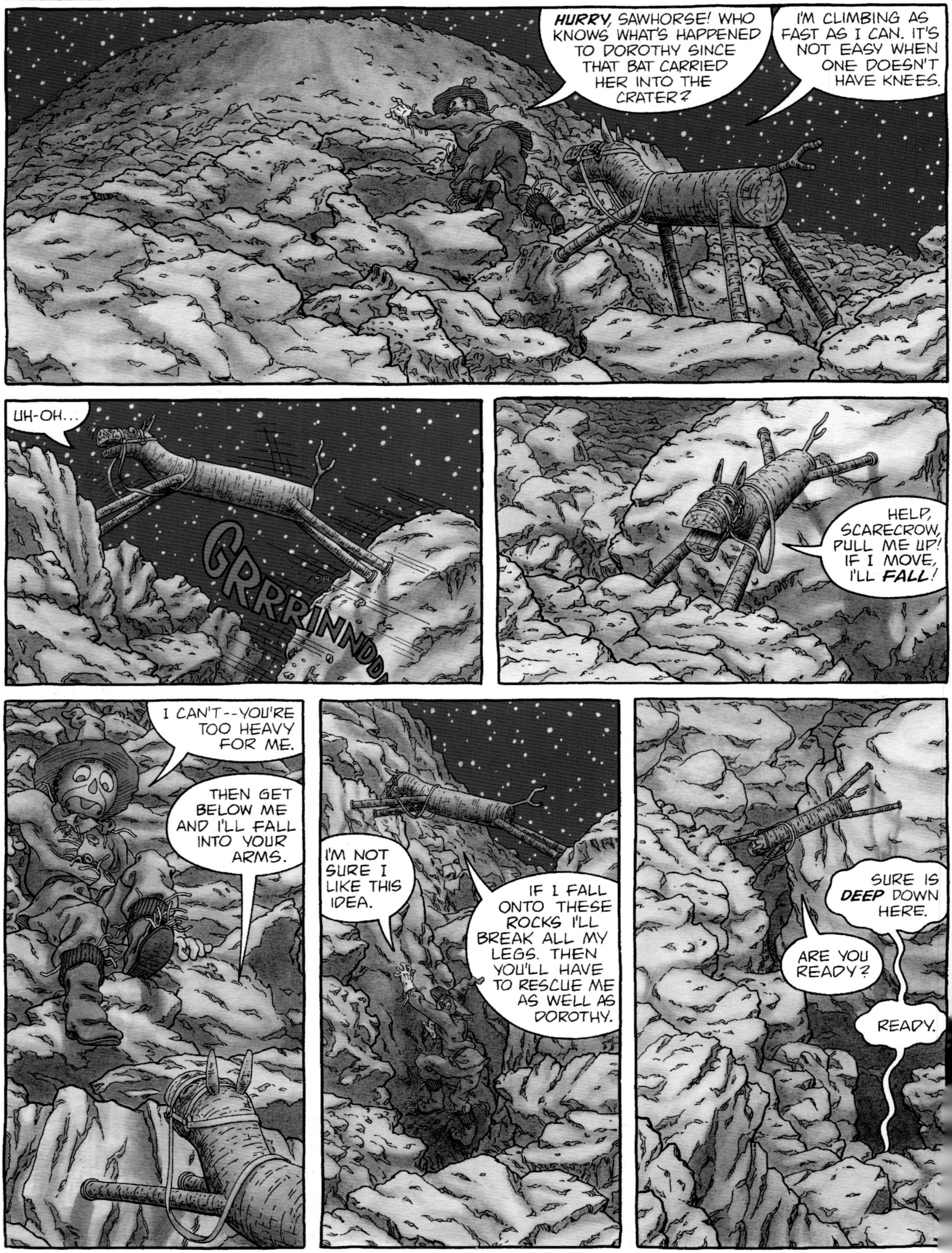

HURRY, SAWHORSE! WHO KNOWS WHAT'S HAPPENED TO DOROTHY SINCE THAT BAT CARRIED HER INTO THE CRATER?
I'M CLIMBING AS FAST AS I CAN. IT'S NOT EASY WHEN ONE DOESN'T HAVE KNEES.
UH-OH...
GRRRINNDD
HELP, SCARECROW, PULL ME UP! IF I MOVE, I'LL FALL!
I CAN'T--YOU'RE TOO HEAVY FOR ME.
THEN GET BELOW ME AND I'LL FALL INTO YOUR ARMS.
I'M NOT SURE I LIKE THIS IDEA.
IF I FALL ONTO THESE ROCKS I'LL BREAK ALL MY LEGS. THEN YOU'LL HAVE TO RESCUE ME AS WELL AS DOROTHY.
SURE IS DEEP DOWN HERE.
ARE YOU READY?
READY.

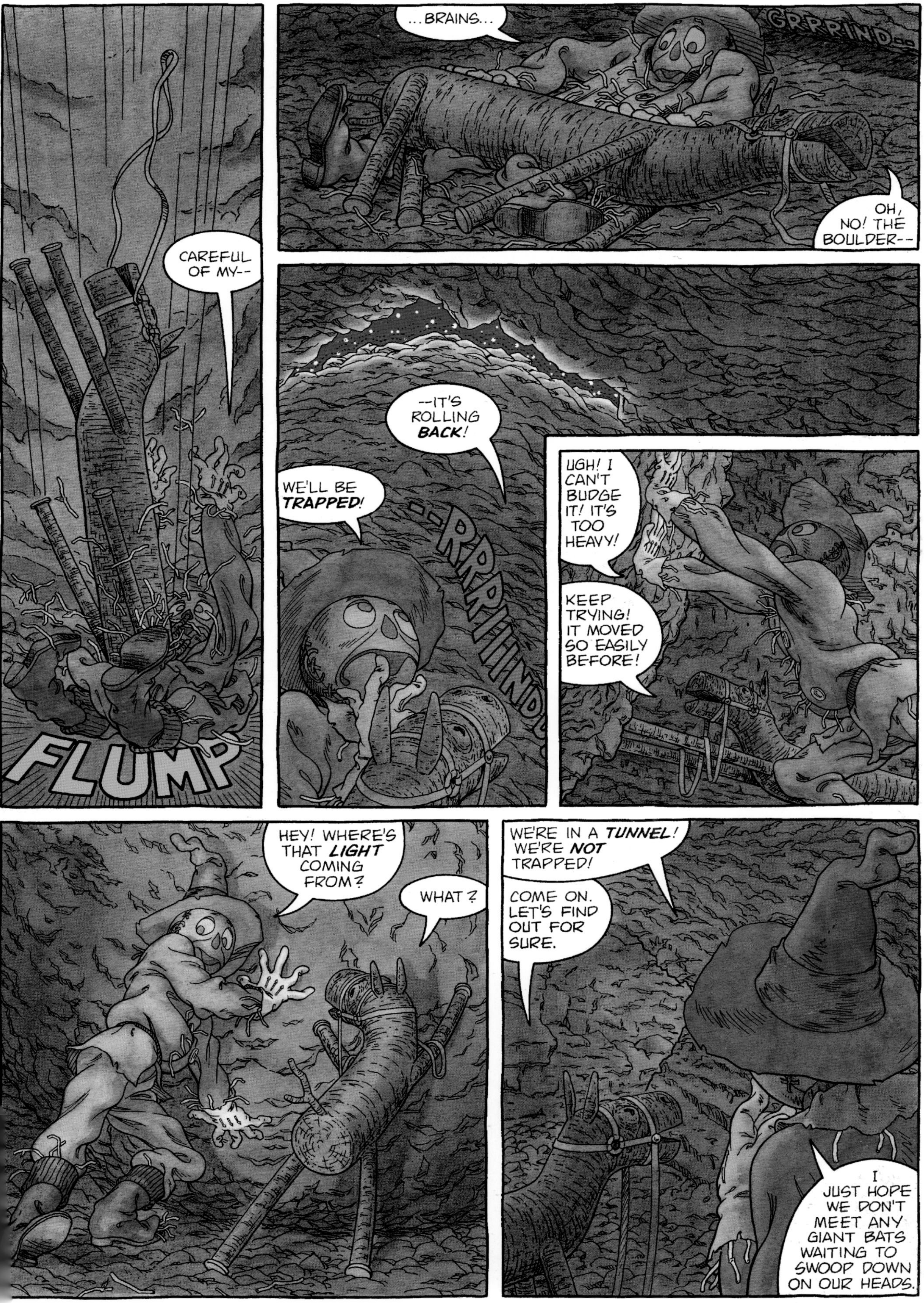
CAREFUL OF MY--
FLUMP
...BRAINS...
GRRRIND...
OH, NO! THE BOULDER--
--IT'S ROLLING BACK!
WE'LL BE TRAPPED!
--RRRIIIND
UGH! I CAN'T BUDGE IT! IT'S TOO HEAVY!
KEEP TRYING! IT MOVED SO EASILY BEFORE!
HEY! WHERE'S THAT LIGHT COMING FROM?
WHAT?
WE'RE IN A TUNNEL! WE'RE NOT TRAPPED!
COME ON. LET'S FIND OUT FOR SURE.
I JUST HOPE WE DON'T MEET ANY GIANT BATS WAITING TO SWOOP DOWN ON OUR HEADS.

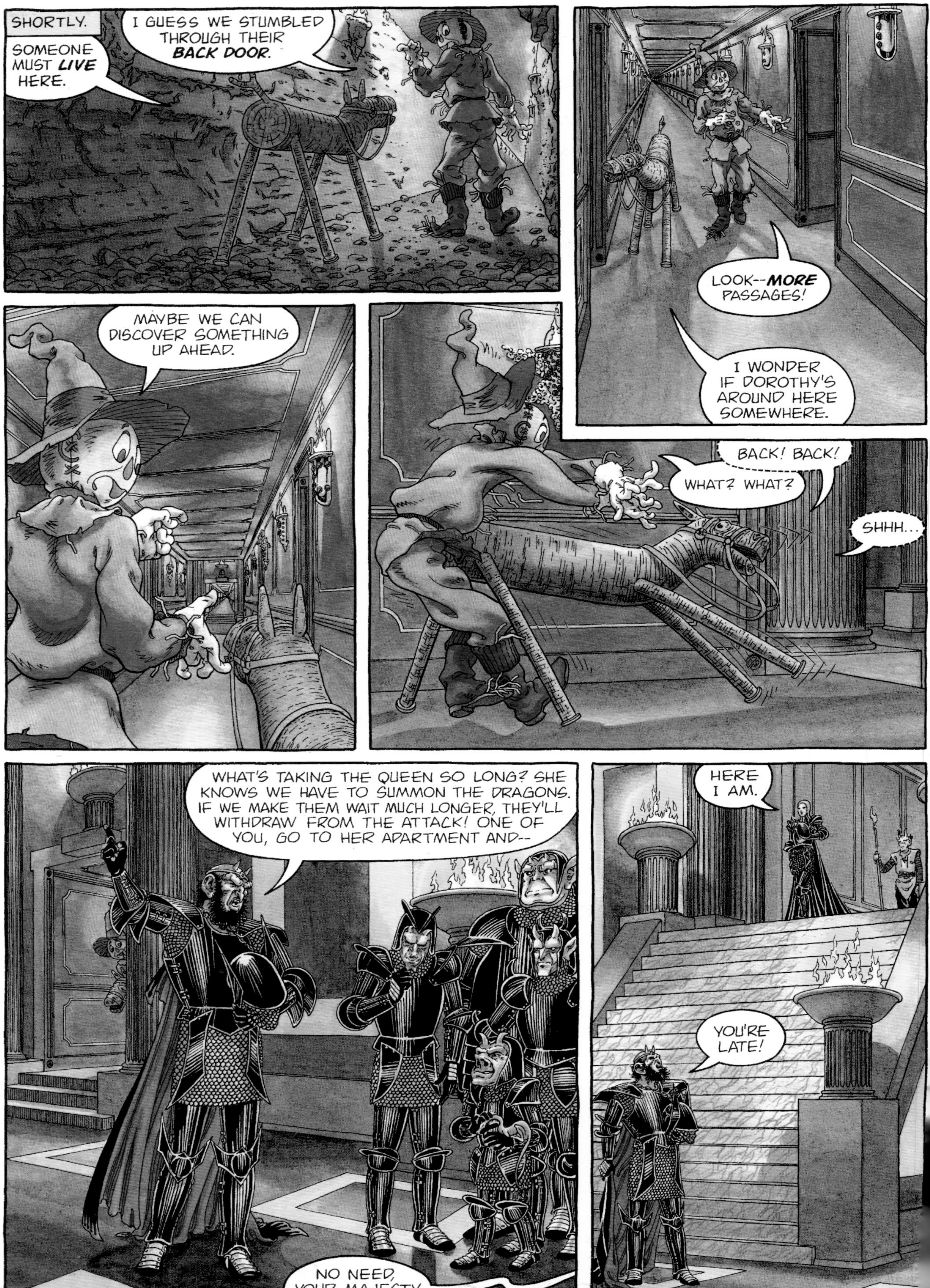
SHORTLY.
SOMEONE MUST **LIVE** HERE.
I GUESS WE STUMBLED THROUGH THEIR **BACK DOOR**.
LOOK--**MORE** PASSAGES!
I WONDER IF DOROTHY'S AROUND HERE SOMEWHERE.
MAYBE WE CAN DISCOVER SOMETHING UP AHEAD.
BACK! BACK!
WHAT? WHAT?
SHHH...
WHAT'S TAKING THE QUEEN SO LONG? SHE KNOWS WE HAVE TO SUMMON THE DRAGONS. IF WE MAKE THEM WAIT MUCH LONGER, THEY'LL WITHDRAW FROM THE ATTACK! ONE OF YOU, GO TO HER APARTMENT AND--
NO NEED, YOUR MAJESTY.
HERE I AM.
YOU'RE LATE!

FORGIVE ME, YOUR MAJESTY.

COME QUICKLY! DAWN DRAWS EVER NEARER, AND WE CANNOT SECRETLY ATTACK BURZEE *AFTER* SUNRISE.

THEY'RE COMING THIS WAY!

I WAS UNFORSEEABLY DELAYED.

HOW STRANGE THAT *TONIGHT* YOU MEET DELAY. YOU'RE NOT HAVING SECOND THOUGHTS I HOPE.

SECOND THOUGHTS, YOUR MAJESTY? NOT *I*!

AT THIS MOMENT MY CONSUMING NEED IS TO *DESTROY* THAT FOREST AND WIPE THE WOOD-NYMPHS FROM MY MEMORY *FOREVER*!

HA-*HA*! VERY GOOD!

ON TO THE *LAVA PITS*!

ARE THEY GONE?

YES, THEY TURNED DOWN ANOTHER HALLWAY.

AWP! WHAT'S THAT?

WOOOSH-SH

183

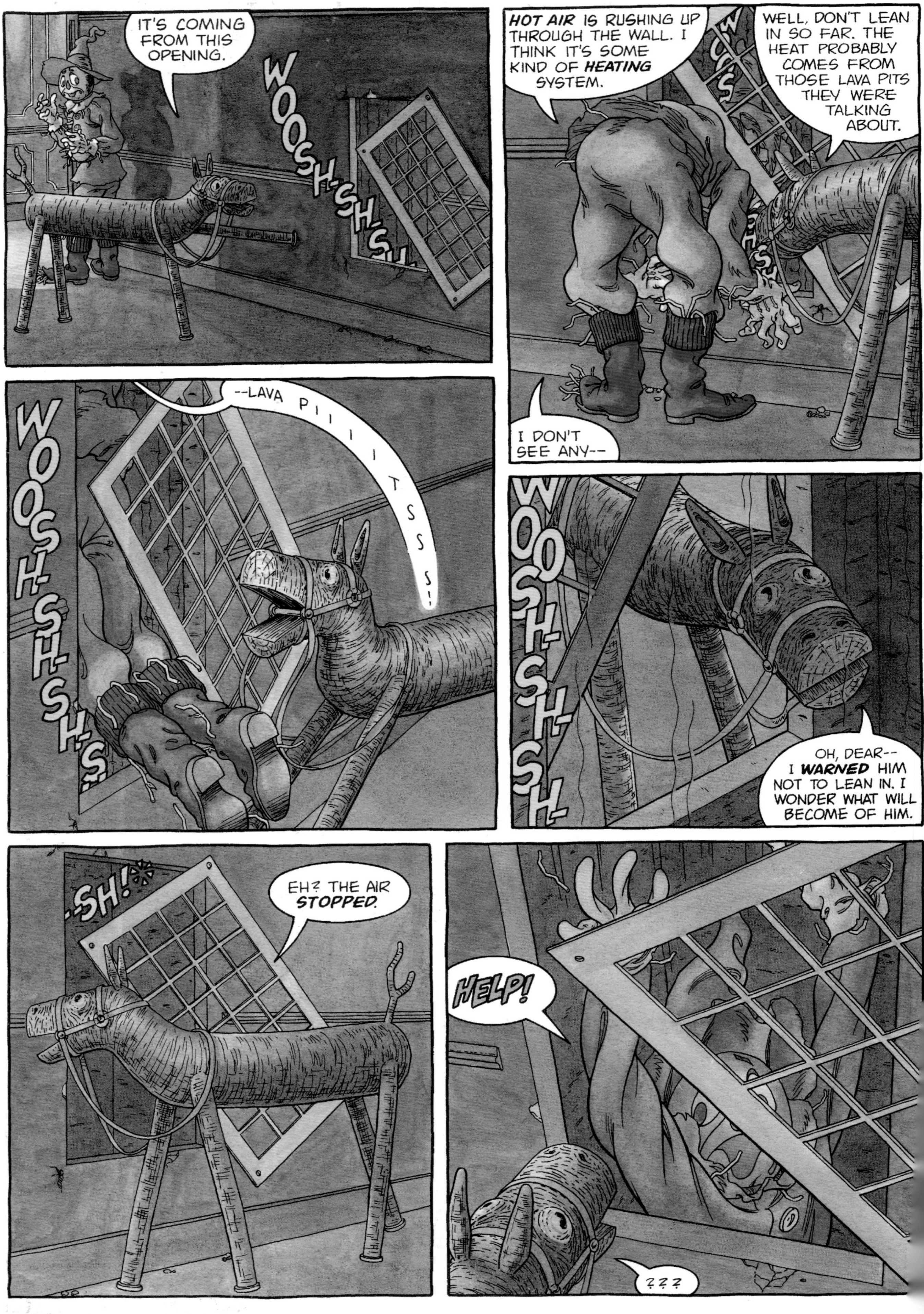
IT'S COMING FROM THIS OPENING.
WOOSH-SH-SH...
HOT AIR IS RUSHING UP THROUGH THE WALL. I THINK IT'S SOME KIND OF HEATING SYSTEM.
WELL, DON'T LEAN IN SO FAR. THE HEAT PROBABLY COMES FROM THOSE LAVA PITS THEY WERE TALKING ABOUT.
I DON'T SEE ANY--
WOOSH-SH-SH-SH-S...
--LAVA PIIIITSSSS!
WOOSH-SH-SH-
OH, DEAR-- I WARNED HIM NOT TO LEAN IN. I WONDER WHAT WILL BECOME OF HIM.
-SH!
EH? THE AIR STOPPED.
HELP!
???

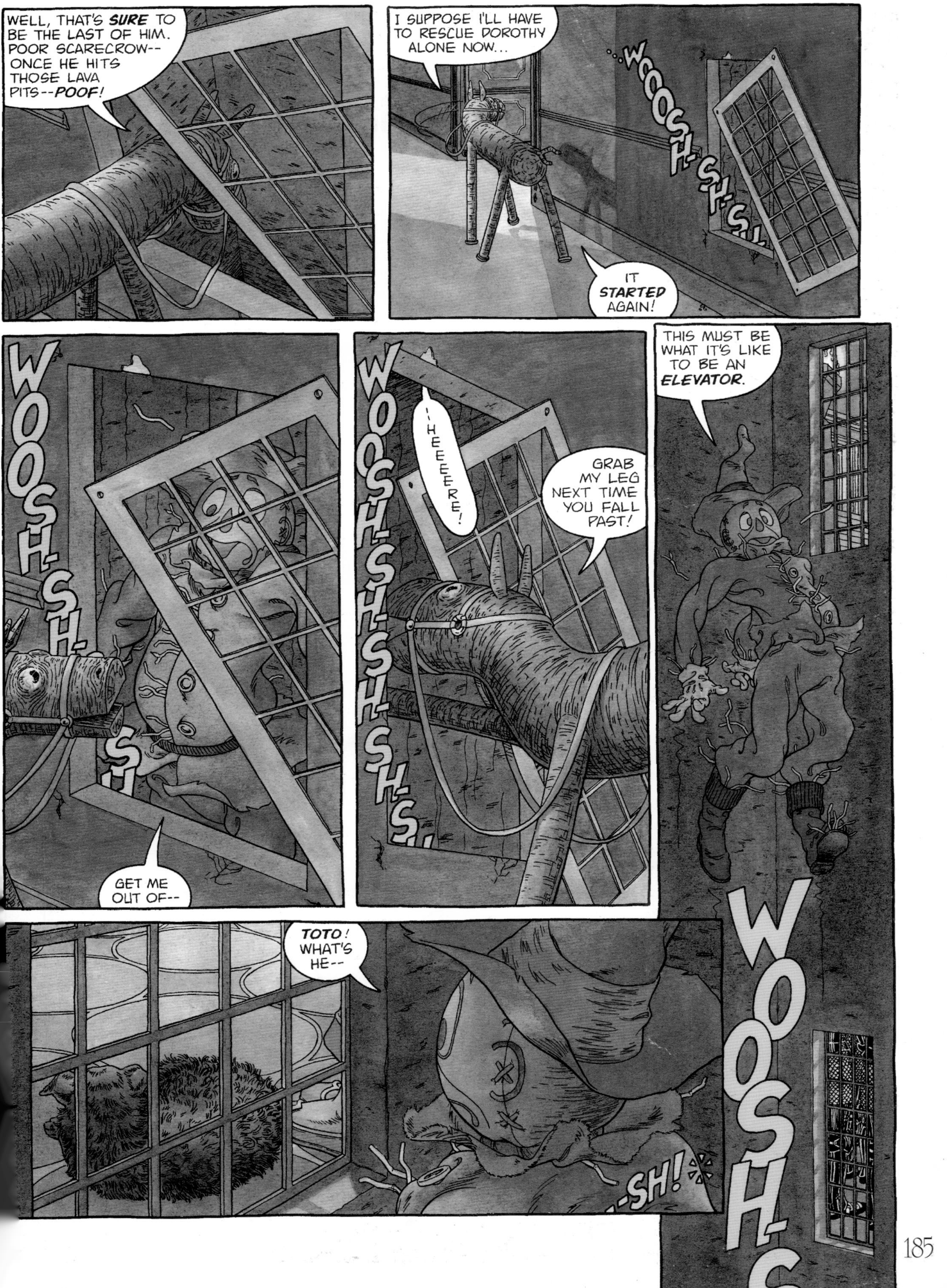
WELL, THAT'S **SURE** TO BE THE LAST OF HIM. POOR SCARECROW-- ONCE HE HITS THOSE LAVA PITS--**POOF**!
I SUPPOSE I'LL HAVE TO RESCUE DOROTHY ALONE NOW...
...WOOOSH-SH-SH...
IT **STARTED** AGAIN!
WOOSH-SH-SH-SH
GET ME OUT OF--
WOOSH-SH-SH-SH-SH-S...
--HEEEERE!
GRAB MY LEG NEXT TIME YOU FALL PAST!
THIS MUST BE WHAT IT'S LIKE TO BE AN **ELEVATOR**.
WOOSH-S
**TOTO**! WHAT'S HE--
-SH!

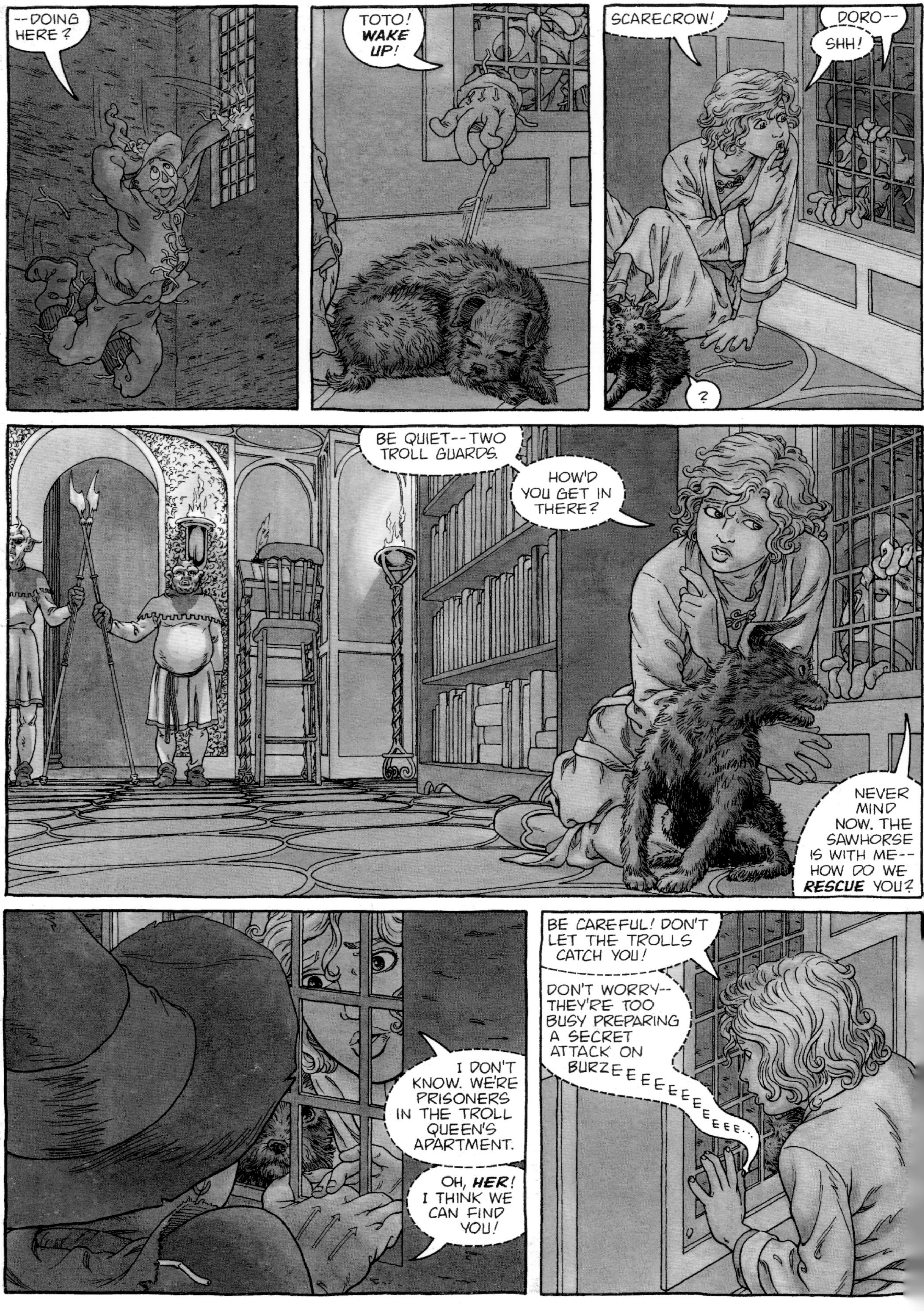
--DOING HERE?
TOTO! **WAKE UP**!
SCARECROW!
DORO--
SHH!
?
BE QUIET--TWO TROLL GUARDS.
HOW'D YOU GET IN THERE?
NEVER MIND NOW. THE SAWHORSE IS WITH ME--HOW DO WE **RESCUE** YOU?
I DON'T KNOW. WE'RE PRISONERS IN THE TROLL QUEEN'S APARTMENT.
OH, **HER**! I THINK WE CAN FIND YOU!
BE CAREFUL! DON'T LET THE TROLLS CATCH YOU!
DON'T WORRY--THEY'RE TOO BUSY PREPARING A SECRET ATTACK ON BURZEEEEEEEEEEEE...

WHAT'S HAPPENED TO HIM? THE AIR CURRENT STOPPED AWHI--

SPLOP

WHO'RE YOU *TALKING* TO?

UH--MY *DOG*--

WELL, *DON'T!*

BURZEE...? ISN'T THAT THE HUGE, OLD FOREST FULL OF MAGICAL BEINGS I'VE HEARD OZMA TALK ABOUT? IF THE TROLLS ARE GOING TO *ATTACK* THE FOREST...

*DOROTHY! TOTO!*

HUNH?

YII!

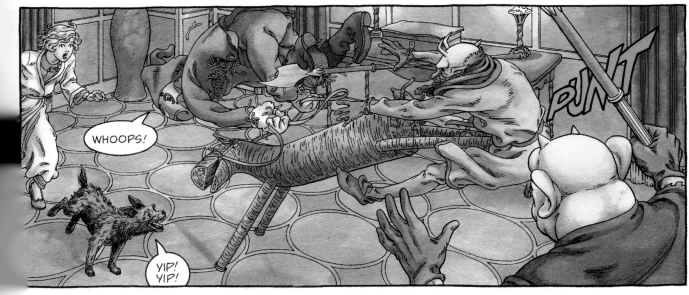

WHOOPS!

PUNT

YIP! YIP!

187

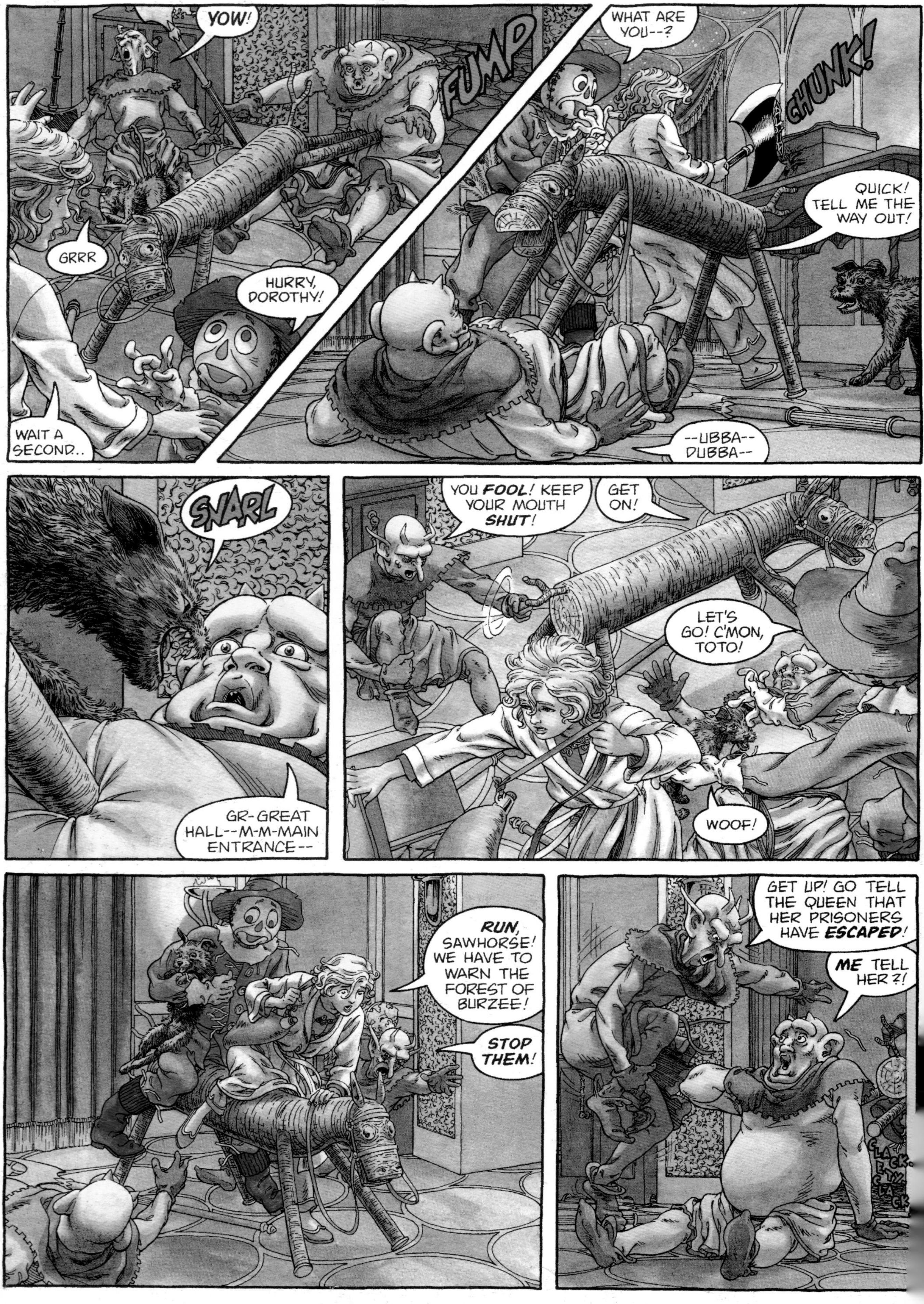
YOW!
FUMP
GRRR
HURRY, DOROTHY!
WAIT A SECOND..
WHAT ARE YOU--?
CHUNK!
QUICK! TELL ME THE WAY OUT!
--UBBA--DUBBA--
SNARL
GR-GREAT HALL--M-M-MAIN ENTRANCE--
YOU **FOOL**! KEEP YOUR MOUTH **SHUT**!
GET ON!
LET'S GO! C'MON, TOTO!
WOOF!
**RUN**, SAWHORSE! WE HAVE TO WARN THE FOREST OF BURZEE!
**STOP THEM**!
GET UP! GO TELL THE QUEEN THAT HER PRISONERS HAVE **ESCAPED**!
**ME** TELL HER?!
CLACK-ETY-CLACK

# Chapter Five — The Chase

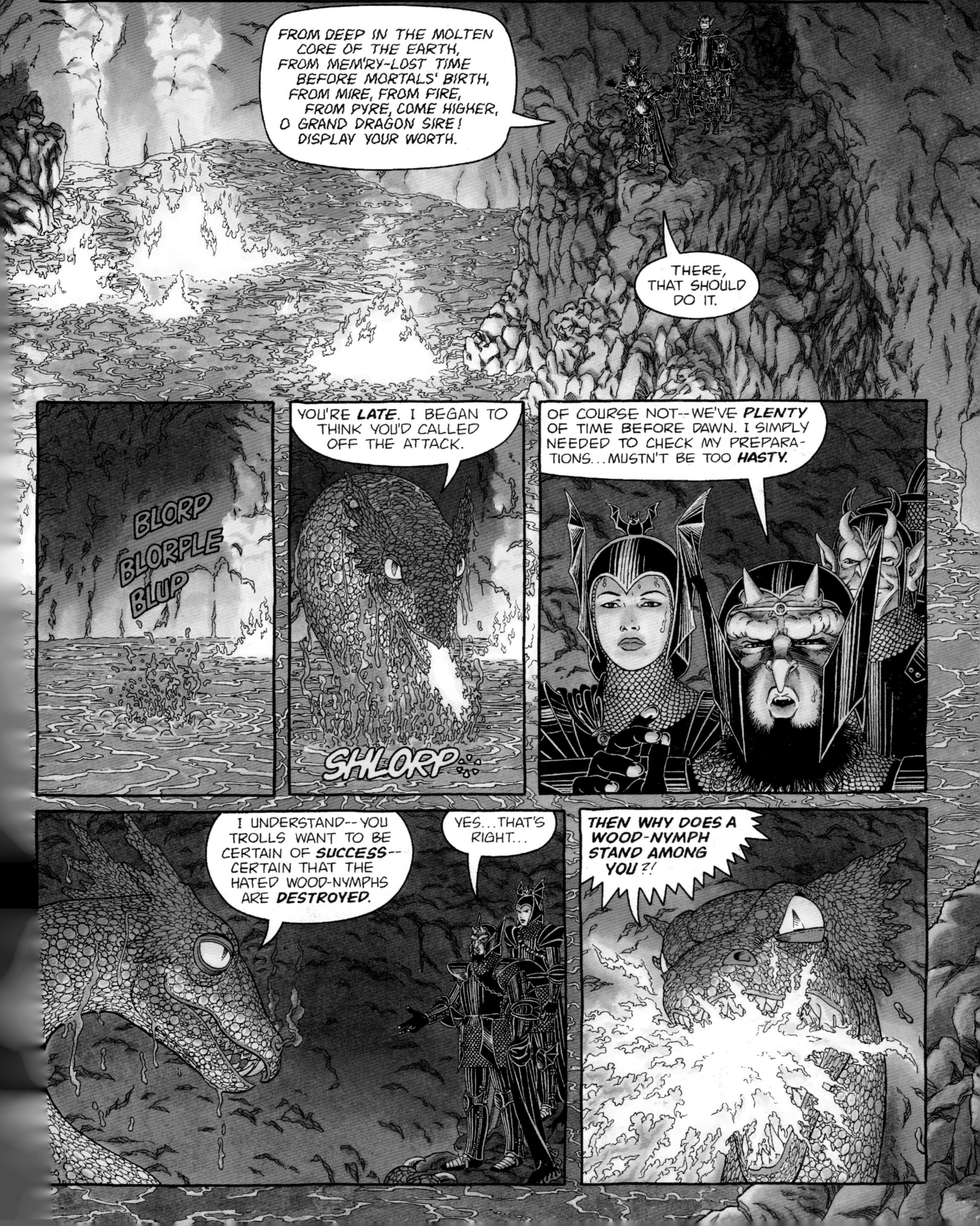

FROM DEEP IN THE MOLTEN CORE OF THE EARTH, FROM MEM'RY-LOST TIME BEFORE MORTALS' BIRTH, FROM MIRE, FROM FIRE, FROM PYRE, COME HIGHER, O GRAND DRAGON SIRE! DISPLAY YOUR WORTH.
THERE, THAT SHOULD DO IT.
BLORP
BLORPLE
BLUP
YOU'RE LATE. I BEGAN TO THINK YOU'D CALLED OFF THE ATTACK.
SHLORP
OF COURSE NOT--WE'VE PLENTY OF TIME BEFORE DAWN. I SIMPLY NEEDED TO CHECK MY PREPARATIONS... MUSTN'T BE TOO HASTY.
I UNDERSTAND--YOU TROLLS WANT TO BE CERTAIN OF SUCCESS--CERTAIN THAT THE HATED WOOD-NYMPHS ARE DESTROYED.
YES... THAT'S RIGHT...
THEN WHY DOES A WOOD-NYMPH STAND AMONG YOU?!

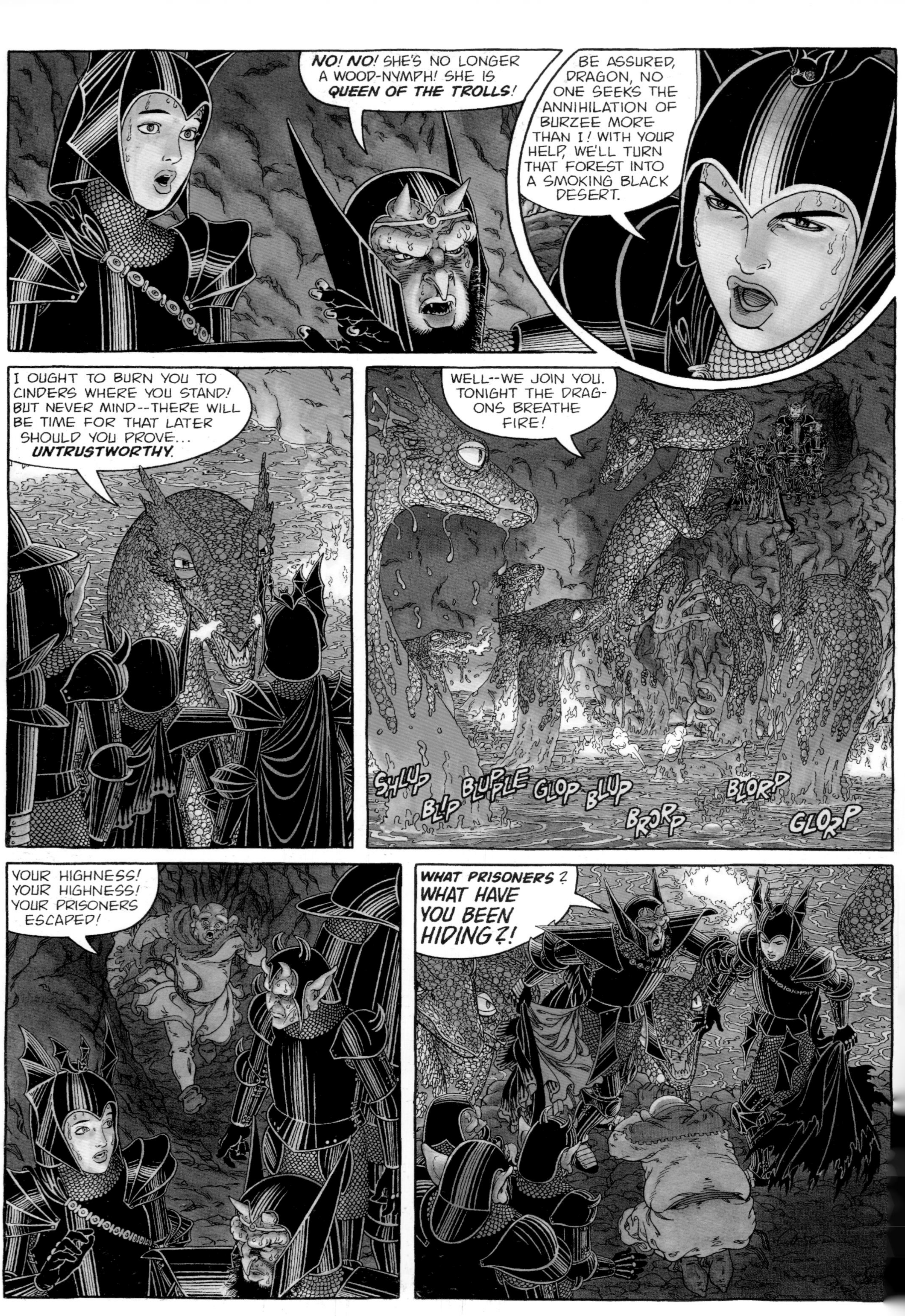

NO! NO! SHE'S NO LONGER A WOOD-NYMPH! SHE IS QUEEN OF THE TROLLS!
BE ASSURED, DRAGON, NO ONE SEEKS THE ANNIHILATION OF BURZEE MORE THAN I! WITH YOUR HELP, WE'LL TURN THAT FOREST INTO A SMOKING BLACK DESERT.
I OUGHT TO BURN YOU TO CINDERS WHERE YOU STAND! BUT NEVER MIND--THERE WILL BE TIME FOR THAT LATER SHOULD YOU PROVE... UNTRUSTWORTHY.
WELL--WE JOIN YOU. TONIGHT THE DRAGONS BREATHE FIRE!
SHLUP
BLIP
BLUPPLE
GLOP
BLUP
BRORP
BLORP
GLORP
YOUR HIGHNESS! YOUR HIGHNESS! YOUR PRISONERS ESCAPED!
WHAT PRISONERS? WHAT HAVE YOU BEEN HIDING?!

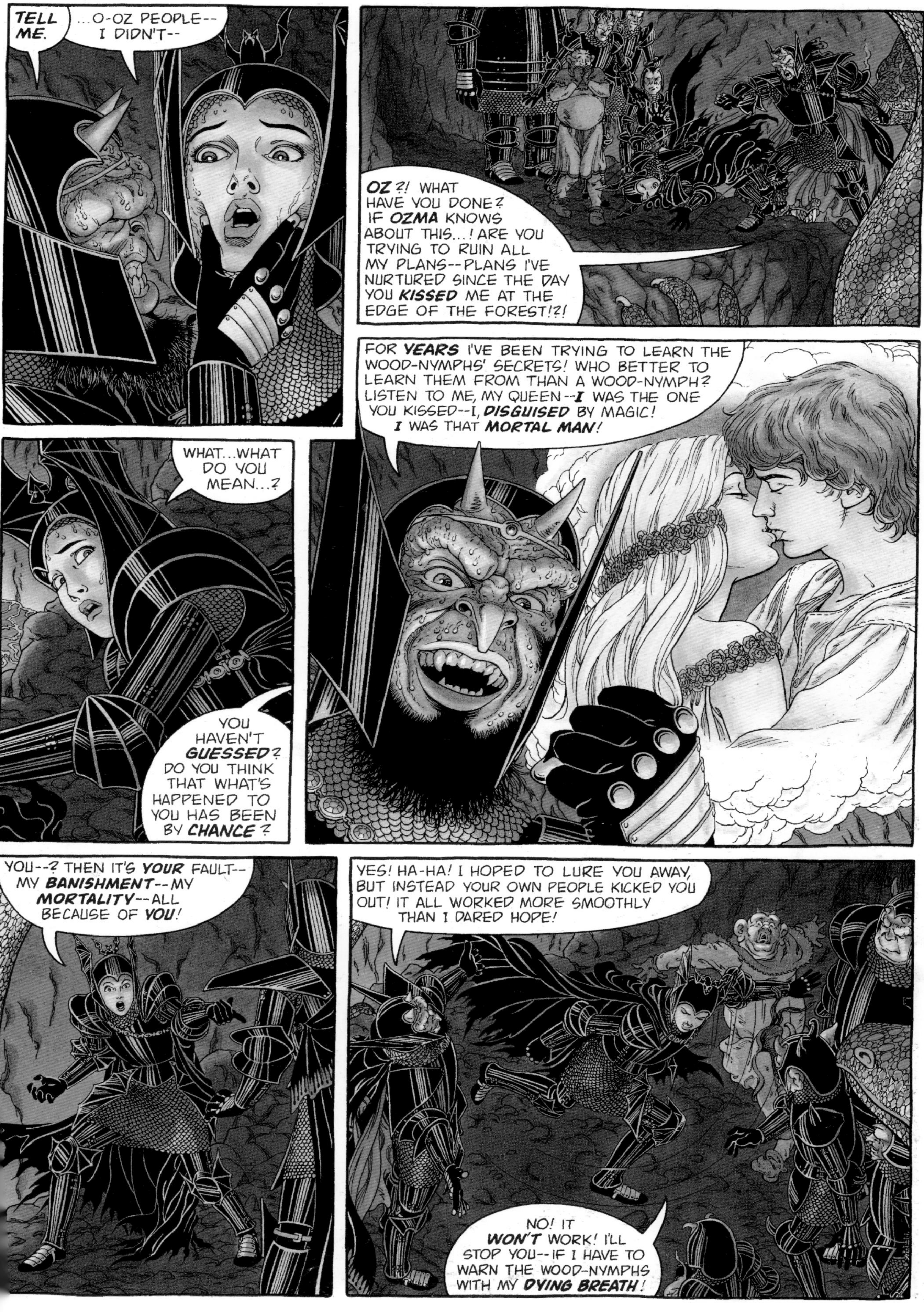
TELL ME.
...O-OZ PEOPLE-- I DIDN'T--
OZ?! WHAT HAVE YOU DONE? IF OZMA KNOWS ABOUT THIS...! ARE YOU TRYING TO RUIN ALL MY PLANS--PLANS I'VE NURTURED SINCE THE DAY YOU KISSED ME AT THE EDGE OF THE FOREST!?!
WHAT...WHAT DO YOU MEAN...?
YOU HAVEN'T GUESSED? DO YOU THINK THAT WHAT'S HAPPENED TO YOU HAS BEEN BY CHANCE?
FOR YEARS I'VE BEEN TRYING TO LEARN THE WOOD-NYMPHS' SECRETS! WHO BETTER TO LEARN THEM FROM THAN A WOOD-NYMPH? LISTEN TO ME, MY QUEEN--I WAS THE ONE YOU KISSED--I, DISGUISED BY MAGIC! I WAS THAT MORTAL MAN!
YOU--? THEN IT'S YOUR FAULT-- MY BANISHMENT--MY MORTALITY--ALL BECAUSE OF YOU!
YES! HA-HA! I HOPED TO LURE YOU AWAY, BUT INSTEAD YOUR OWN PEOPLE KICKED YOU OUT! IT ALL WORKED MORE SMOOTHLY THAN I DARED HOPE!
NO! IT WON'T WORK! I'LL STOP YOU--IF I HAVE TO WARN THE WOOD-NYMPHS WITH MY DYING BREATH!

STOP HER!

YOU REALLY SHOULD HAVE LET ME BURN HER....

FORGET HER-- MY OFFICERS WILL TAKE CARE OF HER. ALL THAT MATTERS NOW IS THAT WE DESTROY THE FOREST. WE MARCH AT ONCE!

VERY GOOD. IF I DON'T BURN SOMETHING SOON I'LL EXPLODE!

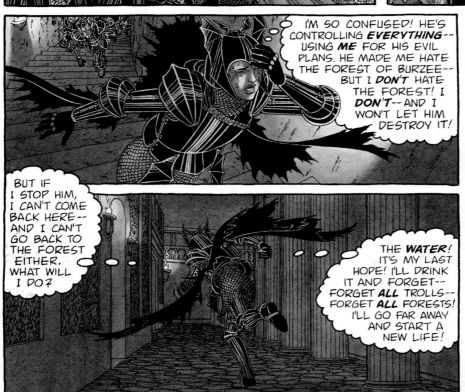
I'M SO CONFUSED! HE'S CONTROLLING *EVERYTHING*-- USING *ME* FOR HIS EVIL PLANS. HE MADE ME HATE THE FOREST OF BURZEE-- BUT I *DON'T* HATE THE FOREST! I *DON'T*-- AND I WON'T LET HIM DESTROY IT!

BUT IF I STOP HIM, I CAN'T COME BACK HERE-- AND I CAN'T GO BACK TO THE FOREST EITHER. WHAT WILL I DO?

THE *WATER*! IT'S MY LAST HOPE! I'LL DRINK IT AND FORGET-- FORGET *ALL* TROLLS-- FORGET *ALL* FORESTS! I'LL GO FAR AWAY AND START A NEW LIFE!

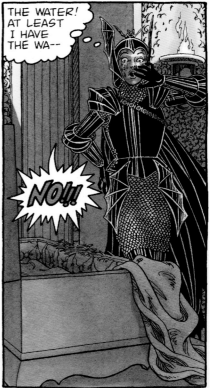
THE WATER! AT LEAST I HAVE THE WA--

*NO!!!*

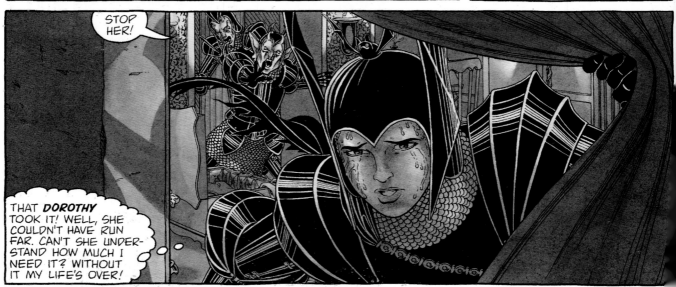
STOP HER!

THAT *DOROTHY* TOOK IT! WELL, SHE COULDN'T HAVE RUN FAR. CAN'T SHE UNDERSTAND HOW MUCH I NEED IT? WITHOUT IT MY LIFE'S OVER!

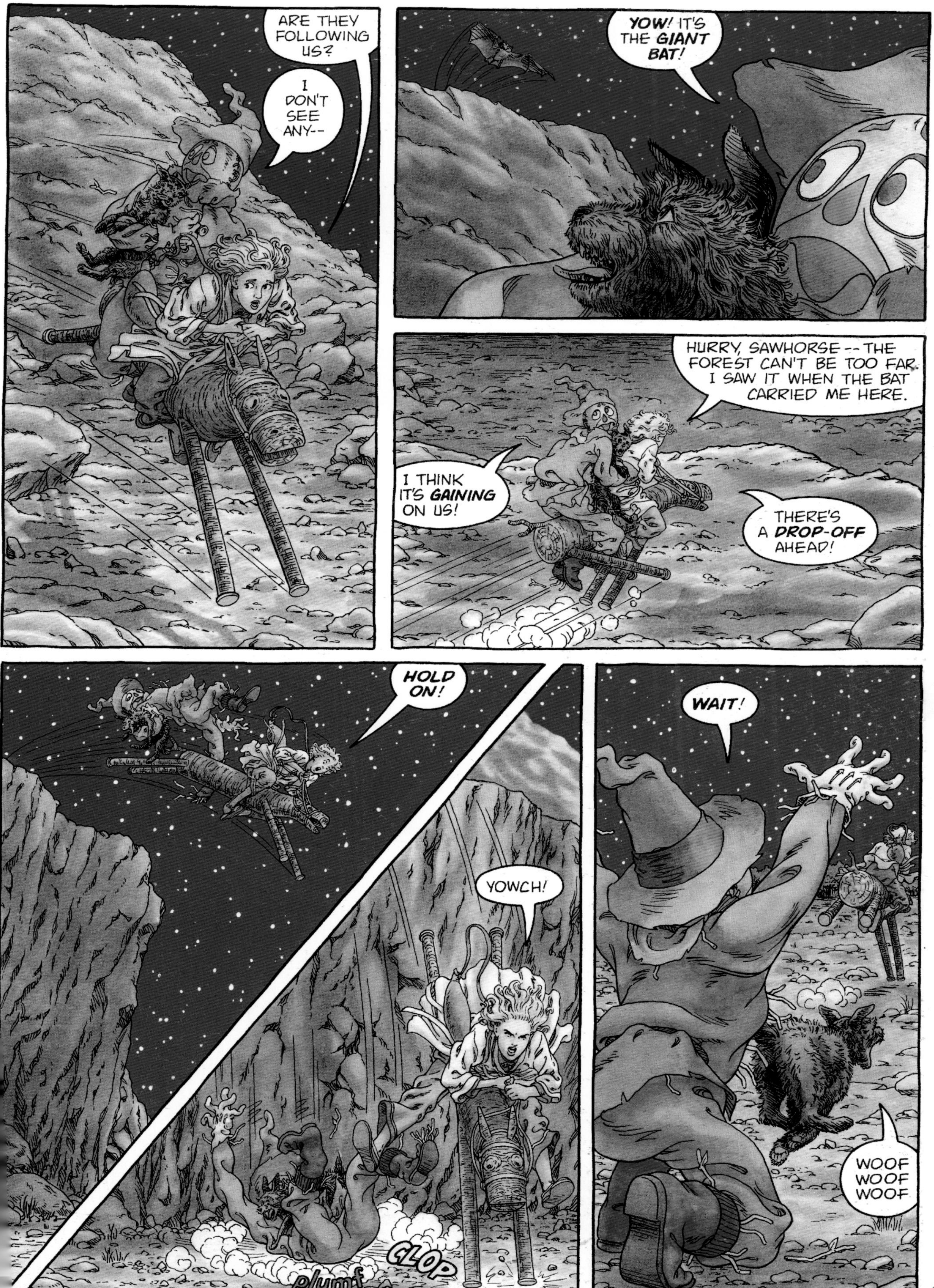

ARE THEY FOLLOWING US?
I DON'T SEE ANY--
YOW! IT'S THE GIANT BAT!
HURRY, SAWHORSE -- THE FOREST CAN'T BE TOO FAR. I SAW IT WHEN THE BAT CARRIED ME HERE.
I THINK IT'S GAINING ON US!
THERE'S A DROP-OFF AHEAD!
HOLD ON!
YOWCH!
GLOP
plumf
WAIT!
WOOF WOOF WOOF

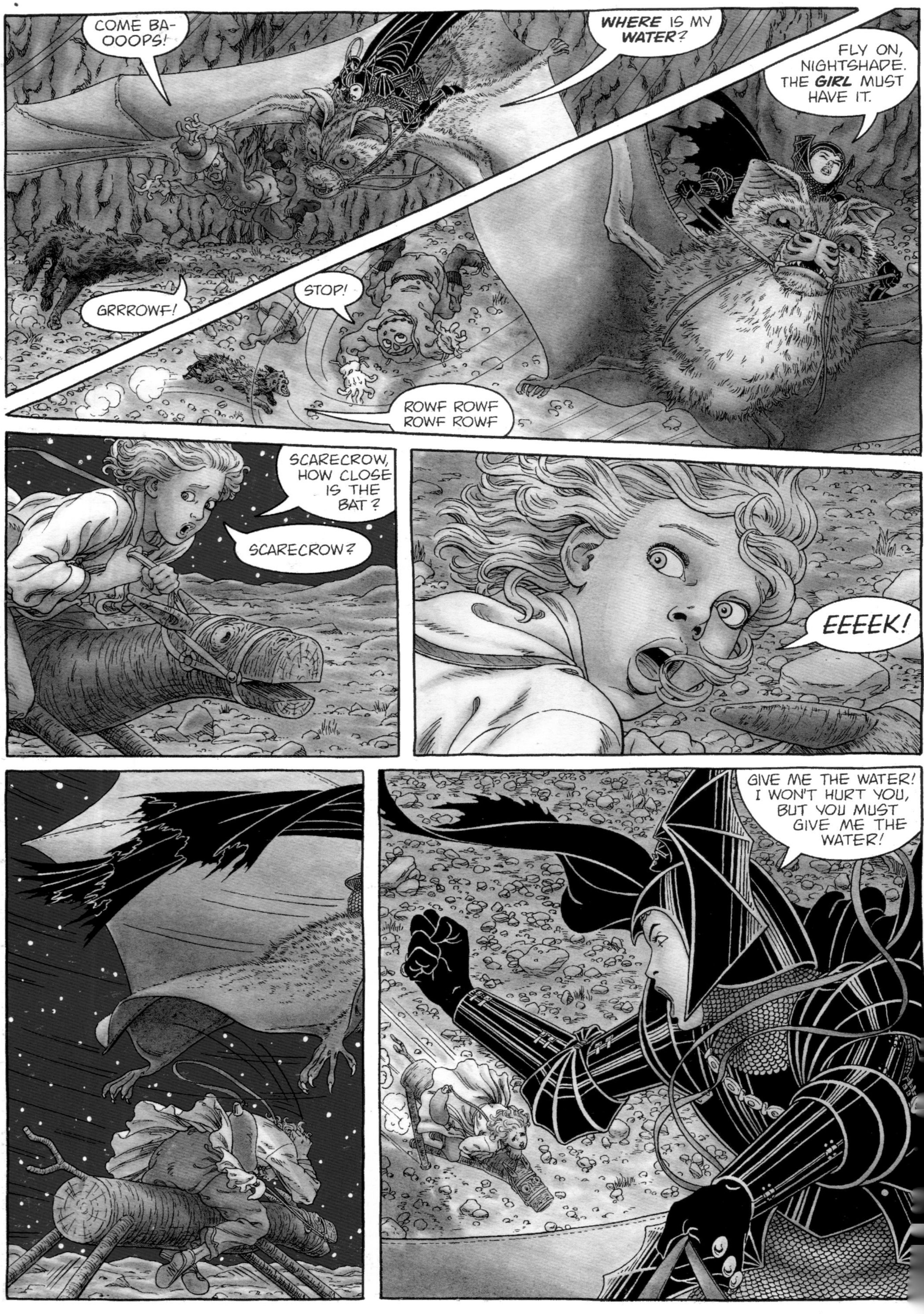

COME BA-OOOPS!
WHERE IS MY WATER?
FLY ON, NIGHTSHADE. THE GIRL MUST HAVE IT.
GRRROWF!
STOP!
ROWF ROWF ROWF ROWF
SCARECROW, HOW CLOSE IS THE BAT?
SCARECROW?
EEEEK!
GIVE ME THE WATER! I WON'T HURT YOU, BUT YOU MUST GIVE ME THE WATER!

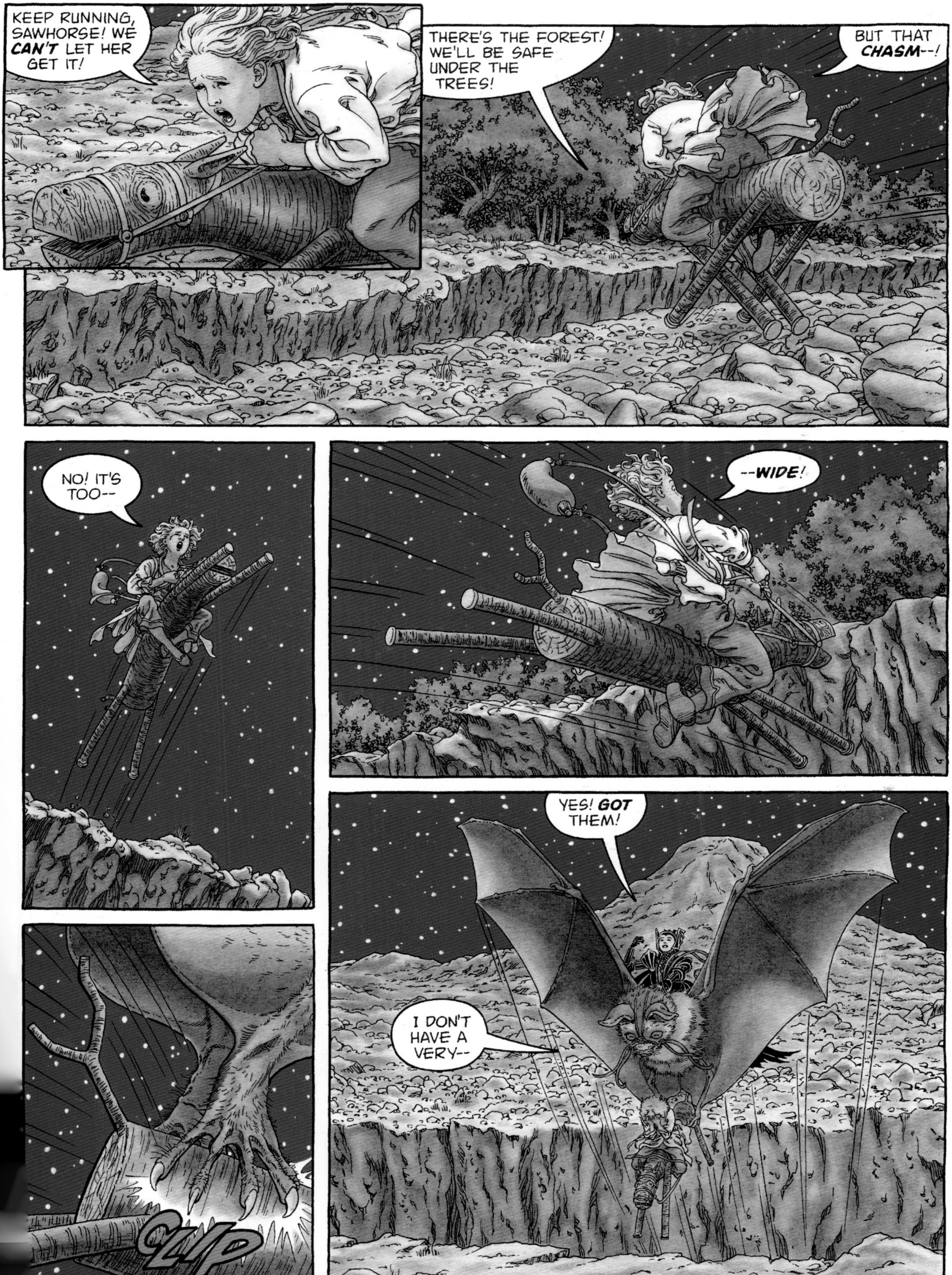
KEEP RUNNING, SAWHORSE! WE CAN'T LET HER GET IT!
THERE'S THE FOREST! WE'LL BE SAFE UNDER THE TREES!
BUT THAT CHASM--!
NO! IT'S TOO--
--WIDE!
CLIP
YES! GOT THEM!
I DON'T HAVE A VERY--

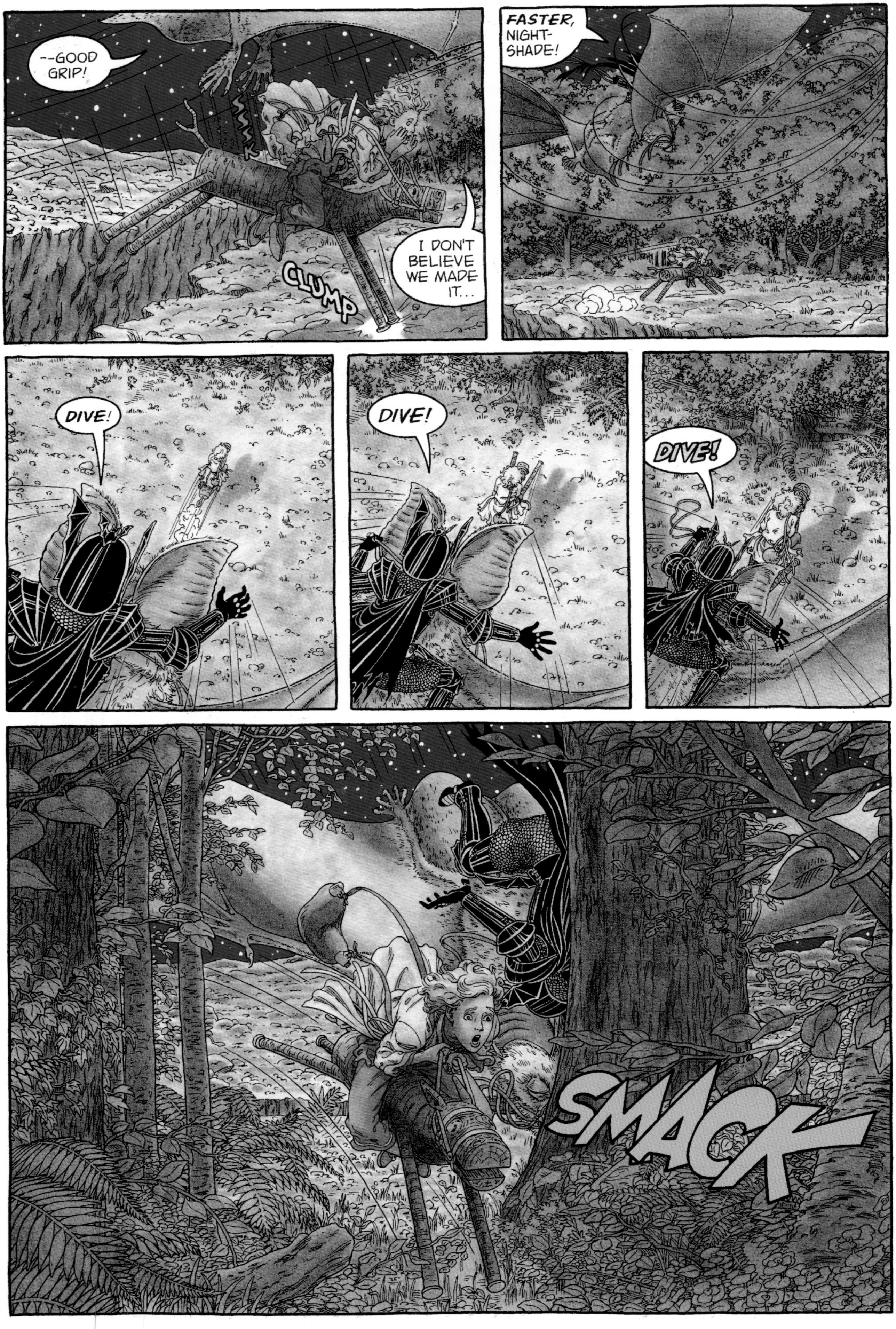
--GOOD GRIP!
CLUMP
I DON'T BELIEVE WE MADE IT...
FASTER, NIGHT-SHADE!
DIVE!
DIVE!
DIVE!
SMACK

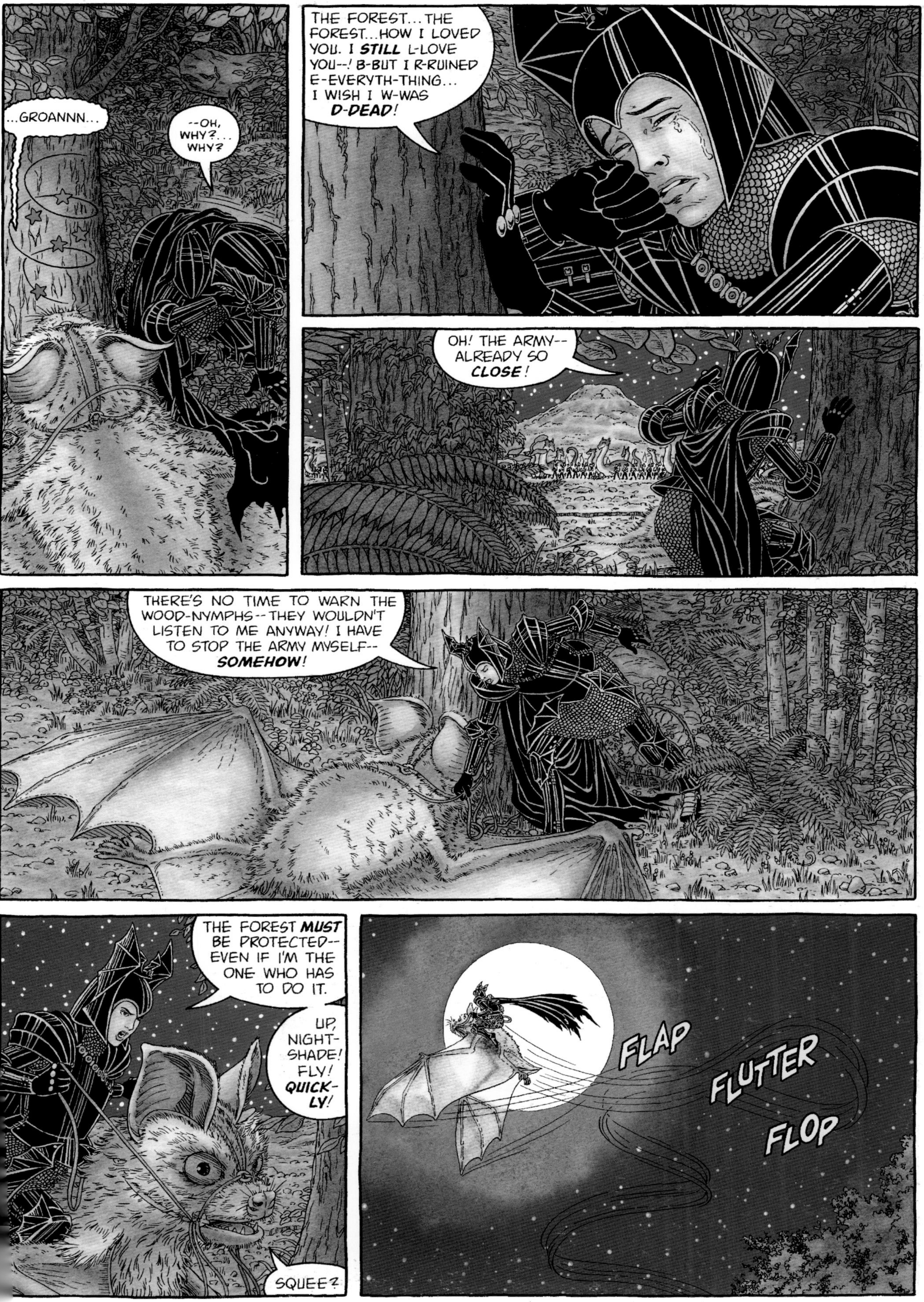
...GROANNN...
--OH, WHY?... WHY?
THE FOREST... THE FOREST... HOW I LOVED YOU. I STILL L-LOVE YOU--! B-BUT I R-RUINED E-EVERYTH-THING... I WISH I W-WAS D-DEAD!
OH! THE ARMY-- ALREADY SO CLOSE!
THERE'S NO TIME TO WARN THE WOOD-NYMPHS--THEY WOULDN'T LISTEN TO ME ANYWAY! I HAVE TO STOP THE ARMY MYSELF-- SOMEHOW!
THE FOREST MUST BE PROTECTED-- EVEN IF I'M THE ONE WHO HAS TO DO IT.
UP, NIGHT-SHADE! FLY! QUICK-LY!
SQUEE?
FLAP
FLUTTER
FLOP

# Chapter Six The Water of Oblivion

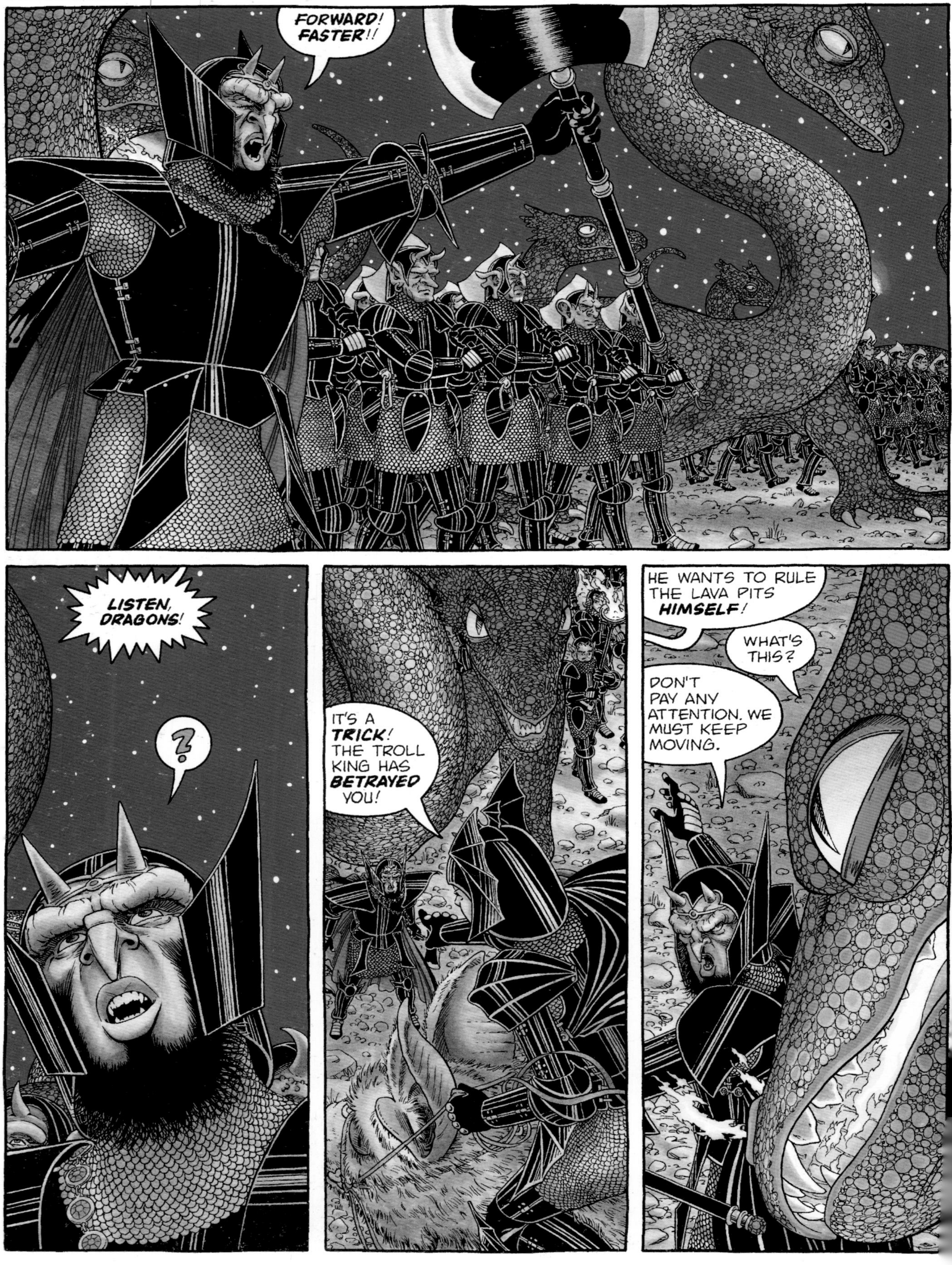
FORWARD! FASTER!!
LISTEN, DRAGONS!
?
IT'S A TRICK! THE TROLL KING HAS BETRAYED YOU!
HE WANTS TO RULE THE LAVA PITS HIMSELF!
WHAT'S THIS?
DON'T PAY ANY ATTENTION. WE MUST KEEP MOVING.

HE'S **LURING** YOU TO BURZEE TO BE **DESTROYED** BY THE WOOD-NYMPHS!

THAT'S NON-SENSE!

THE WOOD-NYMPHS DO HAVE POWERFUL MAGIC, DON'T THEY?

I MAY BE MISTAKEN-- YOU ALL LOOK THE SAME TO ME-- BUT ISN'T THAT THE QUEEN OF THE TROLLS?

YES--SHE **WAS**. BUT SHE'S GONE CRAZY! **YOU** HEARD HER BACK IN THE CAVERN.

KEEP **ON**--DAWN'S NOT FAR OFF.

WAIT A MOMENT, YOU SEEM A LITTLE TOO **EAGER**...

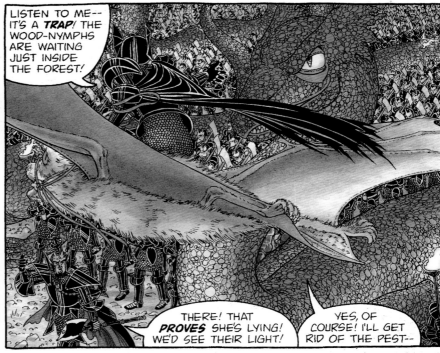

LISTEN TO ME-- IT'S A **TRAP**! THE WOOD-NYMPHS ARE WAITING JUST INSIDE THE FOREST!

THERE! THAT **PROVES** SHE'S LYING! WE'D SEE THEIR LIGHT!

YES, OF COURSE! I'LL GET RID OF THE PEST--

FWOOOSH!

SQUEEE--

OH, NIGHT-SHADE, NIGHT-SHADE, WHAT CAN I DO? THEY'RE STILL ADVANCING.

THAT FELT GOOD!

WHAT'S THAT GLOW?

IT CAN'T BE DAWN YET--

THERE THEY ARE, YOUR MAJESTY.

THE WOOD-NYMPHS!

IT IS A TRAP! TRAITOR

NO!

FWOOM

Krakle

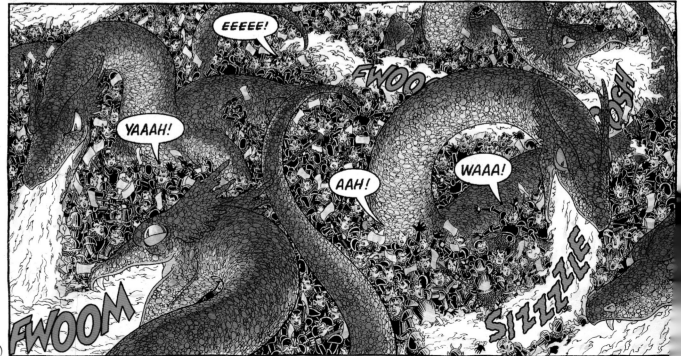

EEEEE!

FWOO

OSH

YAAAH!

AAH!

WAAA!

FWOOM

SIZZZZLE

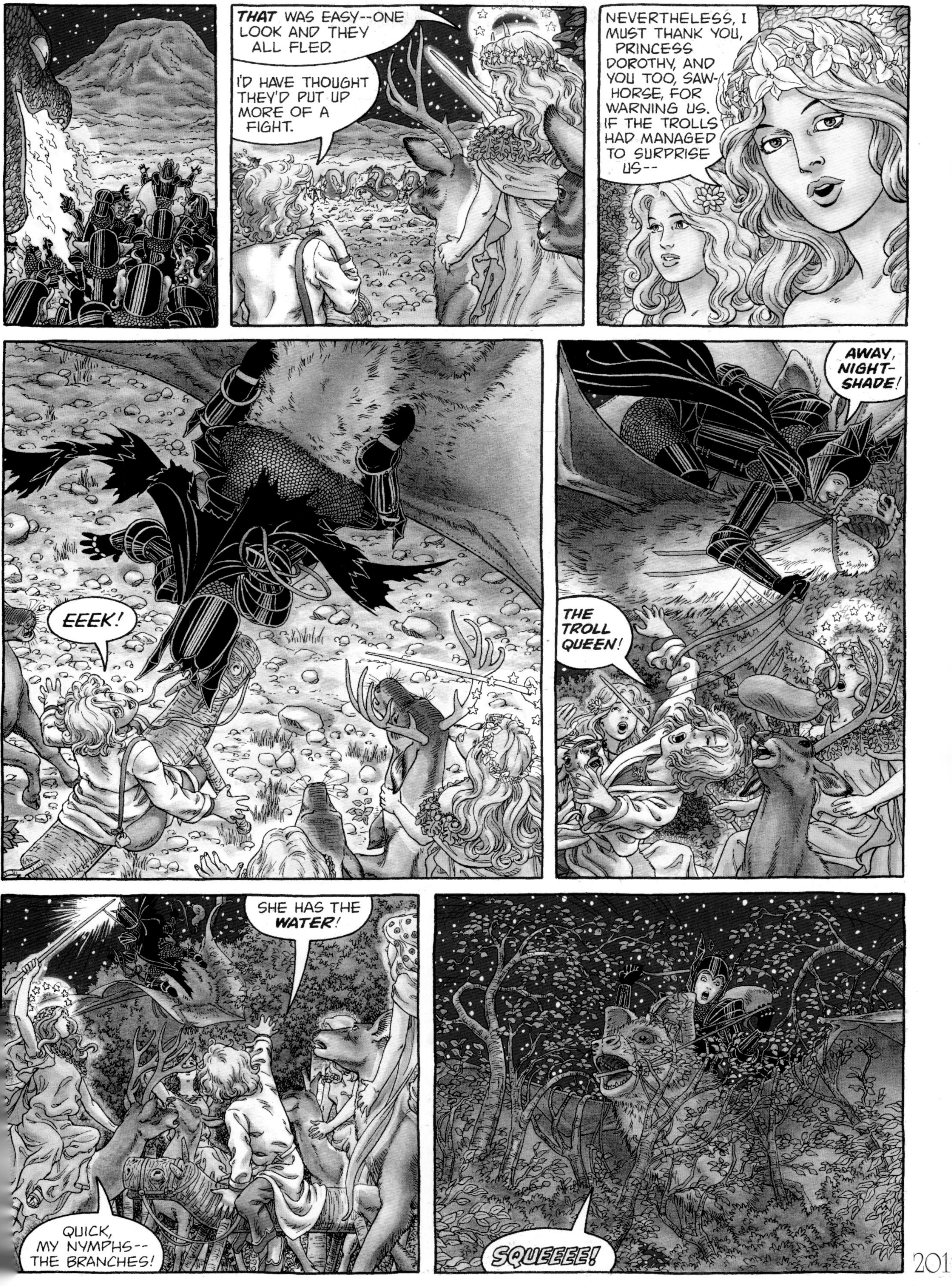

THAT WAS EASY--ONE LOOK AND THEY ALL FLED.
I'D HAVE THOUGHT THEY'D PUT UP MORE OF A FIGHT.
NEVERTHELESS, I MUST THANK YOU, PRINCESS DOROTHY, AND YOU TOO, SAW-HORSE, FOR WARNING US. IF THE TROLLS HAD MANAGED TO SURPRISE US--
EEEK!
AWAY, NIGHT-SHADE!
THE TROLL QUEEN!
SHE HAS THE WATER!
QUICK, MY NYMPHS-- THE BRANCHES!
SQUEEEE!

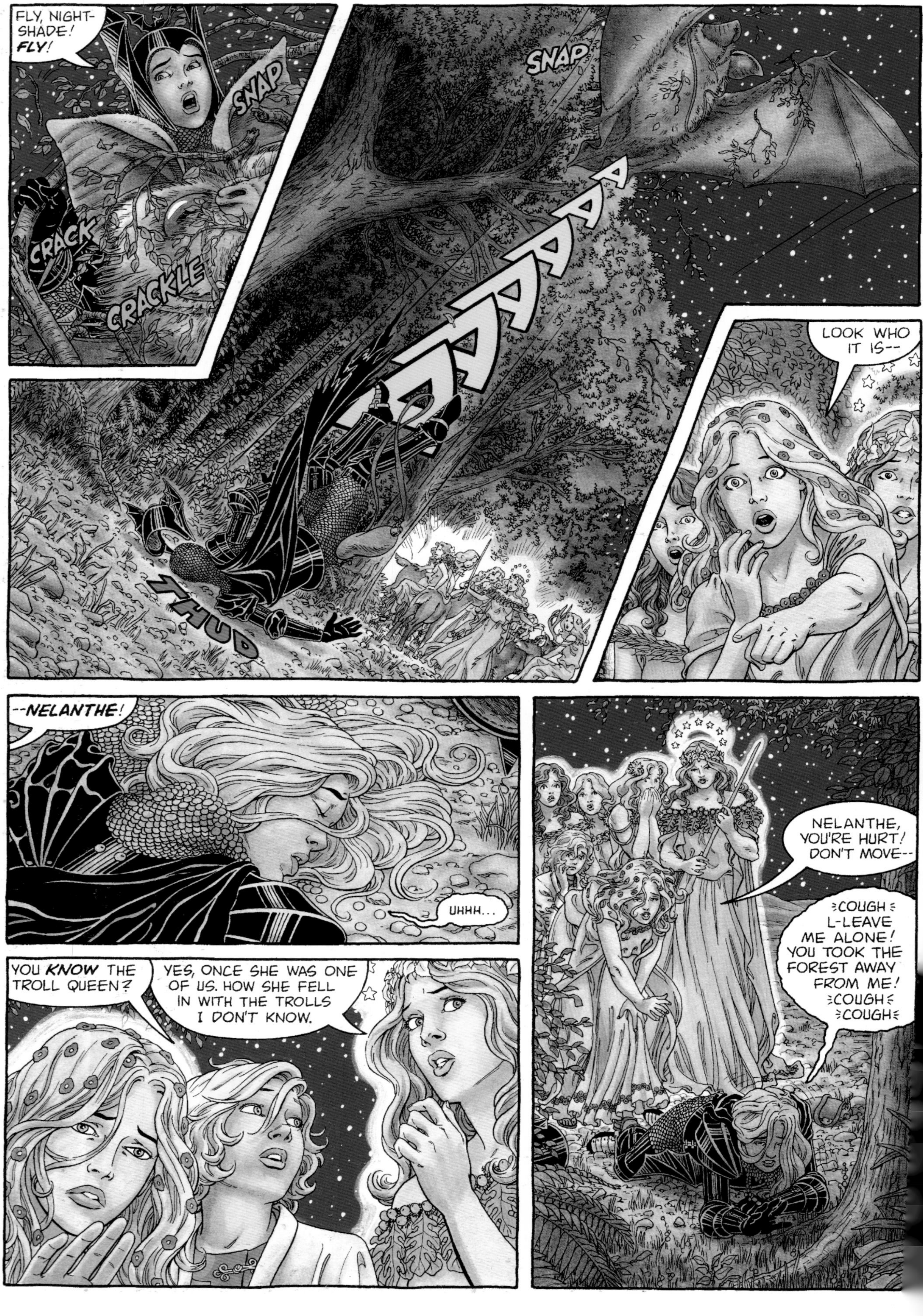
FLY, NIGHT-SHADE! ***FLY!***
SNAP
CRACK
CRACKLE
SNAP
AAAAAAA
THUD
LOOK WHO IT IS--
--***NELANTHE!***
UHHH...
YOU ***KNOW*** THE TROLL QUEEN?
YES, ONCE SHE WAS ONE OF US. HOW SHE FELL IN WITH THE TROLLS I DON'T KNOW.
NELANTHE, YOU'RE HURT! DON'T MOVE--
COUGH L-LEAVE ME ALONE! YOU TOOK THE FOREST AWAY FROM ME! COUGH COUGH

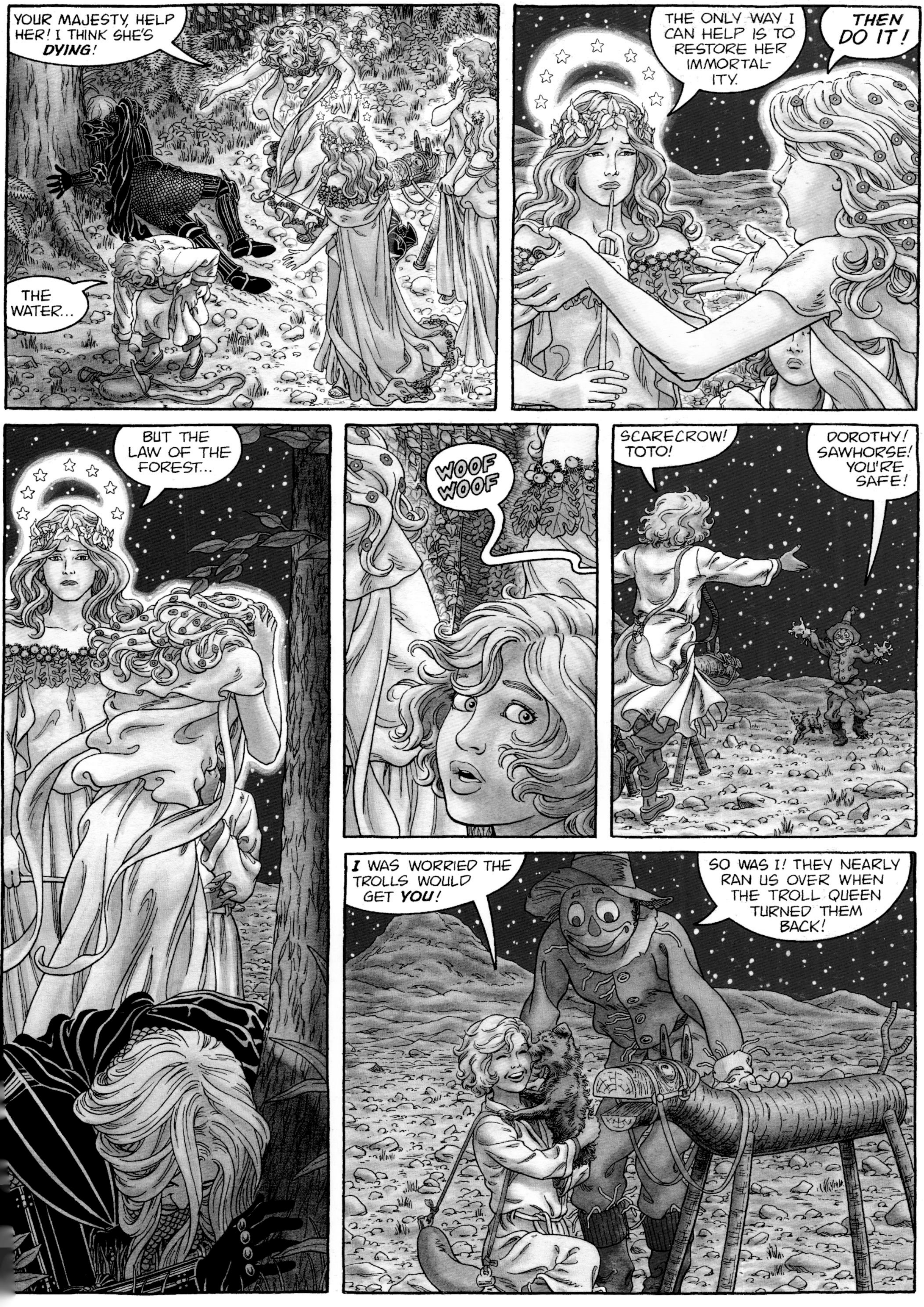
YOUR MAJESTY, HELP HER! I THINK SHE'S **DYING**!
THE WATER...
THE ONLY WAY I CAN HELP IS TO RESTORE HER IMMORTAL-ITY.
**THEN DO IT!**
BUT THE LAW OF THE FOREST...
WOOF WOOF
SCARECROW! TOTO!
DOROTHY! SAWHORSE! YOU'RE SAFE!
**I** WAS WORRIED THE TROLLS WOULD GET **YOU**!
SO WAS I! THEY NEARLY RAN US OVER WHEN THE TROLL QUEEN TURNED THEM BACK!

TROLL QUEEN? YOU MUST MEAN THE **WOOD-NYMPH** QUEEN.

NO, THE **TROLL** QUEEN TRICKED THE DRAGONS INTO ATTACKING THE TROLLS...

WHAT?

BUT THAT MEANS SHE TURNED AGAINST THE TROLLS TO SAVE THE FOREST! THEN SHE HAS **NOTHING LEFT** --EXCEPT...

...EXCEPT THE WATER OF OBLIVION.

BUT I--I **CAN'T** GIVE IT TO HER. OZMA'S FORBIDDEN IT.

CAN IT HELP HER?

I DON'T KNOW, BUT--

AHHHHHHHHH

OH, **SO WHAT** IF IT'S FORBIDDEN. I'LL BE IN DEEP TROUBLE WHEN I GET BACK TO THE EMERALD CITY, BUT I DON'T CARE ANYMORE.

**PLEASE** DRINK IT. YOU WANTED IT SO DESPERATELY.

**NO!**

I--I DON'T WANT IT ANYMORE ⸘COUGH⸘ ⸘COUGH⸘ --ALL I WANT IS THE FOREST--ALL I **EVER** WANTED--ALL I **EVER** LOVED! BUT THEY TOOK IT AWAY, SO I TRIED TO FORGET--BUT I **CAN'T**--I **CAN'T**! AHRGH!

THE FOREST--
THE FOREST--
⸘COUGH COUGH⸘
--UHHHHHHHH....

THIS IS TOO MUCH--I CANNOT ABANDON HER. I'M GOING TO RESTORE HER IMMORTALITY.

YOUR MAJES-TY--!

THE LAW OF THE FOREST!

HOW CAN YOU--?

**SILENCE!**

WHEN I BANISHED NELANTHE MY HEART GRIEVED, BUT HER HEART IS **BREAKING**. IF SHE DIES NOW MY HEART WILL BREAK ALSO.

SHE LOVES THE FOREST DEEPLY. SURELY HER TURNING THE TROLL ARMY BACK PROVES THAT. I RESPECT THE LAW, BUT THE LAW CANNOT SEE A BROKEN HEART. NELANTHE **BELONGS** IN BURZEE-- THAT IS MOST IMPORTANT NOW.

OH, **HURRY**, YOUR MAJESTY--!

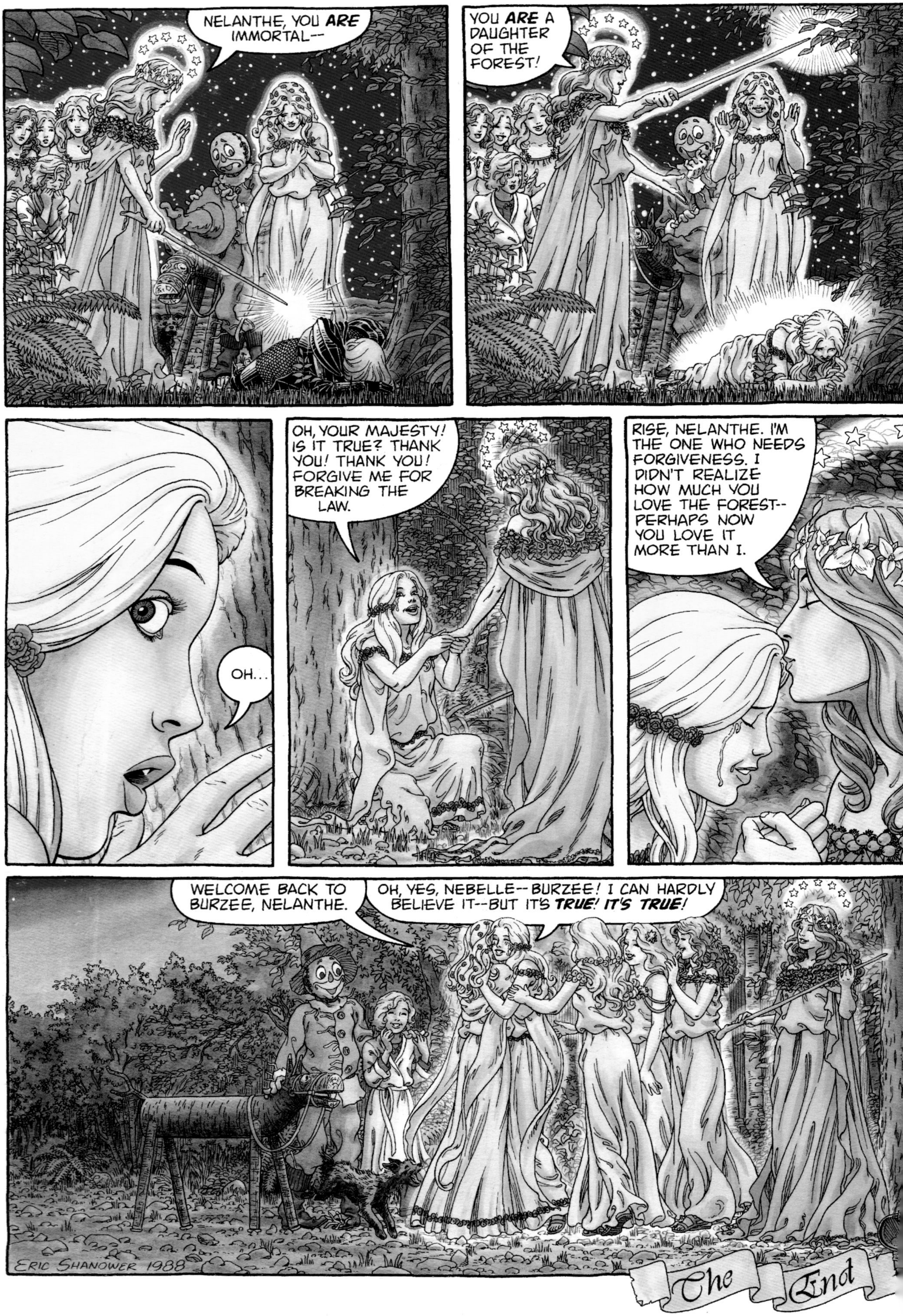

NELANTHE, YOU **ARE** IMMORTAL--
YOU **ARE** A DAUGHTER OF THE FOREST!
OH...
OH, YOUR MAJESTY! IS IT TRUE? THANK YOU! THANK YOU! FORGIVE ME FOR BREAKING THE LAW.
RISE, NELANTHE. I'M THE ONE WHO NEEDS FORGIVENESS. I DIDN'T REALIZE HOW MUCH YOU LOVE THE FOREST--PERHAPS NOW YOU LOVE IT MORE THAN I.
WELCOME BACK TO BURZEE, NELANTHE.
OH, YES, NEBELLE--BURZEE! I CAN HARDLY BELIEVE IT--BUT IT'S ***TRUE! IT'S TRUE!***
ERIC SHANOWER 1988
The End

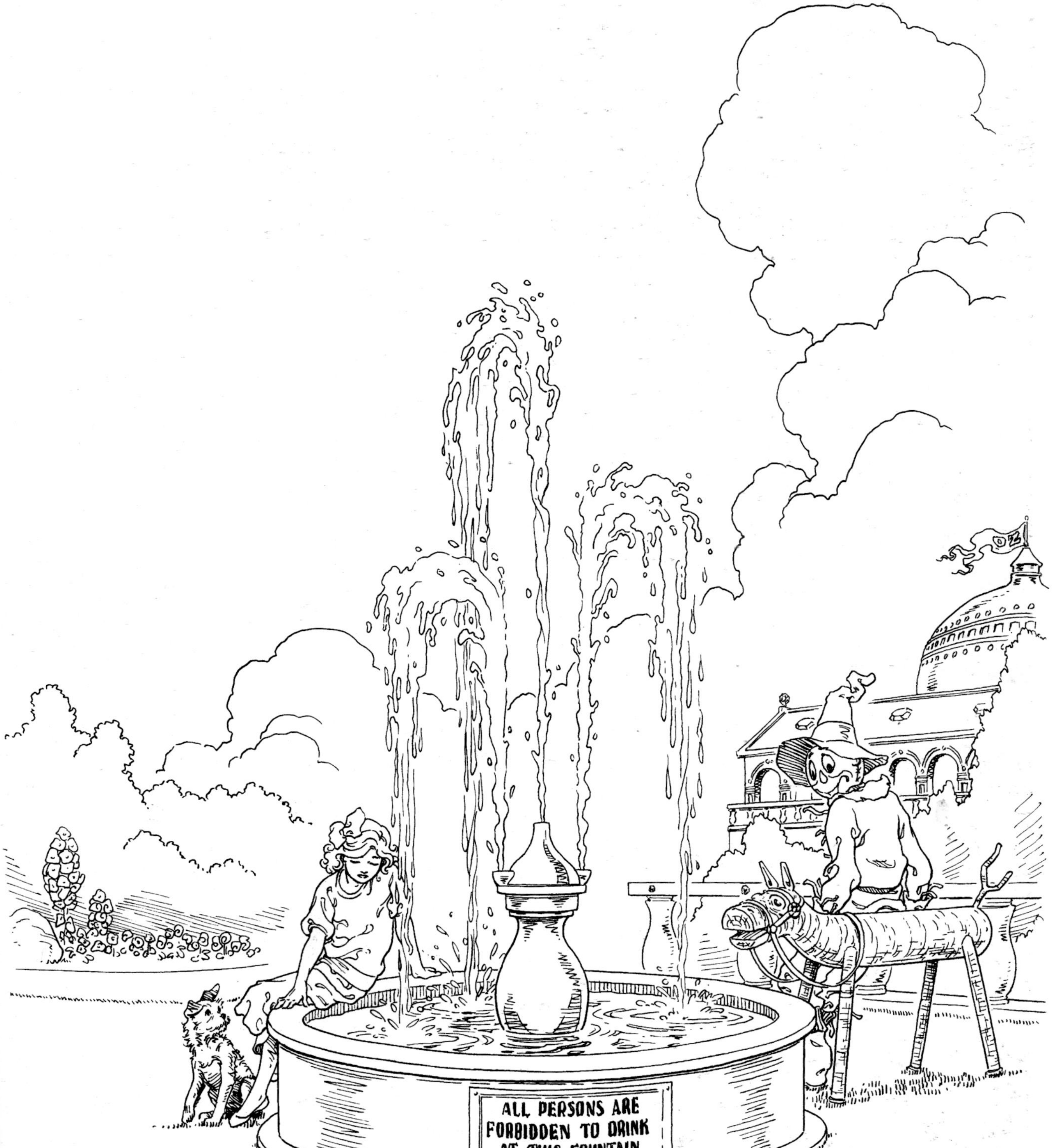
ALL PERSONS ARE FORBIDDEN TO DRINK AT THIS FOUNTAIN

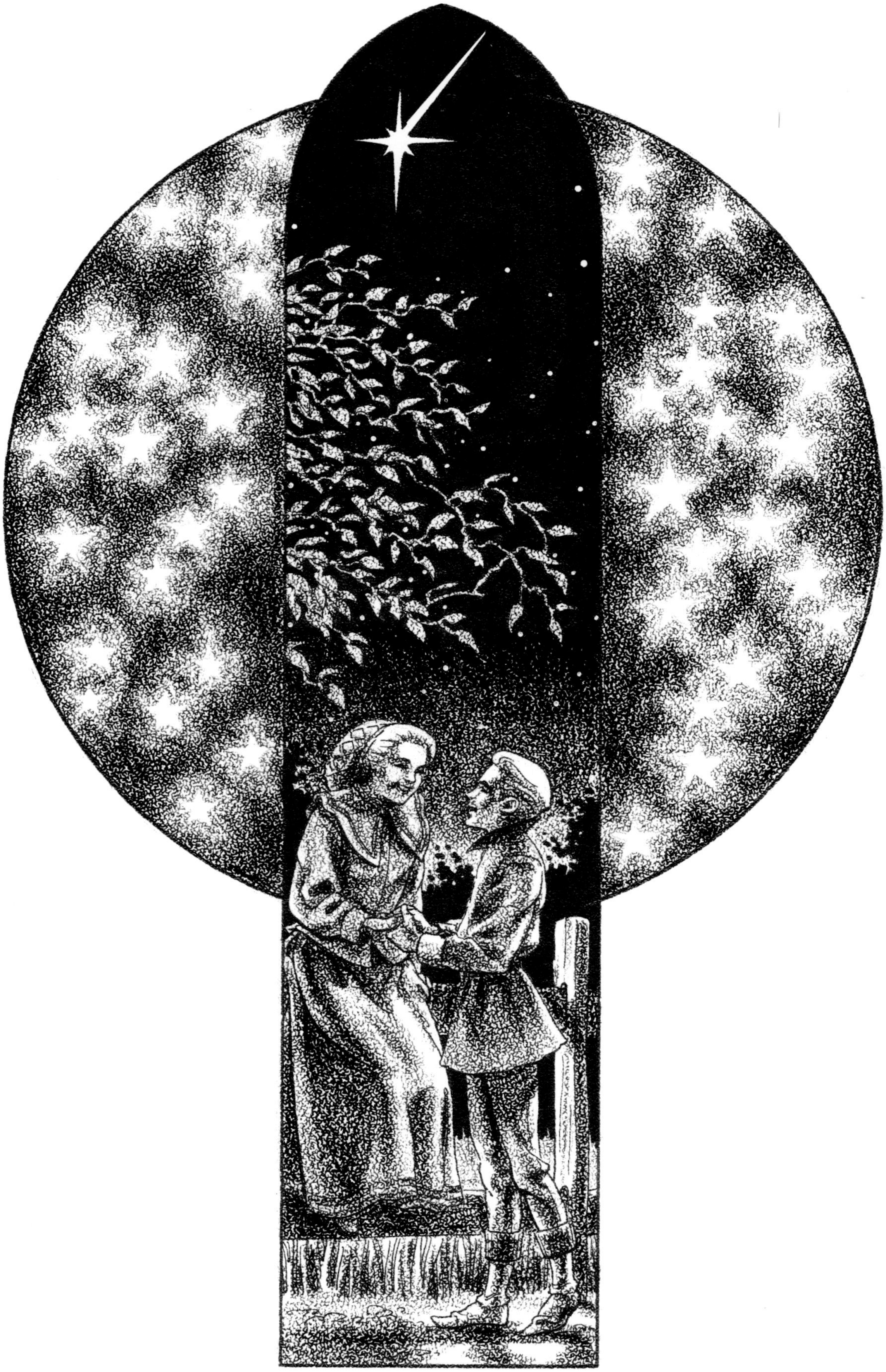

# The Blue Witch of Oz

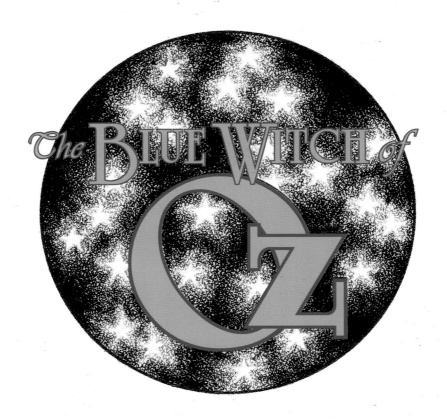

At last,
Elizabeth,
here's one
for you.

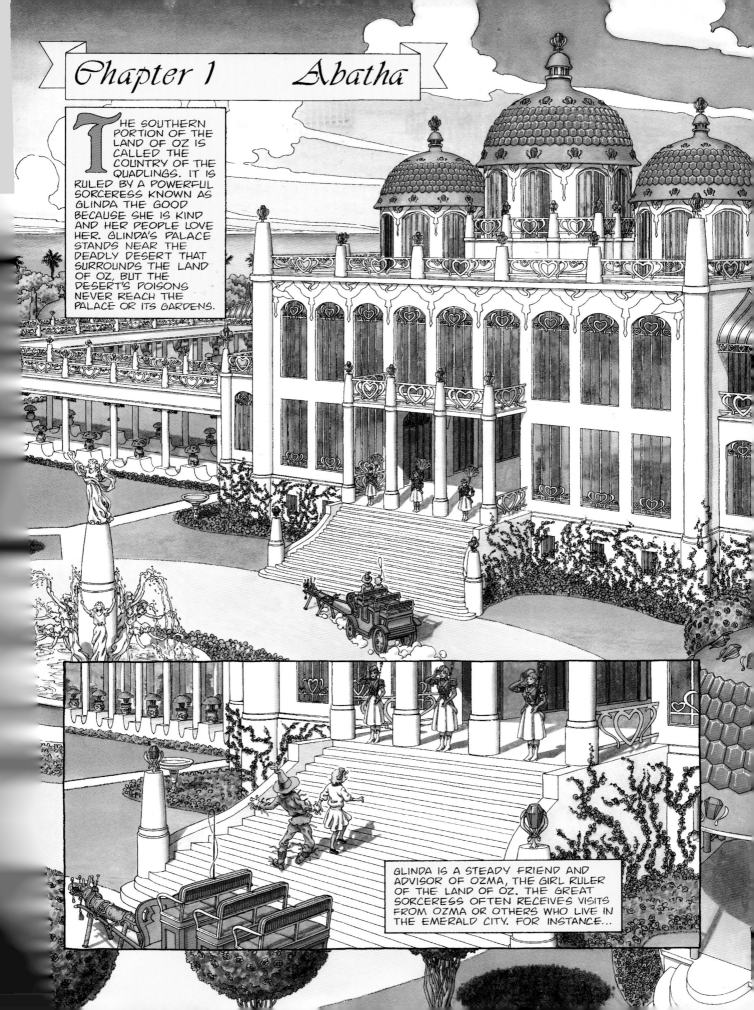

THE SOUTHERN PORTION OF THE LAND OF OZ IS CALLED THE COUNTRY OF THE QUADLINGS. IT IS RULED BY A POWERFUL SORCERESS KNOWN AS GLINDA THE GOOD BECAUSE SHE IS KIND AND HER PEOPLE LOVE HER. GLINDA'S PALACE STANDS NEAR THE DEADLY DESERT THAT SURROUNDS THE LAND OF OZ, BUT THE DESERT'S POISONS NEVER REACH THE PALACE OR ITS GARDENS.

GLINDA IS A STEADY FRIEND AND ADVISOR OF OZMA, THE GIRL RULER OF THE LAND OF OZ. THE GREAT SORCERESS OFTEN RECEIVES VISITS FROM OZMA OR OTHERS WHO LIVE IN THE EMERALD CITY. FOR INSTANCE...

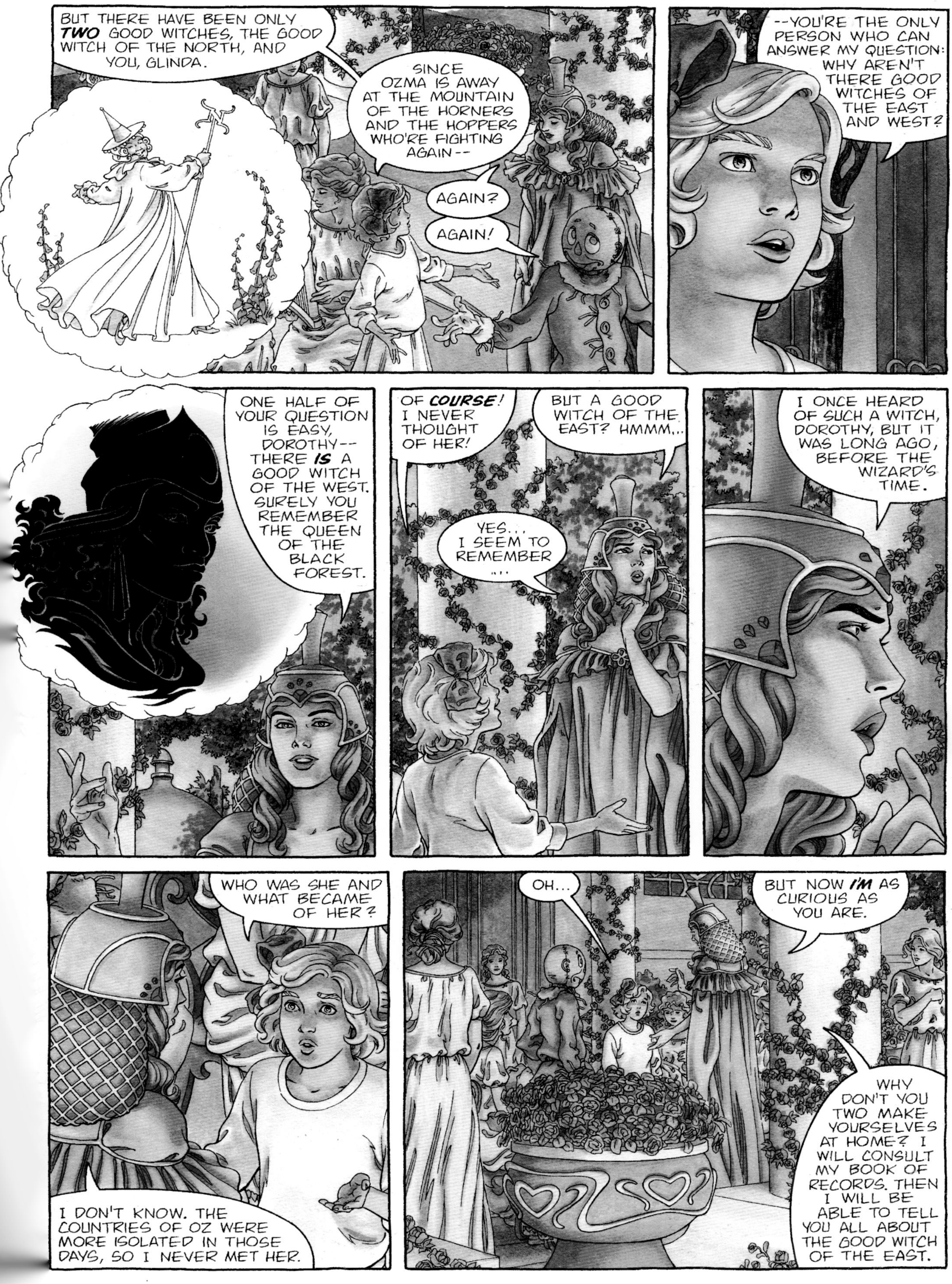
BUT THERE HAVE BEEN ONLY **TWO** GOOD WITCHES, THE GOOD WITCH OF THE NORTH, AND YOU, GLINDA.
SINCE OZMA IS AWAY AT THE MOUNTAIN OF THE HORNERS AND THE HOPPERS WHO'RE FIGHTING AGAIN--
AGAIN?
AGAIN!
--YOU'RE THE ONLY PERSON WHO CAN ANSWER MY QUESTION: WHY AREN'T THERE GOOD WITCHES OF THE EAST AND WEST?
ONE HALF OF YOUR QUESTION IS EASY, DOROTHY-- THERE **IS** A GOOD WITCH OF THE WEST. SURELY YOU REMEMBER THE QUEEN OF THE BLACK FOREST.
OF **COURSE**! I NEVER THOUGHT OF HER!
BUT A GOOD WITCH OF THE EAST? HMMM...
YES... I SEEM TO REMEMBER ...
I ONCE HEARD OF SUCH A WITCH, DOROTHY, BUT IT WAS LONG AGO, BEFORE THE WIZARD'S TIME.
WHO WAS SHE AND WHAT BECAME OF HER?
I DON'T KNOW. THE COUNTRIES OF OZ WERE MORE ISOLATED IN THOSE DAYS, SO I NEVER MET HER.
OH...
BUT NOW **I'M** AS CURIOUS AS YOU ARE.
WHY DON'T YOU TWO MAKE YOURSELVES AT HOME? I WILL CONSULT MY BOOK OF RECORDS. THEN I WILL BE ABLE TO TELL YOU ALL ABOUT THE GOOD WITCH OF THE EAST.

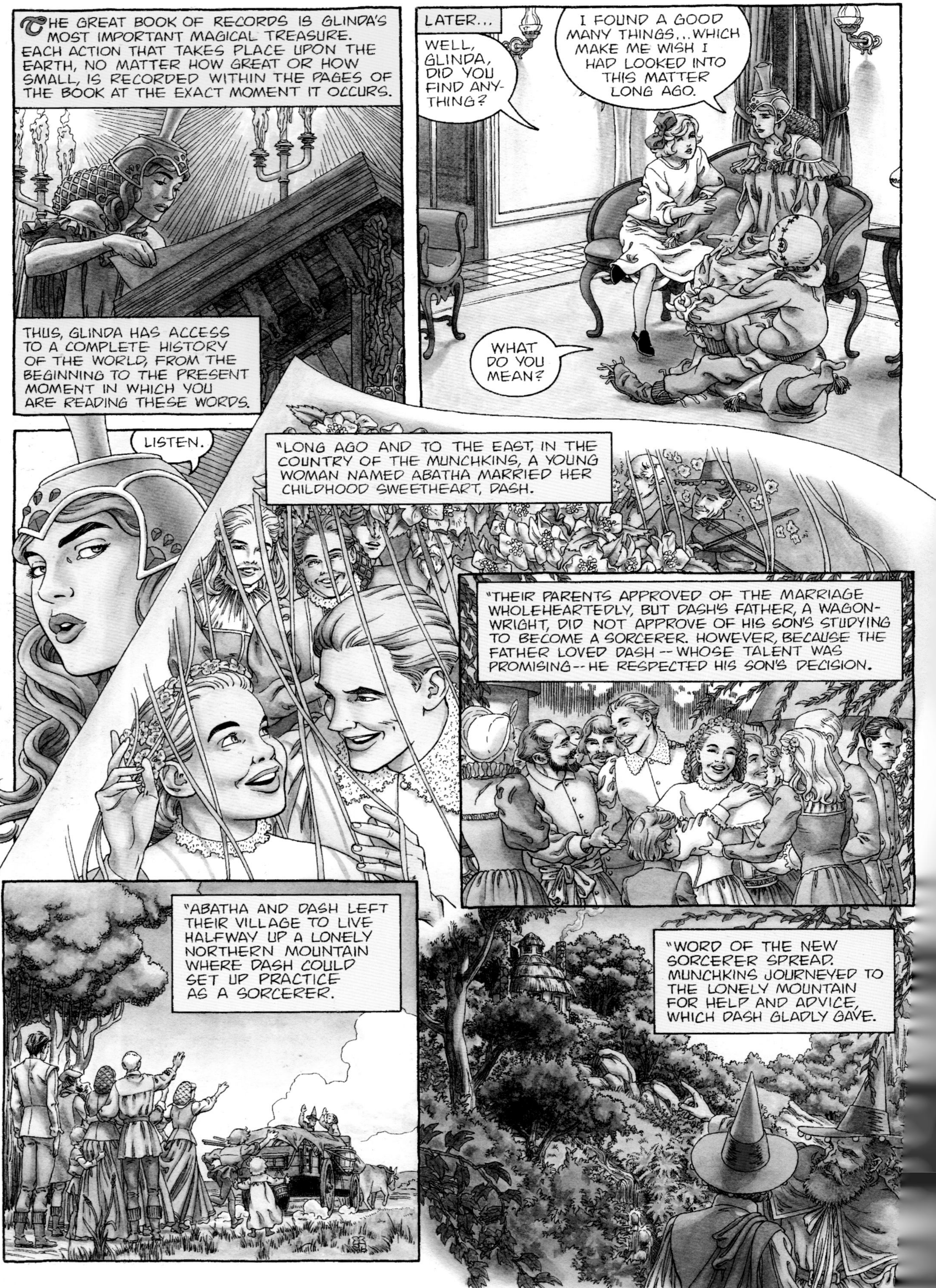
THE GREAT BOOK OF RECORDS IS GLINDA'S MOST IMPORTANT MAGICAL TREASURE. EACH ACTION THAT TAKES PLACE UPON THE EARTH, NO MATTER HOW GREAT OR HOW SMALL, IS RECORDED WITHIN THE PAGES OF THE BOOK AT THE EXACT MOMENT IT OCCURS.
THUS, GLINDA HAS ACCESS TO A COMPLETE HISTORY OF THE WORLD, FROM THE BEGINNING TO THE PRESENT MOMENT IN WHICH YOU ARE READING THESE WORDS.
LATER...
WELL, GLINDA, DID YOU FIND ANY-THING?
I FOUND A GOOD MANY THINGS...WHICH MAKE ME WISH I HAD LOOKED INTO THIS MATTER LONG AGO.
WHAT DO YOU MEAN?
LISTEN.
"LONG AGO AND TO THE EAST, IN THE COUNTRY OF THE MUNCHKINS, A YOUNG WOMAN NAMED ABATHA MARRIED HER CHILDHOOD SWEETHEART, DASH.
"THEIR PARENTS APPROVED OF THE MARRIAGE WHOLEHEARTEDLY, BUT DASH'S FATHER, A WAGON-WRIGHT, DID NOT APPROVE OF HIS SON'S STUDYING TO BECOME A SORCERER. HOWEVER, BECAUSE THE FATHER LOVED DASH -- WHOSE TALENT WAS PROMISING-- HE RESPECTED HIS SON'S DECISION.
"ABATHA AND DASH LEFT THEIR VILLAGE TO LIVE HALFWAY UP A LONELY NORTHERN MOUNTAIN WHERE DASH COULD SET UP PRACTICE AS A SORCERER.
"WORD OF THE NEW SORCERER SPREAD. MUNCHKINS JOURNEYED TO THE LONELY MOUNTAIN FOR HELP AND ADVICE, WHICH DASH GLADLY GAVE.

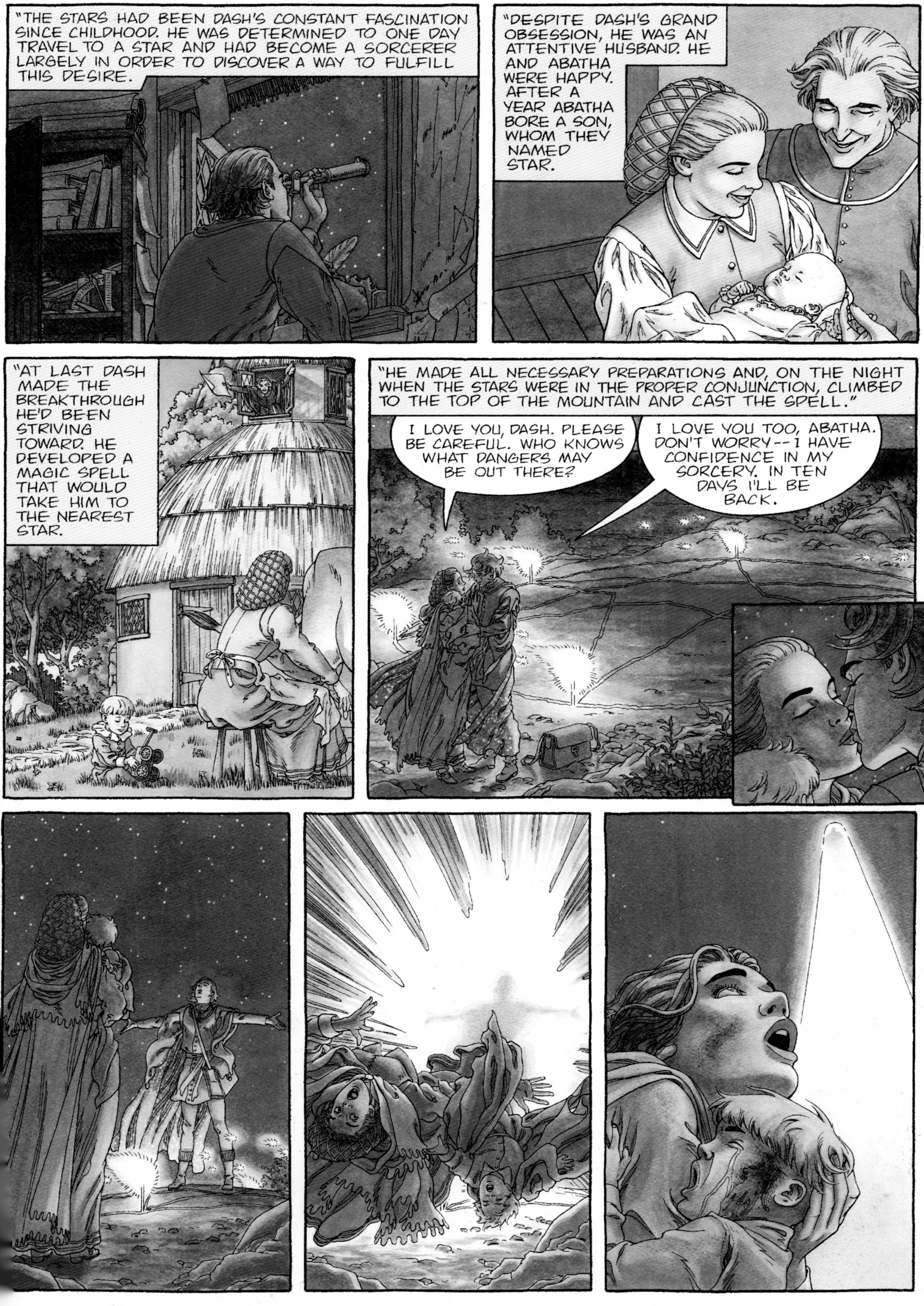
"THE STARS HAD BEEN DASH'S CONSTANT FASCINATION SINCE CHILDHOOD. HE WAS DETERMINED TO ONE DAY TRAVEL TO A STAR AND HAD BECOME A SORCERER LARGELY IN ORDER TO DISCOVER A WAY TO FULFILL THIS DESIRE.
"DESPITE DASH'S GRAND OBSESSION, HE WAS AN ATTENTIVE HUSBAND. HE AND ABATHA WERE HAPPY. AFTER A YEAR ABATHA BORE A SON, WHOM THEY NAMED STAR.
"AT LAST DASH MADE THE BREAKTHROUGH HE'D BEEN STRIVING TOWARD. HE DEVELOPED A MAGIC SPELL THAT WOULD TAKE HIM TO THE NEAREST STAR.
"HE MADE ALL NECESSARY PREPARATIONS AND, ON THE NIGHT WHEN THE STARS WERE IN THE PROPER CONJUNCTION, CLIMBED TO THE TOP OF THE MOUNTAIN AND CAST THE SPELL."
I LOVE YOU, DASH. PLEASE BE CAREFUL. WHO KNOWS WHAT DANGERS MAY BE OUT THERE?
I LOVE YOU TOO, ABATHA. DON'T WORRY--I HAVE CONFIDENCE IN MY SORCERY. IN TEN DAYS I'LL BE BACK.

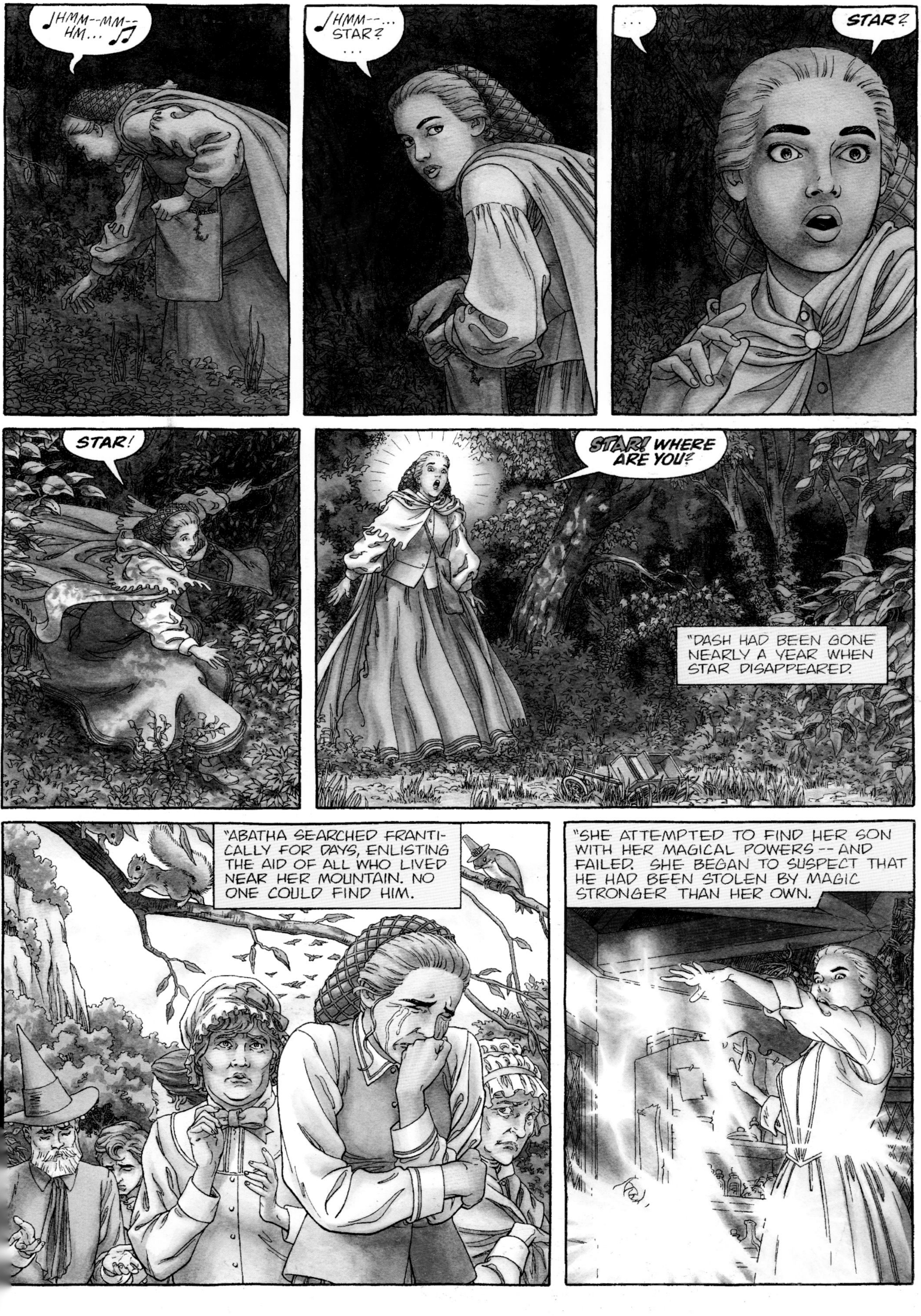
♪HMM--MM--
HM... ♫
♪HMM--...
STAR?
...
...
STAR?
STAR!
STAR! WHERE ARE YOU?
"DASH HAD BEEN GONE NEARLY A YEAR WHEN STAR DISAPPEARED.
"ABATHA SEARCHED FRANTICALLY FOR DAYS, ENLISTING THE AID OF ALL WHO LIVED NEAR HER MOUNTAIN. NO ONE COULD FIND HIM.
"SHE ATTEMPTED TO FIND HER SON WITH HER MAGICAL POWERS -- AND FAILED. SHE BEGAN TO SUSPECT THAT HE HAD BEEN STOLEN BY MAGIC STRONGER THAN HER OWN.

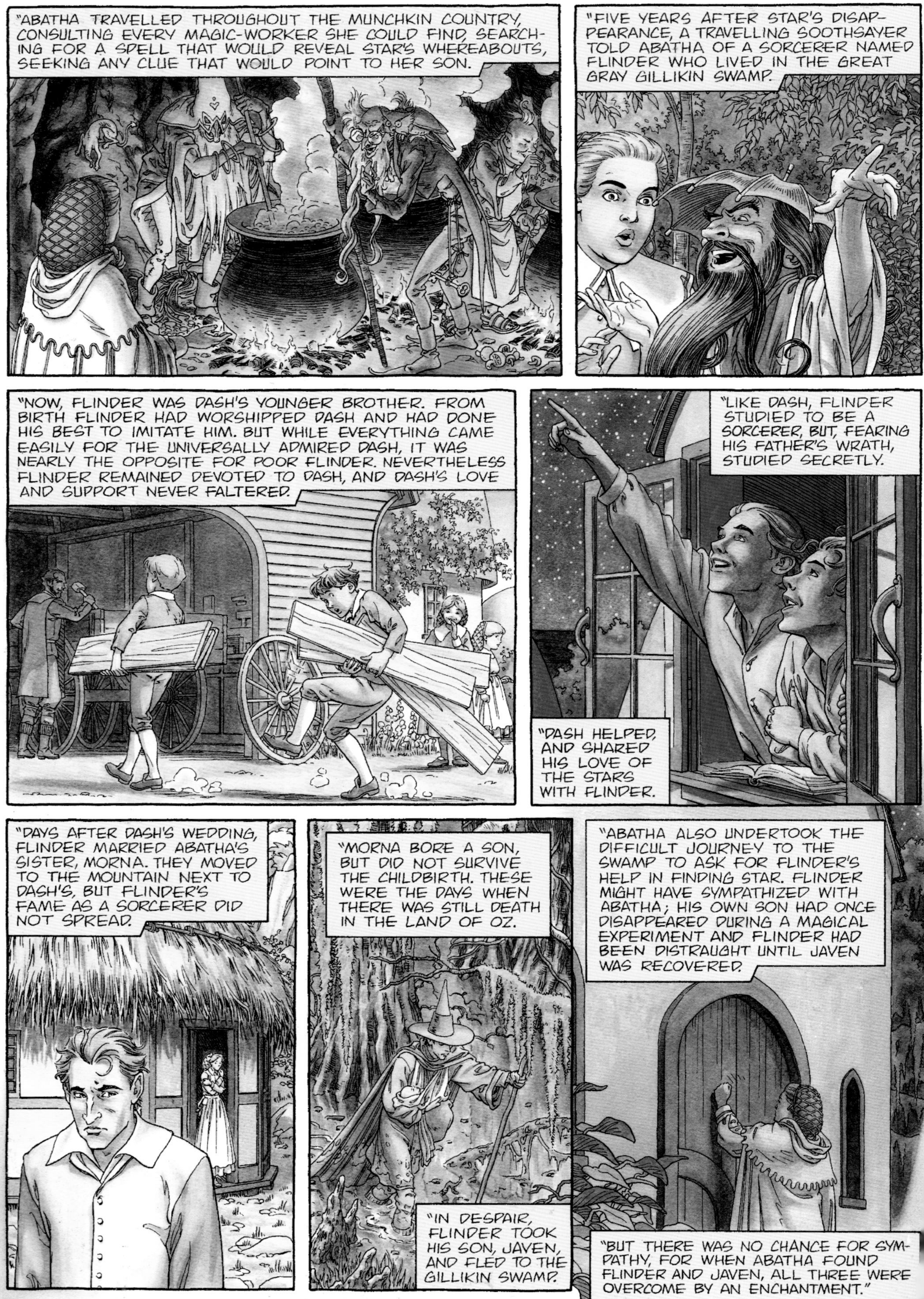
"ABATHA TRAVELLED THROUGHOUT THE MUNCHKIN COUNTRY, CONSULTING EVERY MAGIC-WORKER SHE COULD FIND, SEARCHING FOR A SPELL THAT WOULD REVEAL STAR'S WHEREABOUTS, SEEKING ANY CLUE THAT WOULD POINT TO HER SON.
"FIVE YEARS AFTER STAR'S DISAPPEARANCE, A TRAVELLING SOOTHSAYER TOLD ABATHA OF A SORCERER NAMED FLINDER WHO LIVED IN THE GREAT GRAY GILLIKIN SWAMP.
"NOW, FLINDER WAS DASH'S YOUNGER BROTHER. FROM BIRTH FLINDER HAD WORSHIPPED DASH AND HAD DONE HIS BEST TO IMITATE HIM. BUT WHILE EVERYTHING CAME EASILY FOR THE UNIVERSALLY ADMIRED DASH, IT WAS NEARLY THE OPPOSITE FOR POOR FLINDER. NEVERTHELESS FLINDER REMAINED DEVOTED TO DASH, AND DASH'S LOVE AND SUPPORT NEVER FALTERED.
"LIKE DASH, FLINDER STUDIED TO BE A SORCERER, BUT, FEARING HIS FATHER'S WRATH, STUDIED SECRETLY.
"DASH HELPED, AND SHARED HIS LOVE OF THE STARS WITH FLINDER.
"DAYS AFTER DASH'S WEDDING, FLINDER MARRIED ABATHA'S SISTER, MORNA. THEY MOVED TO THE MOUNTAIN NEXT TO DASH'S, BUT FLINDER'S FAME AS A SORCERER DID NOT SPREAD.
"MORNA BORE A SON, BUT DID NOT SURVIVE THE CHILDBIRTH. THESE WERE THE DAYS WHEN THERE WAS STILL DEATH IN THE LAND OF OZ.
"IN DESPAIR, FLINDER TOOK HIS SON, JAVEN, AND FLED TO THE GILLIKIN SWAMP.
"ABATHA ALSO UNDERTOOK THE DIFFICULT JOURNEY TO THE SWAMP TO ASK FOR FLINDER'S HELP IN FINDING STAR. FLINDER MIGHT HAVE SYMPATHIZED WITH ABATHA; HIS OWN SON HAD ONCE DISAPPEARED DURING A MAGICAL EXPERIMENT AND FLINDER HAD BEEN DISTRAUGHT UNTIL JAVEN WAS RECOVERED.
"BUT THERE WAS NO CHANCE FOR SYMPATHY, FOR WHEN ABATHA FOUND FLINDER AND JAVEN, ALL THREE WERE OVERCOME BY AN ENCHANTMENT."

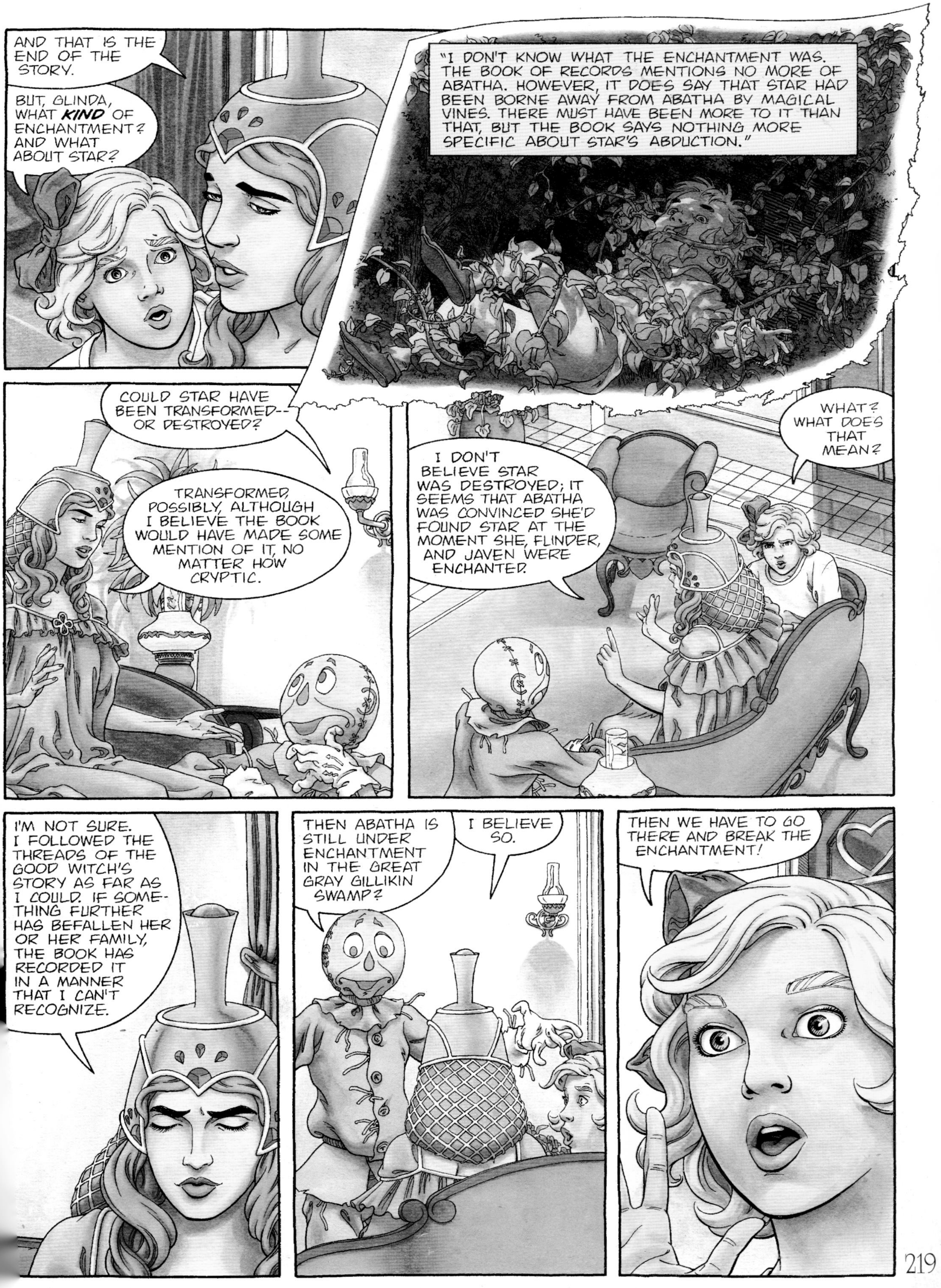
AND THAT IS THE END OF THE STORY.
BUT, GLINDA, WHAT **KIND** OF ENCHANTMENT? AND WHAT ABOUT STAR?
"I DON'T KNOW WHAT THE ENCHANTMENT WAS. THE BOOK OF RECORDS MENTIONS NO MORE OF ABATHA. HOWEVER, IT DOES SAY THAT STAR HAD BEEN BORNE AWAY FROM ABATHA BY MAGICAL VINES. THERE MUST HAVE BEEN MORE TO IT THAN THAT, BUT THE BOOK SAYS NOTHING MORE SPECIFIC ABOUT STAR'S ABDUCTION."
COULD STAR HAVE BEEN TRANSFORMED-- OR DESTROYED?
TRANSFORMED, POSSIBLY, ALTHOUGH I BELIEVE THE BOOK WOULD HAVE MADE SOME MENTION OF IT, NO MATTER HOW CRYPTIC.
I DON'T BELIEVE STAR WAS DESTROYED; IT SEEMS THAT ABATHA WAS CONVINCED SHE'D FOUND STAR AT THE MOMENT SHE, FLINDER, AND JAVEN WERE ENCHANTED.
WHAT? WHAT DOES THAT MEAN?
I'M NOT SURE. I FOLLOWED THE THREADS OF THE GOOD WITCH'S STORY AS FAR AS I COULD. IF SOMETHING FURTHER HAS BEFALLEN HER OR HER FAMILY, THE BOOK HAS RECORDED IT IN A MANNER THAT I CAN'T RECOGNIZE.
THEN ABATHA IS STILL UNDER ENCHANTMENT IN THE GREAT GRAY GILLIKIN SWAMP?
I BELIEVE SO.
THEN WE HAVE TO GO THERE AND BREAK THE ENCHANTMENT!

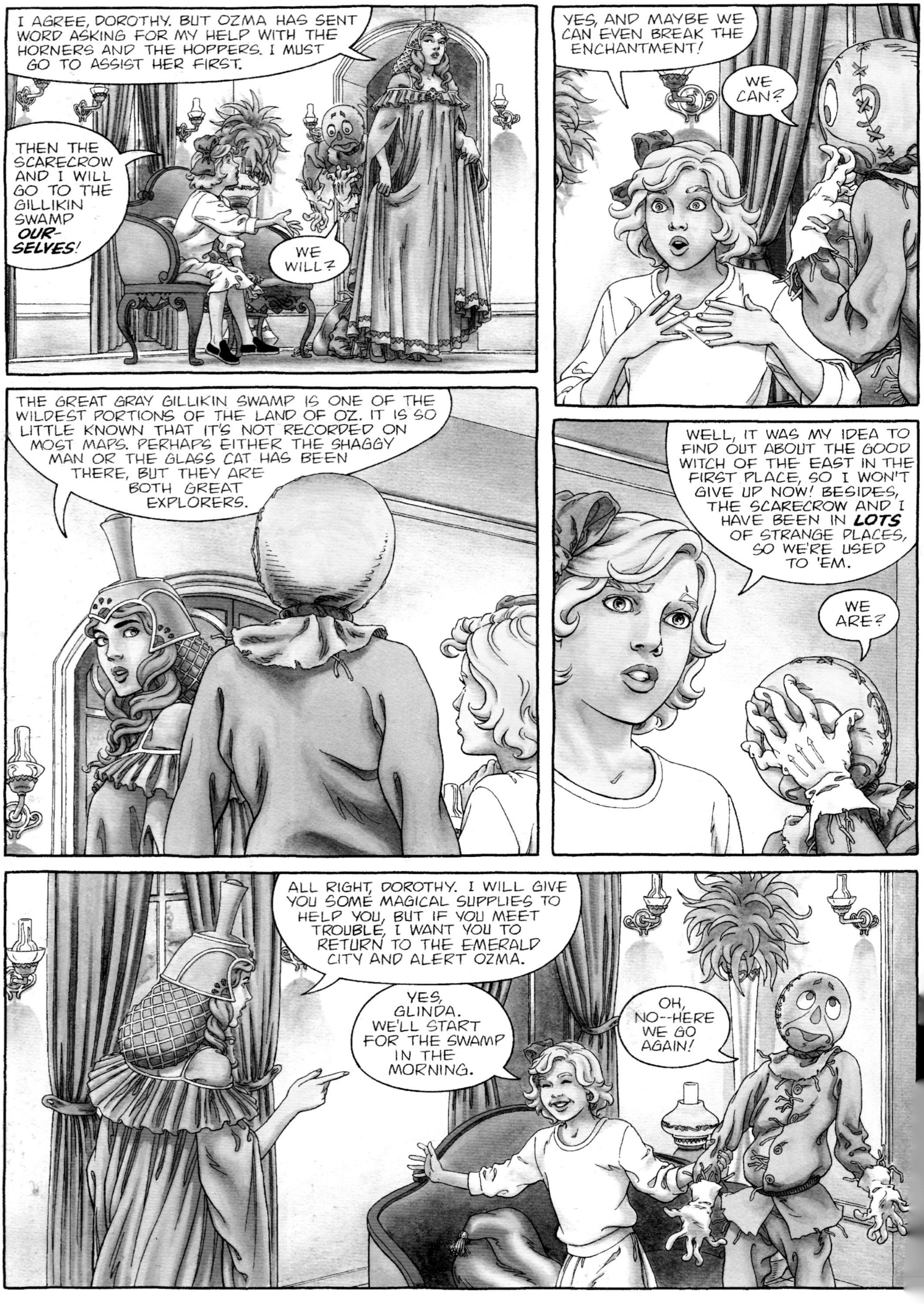
I AGREE, DOROTHY. BUT OZMA HAS SENT WORD ASKING FOR MY HELP WITH THE HORNERS AND THE HOPPERS. I MUST GO TO ASSIST HER FIRST.
THEN THE SCARECROW AND I WILL GO TO THE GILLIKIN SWAMP ***OUR-SELVES***!
WE WILL?
YES, AND MAYBE WE CAN EVEN BREAK THE ENCHANTMENT!
WE CAN?
THE GREAT GRAY GILLIKIN SWAMP IS ONE OF THE WILDEST PORTIONS OF THE LAND OF OZ. IT IS SO LITTLE KNOWN THAT IT'S NOT RECORDED ON MOST MAPS. PERHAPS EITHER THE SHAGGY MAN OR THE GLASS CAT HAS BEEN THERE, BUT THEY ARE BOTH GREAT EXPLORERS.
WELL, IT WAS MY IDEA TO FIND OUT ABOUT THE GOOD WITCH OF THE EAST IN THE FIRST PLACE, SO I WON'T GIVE UP NOW! BESIDES, THE SCARECROW AND I HAVE BEEN IN ***LOTS*** OF STRANGE PLACES, SO WE'RE USED TO 'EM.
WE ARE?
ALL RIGHT, DOROTHY. I WILL GIVE YOU SOME MAGICAL SUPPLIES TO HELP YOU, BUT IF YOU MEET TROUBLE, I WANT YOU TO RETURN TO THE EMERALD CITY AND ALERT OZMA.
YES, GLINDA. WE'LL START FOR THE SWAMP IN THE MORNING.
OH, NO--HERE WE GO AGAIN!

THE FOLLOWING DAY IN THE NORTHERN COUNTRY OF THE GILLIKINS...

THIS IS AS FAR AS I CAN GO WITH THE RED WAGON.

WE'LL HAVE TO CROSS THE MOUNTAINS ON FOOT.

WILL YOU BE OKAY TILL WE GET BACK, SAWHORSE?

OH, YES. I'LL CONTENT MYSELF WITH OBSERVING THE GROWTH PROCESS OF GRASS.

OVER THE HILLS TO THE GILLIKIN *SWAMP*, CARRYING MAGIC SUPPLIES, SOME FOR *CAWMP*, OTHERS FOR BREAKING ENCHANTMENTS, WE *TRAWMP*, DUBIOUS THAT THE SWAMP WON'T BE TOO *DAWMP*, HOPING THE MOISTURE WON'T MAKE MY BRAINS *CRAWMP*, KNOWING THAT SOGGY STRAW'S USELESS--

OH, *STOMP*-- I MEAN *STOP!*

IF THIS CHART IS RIGHT, WE'RE NOT FAR FROM THE SWAMP.

I WONDER WHAT THE ENCHANTMENT COULD BE.

DEADLY DESERT

NEXT MORNING...

SCARECROW, LOOK! THERE IT IS...

221

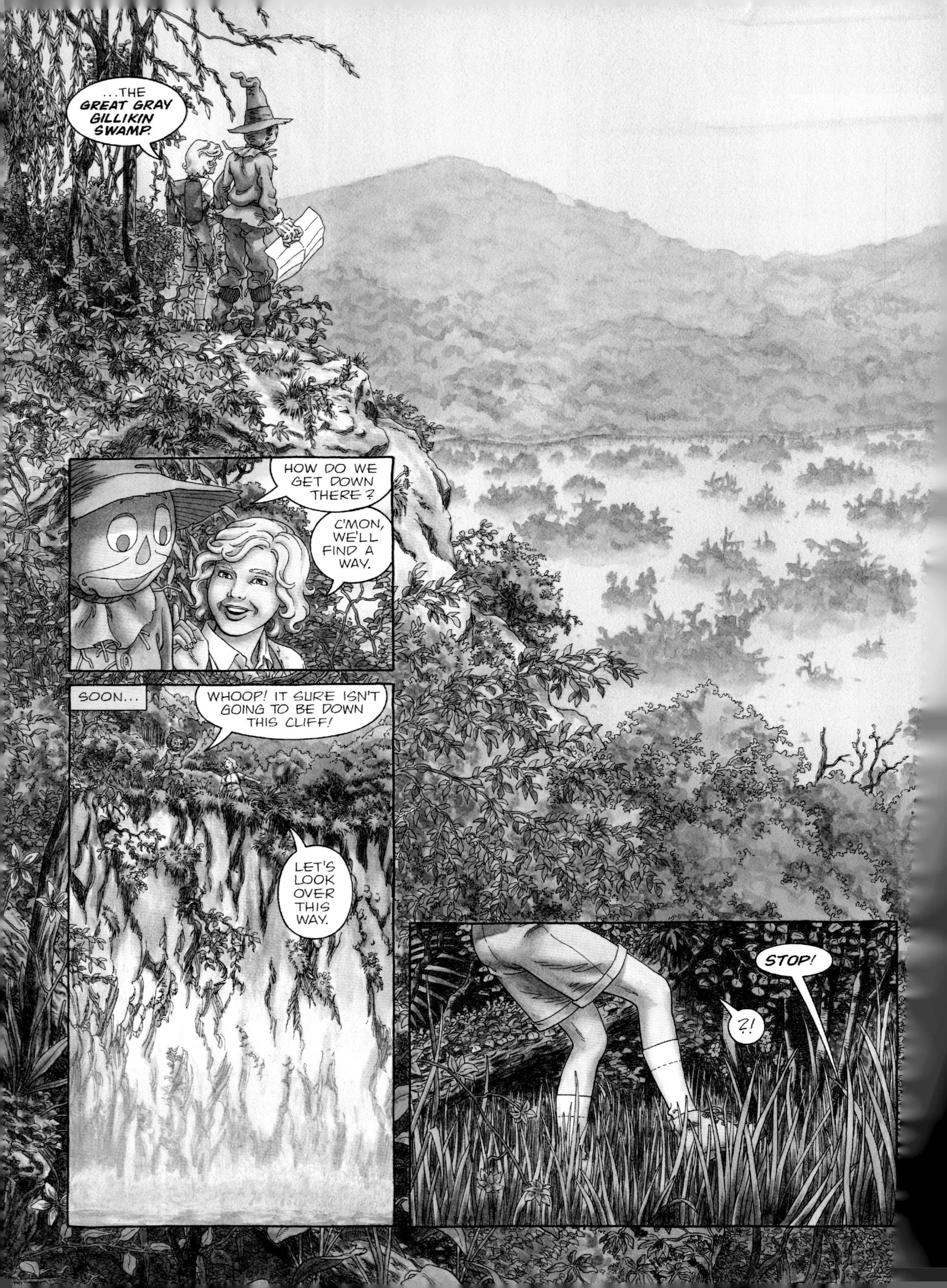
...THE GREAT GRAY GILLIKIN SWAMP.
HOW DO WE GET DOWN THERE?
C'MON, WE'LL FIND A WAY.
SOON...
WHOOP! IT SURE ISN'T GOING TO BE DOWN THIS CLIFF!
LET'S LOOK OVER THIS WAY.
STOP!
?!

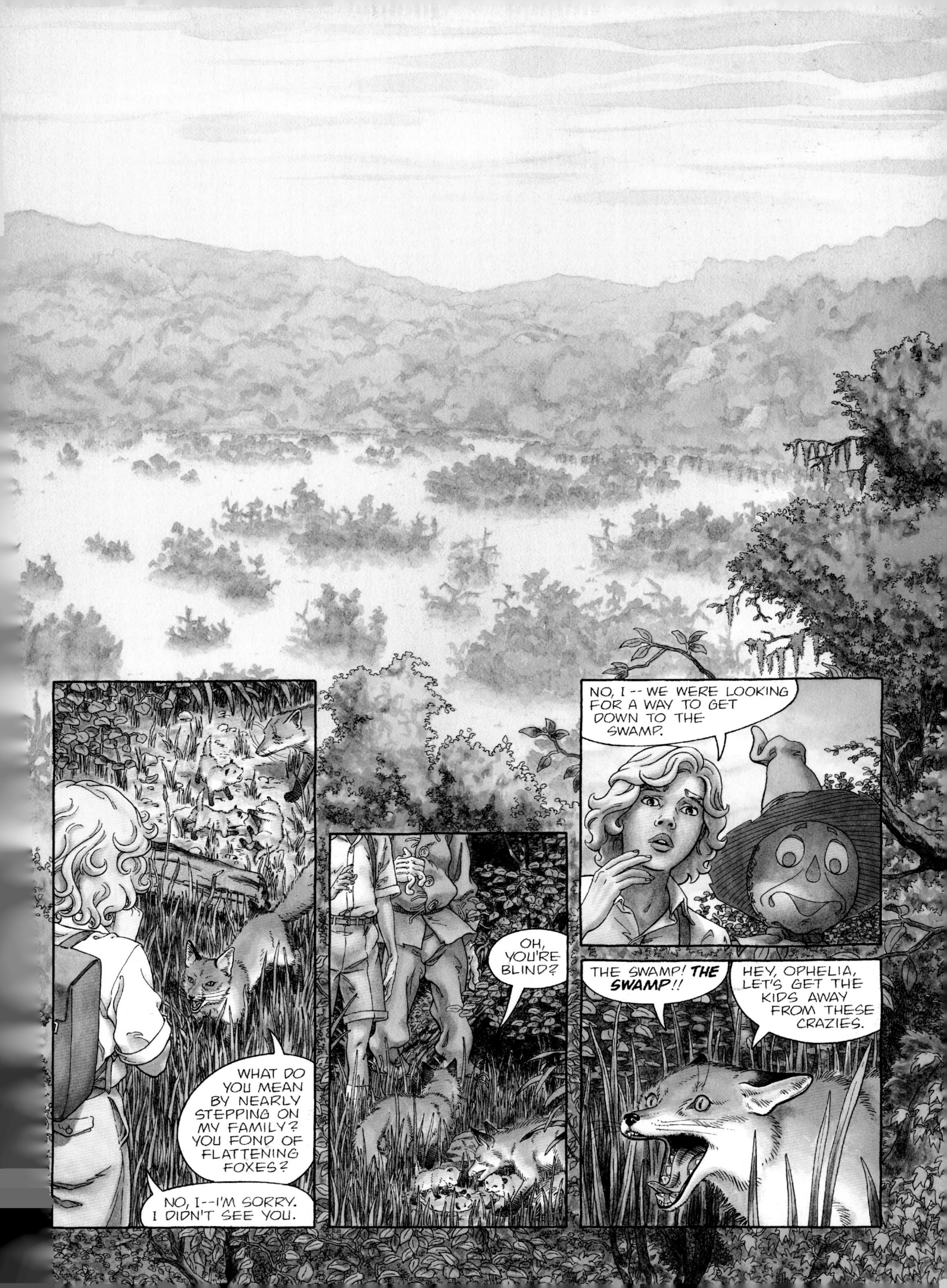
WHAT DO YOU MEAN BY NEARLY STEPPING ON MY FAMILY? YOU FOND OF FLATTENING FOXES?
NO, I--I'M SORRY. I DIDN'T SEE YOU.
OH, YOU'RE BLIND?
NO, I -- WE WERE LOOKING FOR A WAY TO GET DOWN TO THE SWAMP.
THE SWAMP! **THE SWAMP**!!
HEY, OPHELIA, LET'S GET THE KIDS AWAY FROM THESE CRAZIES.

...UNTIL--

COME ONNN... COOOME ONNN...

OH! I FORGOT THE KNAPSACK!

GOT IT! *HURRY,* DOROTHY!

I'M COMING!

QUICK! IT'S DRIFTING AWAY FROM THE CLIFF!

AH, SOLID GROUN--

SQUISH!

...SORT OF.

CRACK!

YII!

SPLUTCH!

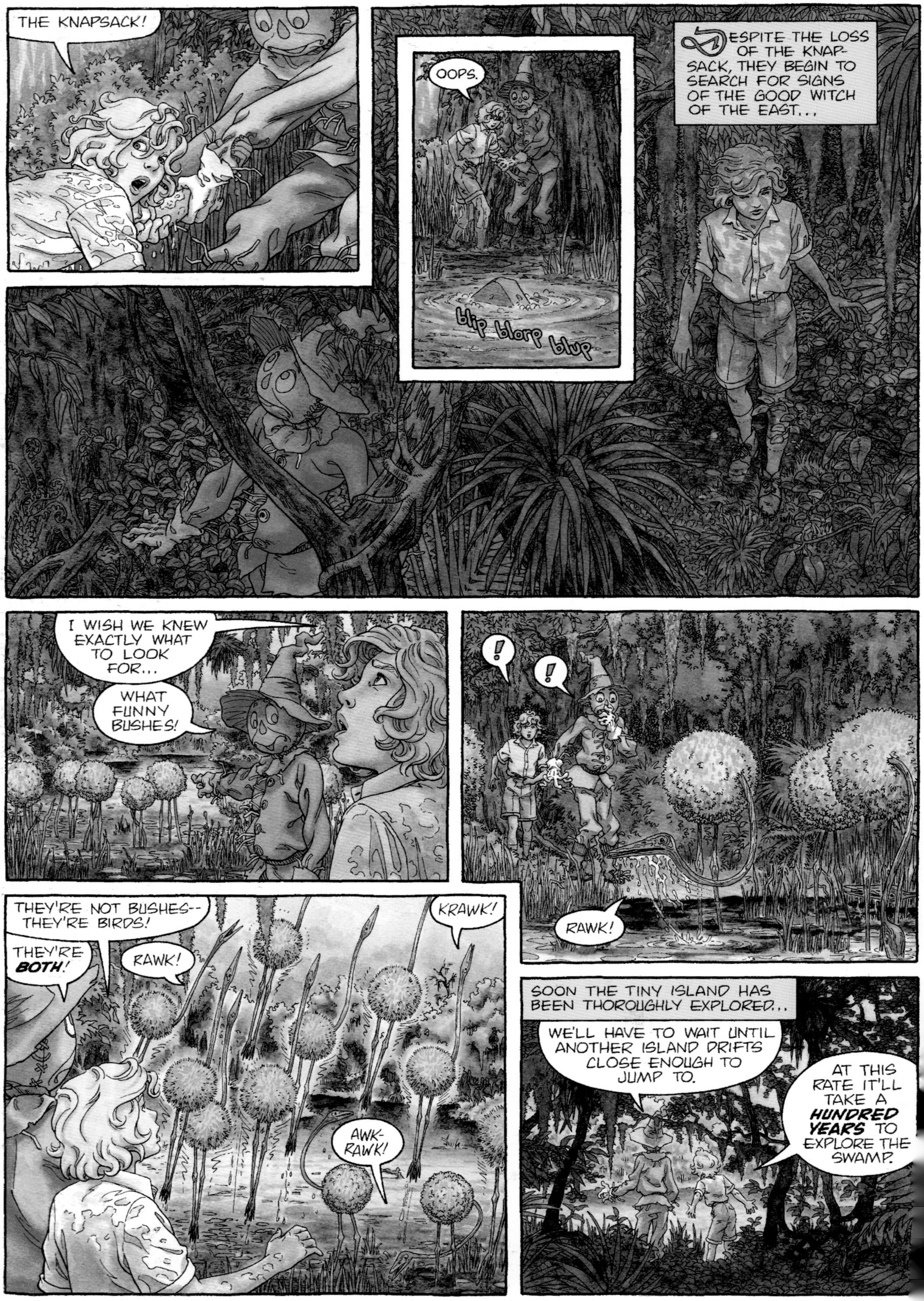
THE KNAPSACK!
OOPS.
blip blorp blup
DESPITE THE LOSS OF THE KNAPSACK, THEY BEGIN TO SEARCH FOR SIGNS OF THE GOOD WITCH OF THE EAST...
I WISH WE KNEW EXACTLY WHAT TO LOOK FOR...
WHAT FUNNY BUSHES!
!
!
RAWK!
THEY'RE NOT BUSHES-- THEY'RE BIRDS!
THEY'RE **BOTH**!
RAWK!
KRAWK!
AWK-RAWK!
SOON THE TINY ISLAND HAS BEEN THOROUGHLY EXPLORED...
WE'LL HAVE TO WAIT UNTIL ANOTHER ISLAND DRIFTS CLOSE ENOUGH TO JUMP TO.
AT THIS RATE IT'LL TAKE A **HUNDRED YEARS** TO EXPLORE THE SWAMP.

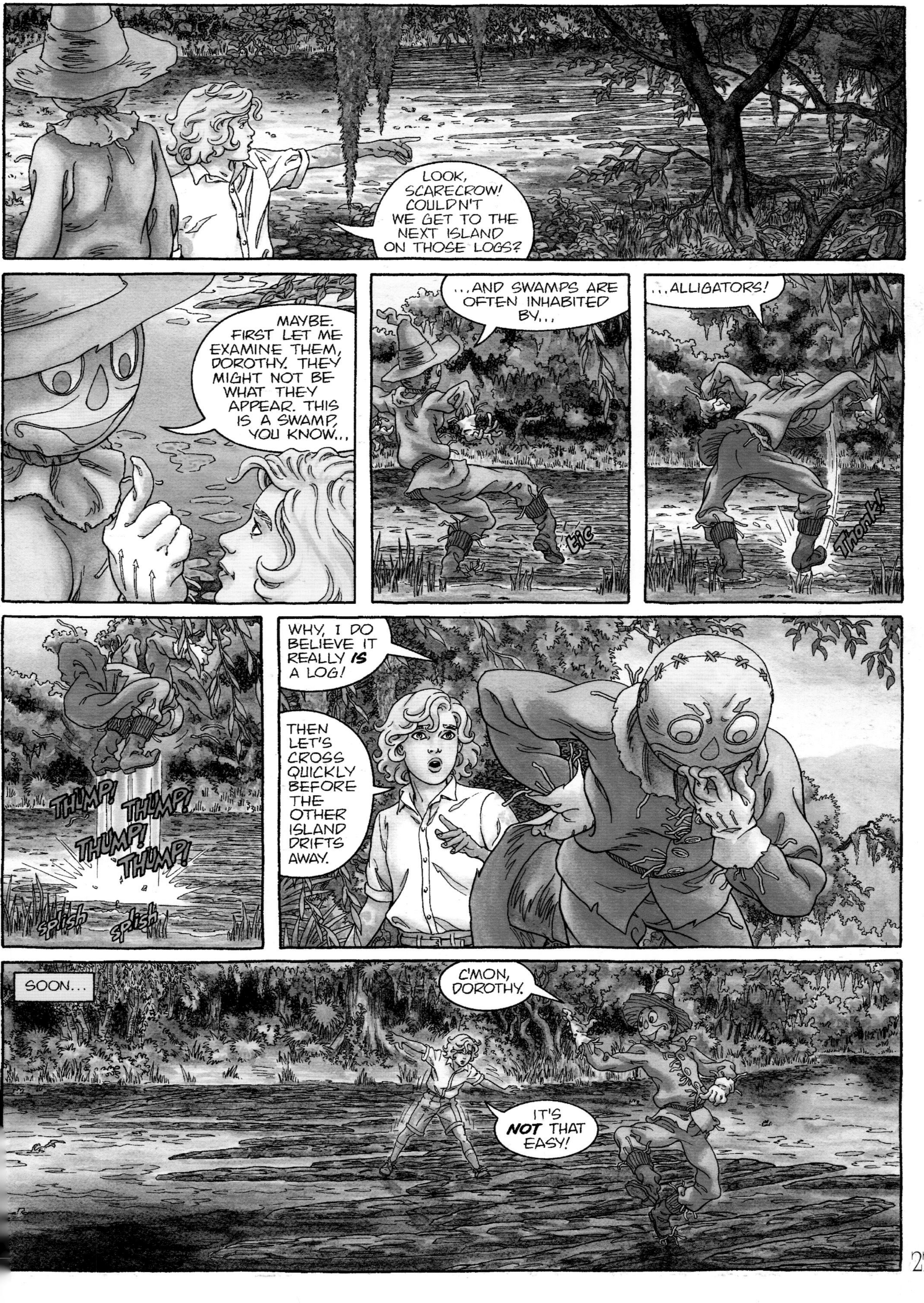

LOOK, SCARECROW! COULDN'T WE GET TO THE NEXT ISLAND ON THOSE LOGS?
MAYBE. FIRST LET ME EXAMINE THEM, DOROTHY. THEY MIGHT NOT BE WHAT THEY APPEAR. THIS IS A SWAMP, YOU KNOW...
...AND SWAMPS ARE OFTEN INHABITED BY...
tic
...ALLIGATORS!
THONK!
THUMP! THUMP! THUMP! THUMP!
splish splish
WHY, I DO BELIEVE IT REALLY **IS** A LOG!
THEN LET'S CROSS QUICKLY BEFORE THE OTHER ISLAND DRIFTS AWAY.
SOON...
C'MON, DOROTHY.
IT'S **NOT** THAT EASY!

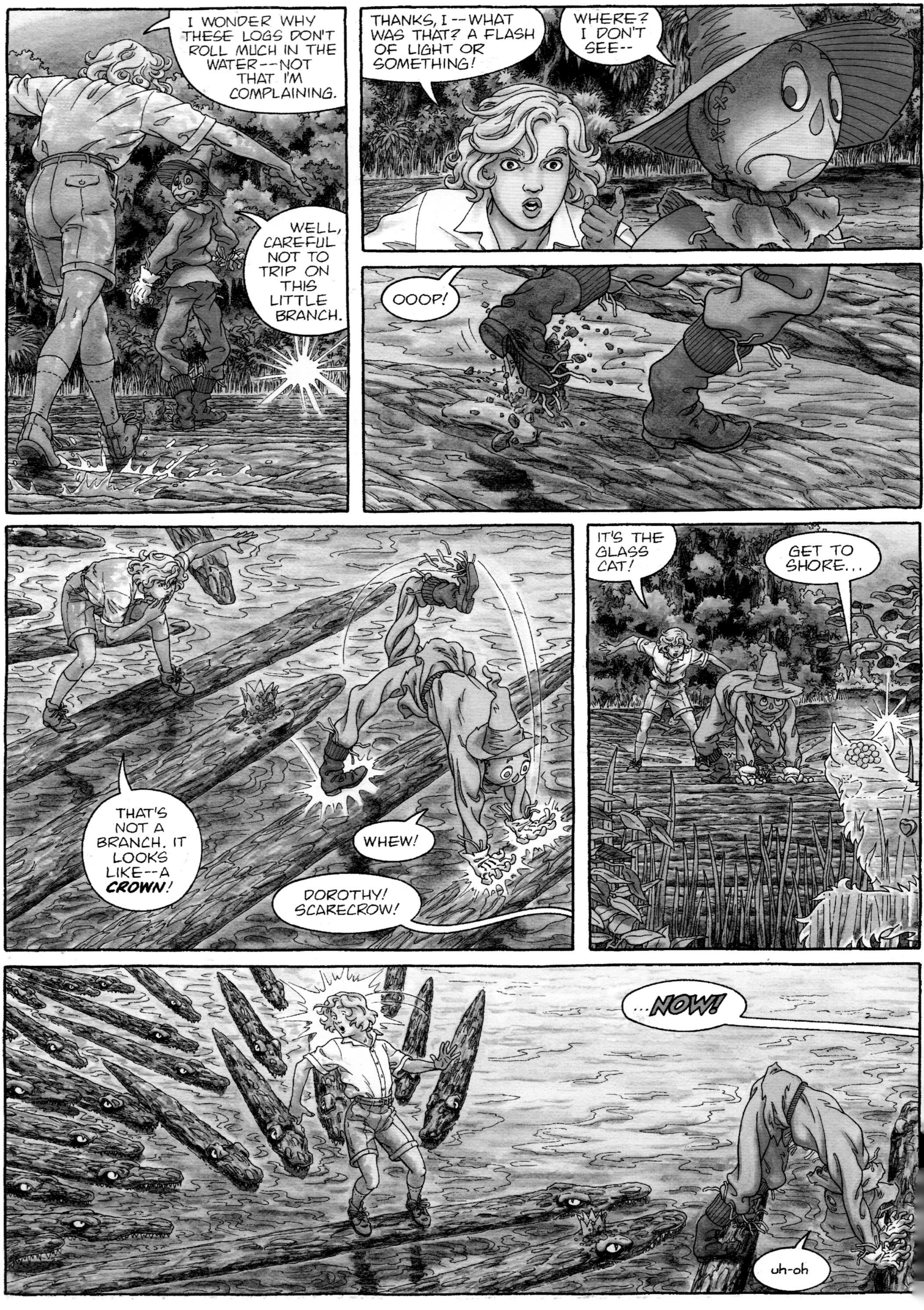
I WONDER WHY THESE LOGS DON'T ROLL MUCH IN THE WATER--NOT THAT I'M COMPLAINING.
WELL, CAREFUL NOT TO TRIP ON THIS LITTLE BRANCH.
THANKS, I--WHAT WAS THAT? A FLASH OF LIGHT OR SOMETHING!
WHERE? I DON'T SEE--
OOOP!
THAT'S NOT A BRANCH. IT LOOKS LIKE--A **CROWN**!
WHEW!
DOROTHY! SCARECROW!
IT'S THE GLASS CAT!
GET TO SHORE...
...NOW!
uh-oh

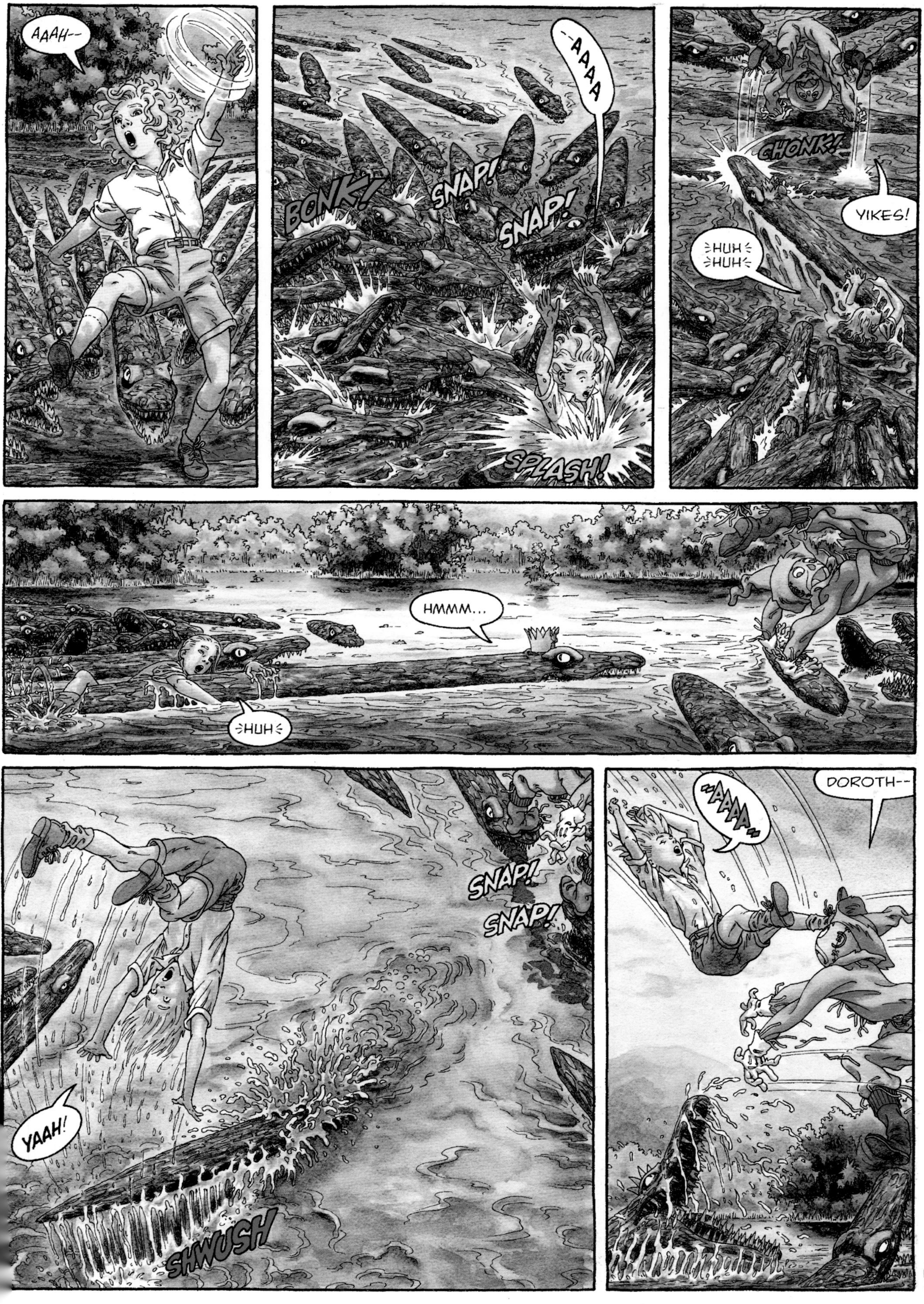
AAAH--
--AAAA
BONK!
SNAP!
SNAP!
SPLASH!
CHONK!
YIKES!
HUH HUH
HMMM...
HUH
SNAP!
SNAP!
YAAH!
SHWUSH
DOROTH--
AAAA

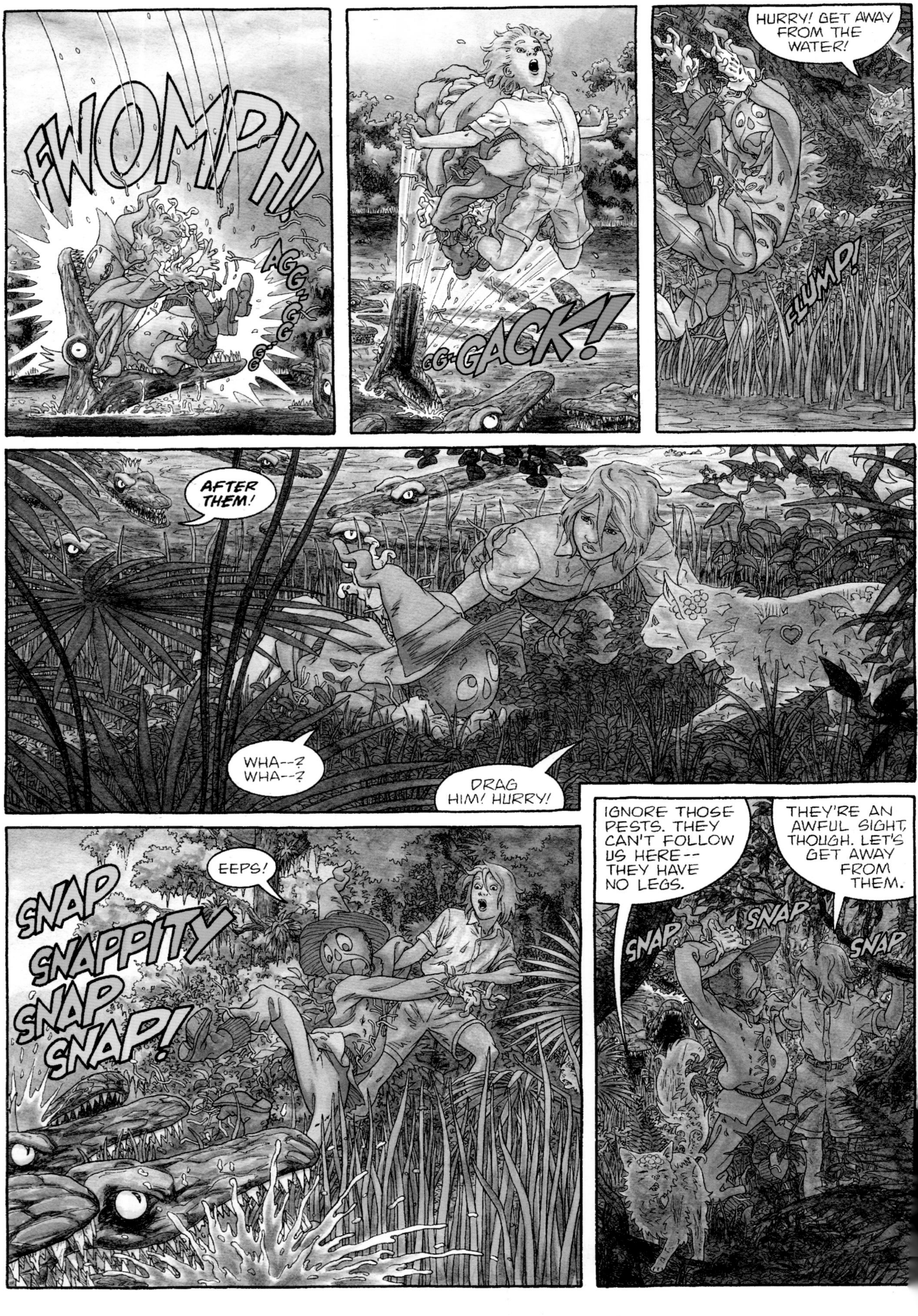
FWOMPH!
AGG-G-G-G
GG-GACK!
HURRY! GET AWAY FROM THE WATER!
FLUMP!
AFTER THEM!
WHA--? WHA--?
DRAG HIM! HURRY!
EEPS!
SNAP SNAPPITY SNAP SNAP!
IGNORE THOSE PESTS. THEY CAN'T FOLLOW US HERE-- THEY HAVE NO LEGS.
THEY'RE AN AWFUL SIGHT, THOUGH. LET'S GET AWAY FROM THEM.
SNAP
SNAP
SNAP

# Chapter 3 The Enchantment

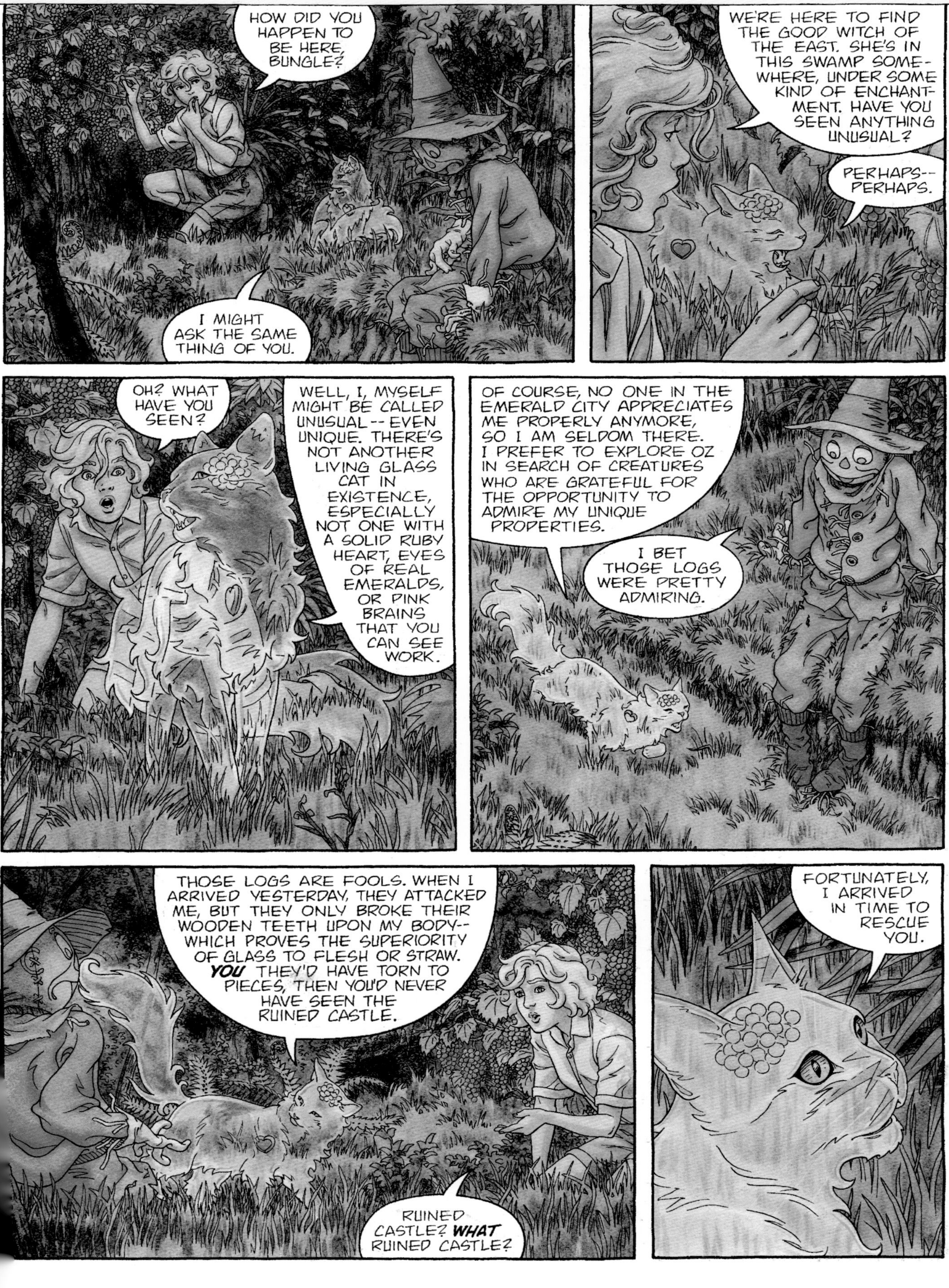
HOW DID YOU HAPPEN TO BE HERE, BUNGLE?
I MIGHT ASK THE SAME THING OF YOU.
WE'RE HERE TO FIND THE GOOD WITCH OF THE EAST. SHE'S IN THIS SWAMP SOMEWHERE, UNDER SOME KIND OF ENCHANTMENT. HAVE YOU SEEN ANYTHING UNUSUAL?
PERHAPS-- PERHAPS.
OH? WHAT HAVE YOU SEEN?
WELL, I, MYSELF MIGHT BE CALLED UNUSUAL -- EVEN UNIQUE. THERE'S NOT ANOTHER LIVING GLASS CAT IN EXISTENCE, ESPECIALLY NOT ONE WITH A SOLID RUBY HEART, EYES OF REAL EMERALDS, OR PINK BRAINS THAT YOU CAN SEE WORK.
OF COURSE, NO ONE IN THE EMERALD CITY APPRECIATES ME PROPERLY ANYMORE, SO I AM SELDOM THERE. I PREFER TO EXPLORE OZ IN SEARCH OF CREATURES WHO ARE GRATEFUL FOR THE OPPORTUNITY TO ADMIRE MY UNIQUE PROPERTIES.
I BET THOSE LOGS WERE PRETTY ADMIRING.
THOSE LOGS ARE FOOLS. WHEN I ARRIVED YESTERDAY, THEY ATTACKED ME, BUT THEY ONLY BROKE THEIR WOODEN TEETH UPON MY BODY-- WHICH PROVES THE SUPERIORITY OF GLASS TO FLESH OR STRAW. YOU THEY'D HAVE TORN TO PIECES, THEN YOU'D NEVER HAVE SEEN THE RUINED CASTLE.
RUINED CASTLE? WHAT RUINED CASTLE?
FORTUNATELY, I ARRIVED IN TIME TO RESCUE YOU.

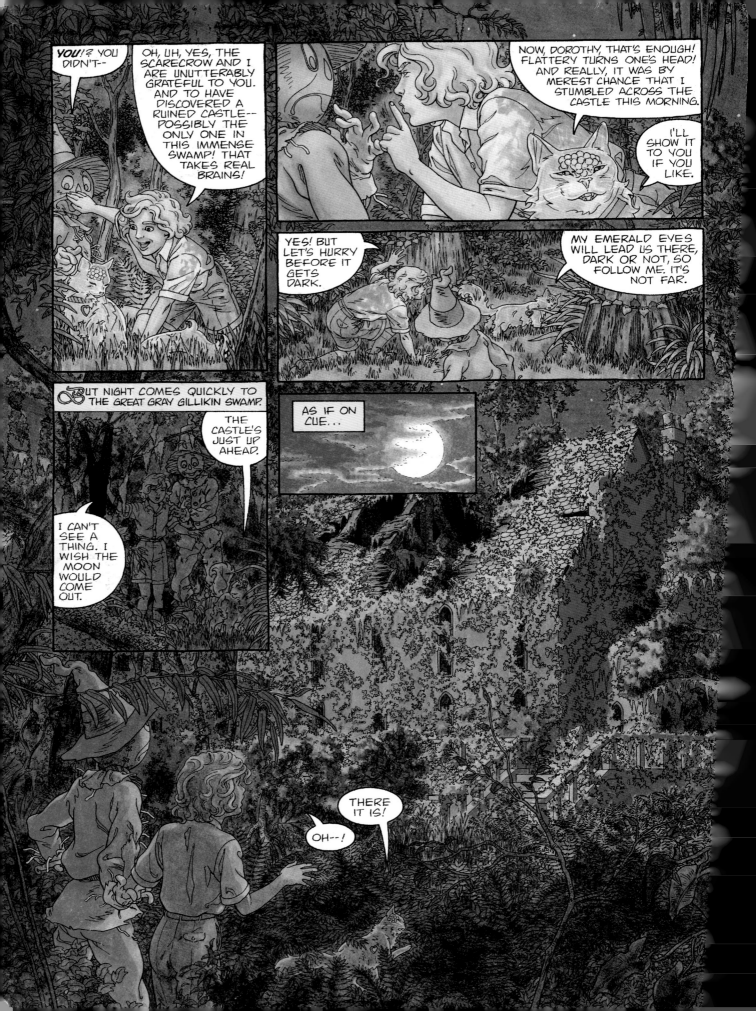

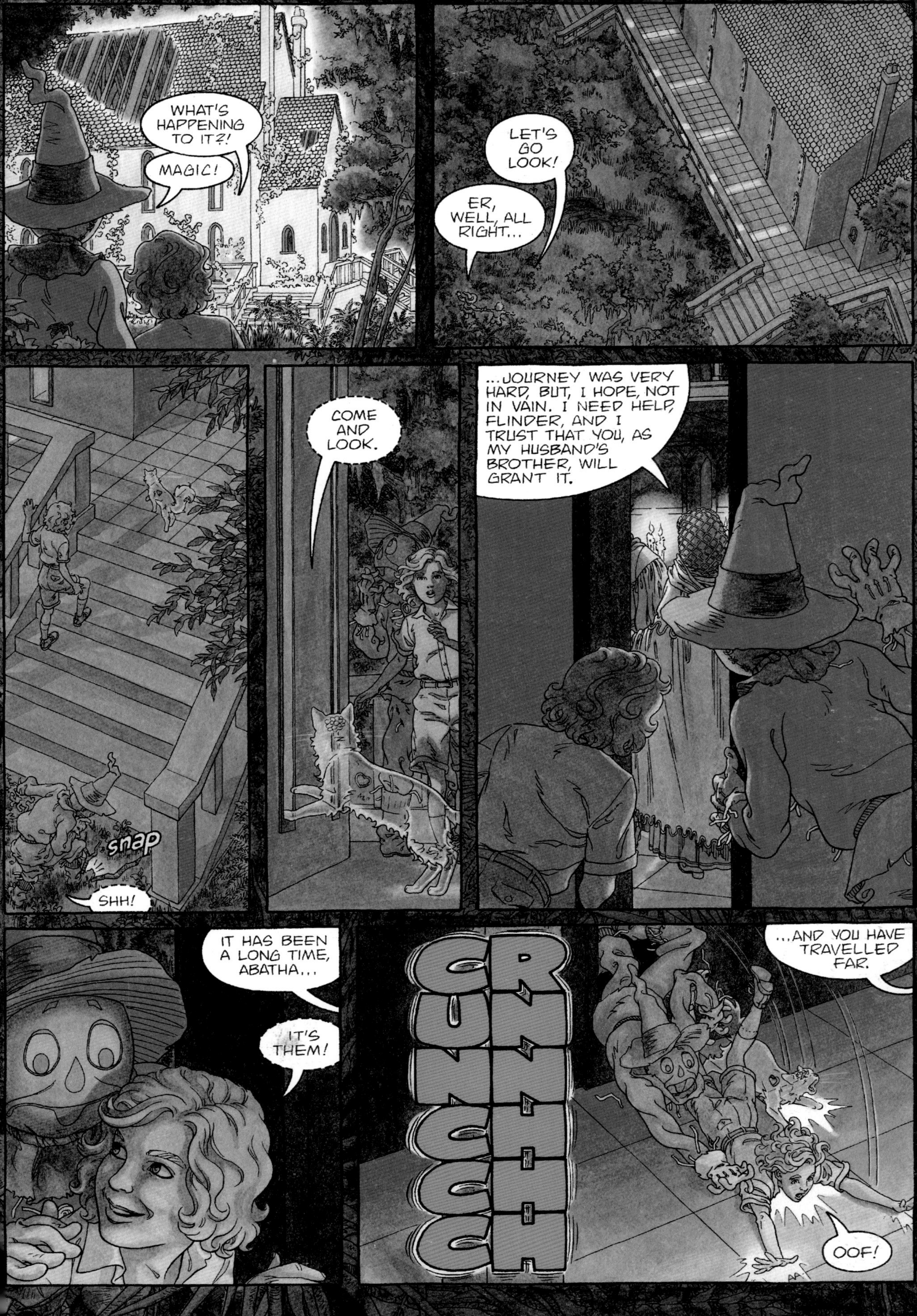
WHAT'S HAPPENING TO IT?!
MAGIC!
LET'S GO LOOK!
ER, WELL, ALL RIGHT...
snap
SHH!
COME AND LOOK.
...JOURNEY WAS VERY HARD, BUT, I HOPE, NOT IN VAIN. I NEED HELP, FLINDER, AND I TRUST THAT YOU, AS MY HUSBAND'S BROTHER, WILL GRANT IT.
IT HAS BEEN A LONG TIME, ABATHA...
IT'S THEM!
CRUNCH CRUNCH
...AND YOU HAVE TRAVELLED FAR.
OOF!

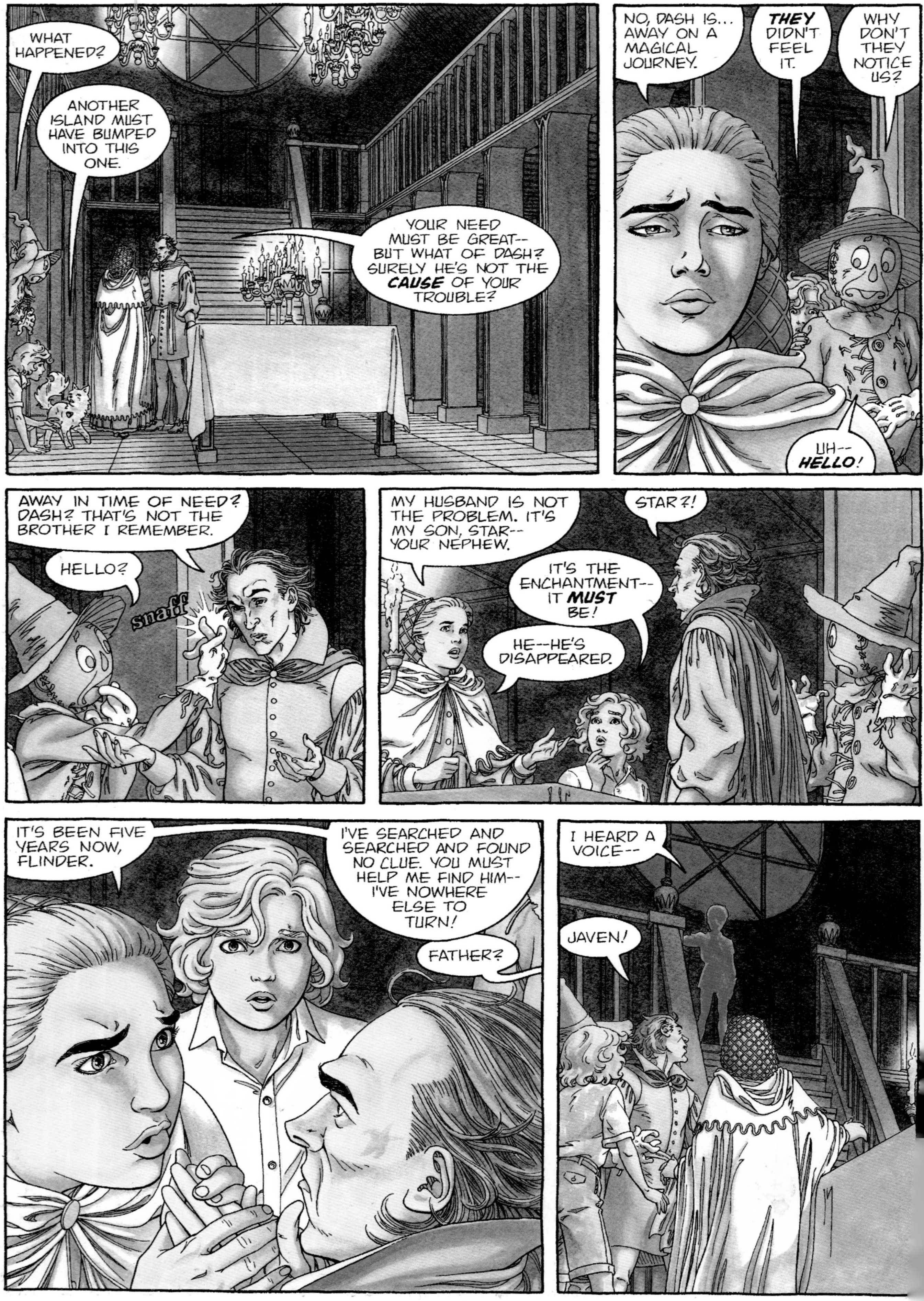
WHAT HAPPENED?
ANOTHER ISLAND MUST HAVE BUMPED INTO THIS ONE.
YOUR NEED MUST BE GREAT-- BUT WHAT OF DASH? SURELY HE'S NOT THE CAUSE OF YOUR TROUBLE?
NO, DASH IS... AWAY ON A MAGICAL JOURNEY.
THEY DIDN'T FEEL IT.
WHY DON'T THEY NOTICE US?
UH-- HELLO!
AWAY IN TIME OF NEED? DASH? THAT'S NOT THE BROTHER I REMEMBER.
HELLO?
snaff
MY HUSBAND IS NOT THE PROBLEM. IT'S MY SON, STAR-- YOUR NEPHEW.
STAR?!
IT'S THE ENCHANTMENT-- IT MUST BE!
HE--HE'S DISAPPEARED.
IT'S BEEN FIVE YEARS NOW, FLINDER.
I'VE SEARCHED AND SEARCHED AND FOUND NO CLUE. YOU MUST HELP ME FIND HIM-- I'VE NOWHERE ELSE TO TURN!
FATHER?
I HEARD A VOICE--
JAVEN!

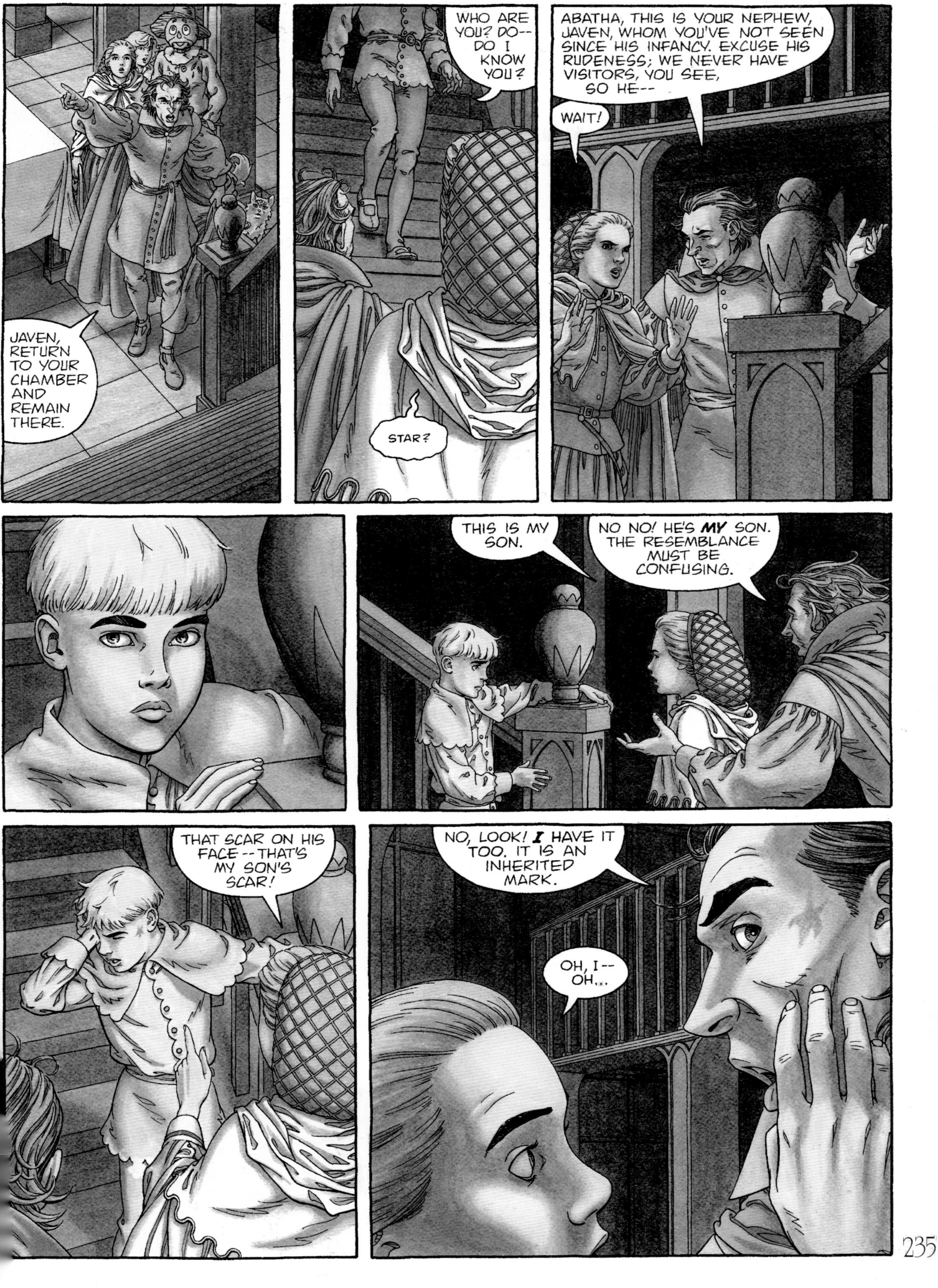

JAVEN, RETURN TO YOUR CHAMBER AND REMAIN THERE.
WHO ARE YOU? DO-- DO I KNOW YOU?
STAR?
ABATHA, THIS IS YOUR NEPHEW, JAVEN, WHOM YOU'VE NOT SEEN SINCE HIS INFANCY. EXCUSE HIS RUDENESS; WE NEVER HAVE VISITORS, YOU SEE, SO HE--
WAIT!
THIS IS MY SON.
NO NO! HE'S **MY** SON. THE RESEMBLANCE MUST BE CONFUSING.
THAT SCAR ON HIS FACE--THAT'S MY SON'S SCAR!
NO, LOOK! **I** HAVE IT TOO. IT IS AN INHERITED MARK.
OH, I-- OH...

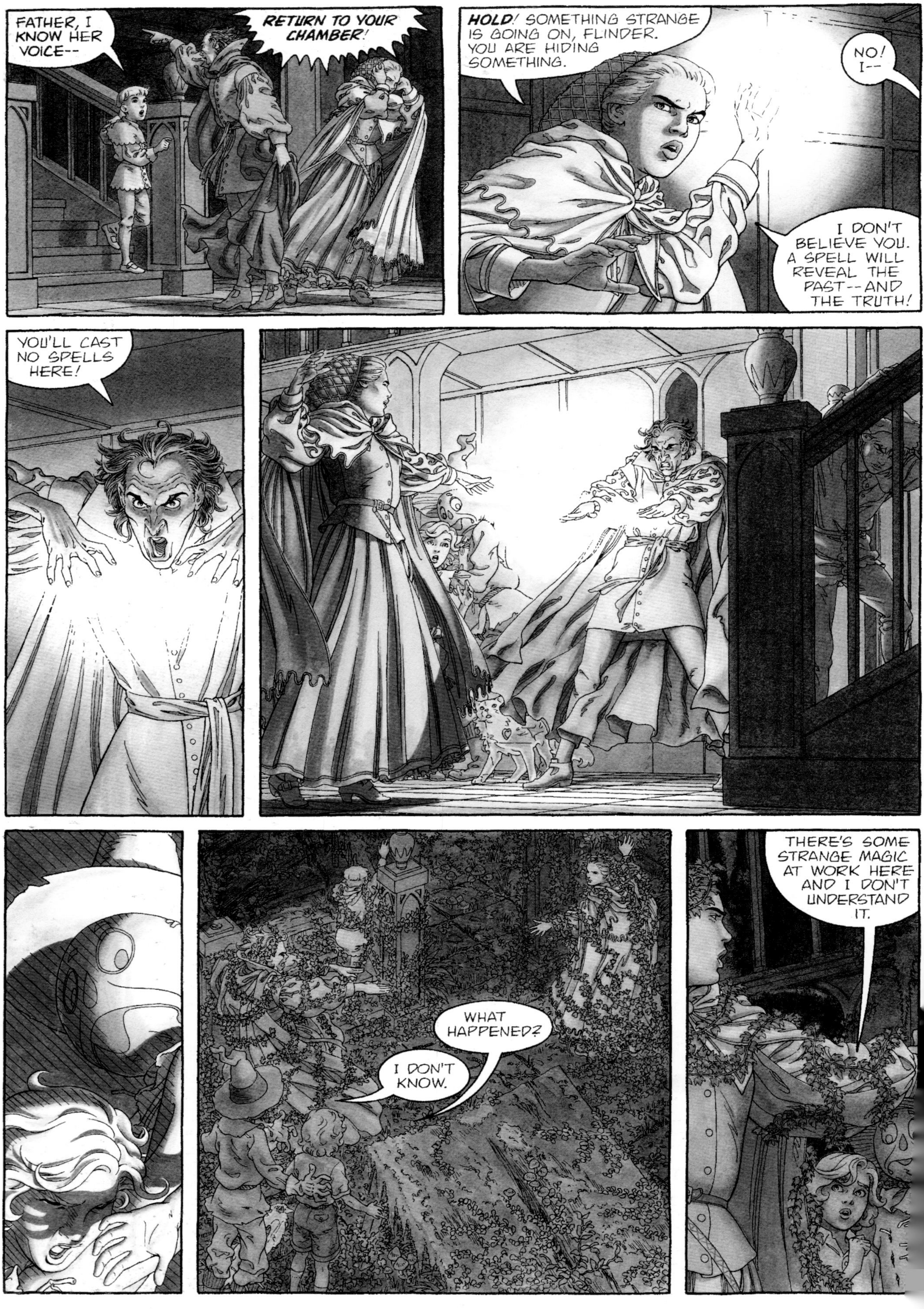

FATHER, I KNOW HER VOICE--
RETURN TO YOUR CHAMBER!
HOLD! SOMETHING STRANGE IS GOING ON, FLINDER. YOU ARE HIDING SOMETHING.
NO! I--
I DON'T BELIEVE YOU. A SPELL WILL REVEAL THE PAST--AND THE TRUTH!
YOU'LL CAST NO SPELLS HERE!
WHAT HAPPENED?
I DON'T KNOW.
THERE'S SOME STRANGE MAGIC AT WORK HERE AND I DON'T UNDERSTAND IT.

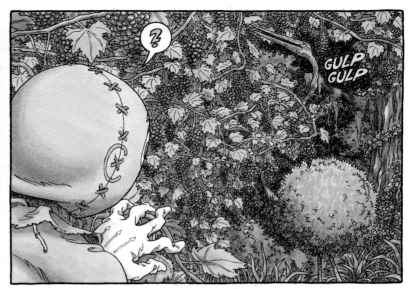

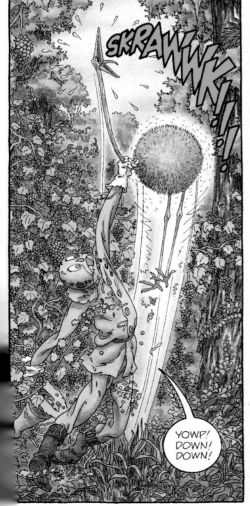

237

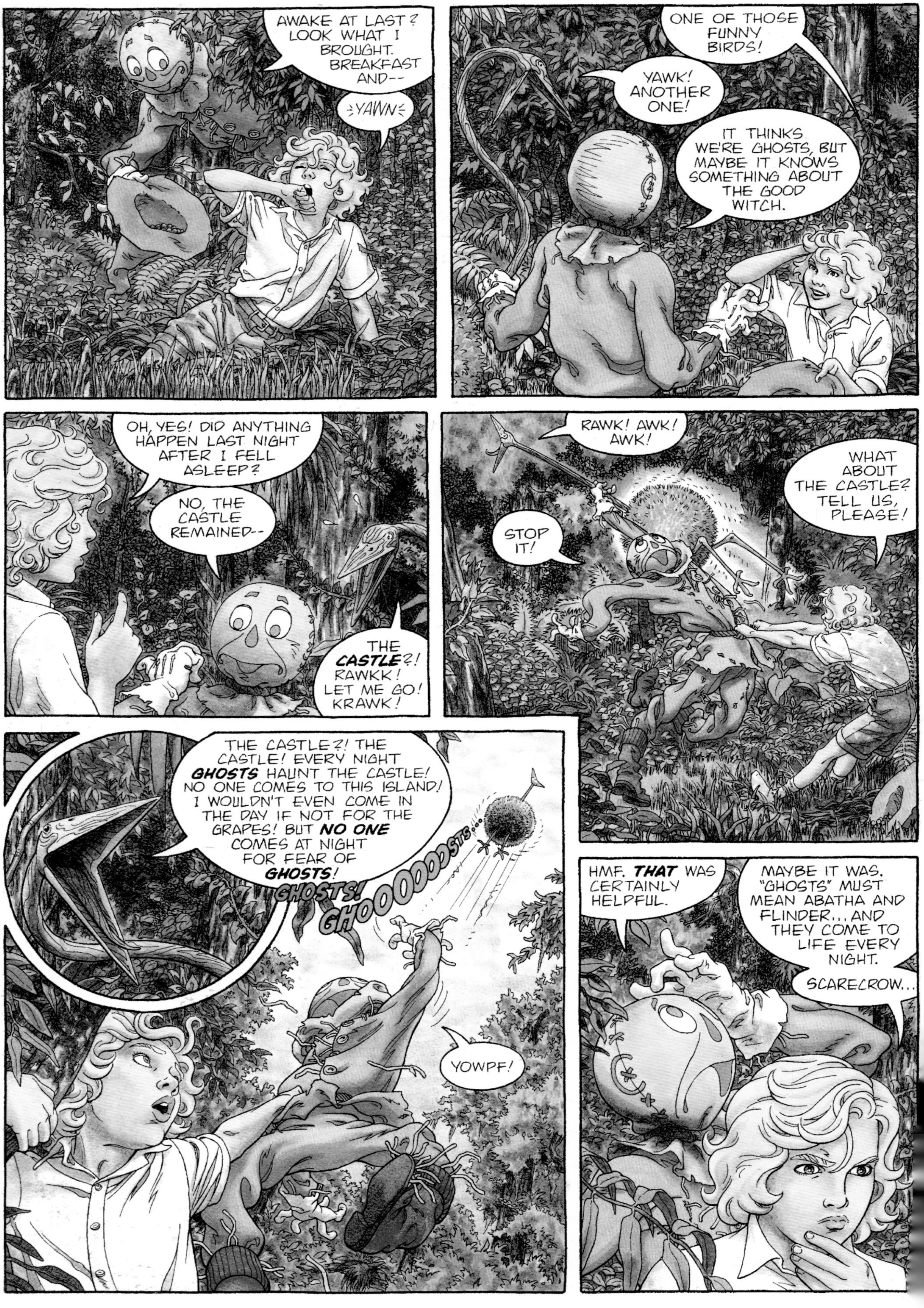
AWAKE AT LAST? LOOK WHAT I BROUGHT. BREAKFAST AND--
YAWN
ONE OF THOSE FUNNY BIRDS!
YAWK! ANOTHER ONE!
IT THINKS WE'RE GHOSTS, BUT MAYBE IT KNOWS SOMETHING ABOUT THE GOOD WITCH.
OH, YES! DID ANYTHING HAPPEN LAST NIGHT AFTER I FELL ASLEEP?
NO, THE CASTLE REMAINED--
THE **CASTLE**?! RAWKK! LET ME GO! KRAWK!
RAWK! AWK! AWK!
STOP IT!
WHAT ABOUT THE CASTLE? TELL US, PLEASE!
THE CASTLE?! THE CASTLE! EVERY NIGHT **GHOSTS** HAUNT THE CASTLE! NO ONE COMES TO THIS ISLAND! I WOULDN'T EVEN COME IN THE DAY IF NOT FOR THE GRAPES! BUT **NO ONE** COMES AT NIGHT FOR FEAR OF **GHOSTS**!
GHOSTS! GHOOOOOOOSTS...
YOWPF!
HMF. **THAT** WAS CERTAINLY HELPFUL.
MAYBE IT WAS. "GHOSTS" MUST MEAN ABATHA AND FLINDER... AND THEY COME TO LIFE EVERY NIGHT.
SCARECROW...

...I THINK I'VE FIGURED OUT THE ENCHANTMENT!

WHAT? TELL ME!

WELL, ABATHA CAST A SPELL TO REPLAY THE PAST. AND FLINDER'S SPELL MUST HAVE BEEN TO FREEZE ABATHA IN PLACE. BUT THE SPELLS DIDN'T WORK AS INTENDED! THEY CRASHED AND EXPLODED, CASTING ALL THREE OF THEM UNDER A COMBINATION OF BOTH SPELLS.

ER--?

DON'T YOU SEE? EVERYTHING'S FROZEN UNTIL THEY REPLAY THEIR LAST SCENE EVERY NIGHT AND ENCHANT THEMSELVES ALL OVER AGAIN! I WISH WE KNEW HOW TO BREAK THE ENCHANTMENT!

MAYBE WE CAN PREVENT THE SPELLS FROM BEING CAST AT ALL. IF WE COULD STOP THEM, THEN THE ENCHANTMENT WOULD BE BROKEN, WOULDN'T IT?

I THINK SO-- HMM...

IF WE HAD A MIRROR, WE COULD DEFLECT THE SPELLS AWAY FROM EACH OTHER.

WE DON'T HAVE A MIRROR, BUT MAYBE WE CAN TURN ABATHA AND FLINDER AWAY FROM EACH OTHER SO THAT THEY CAST THE SPELLS IN THE WRONG DIRECTIONS.

THAT MIGHT WORK! UNDER THE ENCHANTMENT THEY CAN'T SENSE US, SO THEY WON'T NOTICE US TURNING THEM-- BUT WE MUST BE SURE TO TURN THEM SO THAT THE SPELLS HIT THE WALL OR SOMETHING...

RUSTLE RUSTLE

THERE YOU ARE, BUNGLE. GUESS WHAT--WE THINK WE'VE FIGURED OUT A WAY TO BREAK THE ENCHANTMENT.

FORGET ENCHANTMENTS! YOU BETTER FIGURE OUT A WAY OFF THIS ISLAND. THE LOGS ARE STILL SURROUNDING IT, AND THEY'RE NOT ABOUT TO LET YOU GET AWAY.

THAT NIGHT--

NO NO! HE'S **MY** SON THE RESEMBLANCE MUST BE CONFUSING.

THEY'RE ALREADY GOING...

WE'RE NOT TOO LATE...?

THAT SCAR ON HIS FACE-- THAT'S MY SON'S SCAR!

NO, BUT WE DON'T HAVE TIME TO WASTE.

NO, LOOK! **I** HAVE IT TOO. IT IS AN INHERITED MARK.

OH, I-- OH...

FATHER...

...I KNOW HER VOICE--

**RETURN TO YOUR CHAMBER!**

OUCH!

DOROTHY, I--I CAN'T BUDGE HER!

**HOLD!** SOMETHING STRANGE IS GOING ON, FLINDER.

YOU ARE HIDING SOMETHING.

NO, I--

TRY HARDER, SCARECROW! HERE, I'LL HELP.

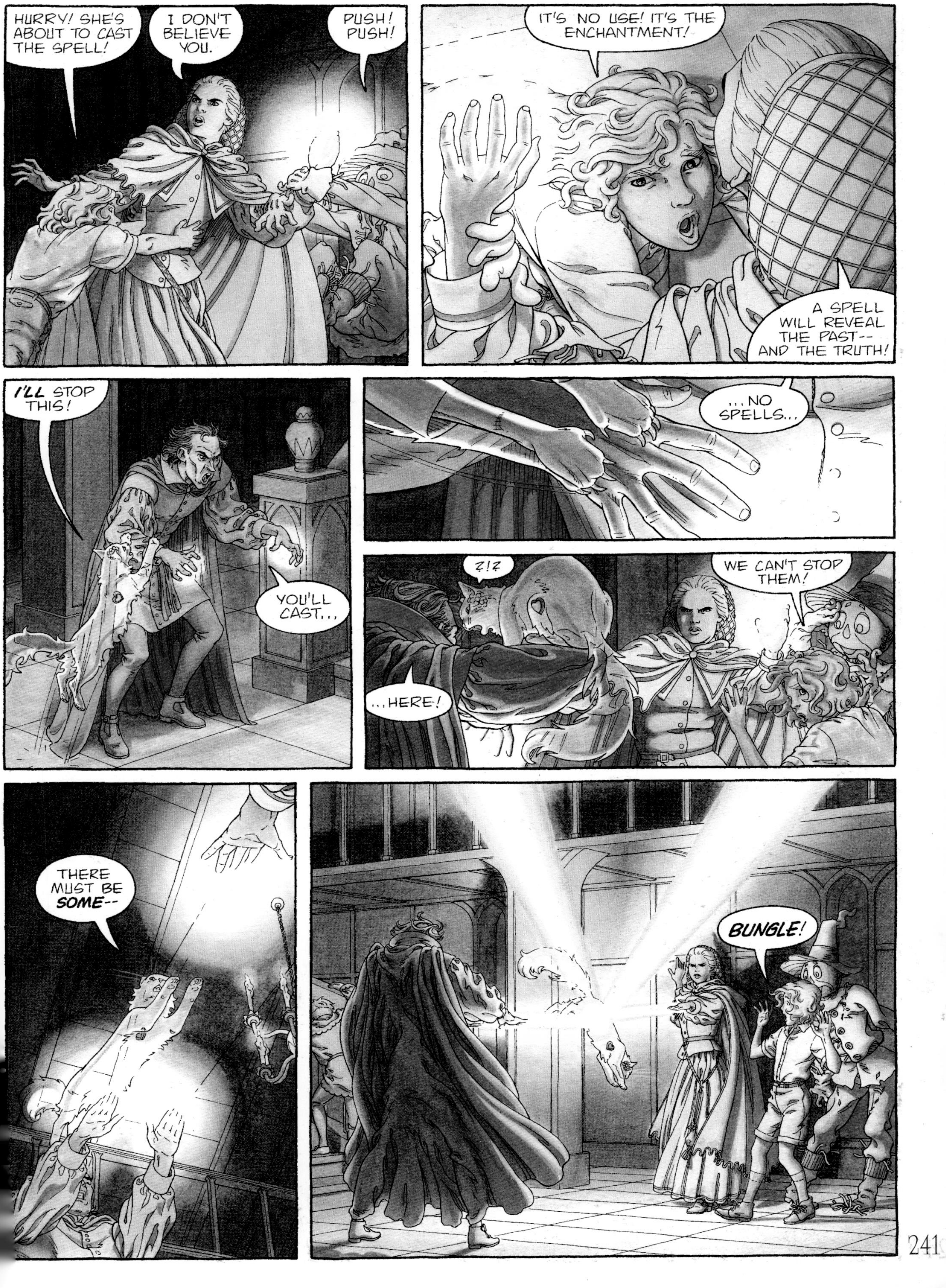
HURRY! SHE'S ABOUT TO CAST THE SPELL!
I DON'T BELIEVE YOU.
PUSH! PUSH!
IT'S NO USE! IT'S THE ENCHANTMENT!
A SPELL WILL REVEAL THE PAST-- AND THE TRUTH!
I'LL STOP THIS!
YOU'LL CAST...
...NO SPELLS...
?!?
WE CAN'T STOP THEM!
...HERE!
THERE MUST BE SOME--
BUNGLE!

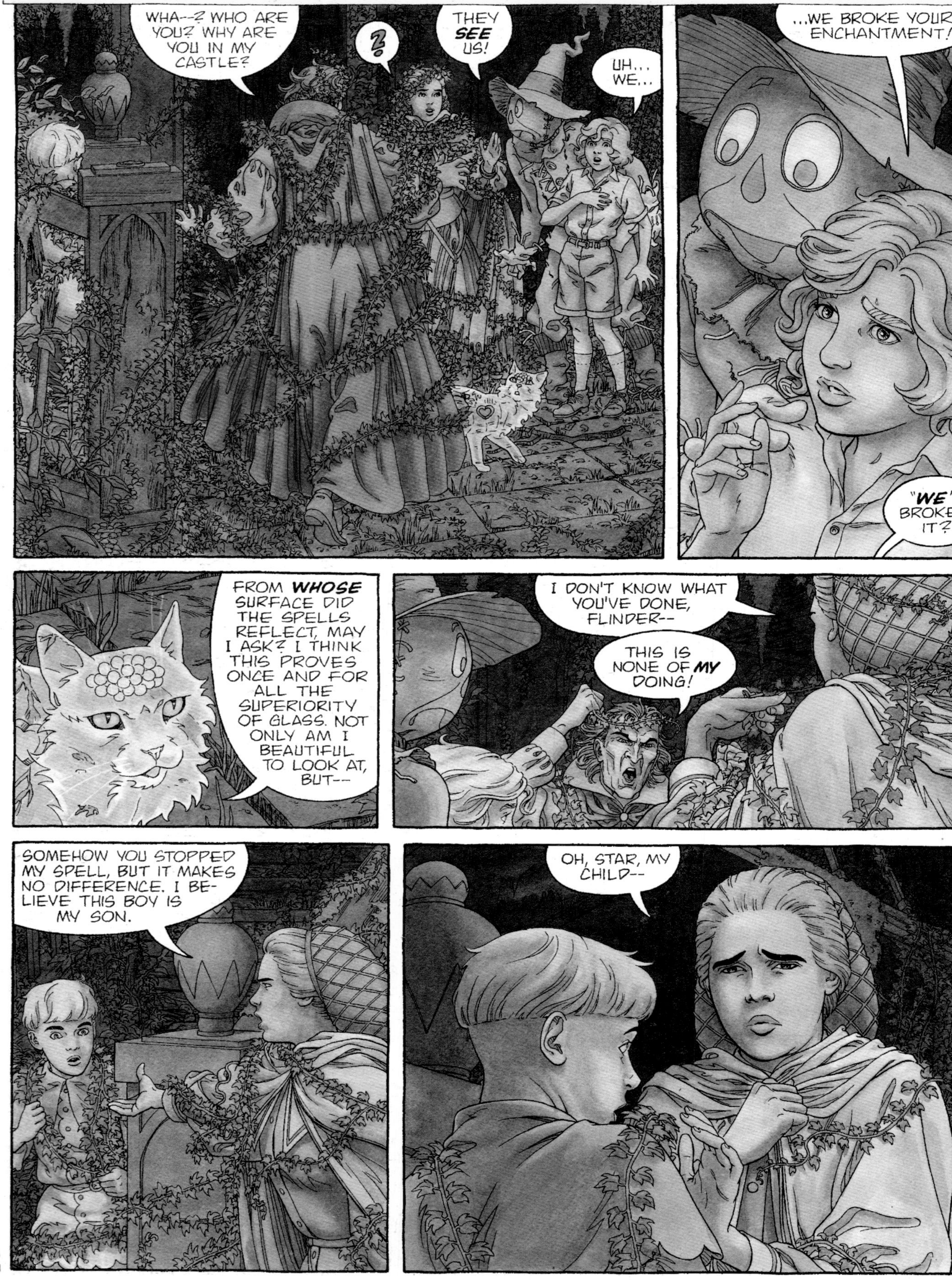
WHA--? WHO ARE YOU? WHY ARE YOU IN MY CASTLE?
?
THEY **SEE** US!
UH... WE...
...WE BROKE YOUR ENCHANTMENT!
"**WE**" BROKE IT?
FROM **WHOSE** SURFACE DID THE SPELLS REFLECT, MAY I ASK? I THINK THIS PROVES ONCE AND FOR ALL THE SUPERIORITY OF GLASS. NOT ONLY AM I BEAUTIFUL TO LOOK AT, BUT--
I DON'T KNOW WHAT YOU'VE DONE, FLINDER--
THIS IS NONE OF **MY** DOING!
SOMEHOW YOU STOPPED MY SPELL, BUT IT MAKES NO DIFFERENCE. I BE-LIEVE THIS BOY IS MY SON.
OH, STAR, MY CHILD--

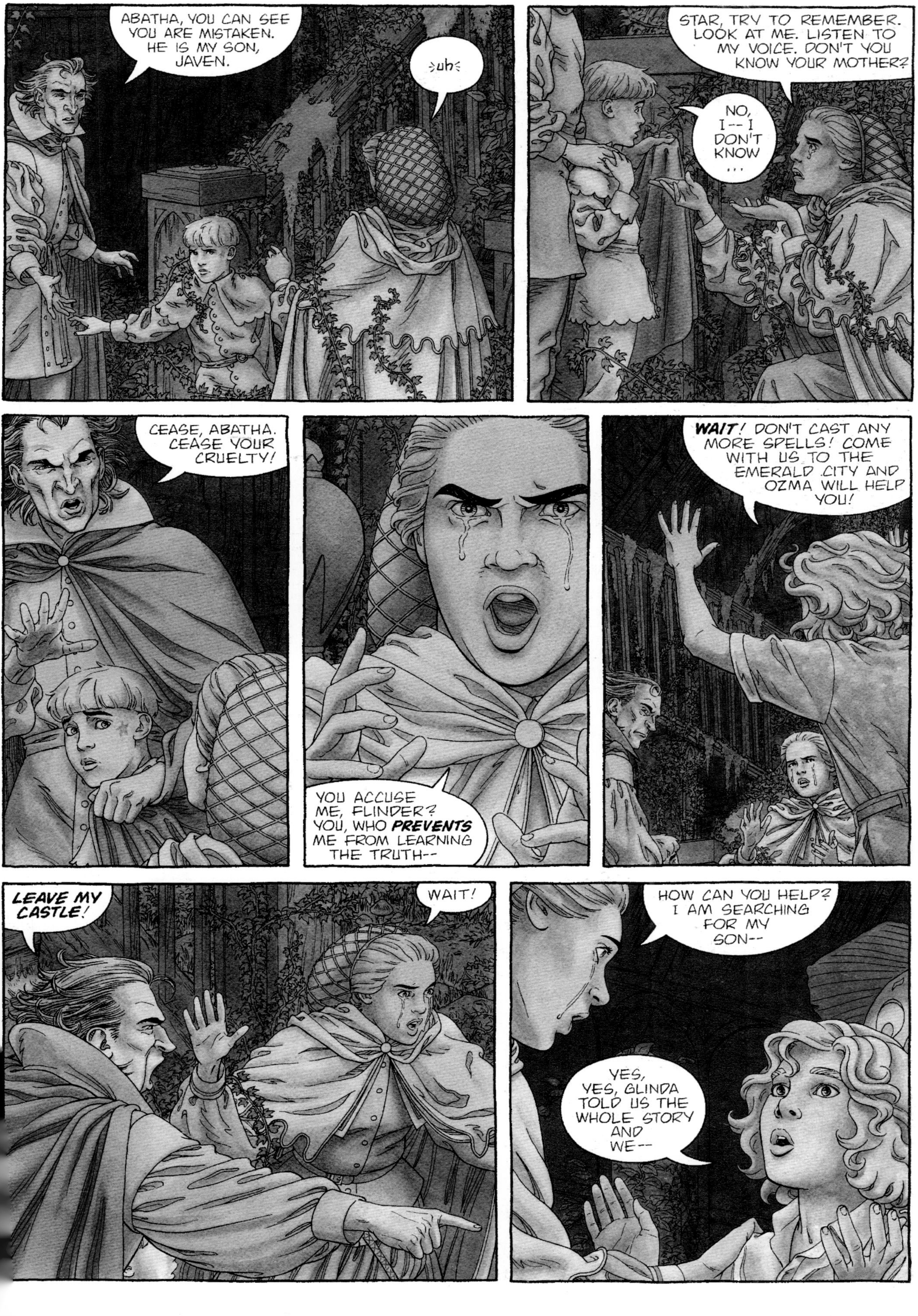
ABATHA, YOU CAN SEE YOU ARE MISTAKEN. HE IS MY SON, JAVEN.
uh
STAR, TRY TO REMEMBER. LOOK AT ME. LISTEN TO MY VOICE. DON'T YOU KNOW YOUR MOTHER?
NO, I-- I DON'T KNOW ...
CEASE, ABATHA. CEASE YOUR CRUELTY!
YOU ACCUSE ME, FLINDER? YOU, WHO **PREVENTS** ME FROM LEARNING THE TRUTH--
**WAIT**! DON'T CAST ANY MORE SPELLS! COME WITH US TO THE EMERALD CITY AND OZMA WILL HELP YOU!
**LEAVE MY CASTLE**!
WAIT!
HOW CAN YOU HELP? I AM SEARCHING FOR MY SON--
YES, YES, GLINDA TOLD US THE WHOLE STORY AND WE--

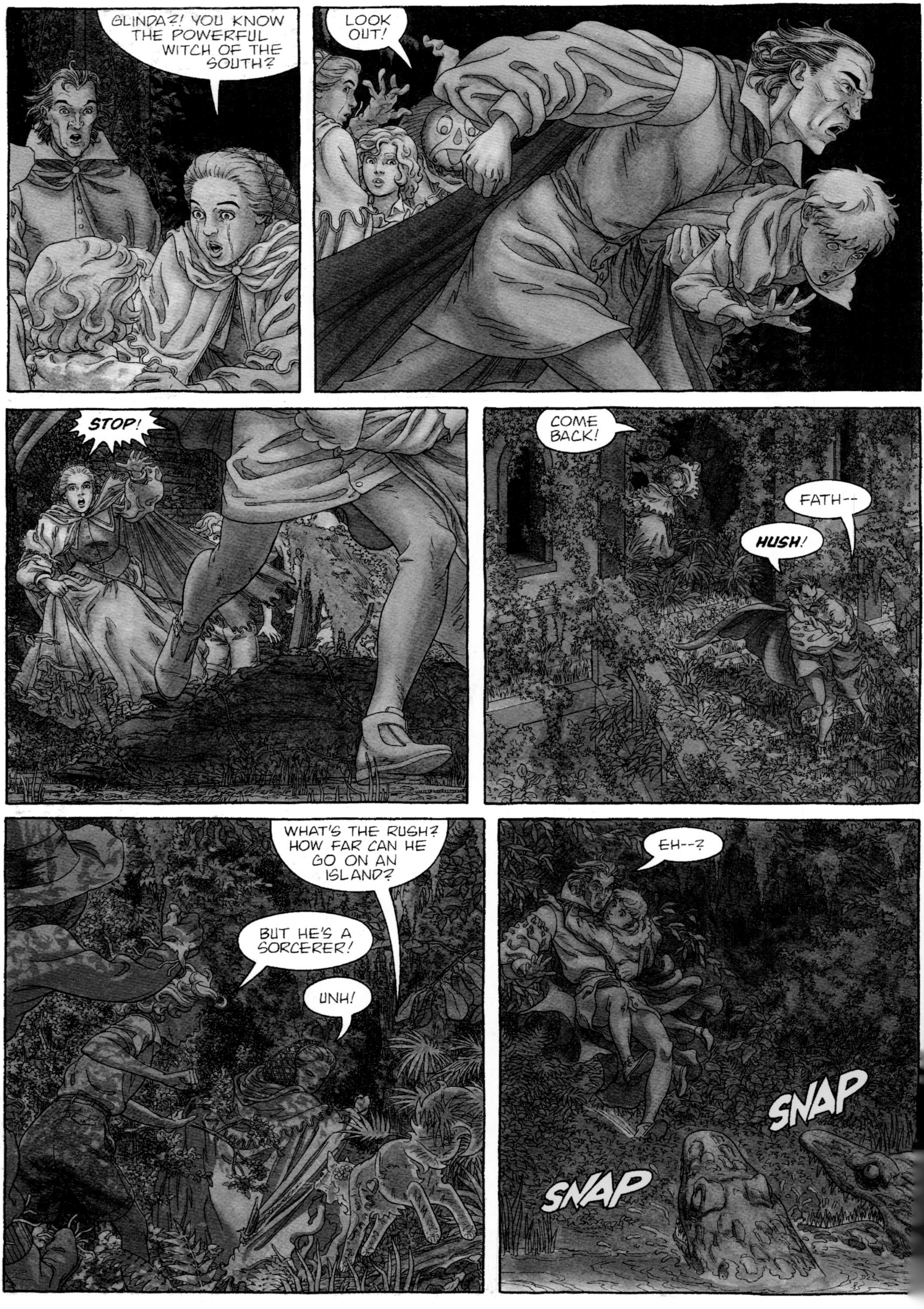
GLINDA?! YOU KNOW THE POWERFUL WITCH OF THE SOUTH?
LOOK OUT!
STOP!
COME BACK!
FATH--
HUSH!
WHAT'S THE RUSH? HOW FAR CAN HE GO ON AN ISLAND?
BUT HE'S A SORCERER!
UNH!
EH--?
SNAP
SNAP

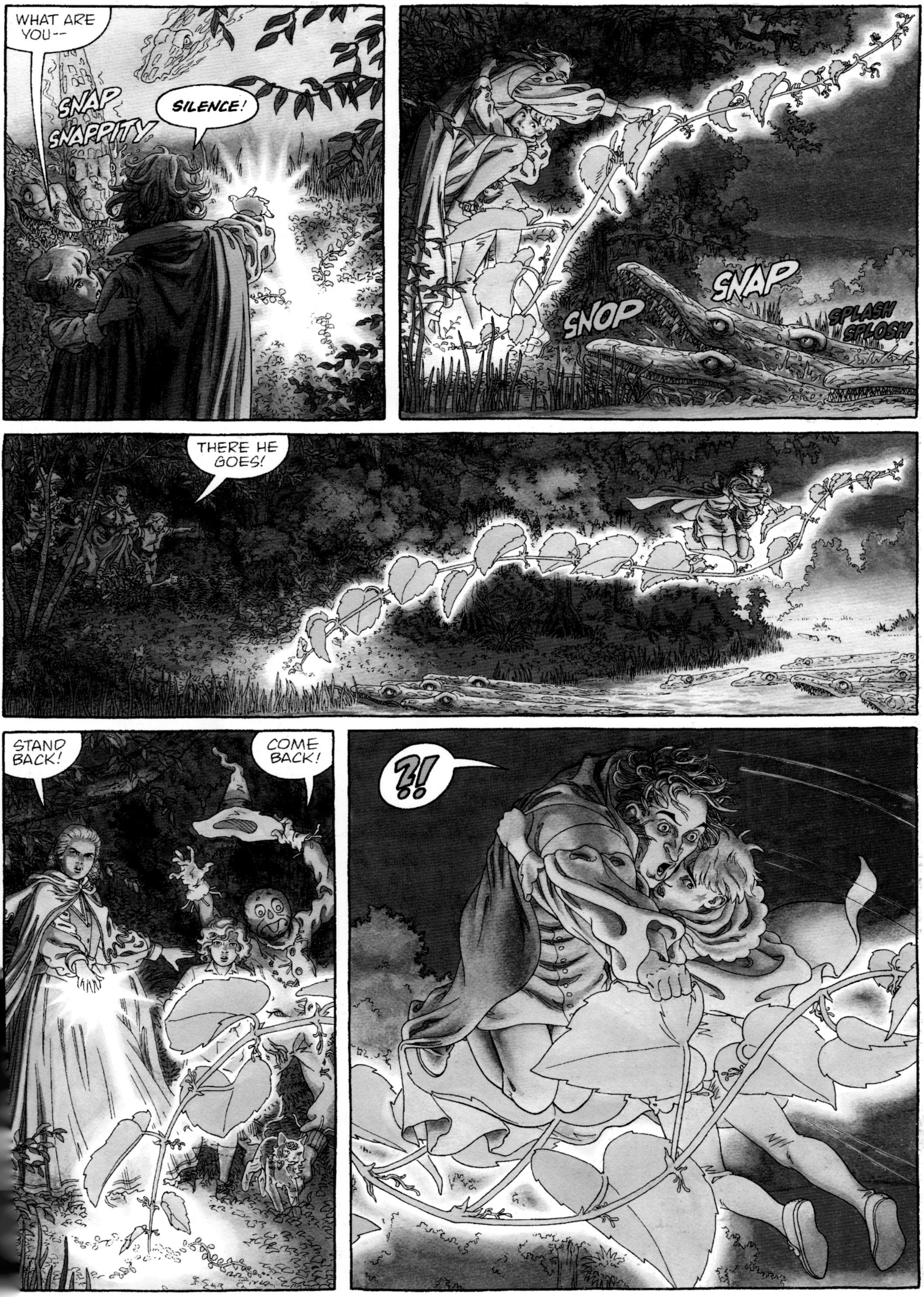

WHAT ARE YOU--
SNAP SNAPPITY
SILENCE!
SNAP
SNOP
SPLASH SPLOSH
THERE HE GOES!
STAND BACK!
COME BACK!
?!

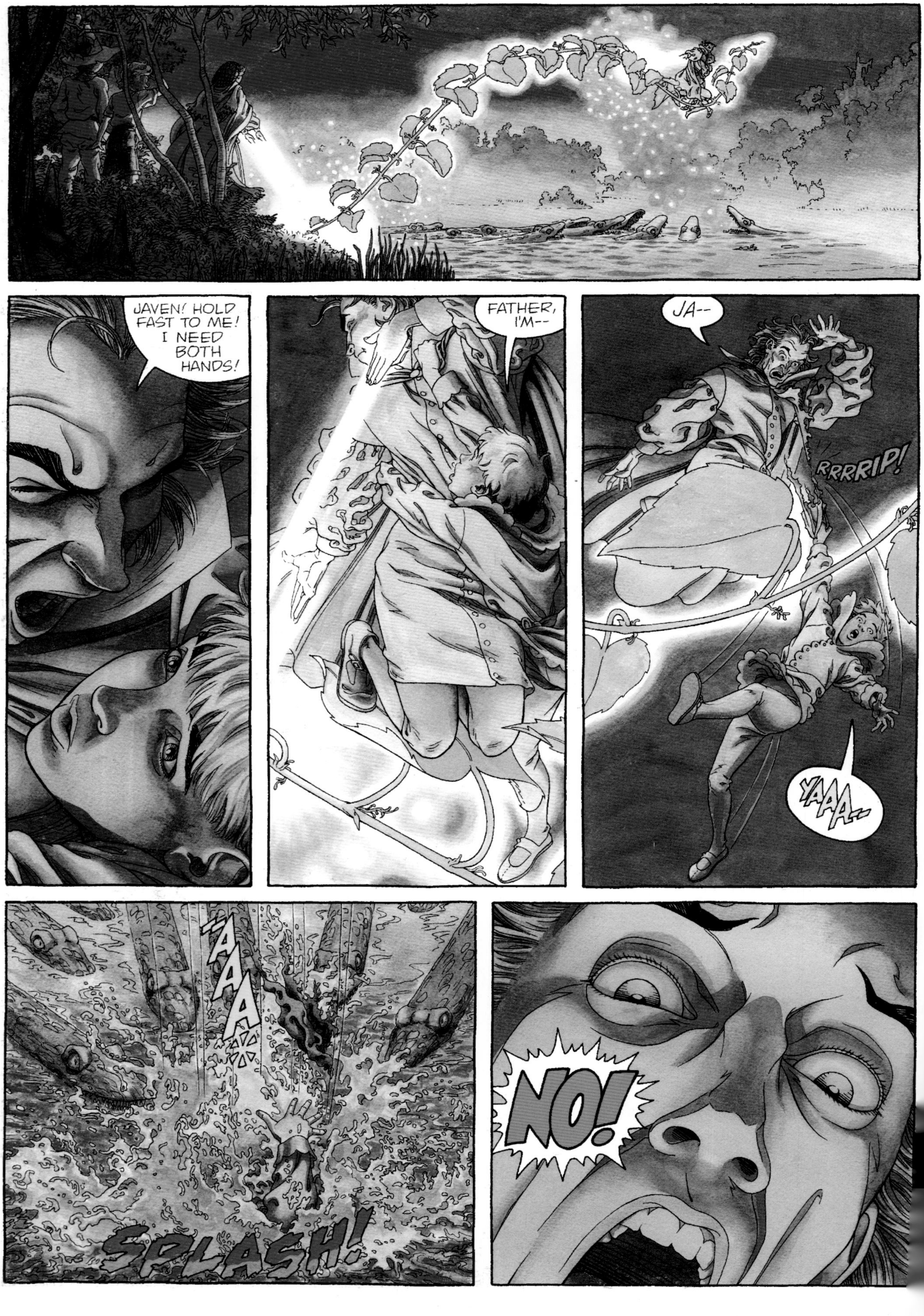
JAVEN! HOLD FAST TO ME! I NEED BOTH HANDS!
FATHER, I'M--
JA--
RRRRIP!
YAAA--
AAA
SPLASH!
NO!

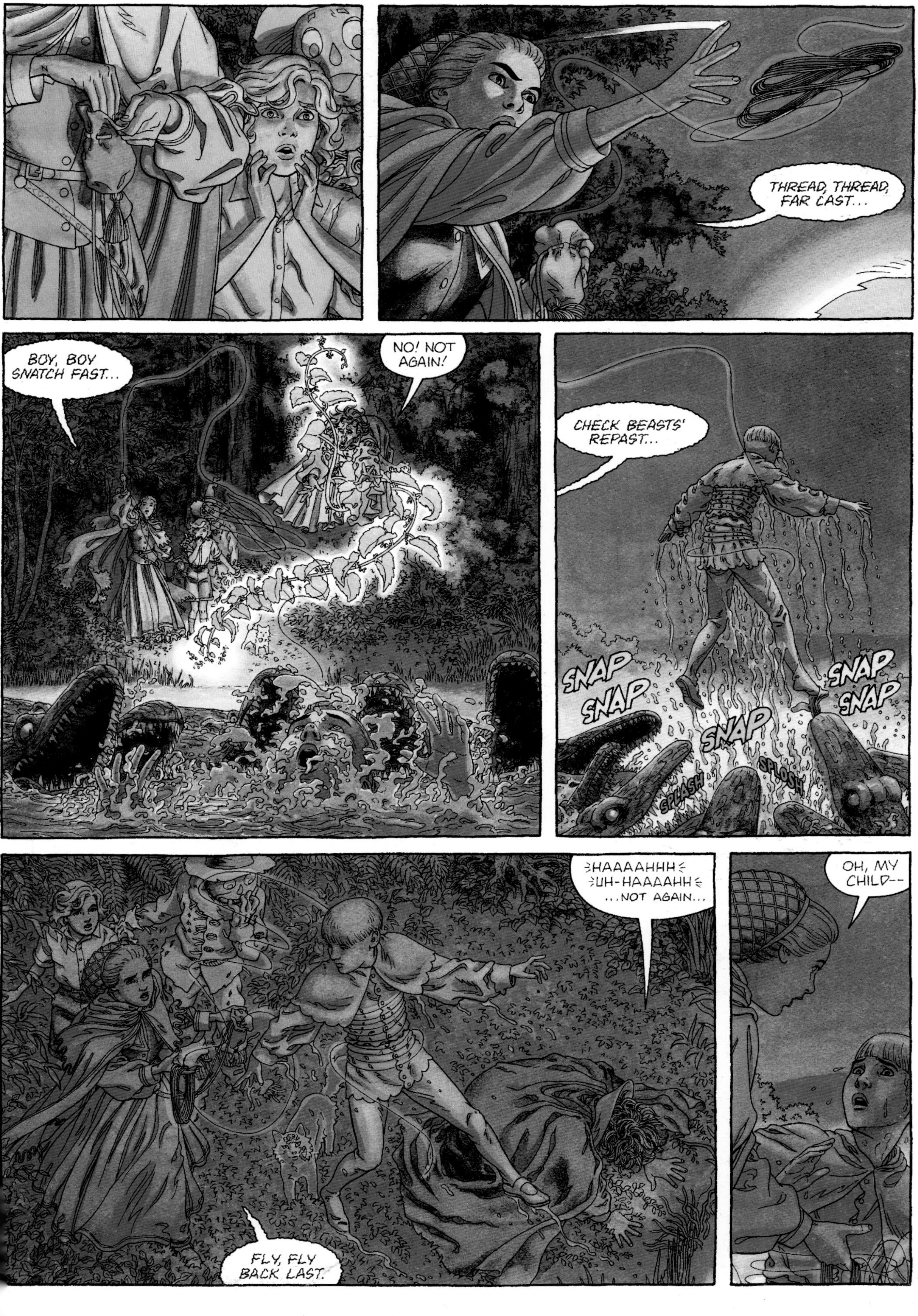
THREAD, THREAD, FAR CAST...
BOY, BOY SNATCH FAST...
NO! NOT AGAIN!
CHECK BEASTS' REPAST...
SNAP SNAP
SNAP SNAP
SNAP
SPLASH
SPLOSH
HAAAAHHH
UH-HAAAAHH
...NOT AGAIN...
FLY, FLY BACK LAST.
OH, MY CHILD--

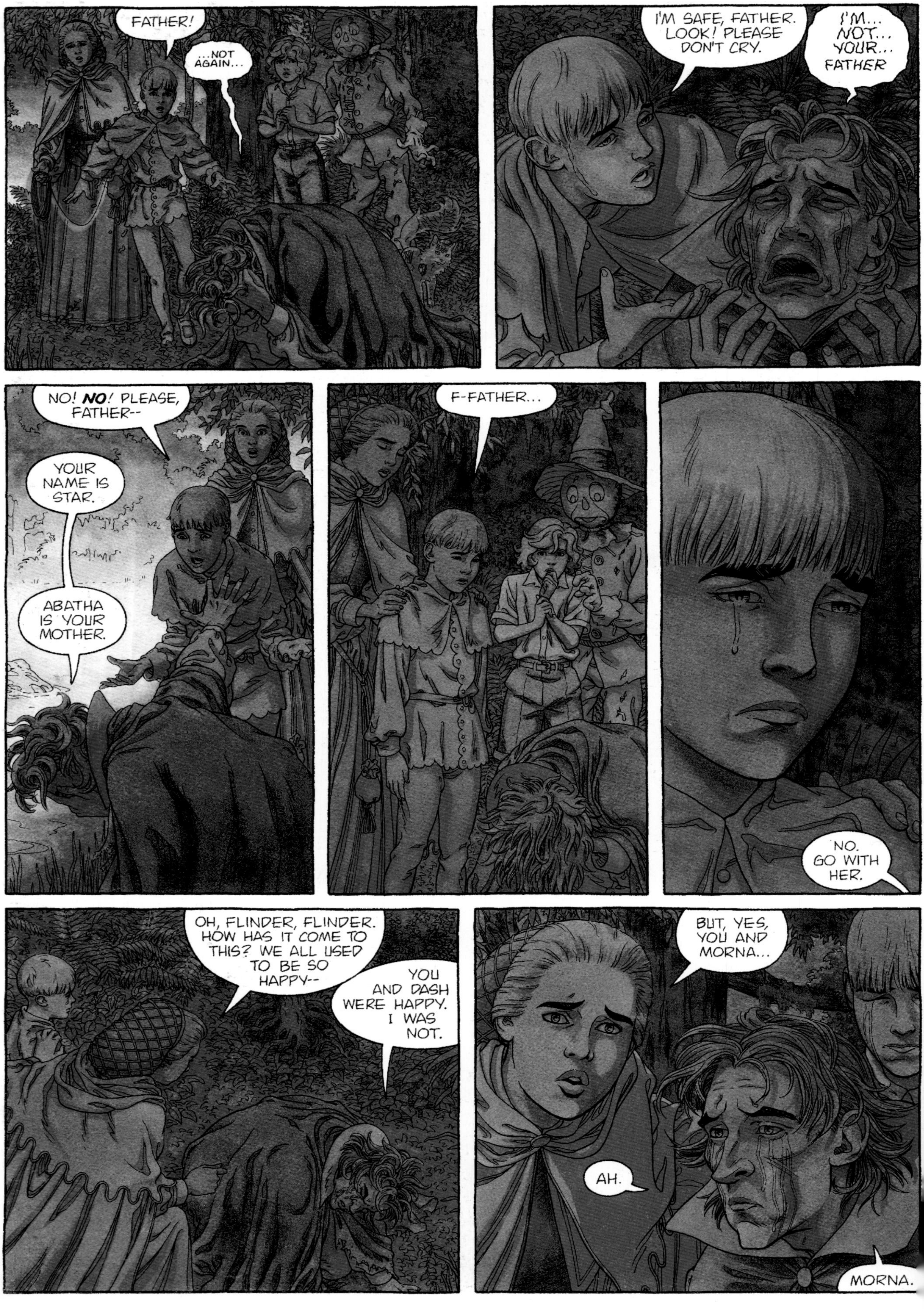
FATHER!
...NOT AGAIN...
I'M SAFE, FATHER. LOOK! PLEASE DON'T CRY.
I'M... NOT... YOUR... FATHER
NO! NO! PLEASE, FATHER--
YOUR NAME IS STAR.
ABATHA IS YOUR MOTHER.
F-FATHER...
NO. GO WITH HER.
OH, FLINDER, FLINDER. HOW HAS IT COME TO THIS? WE ALL USED TO BE SO HAPPY--
YOU AND DASH WERE HAPPY. I WAS NOT.
BUT, YES, YOU AND MORNA...
AH.
MORNA.

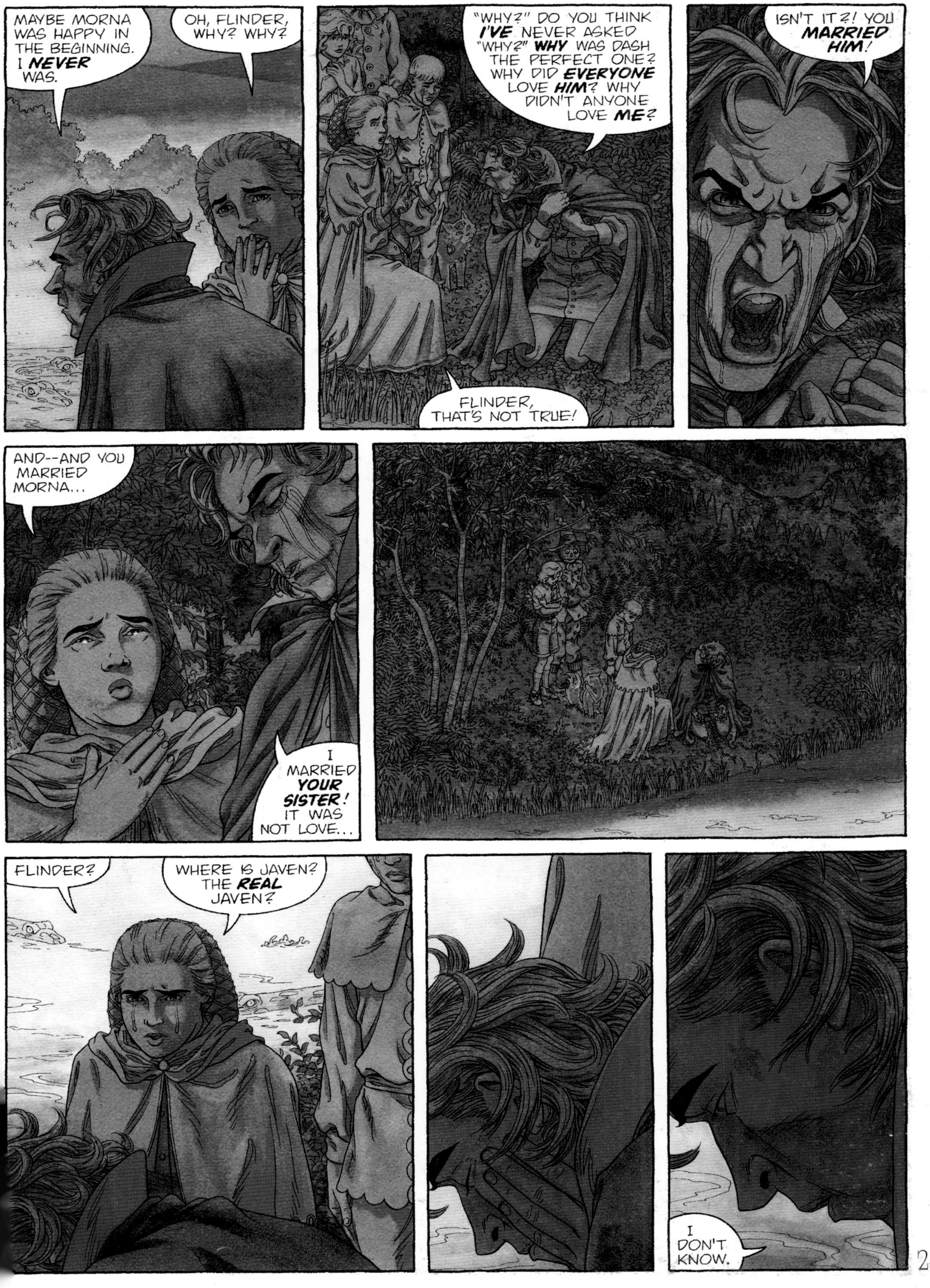

MAYBE MORNA WAS HAPPY IN THE BEGINNING. I **NEVER** WAS.
OH, FLINDER, WHY? WHY?
"WHY?" DO YOU THINK **I'VE** NEVER ASKED "WHY?" **WHY** WAS DASH THE PERFECT ONE? WHY DID **EVERYONE** LOVE **HIM**? WHY DIDN'T ANYONE LOVE **ME**?
FLINDER, THAT'S NOT TRUE!
ISN'T IT?! YOU **MARRIED HIM**!
AND--AND YOU MARRIED MORNA...
I MARRIED **YOUR SISTER**! IT WAS NOT LOVE...
FLINDER?
WHERE IS JAVEN? THE **REAL** JAVEN?
I DON'T KNOW.

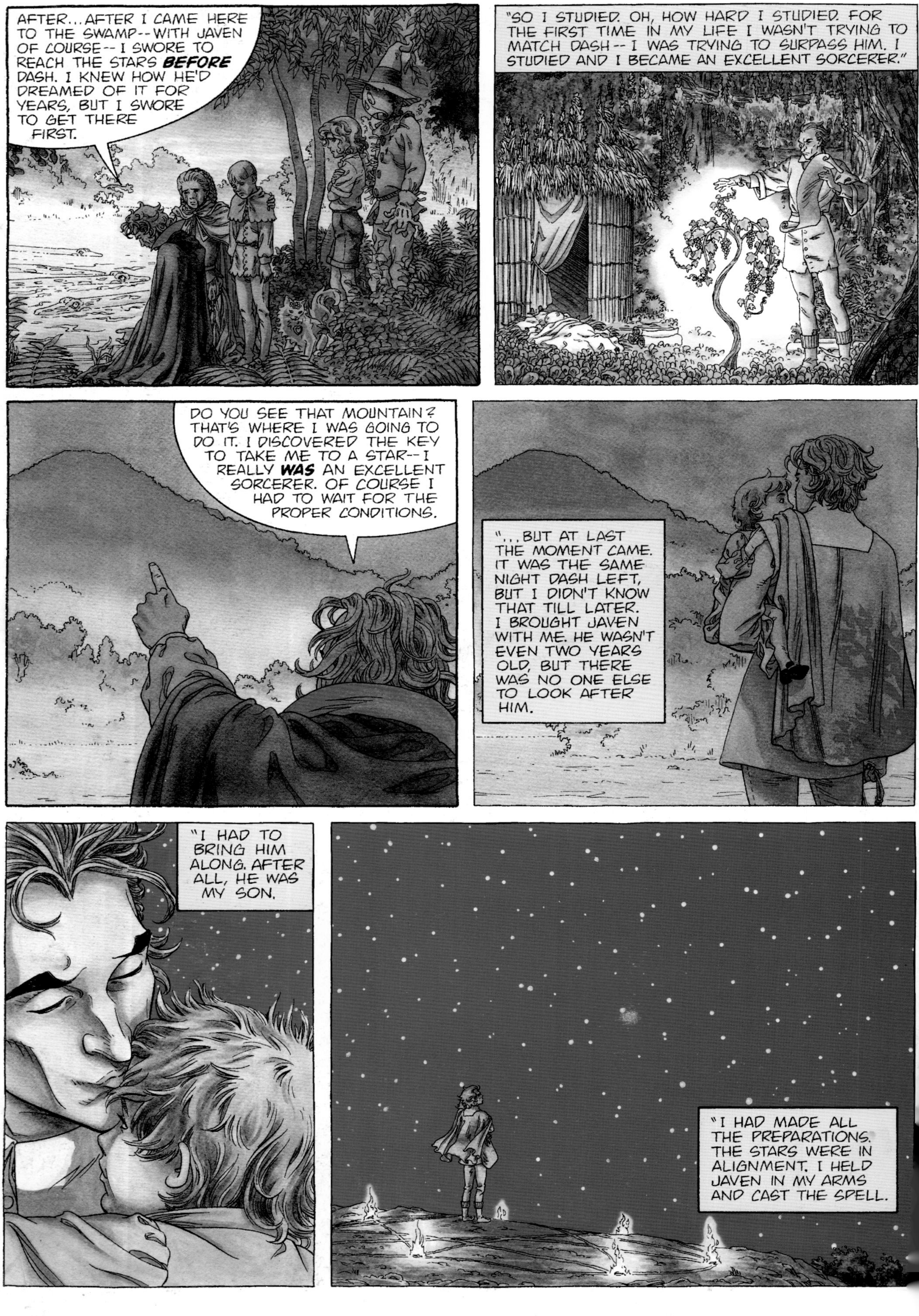
AFTER... AFTER I CAME HERE TO THE SWAMP--WITH JAVEN OF COURSE--I SWORE TO REACH THE STARS **BEFORE** DASH. I KNEW HOW HE'D DREAMED OF IT FOR YEARS, BUT I SWORE TO GET THERE FIRST.
"SO I STUDIED. OH, HOW HARD I STUDIED. FOR THE FIRST TIME IN MY LIFE I WASN'T TRYING TO MATCH DASH--I WAS TRYING TO SURPASS HIM. I STUDIED AND I BECAME AN EXCELLENT SORCERER."
DO YOU SEE THAT MOUNTAIN? THAT'S WHERE I WAS GOING TO DO IT. I DISCOVERED THE KEY TO TAKE ME TO A STAR--I REALLY **WAS** AN EXCELLENT SORCERER. OF COURSE I HAD TO WAIT FOR THE PROPER CONDITIONS.
"...BUT AT LAST THE MOMENT CAME. IT WAS THE SAME NIGHT DASH LEFT, BUT I DIDN'T KNOW THAT TILL LATER. I BROUGHT JAVEN WITH ME. HE WASN'T EVEN TWO YEARS OLD, BUT THERE WAS NO ONE ELSE TO LOOK AFTER HIM.
"I HAD TO BRING HIM ALONG. AFTER ALL, HE WAS MY SON.
"I HAD MADE ALL THE PREPARATIONS. THE STARS WERE IN ALIGNMENT. I HELD JAVEN IN MY ARMS AND CAST THE SPELL.

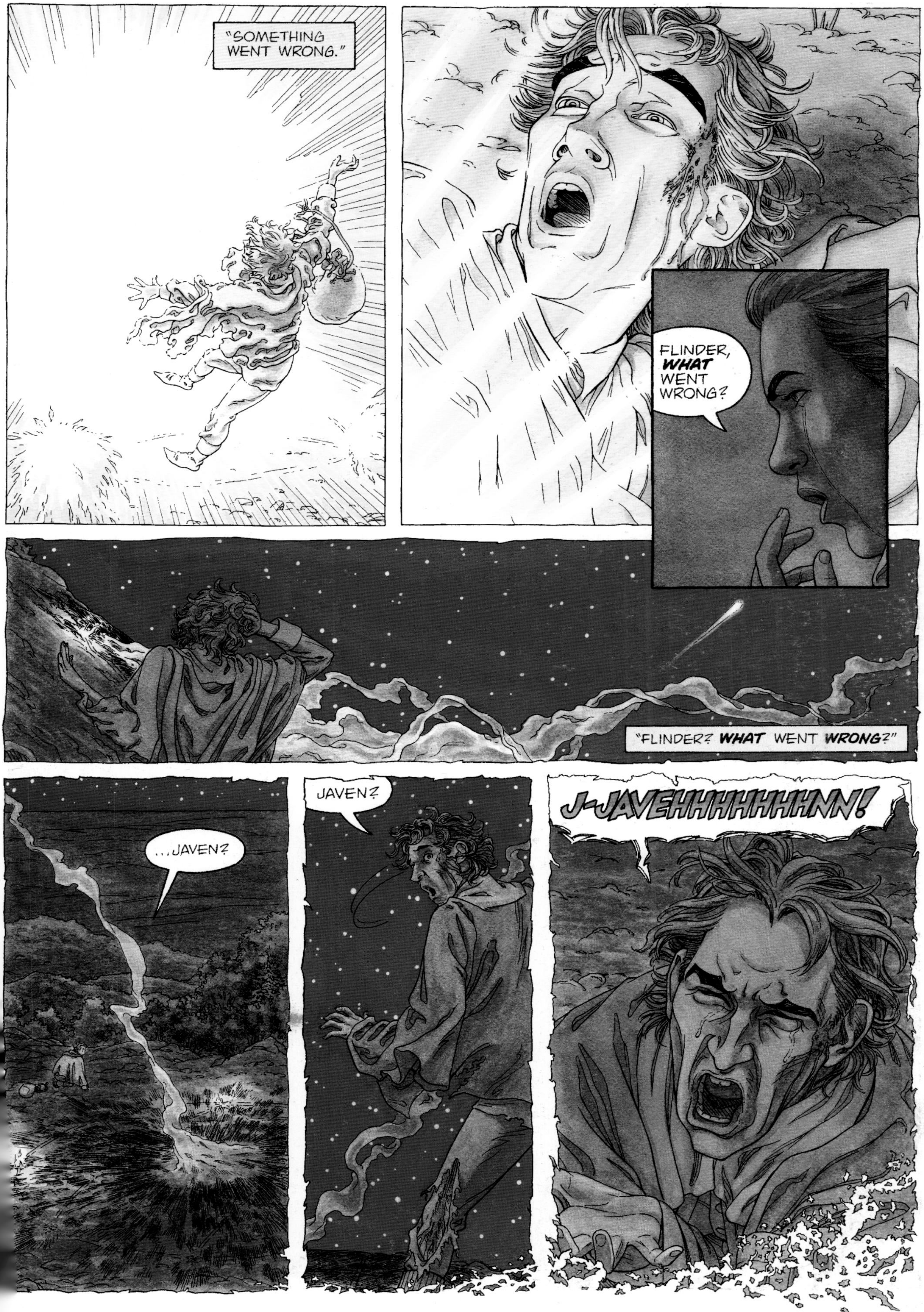
"SOMETHING WENT WRONG."
FLINDER, **WHAT** WENT WRONG?
"FLINDER? **WHAT** WENT **WRONG**?"
...JAVEN?
JAVEN?
J-JAVEHHHHHHHNN!

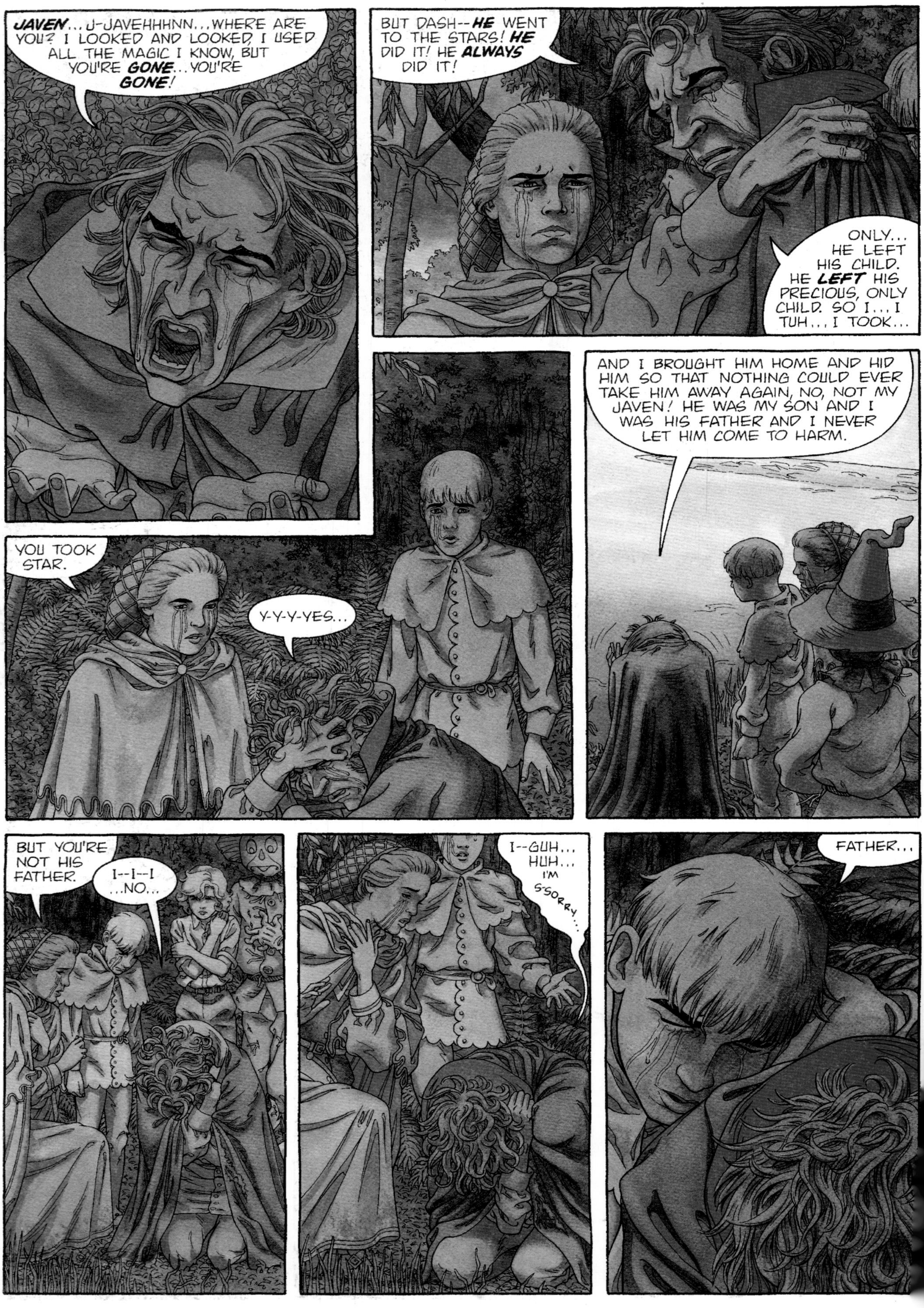

JAVEN... J-JAVEHHHNN...WHERE ARE YOU? I LOOKED AND LOOKED, I USED ALL THE MAGIC I KNOW, BUT YOU'RE GONE...YOU'RE GONE!
BUT DASH--HE WENT TO THE STARS! HE DID IT! HE ALWAYS DID IT!
ONLY... HE LEFT HIS CHILD. HE LEFT HIS PRECIOUS, ONLY CHILD. SO I... I TUH... I TOOK...
AND I BROUGHT HIM HOME AND HID HIM SO THAT NOTHING COULD EVER TAKE HIM AWAY AGAIN, NO, NOT MY JAVEN! HE WAS MY SON AND I WAS HIS FATHER AND I NEVER LET HIM COME TO HARM.
YOU TOOK STAR.
Y-Y-Y-YES...
BUT YOU'RE NOT HIS FATHER.
I--I--I ...NO...
I--GUH... HUH... I'M S'SORRY...
FATHER...

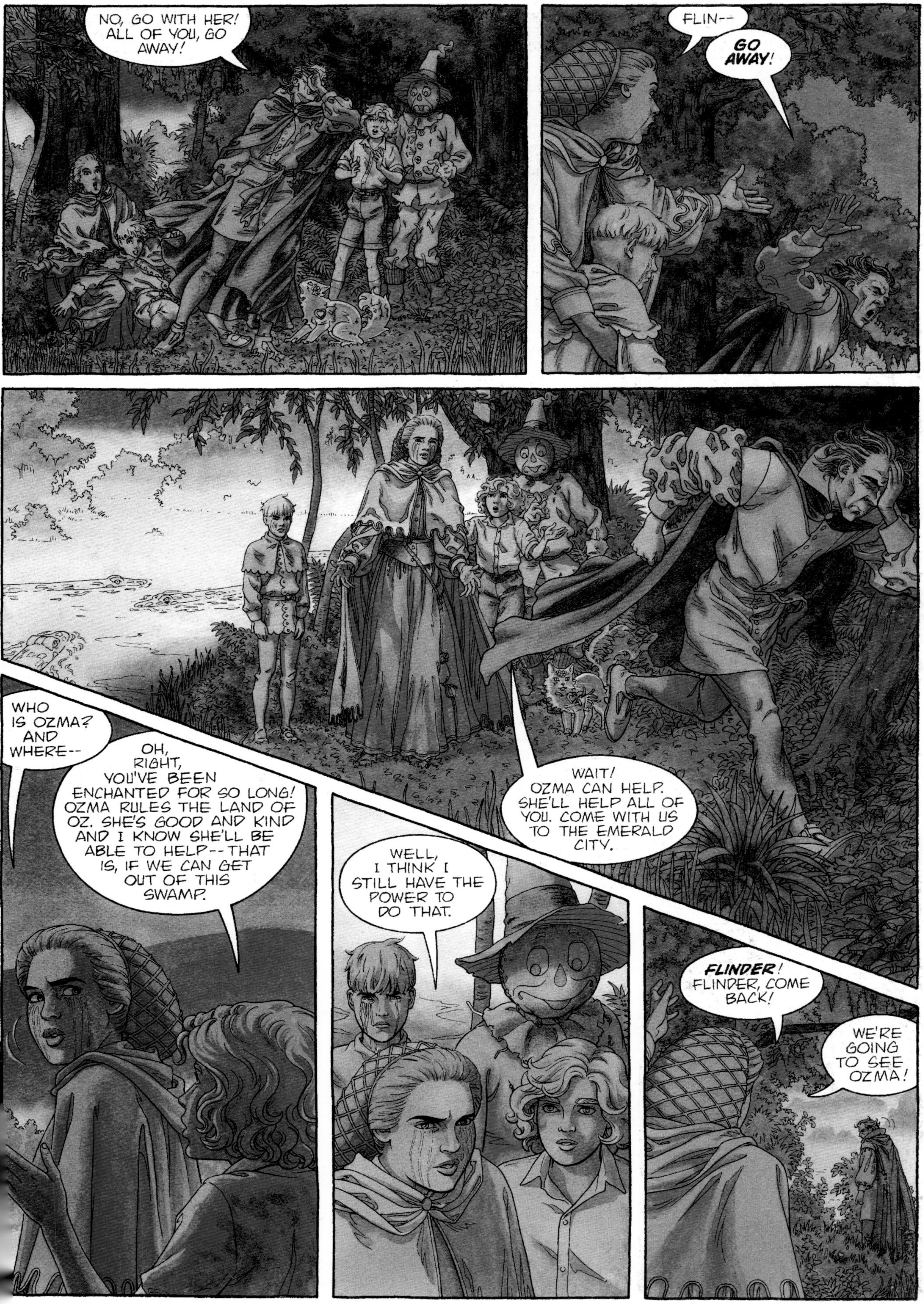
NO, GO WITH HER! ALL OF YOU, GO AWAY!
FLIN--
GO AWAY!
WHO IS OZMA? AND WHERE--
OH, RIGHT, YOU'VE BEEN ENCHANTED FOR SO LONG! OZMA RULES THE LAND OF OZ. SHE'S GOOD AND KIND AND I KNOW SHE'LL BE ABLE TO HELP--THAT IS, IF WE CAN GET OUT OF THIS SWAMP.
WAIT! OZMA CAN HELP. SHE'LL HELP ALL OF YOU. COME WITH US TO THE EMERALD CITY.
WELL, I THINK I STILL HAVE THE POWER TO DO THAT.
FLINDER! FLINDER, COME BACK!
WE'RE GOING TO SEE OZMA!

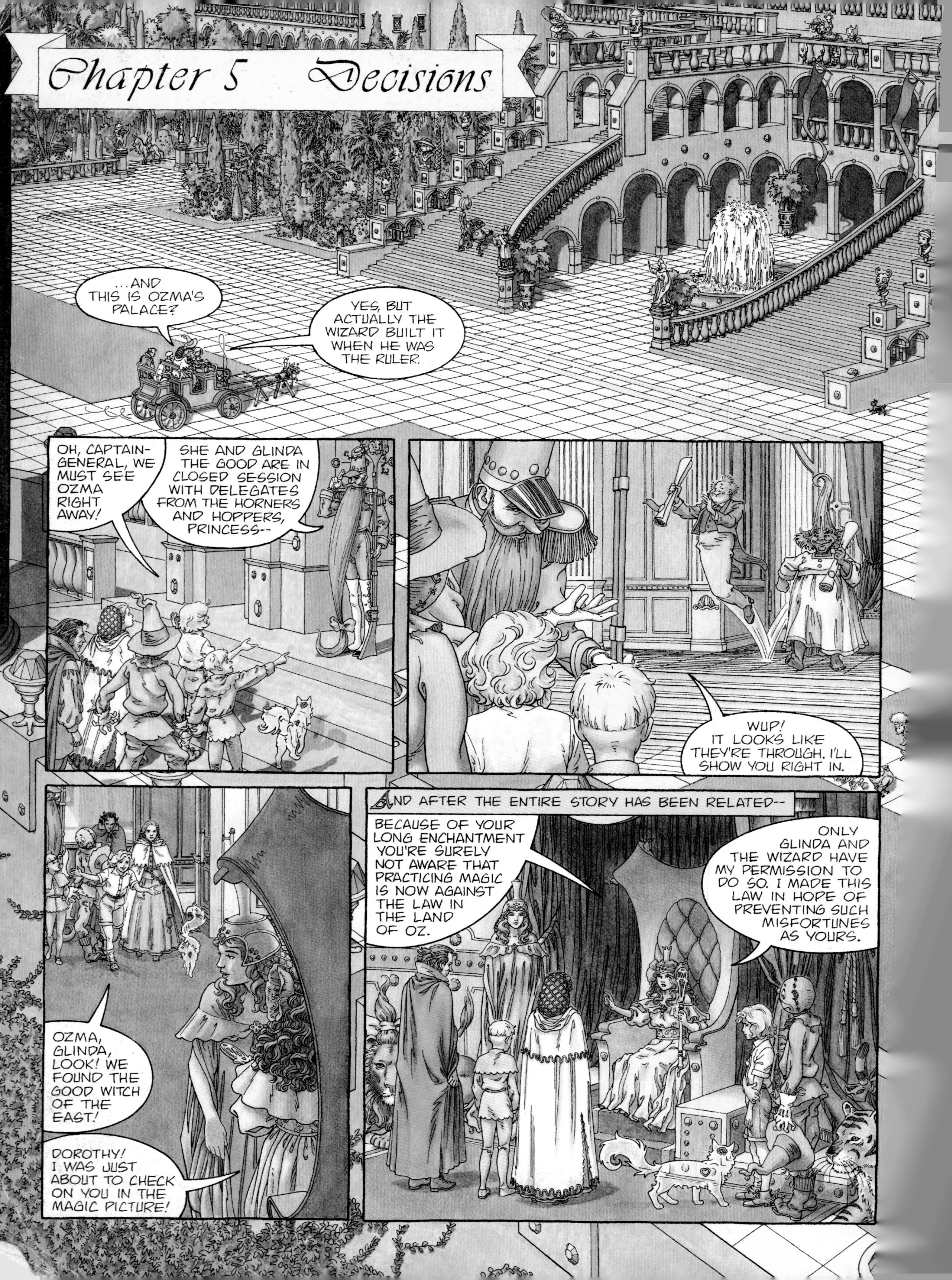
Chapter 5 Decisions
...AND THIS IS OZMA'S PALACE?
YES, BUT ACTUALLY THE WIZARD BUILT IT WHEN HE WAS THE RULER.
OH, CAPTAIN-GENERAL, WE MUST SEE OZMA RIGHT AWAY!
SHE AND GLINDA THE GOOD ARE IN CLOSED SESSION WITH DELEGATES FROM THE HORNERS AND HOPPERS, PRINCESS--
WUP! IT LOOKS LIKE THEY'RE THROUGH. I'LL SHOW YOU RIGHT IN.
OZMA, GLINDA, LOOK! WE FOUND THE GOOD WITCH OF THE EAST!
DOROTHY! I WAS JUST ABOUT TO CHECK ON YOU IN THE MAGIC PICTURE!
AND AFTER THE ENTIRE STORY HAS BEEN RELATED--
BECAUSE OF YOUR LONG ENCHANTMENT YOU'RE SURELY NOT AWARE THAT PRACTICING MAGIC IS NOW AGAINST THE LAW IN THE LAND OF OZ.
ONLY GLINDA AND THE WIZARD HAVE MY PERMISSION TO DO SO. I MADE THIS LAW IN HOPE OF PREVENTING SUCH MISFORTUNES AS YOURS.